T0156151

Communications
in Computer and Information Science 1706

Editorial Board Members

Rationale

The CCIS series is devoted to the publication of proceedings of computer science conferences. Its aim is to efficiently disseminate original research results in informatics in printed and electronic form. While the focus is on publication of peer-reviewed full papers presenting mature work, inclusion of reviewed short papers reporting on work in progress is welcome, too. Besides globally relevant meetings with internationally representative program committees guaranteeing a strict peer-reviewing and paper selection process, conferences run by societies or of high regional or national relevance are also considered for publication.

Topics

The topical scope of CCIS spans the entire spectrum of informatics ranging from foundational topics in the theory of computing to information and communications science and technology and a broad variety of interdisciplinary application fields.

Information for Volume Editors and Authors

Publication in CCIS is free of charge. No royalties are paid, however, we offer registered conference participants temporary free access to the online version of the conference proceedings on SpringerLink (http://link.springer.com) by means of an http referrer from the conference website and/or a number of complimentary printed copies, as specified in the official acceptance email of the event.

CCIS proceedings can be published in time for distribution at conferences or as post-proceedings, and delivered in the form of printed books and/or electronically as USBs and/or e-content licenses for accessing proceedings at SpringerLink. Furthermore, CCIS proceedings are included in the CCIS electronic book series hosted in the SpringerLink digital library at http://link.springer.com/bookseries/7899. Conferences publishing in CCIS are allowed to use Online Conference Service (OCS) for managing the whole proceedings lifecycle (from submission and reviewing to preparing for publication) free of charge.

Publication process

The language of publication is exclusively English. Authors publishing in CCIS have to sign the Springer CCIS copyright transfer form, however, they are free to use their material published in CCIS for substantially changed, more elaborate subsequent publications elsewhere. For the preparation of the camera-ready papers/files, authors have to strictly adhere to the Springer CCIS Authors' Instructions and are strongly encouraged to use the CCIS LaTeX style files or templates.

Abstracting/Indexing

CCIS is abstracted/indexed in DBLP, Google Scholar, EI-Compendex, Mathematical Reviews, SCImago, Scopus. CCIS volumes are also submitted for the inclusion in ISI Proceedings.

How to start

To start the evaluation of your proposal for inclusion in the CCIS series, please send an e-mail to ccis@springer.com.

Sergio Nesmachnow · Luis Hernández Callejo
Editors

Smart Cities

5th Ibero-American Congress, ICSC-CITIES 2022
Cuenca, Ecuador, November 28–30, 2022
Revised Selected Papers

Editors
Sergio Nesmachnow 🆔
Universidad de la República
Montevideo, Uruguay

Luis Hernández Callejo 🆔
Universidad de Valladolid
Soria, Spain

ISSN 1865-0929   ISSN 1865-0937 (electronic)
Communications in Computer and Information Science
ISBN 978-3-031-28453-3   ISBN 978-3-031-28454-0 (eBook)
https://doi.org/10.1007/978-3-031-28454-0

This Springer imprint is published by the registered company Springer Nature Switzerland AG
The registered company address is: Gewerbestrasse 11, 6330 Cham, Switzerland

Preface

This CCIS volume presents selected articles from the 5th edition of the Ibero-American Congress of Smart Cities (ICSC-CITIES 2022), held on November 28–30, 2022 in Cuenca, Ecuador, in a mixed modality, with in-person and online talks and article presentations. This event continues the successful four previous editions of the congress, held in Soria, Spain in 2018 and 2019, Costa Rica in 2020, and Cancún, México, in 2021.

The main goal of ICSC-CITIES 2022 was to provide a forum for researchers, scientists, teachers, decision-makers, postgraduate students and practitioners from different countries in Ibero-America and worldwide to share their current initiatives related to Smart Cities. Articles in this volume address four relevant topics (computational intelligence and urban informatics for smart cities; Internet of Things; optimization, smart production, and smart public services; and smart monitoring and communications) covering several areas of research and applications.

The main program consisted of three round tables, 72 oral presentations and 12 poster presentations from international speakers, highlighting recent developments in areas related to smart cities. Over three hundred distinguished participants from 28 countries gathered presentially or virtually for the congress. The Program Committee of ICSC-CITIES 2022 received 116 manuscripts. 72 submissions were accepted for oral presentation and the best 18 whose contents are within the Computer and Information Science areas were selected to be published in this CCIS volume. All articles have undergone a careful single-blind peer-review process by at least three subject-matter experts before being selected for publication.

We would like to express our deep gratitude to all the contributors to ICSC-CITIES 2022, the congress organizers, and to the authors and reviewers for their endeavors that made the paper-reviewing process efficient and convenient. We also thank the participants of the congress, our institutions, and all readers of this CCIS volume.

December 2022

Sergio Nesmachnow
Luis Hernández Callejo

Organization

General Chairs

Luis Hernández Callejo	Universidad de Valladolid, Spain
Sergio Nesmachnow	Universidad de la República, Uruguay

Track Chairs

Fabián Castillo Peña	Universidad Libre Seccional Cali, Colombia
Ponciano Jorge Escamilla Ambrosio	Instituto Politécnico Nacional, México
Paulo Gondim	Universidade de Brasília, Brazil
Luis Eduardo Tobón	Pontificia Universidad Javeriana, Cali, Colombia
Bernabé Dorronsoro	Universidad de Cádiz, Spain
Ana Ruiz	Universidad San Jorge, Cátedra Mobility Experience, Spain
Humberto Sossa	Instituto Politécnico Nacional, México
Jesús Armando Aguilar Jiménez	Universidad Autónoma de Baja California, México
Victor Alonso Gómez	Universidad de Valladolid, Spain
Sara Gallardo Saavedra	Universidad de Valladolid, Spain
Luis Hernández Callejo	Universidad de Valladolid, Spain
Roberto Villafáfila Robles	Universidad Politécnica de Cataluña, Spain
Irene Lebrusan	Instituto Complutense de Sociología para el Estudio de las Transformaciones Sociales Contemporáneas, Spain
Andrés Navarro	Pontificia Universidad Javeriana, Cali, Colombia
Adriana Correa Guimaraes	Universidad de Valladolid, Spain
Óscar Duque Pérez	Universidad de Valladolid, Spain
Luis Manuel Navas	Universidad de Valladolid, Spain
Jorge Luis Mírez Tarrillo	Universidad Nacional de Ingeniería, Perú
Lorena Parra	Universitat Politècnica de València, Spain
Carlos E. Torres Aguilar	Centro Nacional de Investigación y Desarrollo Tecnológico, México
Daniel Rossit	Universidad Nacional del Sur, Argentina
Pedro Moreno Bernal	Universidad Autónoma del Estado de Morelos, México

Jesús del Carmen Peralta Abarca	Universidad Autónoma del Estado de Morelos, México
Ana Carolina Olivera	CONICET, Argentina
Sergio Nesmachnow	Universidad de la República, Uruguay
Diego Rossit	Universidad Nacional del Sur, Argentina
Mariano Frutos	Universidad Nacional del Sur, Argentina
Teodoro Calonge Cano	Universidad de Valladolid, Spain
Ponciano Jorge Escamilla Ambrosio	Instituto Politécnico Nacional, México
Renzo Massobrio	Universidad de la República, Uruguay and Universidad de Cádiz, Spain
Luis Angelo Steffenel	Université de Reims Champagne-Ardenne, France
Jamal Toutouh	Universidad de Málaga, Spain

Publication Chairs

Luis Hernández Callejo	Universidad de Valladolid, Spain
Sergio Nesmachnow	Universidad de la República, Uruguay
Pedro Moreno Bernal	Universidad Autónoma del Estado de Morelos, México
Diego Rossit	Universidad Nacional del Sur, Argentina

Submission and Conference Management Chair

| Santiago Iturriaga | Universidad de la República, Uruguay |

Program Committee

Adolfo Ruelas Puente	Universidad Autónoma de Baja California, México
Adrian Toncovich	Universidad Nacional del Sur, Argentina
Adriana Correa-Guimaraes	Universidad de Valladolid, Spain
Agustín Laguarda	Universidad de la República, Uruguay
Alejandro Otero	Universidad de Buenos Aires-CONICET, Argentina
Alejandro Paz Parra	Pontificia Universidad Javeriana, Colombia
Alessandra Bussador	Universidade Federal da Integração Latino-Americana, Brazil

Alexander Vallejo Díaz	Santo Domingo Institute of Technology, Dominican Republic
Alexis Acuna	Universidad Autónoma de Baja California, México
Ana Carolina Olivera	Universidad Nacional de Cuyo, Argentina
Ana Ruiz	San Jorge University, Spain
Andrei Tchernykh	CICESE Research Center, México
Andrés Adolfo Navarro Newball	Pontificia Universidad Javeriana, Colombia
Ángel Zorita Lamadrid	Universidad de Valladolid, Spain
Angela Ferreira	Polytechnic Institute of Bragança, Portugal
Antonio Mauttone	Universidad de la República, Uruguay
Antonio Muñoz	University of Málaga, Spain
Armando Huicochea	Research Center for Engineering and Applied Science, México
Bernabe Dorronsoro	Universidad de Cádiz, Spain
Bernardo Pulido-Gaytan	CICESE Research Center, México
Bouras Abdelkarim	Badji Mokhtar University, Algeria
Carlos Grande	Universidad Centroamericana José Simeón Cañas, El Salvador
Carlos Meza Benavides	Anhalt University of Applied Sciences, Germany
Carlos E. Torres	Tecnológico Nacional de México/CENIDET, México
Christian Cintrano	Universidad de Málaga, Spain
Claudio Paz	Universidad Tecnológica Nacional - FRC, Argentina
Claudio Risso	Universidad de la República, Uruguay
Cleonilson Protasio	Federal University of Paraíba, Portugal
Cristina Sáez Blázquez	University of Salamanca, Spain
Daniel Rossit	Universidad Nacional del Sur, Argentina
Daniel H. Stolfi	University of Luxembourg, Luxembourg
David Peña Morales	Universidad de Cádiz, Spain
Deyslen Mariano	Instituto Tecnológico de Santo Domingo, Dominican Republic
Diego Arcos-Aviles	Universidad de las Fuerzas Armadas ESPE, Ecuador
Diego Alberto Godoy	Universidad Gastón Dachary, Argentina
Diego Gabriel Rossit	Universidad Nacional del Sur-CONICET, Argentina
Edgardo Aníbal Belloni	Universidad Gastón Dachary, Argentina
Edith Gabriela Manchego Huaquipaco	Universidad Nacional de San Agustín de Arequipa, Perú
Eduardo Fernández	Universidad de la República, Uruguay
Emmanuel Millan	UNCuyo, Argentina

Enrique González	Universidad de Salamanca, Spain
Esteban Mocskos	Universidad de Buenos Aires, Argentina
Fabian Castillo Peña	Universidad Libre - Cali, Colombia
Francisco David Moya Chaves	Universidad Distrital Francisco José de Caldas, Colombia
Francisco Valbuena	Universidad de Valladolid, Spain
Franco Robledo	Universidad de la República, Uruguay
Gilberto Martinez	CIC-IPN, México
Gina Paola Maestre Gongora	Universidad Cooperativa de Colombia, Colombia
Gustavo Richmond-Navarro	Instituto Tecnológico de Costa Rica, Costa Rica
Ignacio de Godos	Universidad de Valladolid, Spain
Ignacio Martín Nieto	Universidad de Salamanca, Spain
Irene Lebrusán	Harvard University, USA
Ivania Aguirre	University of Cuenca, Ecuador
Jamal Toutouh	Massachusetts Institute of Technology, USA
Javier Rocher	Universitat Politècnica de València, Spain
Jesús Vegas	Universidad de Valladolid, Spain
Jesús Armando Aguilar	Autonomous University of Baja California, México
Jesús Del Carmen Peralta Abarca	Universidad Autónoma del Estado de Morelos, México
Joao Coelho	Instituto Politécnico de Bragança, Portugal
Jonathan Muraña	UDELAR, Uruguay
Jorge Arturo Del Ángel Ramos	Universidad Veracruzana, México
Jorge Mario Cortés-Mendoza	University of Luxembourg, Luxembourg
Jorge Mírez	Universidad Nacional de Ingeniería, Perú
Jorge Nájera	Centro de Investigaciones Energéticas, Medioambientales y Tecnológicas, Spain
José Alberto Hernández	Universidad Autónoma del Estado de Morelos, México
José Ángel Morell Martínez	Universidad de Málaga, Spain
José Antonio Ferrer	CIEMAT, Spain
José-Ramón Aira	Universidad de Valladolid, Spain
Juan Chavat	Universidad de la República, Uruguay
Juan Espinoza	Universidad de Cuenca, Ecuador
Juan Francisco Cabrera Sánchez	Universidad de Cádiz, Spain
Juan Humberto Sossa Azuela	CIC-IPN, México
Juan José Tarrio	Comisión Nacional de Energía Atómica, Argentina
Juan Manuel Ramírez Alcaraz	Universidad de Colima, México
Juan Mauricio	Universidade Federal da Paraíba, Brazil
Juan Pavón	Universidad Complutense de Madrid, Spain

Renato Andara	Universidad Nacional Experimental Politécnica Antonio José de Sucre, Venezuela
Renzo Massobrio	Universidad de la República, Uruguay
Ricardo Beltrán	Centro de Investigación en Materiales Avanzados, México
Roberto Villafafila	Universitat Politècnica de Catalunya, Spain
Rodrigo Porteiro	UTE, Uruguay
Rogelio Vargas Lopez	Universidad Autónoma de Guadalajara, México
Santiago Iturriaga	Universidad de la República, Uruguay
Sara Gallardo-Saavedra	Universidad de Valladolid, Spain
Sergio Nesmachnow	Universidad de la República, Uruguay
Sesil Koutra	University of Mons, Belgium
Silvia Soutullo	CIEMAT, Spain
Teodoro Calonge	Universidad de Valladolid, Spain
Teresa Batista	Universidade de Évora, Portugal
Tiago Carneiro Pessoa	INRIA, France
Vanessa Guimarães	CEFET/RJ, Brazil
Vicente Leite	Instituto Politécnico de Bragança, Portugal
Vicente Canals	Universidad de las Islas Baleares, Spain
Víctor Alonso Gómez	Universidad de Valladolid, Spain
Víctor Manuel Padrón Nápoles	Universidad Europea de Madrid, Spain

Reviewers

Abelardo Contreras Panibra	Universidad Nacional de Ingeniería, Perú
Adalberto Ospino	Universidad de la Costa, Colombia
Adolfo Heriberto Ruelas Puente	Universidad Autónoma de Baja California, México
Adrián Toncovich	Universidad Nacional del Sur, Argentina
Adrian Criollo	Universidad Politécnica Salesiana, Ecuador
Alberto Redondo	Universidad de Valladolid, Spain
Alejandro Paz Parra	Universidad Santiago de Cali, Colombia
Alejandro César López Bolaños	Universidad Nacional Autónoma de México, México
Alejandro Otero	Universidad de Buenos Aires-CONICET, Argentina
Alessandra Bussador	Centro Universitário Dinâmica das Cataratas, Brazil
Alexander Vallejo Díaz	Instituto Tecnológico de Santo Domingo, Dominican Republic
Alexis Acuña Ramírez	Universidad Autónoma de Baja California, México

Alfonso García Alvaro	Universidad de Valladolid, Spain
Alicia Martínez Rebollar	Tecnológico Nacional de México/Centro Nacional de Investigación y Desarrollo Tecnológico, México
Alvaro Jaramillo Duque	Universidad de Antioquia, Colombia
Amaia Arrinda	University of the Basque Country, Spain
Américo Vicente Teixeira Leite	Instituto Politécnico de Bragança, Portugal
Ana Ruiz Varona	Universidad San Jorge, Spain
Ana Carolina Olivera	CONICET-Universidad Nacional de Cuyo, Argentina
Ana Lilia Sanchéz Brito	Tecnológico Nacional de México/Centro Nacional de Investigación y Desarrollo Tecnológico, México
Andrei Tchernykh	CICESE Research Center, Mexico
Andrés Adolfo Navarro Newball	Pontificia Universidad Javeriana Cali, Colombia
Andrés Llombart	CIRCE - Research Centre, Spain
Andres Montero-Izquierdo	Universidad de Cuenca, Ecuador
Ângela Ferreira	Instituto Politécnico de Bragança, Portugal
Angeles Dennis Figueroa-Negrete	Universidad Autónoma del Estado de Morelos, México
Antonella Cavallin	Universidad Nacional del Sur, Argentina
Antonio Daniel Mauttone Vidales	Universidad de la República, Uruguay
Araceli Ávila Hernández	Centro Nacional de Investigación y Desarrollo Tecnológico, México
Armando Huicochea Rodríguez	Universidad Autónoma del Estado de Morelos, México
Bernabe Dorronsoro	Universidad de Cádiz, Spain
Bernardo Pulido Gaytan	CICESE Research Center, México
Bouras Abdelkarim	Badji Mokhtar University, Algeria
Carlos Enrique Torres Aguilar	Tecnológico Nacional de México/Centro Nacional de Investigación y Desarrollo Tecnológico, México
Carlos Miguel Jiménez-Xamán	Tecnológico Nacional de México/Centro Nacional de Investigación y Desarrollo Tecnológico, México
Carmen Alonso-Garcia	CIEMAT - Centro de Investigaciones Energéticas, Medioambientales y Tecnológicas, Spain
Carolina Solis Maldonado	Universidad Veracruzana, México
César Alejandro Varela Boydo	Centro Nacional de Investigación y Desarrollo Tecnológico, México
Cindy Espinoza Aguirre	Universidad de Cuenca, Ecuador
Claudio J. Paz	Universidad Tecnológica Nacional - FRC, Argentina

Consuelo Gines Palestino	Tecnológico Nacional de México Campus Tepexi, México
Cristina Sáez Blázquez	Universidad de León, Spain
Daniel Rossit	Universidad Nacional del Sur-CONICET, Argentina
Daniel Stolfi	SnT - University of Luxembourg, Luxembourg
Daniel Moringo-Sotelo	Universidad de Valladolid, Spain
Danielle Rodrigues de Moraes	Centro Federal de Educação Tecnológica Celso Suckow da Fonseca, Brazil
David Peña Morales	Universidad de Cádiz, Spain
David de la Vega	University of the Basque Country, Spain
David Guillermo Pasillas Banda	Universidad de Guadalajara, México
David Peña	Universidad de Cádiz, Spain
David Zabala-Pedraza	Instituto Tecnológico de Santo Domingo, Dominican Republic
Deyslen Mariano Hernández	Instituto Tecnológico de Santo Domingo, Dominican Republic
Diana Sánchez-Partida	Universidad Popular Autónoma del Estado de Puebla, México
Diego Rossit	Universidad Nacional del Sur-CONICET, Argentina
Diego Arcos Avilés	Universidad de las Fuerzas Armadas ESPE, Ecuador
Diego Alberto Godoy	Universidad Gastón Dachary, Argentina
Diego Enrique Morales Polanco	Instituto Tecnológico de Santo Domingo, Dominican Republic
Diego Luis Linares	Pontificia Universidad Javeriana, Colombia
Edgar Vázquez Beltrán	Universidad de Sonora, México
Edgar Vicente Macias Melo	Universidad Juárez Autónoma de Tabasco, México
Edith Gabriela Manchego Huaquipaco	Universidad Nacional de San Agustín de Arequipa, Perú
Egor Shiriaev	North-Caucasus Federal University, Russia
Enrique González González	Universidad de Salamanca, Spain
Esteban Zalamea	Universidad de Cuenca, Ecuador
Estefani Mendoza	Universidad Nacional de Ingeniería, Perú
Fabián Castillo Peña	Universidad Libre de Colombia, Colombia
Fabio Miguel	Universidad Nacional de Río Negro, Argentina
Francisco Chicano	Universidad de Málaga, Spain
Francisco José Sánchez Pacheco	Universidad de Málaga, Spain
Fredy Dulce	Universidad del Valle, Colombia
Gabriel Marro	Universidad San Jorge, Spain

Genesis Sanchez-Sosa	Instituto Tecnológico de Santo Domingo, Dominican Republic
Gilberto Martinez	CIC-IPN, México
Gina Maestre Gongora	Universidad Cooperativa de Colombia, Colombia
Guillermo Pérez	Escuela Politécnica Nacional, Ecuador
Gustavo Richmond-Navarro	Instituto Tecnológico de Costa Rica, Costa Rica
Gustavo Adolfo Gómez Ramírez	Instituto Tecnológico de Costa Rica, Costa Rica
Gustavo Navarro	Centro de Investigaciones Energéticas, Medioambientales y Tecnológicas, Spain
H. Amaris	Universidad Carlos III de Madrid, Spain
Harold Vacca	Universidad Distrital Francisco José de Caldas, Colombia
Hector Felipe Mateo Romero	Universidad de Valladolid, Spain
Heidi Paola Díaz Hernández	Universidad Juárez Autónoma de Tabasco, México
Hugo Estrada	Tecnológico Nacional de México/Centro Nacional de Investigación y Desarrollo Tecnológico, México
Hugo J. Bello	Universidad de Valladolid, Spain
Hugo Sanchez	Anhalt University of Applied Sciences, Germany
Ignaciode Godos Crespo	Universidad de Valladolid, Spain
Irene Lebrusán Murillo	Universidad de Salamanca/Universidad Carlos III de Madrid, Spain
Irene Acosta	Universidad Regional Amazónica, Ecuador
Irene Marisol Revelo Portilla	Pontificia Universidad Católica de Ecuador, Ecuador
Irma Yazmín Hernández Báez	Universidad Politécnica del Estado de Morelos, México
Ismael Minchala	Universidad de Cuenca, Ecuador
Ítalo Bove	Universidad de la República, Uruguay
Itziar Angulo	University of the Basque Country, Spain
Ivan Alonso de Miguel	Universitat de les Illes Balears, Spain
Ivania Carolina Aguirre Pardo	Universidad de Cuenca, Ecuador
Ivonne Yazmín Arce García	Universidad Autónoma del Estado de Morelos, México
J. Guadalupe Velásquez-Aguilar	Universidad Autónoma del Estado de Morelos, México
Jacinto Vidal-Noguera	Universitat de les Illes Balears, Spain
Jaime Paul Ayala	Universidad de las Fuerzas Armadas ESPE, Ecuador
Jamal Toutouh El Alamin	Universidad de Málaga, Spain
Javier Rocher Morant	Universitat Politècnica de València, Spain

Jesús Armando Aguilar Jiménez	Universidad Autónoma de Baja California, México
Jesús del Carmen Peralta Abarca	Universidad Autónoma del Estado de Morelos, México
João Paulo Coelho	Instituto Politécnico de Bragança, Portugal
Jonathan Muraña SIlvera	Universidad de la República, Uruguay
Jorge Nájera Álvarez	CIEMAT, Spain
Jorge del Ángel	Universidad Veracruzana, México
Jorge Gomez-Sanz	Universidad Complutense de Madrid, Spain
Jorge López-Rebollo	Universidad de Salamanca, Spain
Jorge Mírez	Universidad Nacional de Ingeniería, Perú
Jorge-Mario Cortes-Mendoza	University of Luxembourg, Luxembourg
José Alberto Hernández Aguilar	Universidad Autónoma del Estado de Morelos, México
José Ángel Morell Martínez	Universidad de Málaga, Spain
José Antonio Ferrer Tévar	Centro de Investigaciones Energéticas, Medioambientales y Tecnológicas, Spain
Jose Duran	Instituto Tecnológico de Santo Domingo, Dominican Republic
Jose Ignacio Morales Aragonés	Colegio Oficial de Ingenieros de Telecomunicación, Spain
José Ramón Aira Zunzunegui	Universidad Politécnica de Madrid, Spain
Jose-Isidro Hernandez-Vega	Tecnológico Nacional de México, México
Juan Pavón	Universidad Complutense de Madrid, Spain
Juan Carlos Frechoso	Universidad de Valladolid, Spain
Juan Francisco Cabrera Sánchez	Universidad de Cádiz, Spain
Juan Gabriel Ordoñez	Universidad de Nariño, Colombia.
Juan Irving Vasquez Gomez	Instituto Politécnico Nacional, México
Juan Manuel Ramírez Alcaraz	Universidad de Colima, México
Juan Moises Mauricio Villanueva	Universidade Federal da Paraíba, Brazil
Juan Pablo Chavat Pérez	Universidad de la República, Uruguay
Juan Rodríguez	Universidad de la República, Uruguay
Karla María Aguilar Castro	Universidad Juárez Autónoma de Tabasco, México
Laene Oliveira Soares	Centro Federal de Educação Tecnológica Celso Suckow da Fonseca, Brazil
Laura Rosa Guerra Torrealba	Pontificia Universidad Católica de Ecuador, Ecuador
Leonardo Cardinale Villalobos	Tecnológico de Costa Rica, Costa Rica
Lidia Sanz-Molina	Universidad de Valladolid, Spain
Lluc Crespí-Castañer	Universitat de les Illes Balears, Spain
López Cintrano	Universidad de Málaga, Spain

Luis Antonio González Uribe	Universidad Autónoma de Baja California, México
Luis Armando Marrone	Universidad Nacional de La Plata, Argentina
Luis Tobón	Pontificia Universidad Javeriana Cali, Colombia
Luis Gerardo Montané Jiménez	Universidad Veracruzana, México
Luis González Uribe	Universidad Autónoma de Baja California, México
Luis Manuel Navas Gracia	Universidad de Valladolid, Spain
Luis Miguel Quishpe	Universidad Regional Amazónica, Ecuador
Ma. Eloisa Gurruchaga Rodríguez	Instituto Tecnológico de Orizaba, México.
Manuel Ángel González Delgado	Universidad de Valladolid, Spain
Marcelo García Luyo	Universidad Nacional de Ingeniería, Perú
Marcia Eugenio	Universidad de Valladolid, Spain
Marcos Blanco	Centro de Investigaciones Energéticas, Medioambientales y Tecnológicas, Spain
María Sánchez Aparicio	Universidad de Salamanca, Spain
María Teresa Cepero García	Universidad Veracruzana, México
Maria Teresa Folgôa Batista	Universidade de Évora e CIMAC, Portugal
Maria Victoria Reyes Vargas	Universidad Regional Amazónica, Ecuador
Martín Draper	Universidad de la República, Uruguay
Martin Solis Solis	Instituto Tecnológico de Costa Rica, Costa Rica
Matías Galnares	Universidad de la República, Uruguay
Melva Inés Gomez Caicedo	Fundación Universitaria los Libertadores, Colombia
Mercedes Gaitan	Fundación Universitaria Konrad Lorenz, Colombia
Miguel Dávila	Universidad de Valladolid, Spain
Miguel Angel Che-Pan	Tecnológico Nacional de México/Centro Nacional de Investigación y Desarrollo Tecnológico, México
Miguel Angel González	Universidad de Valladolid, Spain
Miguel Angel Muñoz Garcia	Universidad Politécnica de Madrid, Spain
Miguel Aybar	Instituto Tecnológico de Santo Domingo, Dominican Republic
Miguel Mendieta	Universidad Politécnica Salesiana, Ecuador
Miriam Navarrete Procopio	Universidad Autónoma del Estado de Morelos, México
Miriam González Dueñas	Universidad de Guadalajara, México
Moisés Montiel González	Universidad Autónoma del Estado de Morelos, México
Natalia Nuño-Villanueva	Universidad de Salamanca, Spain
Neiel Israel Leyva Santes	Barcelona Supercomputing Center, Spain

Noelia Pinto	Universidad Tecnológica Nacional, Argentina, Argentina
Noelia Uribe-Perez	Tecnalia Research & Innovation, Spain
Olga Quevedo	Universidad de Guayaquil, Ecuador
Óscar Duque Pérez	Universidad de Valladolid, Spain
Oscar Izquierdo Monge	Centro de Investigaciones Energéticas, Medioambientales y Tecnológicas, Spain
Pablo Monzon	Universidad de la República, Uruguay
Pablo Collazzo	University for Continuing Education Krems, Austria
Pablo Daniel Godoy	Universidad Nacional de Cuyo, Argentina
Pablo de Frutos	Universidad de Valladolid, Spain
Paola Duque Sarango	Universidad Politécnica Salesiana, Ecuador
Paolo Piantanida	Politecnico di Torino, Itália
Patricia Ruiz Villalobos	University of Cadiz, Spain
Paul Ayala	Universidad de las Fuerzas Armadas ESPE, Ecuador
Paula Guerra	Kennesaw State University, USA
Paula Peña Carro	Centro de Investigaciones Energéticas, Medioambientales y Tecnológicas, Spain
Paula de Andrés Anaya	Universidad de Salamanca, Spain
Paulo R. L. Gondim	Universidade de Brazilia, Brazil
Pedro Moreno-Bernal	Universidad Autónoma del Estado de Morelos, México
Pedro Antonio Martin-Cervantes	Universidad de Valladolid, Spain
Ramiro José Espinheira Martins	Superior School of Technology and Management-IPB, Portugal
Ramsés David Villalobos Núñez	Universidad Nacional de Ingeniería, Perú
Raúl Alberto López Meraz	Unidad de Ingeniería y Ciencias Químicas/ Universidad Veracruzana, México
Raúl Maján Navalón	Tierra Sin Males, Spain
Renato Alejandro Andara Escalona	Universidad Nacional Experimental Politécnica Antonio José de Sucre, Venezuela
Renzo Massobrio	Delft University of Technology, Netherlands
Ricardo Beltran-Chacon	Centro de Investigación en Materiales Avanzados, Mexico.
Ricardo Peña	Instituto Tecnológico de Santo Domingo, Dominican Republic
Roberto Villafáfila Robles	Universidad Politécnica de Cataluña, Spain
Rodolfo Omar Domínguez García	Universidad de Guadalajara, México
Rogelio Vargas López	Universidad Autónoma de Guadalajara, México
Ronney Boloy	Centro Federal de Educação Tecnológica Celso Suckow da Fonseca, Brazil

Ruby Gines Palestino	Tecnológico Nacional de México, México
Ryszard Edward Rozga Luter	Universidad Autónoma Metropolitana, México
Samanta López Salazar	Tecnológico Nacional de México/Centro Nacional de Investigación y Desarrollo Tecnológico, México
Samuel Borroy	CIRCE Research Centre, Spain
Santiago Damian Quishpe Morales	Pontificia Universidad Católica de Ecuador, Ecuador
Santiago Pindado	Universidad Politécnica de Madrid, Spain
Sara Gallardo Saavedra	Universidad de Valladolid, Spain
Saúl Islas Pereda	Universidad Autónoma de Baja California, México
Silvia Soutullo Castro	CIEMAT, Spain
Sinuhe Gines Palestino	Tecnológico Nacional de México, México
Susana Gómez Redondo	Universidad de Valladolid, Spain
Teodoro Calonge Cano	Universidad de Valladolid, Spain
Thania Guadalupe Lima Tellez	Universidad de Sonora, México
Tiago Carneiro Pessoa	Interuniversity Microelectronics Centre, Belgium
Vanessa de Almeida Guimarães	Centro Federal de Educação Tecnológica Celso Suckow da Fonseca - CEFET/RJ, Brazil
Verónica Pinos-Vélez	Universidad de Cuenca, Ecuador
Vicente José Canals Guinand	Universidad de las Islas Baleares, Spain
Víctor Alonso Gómez	Universidad de Valladolid, Spain
Víctor Hernández Andrés	Universidad de Valladolid, Spain
Víctor Manuel Padrón Nápoles	Universidad Europea de Madrid, Spain
Víctor Martínez	Universitat de les Illes Balears, Spain
Yanitzia Reyes Cárcamo	Tecnológico Nacional de México, México
Yuri Humberto Merizalde Zamora	Universidad de Guayaquil, Ecuador

Contents

Computational Intelligence and Urban Informatics for Smart Cities

Synthetic Dataset of Electroluminescence Images of Photovoltaic Cells
by Deep Convolutional Generative Adversarial Networks 3
    Héctor Felipe Mateo Romero, Miguel Angel González Rebollo,
    Valentín Cardeñoso-Payo, Victor Alonso Gomez, Hugo Jose Bello,
    Alberto Redondo Plaza, and Luis Hernandez Callejo

Walking Accessibility to the Public Transport Network in Montevideo,
Uruguay 17
    Sara Perera and Renzo Massobrio

Artificial Intelligence for Automatic Building Extraction from Urban
Aerial Images 31
    Lucas González, Jamal Toutouh, and Sergio Nesmachnow

Distribution of Police Patrols as a Covering Problem in Smart Cities:
Fuengirola Use Case 46
    Jamal Toutouh, Francisco Chicano, and Rodrigo Gil-Merino

Super Resolution Generative Adversarial Network for Velocity Fields
in Large Eddy Simulations 61
    Maximiliano Bove, Sergio Nesmachnow, and Martín Draper

Deep Neural Networks for Global Horizontal Irradiation Forecasting:
A Comparative Study 77
    Cristian Arbeláez-Duque, Alejandro Duque-Ciro,
    Walter Villa-Acevedo, and Álvaro Jaramillo-Duque

Internet of things

IoT Platform for Monitoring Nutritional and Weather Conditions
of Avocado Production 95
    Pedro Moreno-Bernal, Paris Arizmendi-Peralta,
    José Alberto Hernández-Aguilar, Jesús del Carmen Peralta-Abarca,
    and J. Guadalupe Velásquez-Aguilar

IoT System for Thermographic Data Acquisition of Photovoltaic
Installations 110
  Leonardo Cardinale-Villalobos, Luis Antonio Solís-García,
  and Luis Alonso Araya-Solano

A New Approach to Automate the Connectivity of Electronic Devices
with an IoT Platform 123
  Juan José Flores-Sedano, Hugo Estrada-Esquivel,
  Alicia Martínez Rebollar, and Juan José Jassón Flores Prieto

Optimization, Smart Production, and Smart Public Services

Lean Office Approach for *muda* Identification in the Admission Process
of University Students 143
  Jesús del Carmen Peralta-Abarca, Pedro Moreno-Bernal,
  and Viridiana Aydeé León-Hernández

Smart Mobility for Public Transportation Systems: Improved Bus
Timetabling for Synchronizing Transfers 158
  Claudio Risso, Sergio Nesmachnow, and Diego Rossit

Classification of Polyethylene Terephthalate Bottles in a Recycling Plant 173
  Diego Alberto Godoy, Enrique Marcelo Albornoz, Ricardo Selva,
  Nicolas Ibarra, and Cesar Gallardo

Synthesized Data Generation for Public Transportation Systems 185
  Federico Gómez and Sergio Nesmachnow

Analysis of Public Transportation in Montevideo, Uruguay During
the COVID-19 Pandemic 200
  Andrés Collares, Diego Helal, Sergio Nesmachnow,
  and Andrei Tchernykh

Big Data Trends in the Analysis of City Resources 215
  Regina Gubareva and Rui Pedro Lopes

Smart Monitoring and Communications

Detecting Air Conditioning Usage in Households Using Unsupervised
Machine Learning on Smart Meter Data 233
  Rodrigo Porteiro and Sergio Nesmachnow

SNS-Based Secret Sharing Scheme for Security of Smart City
Communication Systems 248
   Andrei Gladkov, Egor Shiriaev, Andrei Tchernykh, Maxim Deryabin,
   Ekaterina Bezuglova, Georgii Valuev, and Mikhail Babenko

Application of LPWAN Technologies Based on LoRa in the Monitoring
of Water Sources of The Andean Wetlands 264
   Luis González, Andrés Gonzales, Santiago González,
   and Alonso Cartuche

Author Index 279

Computational Intelligence and Urban Informatics for Smart Cities

Synthetic Dataset of Electroluminescence Images of Photovoltaic Cells by Deep Convolutional Generative Adversarial Networks

Héctor Felipe Mateo Romero(✉), Miguel Angel González Rebollo,
Valentín Cardeñoso-Payo, Victor Alonso Gomez, Hugo Jose Bello,
Alberto Redondo Plaza, and Luis Hernandez Callejo

University of Valladolid, Valladolid, Spain
{hectorfelipe.mateo,victor.alonso.gomez,hugojose.bello,
luis.hernandez.callejo}@uva.es, mrebollo@eii.uva.es, valen@infor.uva.es

Abstract. This article presents a different way of obtaining images of solar cells using Artificial Intelligence techniques such as Generative Adversarial Neural Networks (GANs). This will improve the maintenance of Photovoltaic Systems in different places like Smart Cities. The original data has been obtained manually and preprocessed to create better images. The GAN architecture used is known as Deep Convolutional GAN since it performs better than other GANs. The synthetic images were labeled and analyzed to ensure their quality.

Keywords: Generative Adversarial Neural Networks · Photovoltaics · Artificial Intelligence · Synthetic Data · Electroluminescence

1 Introduction

A smart city [1] can be defined as an urban area highly developed in terms of infrastructure, communications, and sustainability. These cities need high amounts of electricity. Two factors are increasing the importance of renewable energies: the rise in the cost of traditional energies and the effects that fossil fuels have on the environment. Solar energy is one of the most important sources due to its facility being installed in different places such as rooftops.

The maintenance of the solar panels is not a trivial issue [2]. Their performance depends on different conditions, which makes necessary a mechanism to control and optimize the production. Solar modules are also vulnerable to phenomena that can reduce or even nullify the production of one cell or even the whole module in the worst cases. This is usually dealt with human labor, checking each module in a certain time.

Artificial intelligence is also applied to deal with this kind of problem. The problem is that AI models need a lot of amounts of data to train [7]. This problem is more critical in this area since it is not easy to obtain the data.

S. Nesmachnow and L. Hernández Callejo (Eds.): ICSC-CITIES 2022, CCIS 1706, pp. 3–16, 2023.
https://doi.org/10.1007/978-3-031-28454-0_1

To solve this problem, we present a new approach: we will use Artificial Intelligence, Generative Adversarial Networks (GANs), to generate new data. This article offers a synthetic dataset ready to be used with models, the images will have associated a value according to their performance. This dataset can also be used alone to analyze characteristics, defects, or properties of cells.

GANs have been used in other works to generate synthetic data [3]. They have been applied to PV systems for solving others problems [4]. They also have been used to generate EL images of PV cells [5,6] but these images were created for fault detection, they do not provide information about the IV curve or the power.

In Sect. 2 the Generative Adversarial Networks are explained, in Sect. 3 the methodology that was followed to generate the dataset is commented and in Sect. 4 we present the synthetic dataset. Finally, we present our conclusions in Sect. 5.

2   Generative Adversarial Networks

Generative Adversarial Networks (GANs) are an emerging technology that has been mainly applied to semi-supervised and unsupervised learning. A GAN can be defined as a pair of networks competing against each other [8], one of the networks is known as the Generator, which tries to create realistic new data, and the other one is the discriminator which has to decide which data is real and which data has been forged.

A key feature of these systems is that the generator network does not have access to real data. Its only feedback about the results of the forgery comes from the discriminator. The discriminator has access to both real and fake data. The loss is computed based on the number of times that the discriminator is deceived by the fake data. This loss is also provided to the generator to improve the quality of the forged images (see Fig. 1).

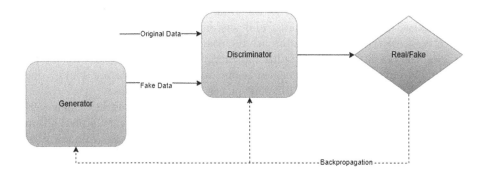

Fig. 1. Diagram of a GAN

The networks working as generators and discriminators are usually implemented by deep Feedforward Networks but there are also more complex architectures based on convolutional or other kinds of layers. These advanced architectures and layers can improve the quality of the forged data.

Deep Convolutional GAN

One of the most interesting improvements of the basic GAN is the Deep Convolutional GAN [9]. Its contributions consisted of a set of constraints on the conventional Convolutional GANs to provide more stable training in almost every setting. The most important guidelines were the utilization of batch normalization in both the generator and discriminator and the removal of fully connected hidden layers.

Another key aspect of the article is the usage of convolutional transposed layers(fractional-stridden) instead of stridden convolutional layers. This is applied to the generator network to increase the size of the images.

3 Methodology

The creation of the synthetic dataset has been a complex process due to the nature of the problem. The gathering of the original data has been realized with a manual process and the data needed different methods of preprocessing. Finally, the labeling of the synthetic images has been done based on the IV curve of the original data.

3.1 Data Gathering

The first part of every research is obtaining data. There are some public datasets available in the bibliography but they are not suitable for this problem since they lack of the Intensity-Voltage (IV) curve that is associated with each PV cell. For the measurements for the IV curve, a device we have used the device with the capacity of measuring the IV curve of a single PV cell [11]. The images of the PV cells were obtained with the electroluminescence (EL) camera Hamamatsu InGaAs C12741-03. It is known that this technique is highly effective for detecting defects on PV modules or cells [10]. and it is widely used in other works related to PV systems. In the Fig. 2 different photographs of the device and the camera are presented.

(a) Device to measure the IV curve

(b) Ingaas Camera

(c) Setting for capturing the images

Fig. 2. Devices used to obtain the data.

The cells were shadowed with different artificial defects, in order to improve the amount of data. The shadows were created aiming to imitate different defects or problems found on solar farms (Fig. 3).

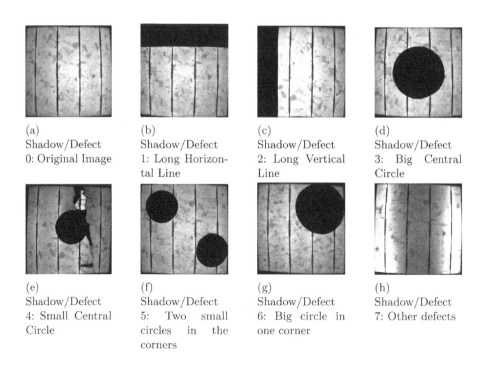

(a)
Shadow/Defect
0: Original Image

(b)
Shadow/Defect
1: Long Horizontal Line

(c)
Shadow/Defect
2: Long Vertical Line

(d)
Shadow/Defect
3: Big Central Circle

(e)
Shadow/Defect
4: Small Central Circle

(f)
Shadow/Defect
5: Two small circles in the corners

(g)
Shadow/Defect
6: Big circle in one corner

(h)
Shadow/Defect
7: Other defects

Fig. 3. Different Techniques to photography modules.

We obtained 602 different images with their corresponding IV curves.

3.2 Image Preprocessing

The obtained images suffered from different problems:

- Dead pixels and luminous noise: The camera has some dead pixels due to its usage, there is also a bit of luminous noise produced by leaks in the insulation of the device. These two phenomena are harmful to the quality of the images even though they are almost not visible to the human eye, so it is important to remove or reduce their presence. To solve this problem, we captured an image before giving power to the PV cell for performing the EL image. This enabled us to perform a subtraction of the noise from each captured image.
- Images with poor lighting: Most of the libraries and programs have problems understanding the scale of the histogram of an image, not knowing with the value is supposed to be white. We can see in Fig. 4a, 4b how the channels of the images only occupy a tiny fraction of all of the possible values. To fix this problem we have performed a min-max standardization, subtracting the minimum value and dividing the maximum value found in the image. The resulting image can be seen in Fig. 4c and Fig. 4d.

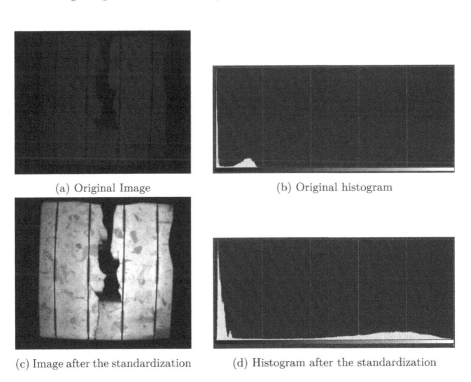

(a) Original Image   (b) Original histogram

(c) Image after the standardization   (d) Histogram after the standardization

Fig. 4. Image before and after applying the fix in the color.

– Black surrounding Areas: As it can be seen in Fig. 4c, the cells are surrounded by a black area, this is caused due to the lens of the camera since it is also capturing the walls of the insulated area. The issue was solved by performing a change of perspective. First of all, we applied different filters to remove the details and obtain the maximum contour polygon of the cell. After that, we performed a Hough Transform to find the corners of the cell. In some cells, we needed to make minor fixes before the transformation due to their defects or black areas. The results of the transformation can be seen in Fig. 5.

Since the process was applied to every image, we obtained 602 processed images.

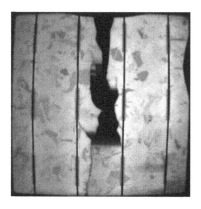

Fig. 5. Cell after removing the black contour

3.3   Creation of the Synthetic Images

As commented before, we have used Deep Convolutional Generative Adversarial Network. The model is composed of two different networks: generative and discriminator.

The architecture of the generative network can be seen in Fig. 7. The input of this network is a random noise with a Normal distribution and produces an image of the desired size. In Fig. 6 we can see the output before and after the training. The network has Convolutional Transpose Layers of different sizes to improve its generative properties. It also uses Batch Normalization [13] and the Leaky Relu function [14]. Other important parameters can be found in Table 1.

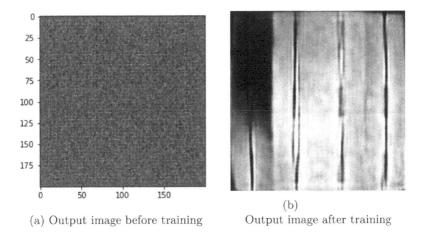

(a) Output image before training

(b)
Output image after training

Fig. 6. Differences in the output images before and after the training.

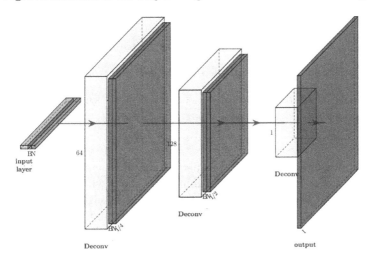

Fig. 7. Architecture of the generator network

Table 1. Hyperparameters for the generator network

Activation function	Loss function	Learning rate	Epochs	Batch size	Output size
Leaky relu	Cross entropy	$5 * 10^{-5}$	800	4	200×200

The architecture of the discriminator network can be seen in Fig. 8. The input is an image of the desired size. The single output determines if the image is a real cell or a fake image. The network uses convolutional layers to find the patterns and features of the images. It also uses dropout and batch normalization to improve its generalization capacities. Other important parameters can be found in Table 2.

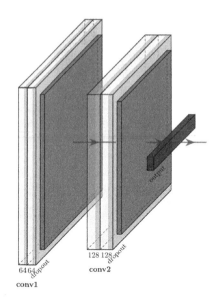

Fig. 8. Architecture of the discriminator network

Table 2. Hyperparameters for the discriminator network

Activation function	Loss function	Learning rate	Epochs	Batch size	Input size
Leaky relu	Cross entropy	$5 * 10^{-5}$	800	4	200×200

The training of both networks was performed simultaneously. We used all the images for training the GAN. The training loop starts with the generator being provided for seed as input. The generator produces a cell from that seed. After that, the discriminator is used to classify real images and fake images. The loss is computed for each of the networks, based on the results of the discriminator. In Fig. 9 we can observe the evolution of the loss in both networks. In the first epochs, the loss of the discriminator is high, until it learns to detect the real images. At that moment the loss of the generator reaches its peak since almost any fake image is being classified as real. After that, the generator improves steadily its images reaching its lower loss near epoch 400. During that time the performance of the discriminator worsens since it gets difficult to differentiate between real and fake images. It reaches its highest loss near epoch 400.

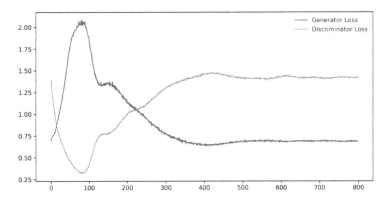

Fig. 9. Evolution of the loss of generator and discriminator

The training took 2 h and 41 min with a CPU AMD Ryzen 7 5800H, 16 GB of RAM, and a GPU Nvidia Geforce GTX 1650.

After the training, the generator network is used to generate 10000 images. Each image is produced by a different random seed. In Fig. 10 we can see some of the generated images.

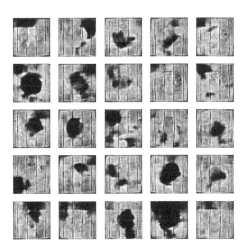

Fig. 10. Multiple generated images

3.4 Labeling

The process of labeling the synthetic images was not trivial. The main problem was related to the nature of the labels of the original images. The labels are based on the energetic production of the cells which is measured with the IV curve. Synthetic cells are not physical cells, so it is not possible to measure their curves. To solve this problem we have created a regression model based on Random Forest (RF) [12]. The tuning of the hyperparameters has been done of this RF with GridSearchCV using the Sklearn library We can see the results of the optimization for RF in Table 3. The RF model is trained with the complete original dataset (602 images).

Table 3. Best hyperparameters found for Random Forest: n_estimators $\in$ $[20, 500]$, max_depth $\in [0, 10]$, min_samples_split $\in [1, 10]$, min_samples_leaf$\in [1, 10]$, min_weight_fraction_leaf $\in [0, 0.8]$

n_estimators	max_depth	min_samples_split	min_samples_leaf	min_weight_fraction_leaf
200	10	1	1	0

The training data of this model was composed of different features extracted from the original 604 images (Table 4) and was divided into training and validation (66%/33%), we decided to use only two different sets due to our limitation in data. The target variable was the power produced by each cell, standardized between 0 and 1.

Table 4. Features for Random Forest Regressor

Mean	Median	Mode	Variance	Std
Roughness	Blacks	Burned whites	Others	peaks_number
Peaks distance	Peak 0 height	Peak 0 width	Peak 1 height	Peak 1 width

The model performed a Mean Absolute Error (MAE) of 0.041 and a Mean Squared Error (MSE) of 0.0038 in the validation dataset. The predictions of the generated dataset can be seen in Fig. 11. Finally, the images were divided in two according to their power (class 0 > 0.8 and class 1 ≤ 0.8). 6963 images were classified as class 0 and 3037 as class 1.

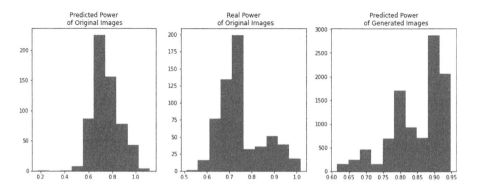

Fig. 11. Histogram of predicted labels of the generated dataset

4   Results

The dataset is divided into two folders according to each class: class 0 represents the images that have a relative power output of at least 0.8. As we have said before the dataset is divided into 6963 of class 0 and 3037 of class 1. The cells in the class are producing enough electricity even if some of them have some kinds of defects (Fig. 12a). class 1 represents the images that have a relative power output of less than 0.8. The cells in that class are underperforming due to their defects (Fig. 12b).

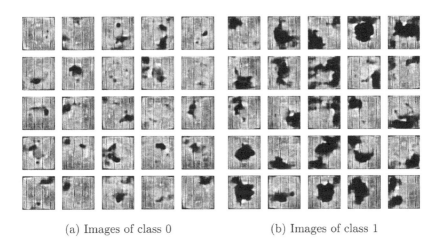

(a) Images of class 0   (b) Images of class 1

Fig. 12. Different generated images of both classes.

We can also observe that the generated images present different defects from the original images. This improves the diversity of defects in the datasets. Even if the images seem to be quite different than the original we can observe that the average of all of the histograms of the images for each class presents a similar structure. The images of class 0 (Fig. 13a) mostly present gray-white colors but in some cases present minor defects that are reflected in the peaks of the black areas. The images of class 1 (Fig. 13b) present a high amount of black pixels due to their high amount of shadows or defects. The generated images have a peak with a higher height than the peak found in the original images but in contrast, the peak in the original images is wider.

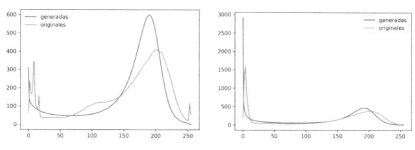

(a) Histogram of the images of class 0   (b) Histogram of the images of class 1

Fig. 13. Different generated images of both classes.

In Fig. 14 we can see a generated cell with its histogram and an original cell with present a similar defect. We can observe that their histogram is also similar, they present the same amount of peaks and are in a similar position.

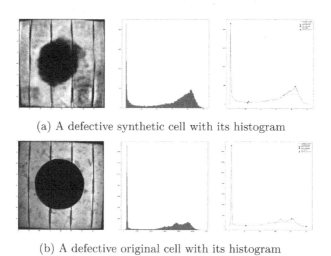

(a) A defective synthetic cell with its histogram

(b) A defective original cell with its histogram

Fig. 14. Comparison of a defective synthetic cell and a defective original cell

In Fig. 15 we can also observe it with the synthetic cells that have almost no defects and an original without them either. Their histogram is also quite similar since their most important peak is placed around the same area.

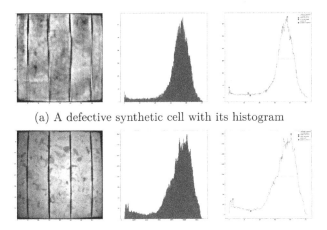

(a) A defective synthetic cell with its histogram

(b) A defective original cell with its histogram

Fig. 15. Comparison of a defective synthetic cell and a defective original cell

The dataset can be downloaded from https://github.com/hectorfelipe98/Synthetic-PV-cell-dataset. We also provide a file that relates each image with its label and its output power.

5 Conclusions and Future Work

This work has shown that it is possible to create new PV datasets using the newest Artificial Intelligence Techniques. The process is not straightforward since it needs different techniques to prepare the data. The labeling of the new images is a complex process since it is not possible to ask a domain expert.

The obtained images present more kinds of defects than the originals. This can be used to train models to improve their generalization capacity.

In future research work, we will try to improve the original dataset, creating new kinds of shadows or defects and trying to make the data more realistic. Another important aspect to improve are the processes to prepare the data, in order to obtain better images. Finally, new architectures or models need to be tested to improve the generation of the images.

Acknowledgements. This study was supported by the University of Valladolid with the predoctoral contracts of 2020, co-funded by Santander Bank. It has been also supported by Cátedra CeI Caja Rural de Soria. Finally, we have to thank the MOVILIDAD DE DOCTORANDOS Y DOCTORANDAS UVa 2022 from the University of Valladolid.

References

1. Kim, J.H.: Smart city trends: a focus on 5 countries and 15 companies. Cities **123**, Article Number 103551 (2022). https://doi.org/10.1016/j.cities.2021.103551
2. Hernández-Callejo, L., Gallardo-Saavedra, S., Alonso-Gómez, V.: A review of photovoltaic systems: design, operation, and maintenance. Solar Energy **188**, 426–440 (2019). https://doi.org/10.1016/j.solener.2019.06.017. ISSN 0038-092X
3. Creswell, A., White, T., Dumoulin, V., Arulkumaran, K., Sengupta, B., Bharath, A.A.: Generative adversarial networks: an overview (2017)
4. Schreiber, J., Jessulat, M., Sick, B.: Generative adversarial networks for operational scenario planning of renewable energy farms: a study on wind and photovoltaic. In: Tetko, I.V., Kůrková, V., Karpov, P., Theis, F. (eds.) ICANN 2019. LNCS, vol. 11729, pp. 550–564. Springer, Cham (2019). https://doi.org/10.1007/978-3-030-30508-6_44
5. Shou, C., et al.: Defect detection with generative adversarial networks for electroluminescence images of solar cells. In: Proceedings - 2020 35th Youth Academic Annual Conference of Chinese Association of Automation, YAC 2020, pp. 312–317 (2020). https://doi.org/10.1109/YAC51587.2020.9337676
6. Luo, Z., Cheng, S.Y., Zheng, Q.Y.: GAN-based augmentation for improving CNN performance of classification of defective photovoltaic module cells in electroluminescence images. In: IOP Conference Series: Earth and Environmental Science, vol. 1, p. 012106 (2019). https://doi.org/10.1088/1755-1315/354/1/012106
7. Du, X., Cai, Y., Wang, S., Zhang, L.: IEEE 2016 31st Youth Academic Annual Conference of Chinese Association of Automation (YAC), pp. 159–164 (2016)
8. Goodfellow, I., et al.: Generative adversarial networks. In: Advances in Neural Information Processing Systems, vol. 3 (2014). https://doi.org/10.1145/3422622
9. Radford, A., Metz, L., Chintala, S.: Unsupervised representation learning with deep convolutional generative adversarial networks. In: ICLR (2016)
10. Gallardo-Saavedra, S., et al.: Nondestructive characterization of solar PV cells defects by means of electroluminescence, infrared thermography, I-V curves and visual tests: experimental study and comparison. Energy **205**, 117930 (2020). ISSN 0360-5442 (2020). https://doi.org/10.1016/j.energy.2020.117930
11. Morales-Aragonés, J.I., Gómez, V.A., Gallardo-Saavedra, S., Redondo-Plaza, A., Fernández-Martínez, D., Hernández-Callejo, L.: Low-cost three-quadrant single solar cell I-V tracer. Appl. Sci. **12**, 6623 (2022). https://doi.org/10.3390/app12136623
12. Ho, T.K.: Random decision forests. In: Proceedings of 3rd International Conference on Document Analysis and Recognition, vol. 1, pp. 278–282 (1995)
13. Ioffe, S., Szegedy, C.: ICML'15: Proceedings of the 32nd International Conference on International Conference on Machine Learning, vol. 37, pp. 448–456 (2015)
14. Maas, A.L., Hannun, A.Y., Ng, A.Y.: Computer science D empirical evaluation of rectified activations in convolution network. https://arxiv.org/pdf/1505.00853.pdf
15. Srivastava, N., Hinton, G., Krizhevsky, A., Sutskever, I., Salakhutdinov, R.: Dropout: a simple way to prevent neural networks from overfitting. J. Mach. Learn. Res. **15**, 1929–1958 (2014)

Walking Accessibility to the Public Transport Network in Montevideo, Uruguay

Sara Perera[1] and Renzo Massobrio[1,2,3]

[1] Facultad de Ingeniería, Universidad de la República, 11300 Montevideo, Uruguay
{sara.perera,renzom,sergion}@fing.edu.uy
[2] Transport and Planning Department, Delft University of Technology,
2628 Delft, CN, The Netherlands
[3] Departamento de Ingeniería Informática, Universidad de Cádiz,
11519 Puerto Real, Spain

Abstract. Public transport plays a key role in expanding the distances that people can travel using active modes of transport. Studying walking accessibility to public transportation systems is highly relevant, since the walk to stops/stations can be particularly challenging for children, the elderly, citizens with disabilities, and for the general population during bad weather conditions or in pedestrian-unfriendly cities. This work presents a study on walking accessibility for the public transport system in Montevideo, Uruguay. The proposed methodology combines information of the bus stops and lines that operate in the city, the road infrastructure, and demographic information of the city to compute walking accessibility indicators to the public transport system. The results of the analysis suggest that over 95.5% of the population can access at least one stop when walking up to 400 m. However, these values are not evenly distributed among the population, with young citizens and men showing lower levels of coverage compared to their counterparts.

Keywords: Accessibility · Walking · Public transport

1 Introduction

The organization of transport systems condition the mobility of people, limiting their ability to participate in society and generating different forms of social exclusion [2]. In particular, geographic exclusion consists in the lack of auto-mobility and access to public transport systems. The importance of ensuring mobility for non-automobile users to reach destinations beyond normal walking range is key for the mitigation of this type of exclusion.

Public transport systems complement the use of active modes of transport (e.g., walking, cycling) by extending their range. Thus, an increase in the use of public transport can deliver significant health benefits, as this mode almost

S. Nesmachnow and L. Hernández Callejo (Eds.): ICSC-CITIES 2022, CCIS 1706, pp. 17–30, 2023.
https://doi.org/10.1007/978-3-031-28454-0_2

always includes a stage with physical activity [14]. In particular, studying walking accessibility to public transport is relevant since the majority of users access networks in this manner. Passengers make their route choice based on the entire trip, including entering and exiting the public transport network [3], and tend to have an aversion towards long walks. However, passengers accept longer access and egress distances to/from the public transport network when the characteristics of the transport service (e.g., speed and frequency) improve [3]. Moreover, time is valued differently by passengers on each part of the trip. It is estimated that passengers value walking time up to 1.65 times more compared to in-vehicle time [1]. Therefore, a reduction in access times would render a greater reduction in the perceived total travel time for passengers.

This work presents a study on walking accessibility from a potential mobility approach using Montevideo, Uruguay, as a case study. The main objective is to provide accessibility indicators for Montevideo's public transport bus network that measure how easy/hard is for citizens in different parts of the city to access the public transport system by walking. For this purpose, several sources of information are combined, including bus lines, bus stops, road infrastructure and population distribution in the city. Through a geospatial analysis, three accessibility indicators are computed. The results obtained are inline with figures reported by the transit authorities while also allowing for a finer-grain analysis throughout the city.

The remainder of this article is organized as follows. First, Sect. 2 provides a review of relevant literature on the subject. Next, Sect. 3 presents the methodology to compute the accessibility indicators. Then, Sect. 4 presents the case study and discusses the results of the indicators. Finally, Sect. 5 summarises the main outcomes and potential lines of future work.

2   Related Work

Studies of walking as a mean of access to public transport networks are classified into two approaches: studies of observed mobility and studies of potential mobility. Observed mobility studies seek to accurately measure the distance or time walked by users to access a public transport network. Most related works with this approach are based on survey information, where passengers declare their point of origin and point of entry to the public transport network [4,5,13].

In contrast, the research reported in this article is categorized in the literature of potential mobility. One of the most widespread methods to capture the potential mobility of individuals is related to the concept of accessibility [6]. In general, accessibility indicators are based on identifying the number of opportunities that an individual has under certain cost parameters associated with the transited networks (e.g., time, distance). Studying walking accessibility to public transport networks implies considering each stop in the system as an opportunity and walking through the road infrastructure as the access method. The standard procedure consists in evaluating the coverage of the transport network through the proportion of the population that is able to access the network by walking up to a certain distance threshold.

An interesting approach was proposed by Langford et. al, which studied the accessibility to the public transport system of South Wales, UK [10]. The authors introduced an accessibility measure based on enhanced *floating catchment* techniques, which capture many detailed aspects of accessibility. The method is a particular case of a gravitational model used to measure spatial interaction. Using information about public transport schedules and stop locations, the authors calculated a walking accessibility indicator to the transport system through geospatial analysis tools. The proposed indicator incorporates aspects of proximity, frequency, demand and availability of the public transport service. The authors concluded that their approach provides considerably more analytical detail than traditional approaches based on calculating the percentage of population covered using Euclidean buffers and area-ratio overlays.

When calculating the distance people walk to access public transport, several approaches exist in the literature to measure the distance from the point of origin to the point of entry to the transport system. The standard procedure in most recent works seems to be to use the shortest distance traveled through the road network from origin to the stop/station of entry [4,5,13]. Many guidelines in the literature suggest using a threshold distance of 400 m [4,13]. However, the origin of this value is unclear; although it might be related to the work of Neilson and Fowler [4]. Several works have shown that this assumption is quite realistic on average. A study done in The Hague, Netherlands, suggests that the median distance walked as a feeding method for the public transport system is 380 m [13]. Similarly, for Sydney, Australia, the median walking distance was estimated to be 364 m for the bus system [4]. Nevertheless, both works highlight that these median values indicate that exactly half of the respondents travel beyond the 400 m threshold used as a rule of thumb.

For the specific case study used in this work—Montevideo, Uruguay—there are no prior studies on walking accessibility to public transport to the best of our knowledge. Some previous works have addressed accessibility to employment opportunities [8], to hospitals [9] and to education centers [7] using public transport, but were not focused on the access/egress to the public transport network. Also, a household mobility survey was conducted in 2016 to obtain a large-scale image of the mobility in the city, considering all modes of transportation and incorporating the metropolitan area of the city [11]. In this survey, participants were asked to provide rough estimates of their walk to stops for those trips involving public transport. Lastly, some figures have been suggested by the transport authorities in the press stating that nearly 97% of Montevideo's population is covered by the public transport network when considering a walking threshold of 400 m [12]. These figures confirm that Montevideo's city planners also assume a fixed distance of 400 m—as guidelines in the literature suggest—and provide a reference accessibility value for comparison.

3   Methodology

This section describes the methodology applied to calculate the indicators of walking accessibility to public transport systems. The workflow is based upon the reviewed literature albeit slightly adapted to the specific case study addressed in this work.

The following data sets are needed to compute the walking accessibility to public transport indicators:

– Zoning of the studied area
– Road network of the studied area
– Population of each zone
– Geographical location of stops
– List of public transport lines that operate on each stop

Indicators are based on a service area (sa) geospatial analysis. This method consists in delimiting the portion of the road network (RN) from which the stop can be reached within a fixed walking distance threshold (d). An example of service area calculation is shown in Fig. 1. The road network is displayed in grey, the stop is marked with a blue dot, and an example service area for the stop is defined in orange. Since bus stops are located in the sidewalk, it is necessary to first project them to the nearest point in the road network.

For notation purposes we will define the service area for a bus stop s_i, given the road network RN and a threshold walking distance d as:

$$SA_i = sa(s_i, RN, d) \tag{1}$$

As outlined in the review of related works, there seems to be a consensus among city planners of using $d=400$ m as the walking distance threshold to access public transport networks.

Then, to calculate accessibility indicators in an aggregated way, a zoning of the area of study must be provided. Depending on the nature of the analysis, coarser or finer zonifications may be considered. Since the road network itself can be used as the delimitation of the zones, it is advisable to take a small buffer for each zone in order to consider roads right in the edge of the zone. Figure 2 shows an example of a zone that correspond to a block; the buffer plotted in orange allows considering the portion of road that delimits the zone within it. Without this buffer, no portion of the road network would be considered to be inside the zone.

Given a pre-defined set of zones $z_1, z_2, ..., z_n$, the portion of the road network within each zone is considered as $rn_1, rn_2, ..., rn_n$. Thus, a formulation is given in Eq. 2, where $\cap$ is the geospatial intersection operation and $b(z_j, B)$ is the resulting polygon of applying a geospatial buffer operation of B units to zone z_j.

$$rn_j = RN \cap b(z_j, B) \tag{2}$$

Thus, with the previous formulations, the definition of whether a stop s_i covers a zone z_j can be defined:

$$s_i \text{ covers } z_j \iff rn_j \cap SA_i \neq \emptyset \tag{3}$$

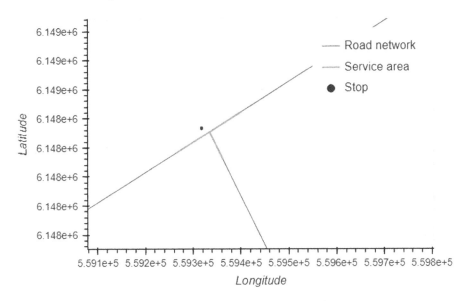

Fig. 1. Service area analysis example

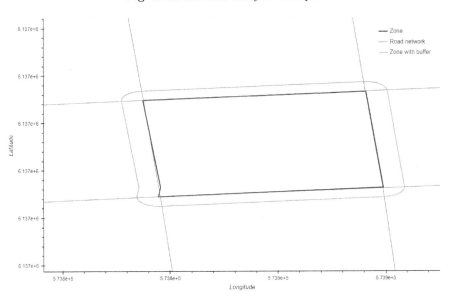

Fig. 2. Zone with buffer example

Also, given the aforementioned road network portions and the service area of each stop, the overlap between these can be computed to determine the coverage c_j at the zone level:

$$c_j = (SA_1 \cup SA_2 \cup ... \cup SA_n) \cap rn_j \qquad (4)$$

Summarizing, three accessibility indicators at the zone level are defined:

1. **Number of bus stops covering each zone at d ≤ 400 m:** corresponding to the number of bus stops that comply with Eq. 3

2. **Number of bus lines covering each zone at d ≤ 400 m:** calculated as the count of different bus lines that operate on bus stops that comply with Eq. 3

3. **Percentage of population within the zone covered by at least one bus stop at d ≤ 400 m:** assuming a uniform spatial distribution of the population in the road segments of each zone, coverage can be estimated through Eq. 4

4   Case Study: Montevideo, Uruguay

This section presents the results of the analysis of walking accessibility to the public transport network in Montevideo, Uruguay.

4.1   City and Public Transport System Overview

Montevideo is the capital and most populated city of Uruguay. It is situated on the southern coast of the country. It has a population of 1,3 million, which constitutes 40% of Uruguay's total population. The size of Montevideo is $201 \, \text{km}^2$ and therefore, has roughly 6.5 thousand inhabitants per km^2. It is a sparsely populated urban area compared to other large cities in Latin American.

The Statistics National Institute (INE) has divided the Uruguayan territory for statistical purposes. Three levels of division are considered:

– Section: Montevideo is divided into 27 Sections, according to the limits established in the 1963 Census. Sections are shown in Fig. 3 with dark blue lines.
– Segment: each Section is subdivided into Segments, which consist of a set of blocks. Montevideo is comprised of 1 063 Segments, which are marked in blue in Fig. 3.
– Zone: is the smallest identifiable zoning defined by INE. Each Segment is divided into several Zones. In densely populated parts of the city Zones usually coincide with a single block. In more rural areas, Zones correspond to portions of territory defined by natural or artificial limits (e.g., watercourses, highways, local roads, railways). Figure 3 shows the 13 608 Zones of Montevideo in sky blue.

In this work Zones are used to compute the walking accessibility indicators, which are the finer-grain zoning division available for the city.

The public transport system in Montevideo is based on buses. Public transport plays an important role in the city. Results from the Mobility Survey of the Metropolitan Area of Montevideo 2016 show that bus trips represent 25% of all trips [11]. Figure 4 outlines the road network, bus lines and bus stops of Montevideo. It is easy to distinguish the central parts of the city as the density of bus stops increases and most lines converge to it.

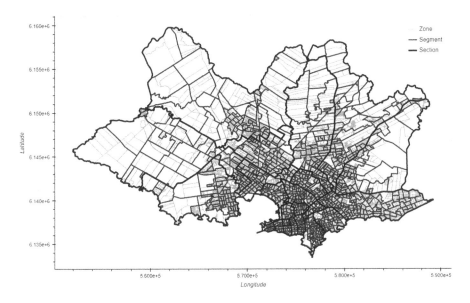

Fig. 3. Division of Montevideo in sections, segments, and zones.

4.2   Software and Tools

Service area analysis was made with QGIS through its algorithm provider using the function *service area*. Similarly, the buffer of Zones was carried out using the vector spatial analysis tool of QGIS. On the other hand, the computation of the accessibility indicators were made through Jupyter Notebooks, which offer a programming ecosystem that integrates data, code and results. Geospatial information was handled through the *Pandas* and *Geopandas* libraries and visualizations were created using the *Bokeh* library.

4.3   Data Sources and Data Cleansing

The main data sources were obtained through the open data catalog of the Municipality of Montevideo. All data sets obtained from this source were downloaded on 3/18/2022. The datasets used correspond to the bus lines and bus stops of the public transport system, the road network of Montevideo, and the population data from the 2011 census for the three existing zoning levels: Section, Segment and Zone.

Bus Stops and Bus Lines. Cleaning the bus lines and stops data comprised a series of consistency checks. A first approach with the data was enough to rule out a line that is active only during the Carnival season in Montevideo and was therefore removed from the lines and stops data set. Another verification carried out was through a full join between the data set of lines and the data set of stops, to check that all lines have associated stops and that all stops have

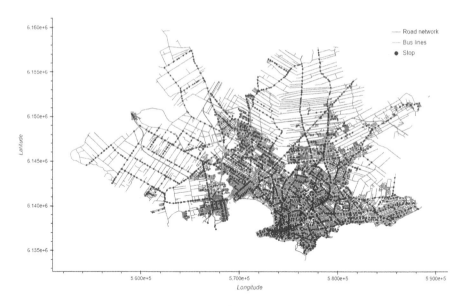

Fig. 4. Montevideo: road network and public transport system

at least one corresponding bus line. As a result of this analysis, one line was removed because it did not have corresponding stops in the set of bus stops. Finally, all the bus stops that were located outside of Montevideo were removed and the lines that operate beyond the department were cut short. In conclusion, the remaining data set of bus lines has 634 different lines; and the set of bus stops is comprised of a total of 4 643 unique stops.

Montevideo Road Network. The cleansing process of the Montevideo road network consisted simply in correcting invalid geometry errors using the prede-fined Check Validity function provided by the QGIS topology checker plugin.

4.4   Accessibility Indicators

The three accessibility indicators were computed according to the methodology, using the finest zoning available for the city, and considering a buffer of 10 m for each Zone as described in the methodology.

The first indicator shows the number of bus stops that cover each Zone considering a walking distance of 400 m or less. Results are shown in the map of Fig. 5, where darker shades of blue indicate a higher number of bus stops reachable from the Zone. The city center (south central area in the map) can be easily distinguished given the higher density of bus stops. Some peripheral Zones also stand out, since Zones in the periphery are larger in area and thus may have access to a higher absolute number of bus stops.

The mean number of bus stops accessible by a given Zone is 9.2; whereas the median is 9.0. A histogram of the distribution of the number of bus stops

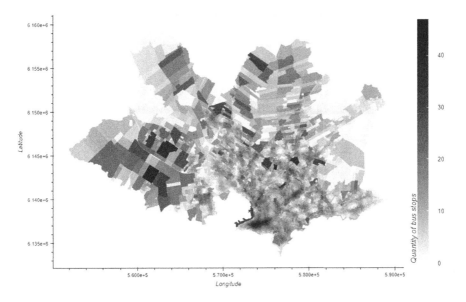

Fig. 5. Number of bus stops accessible when walking up to 400 m per Zone (Color figure online)

is presented in Fig. 6. The *saw-tooth* shape of the distribution can be explained by the fact that bus stops tend to be placed on each side of the road to service both directions of bus lines. Thus, it is more likely to reach an even number of bus stops (i.e., for inbound and outbound bus lines).

Next, we calculate the second accessibility indicator, i.e., the number of bus lines that are accessible for each Zone when considering a walk of 400 m or less. Results are shown in the choropleth map in Fig. 7, where darker colors indicate that a larger number of lines are accessible for that Zone.

The city center in this map stands out compared to other areas since many different bus lines converge to it. Also, the main arteries of the city (going East and North from the city center) can be distinguished because of the density of bus lines that operate over those main roads. Moreover, comparing Fig. 5 with Fig. 7, a softening of peripheral areas can be appreciated, suggesting that while some Zones in the periphery access a large number of stops, these stops provide service to a small number of bus lines. The mean number of lines is 16.7 and the median is 10.0. The distribution of the number of bus lines accessible is shown in the histogram in Fig. 8.

The third and last accessibility indicator illustrates the percentage of population of each Zone covered by the union of service areas. Results are shown in Fig. 9. Key results are that the mean coverage is 94.1% and the median is 100%. An histogram of the distribution of coverage is shown in Fig. 10 and shows that, for most Zones, 100% of their population have access to a bus stop walking 400 m or less. Given the assumption that the population is evenly distributed

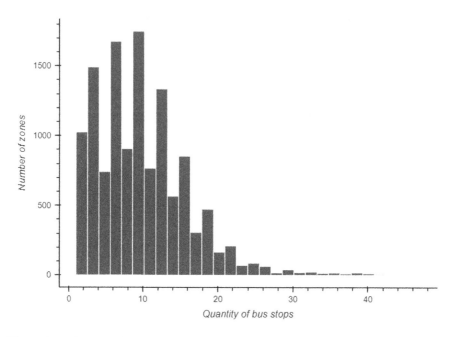

Fig. 6. Distribution of the number of bus stops accessible when walking up to 400 m

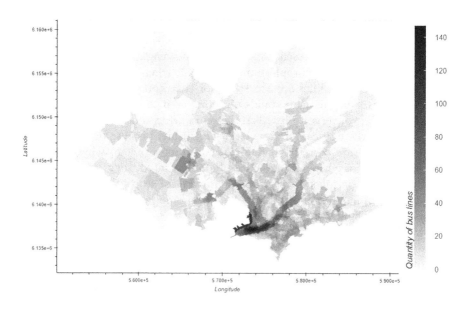

Fig. 7. Number of bus lines accessible when walking up to 400 m per Zone

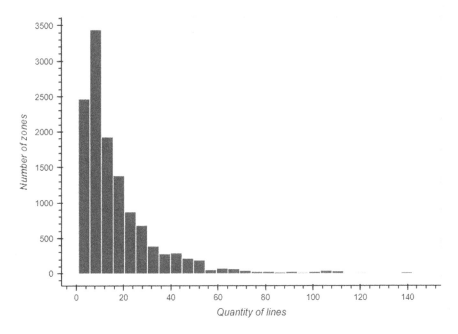

Fig. 8. Distribution of bus lines accessible when walking up to 400 m

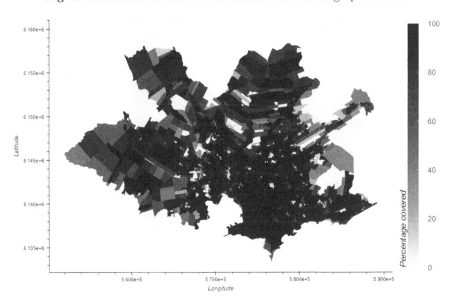

Fig. 9. % of population with access to a bus stop when walking up to 400 m per Zone

on the road network, the percentage of Montevideo's population covered by at least one bus stop at 400 m or less is 95,5%. When considering the population split by gender, women (95.7%) present a slightly higher percentage of coverage

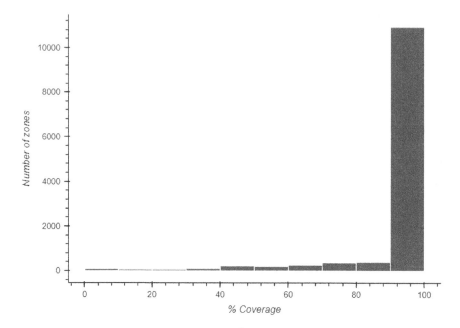

Fig. 10. Distribution of the % of population with access to a bus stop when walking up to 400 m

than men (95.3%). In regards to age, young citizens (0 to 14 years old) present the lowest levels of accessibility with a coverage of 93.9% whereas senior citizens present the best values of accessibility with 95.6%.

5   Conclusions and Future Work

This work presented a study on walking accessibility to public transport systems using Montevideo, Uruguay, as a case study. As public transport in Montevideo is based on buses, the main data sets considered are bus stops and lines. The analysis was performed using the smallest zoning available for the city which is roughly equivalent to blocks in densely populated areas of the city. Through a service area analysis using geospatial tools we estimated the coverage of Montevideo's public transport bus network. The implemented methodology accounts for the actual walk that passenger do through the road network, improving other simpler estimations based on straight line distances and buffer areas.

The main finding of the analysis is that 95,5% of Montevideo's population can access at least one bus stop when walking up to 400 m. However, when considering the number of different bus lines that operate on these stops, results show that areas in the outskirts of the city have access to fewer bus lines compared to downtown areas. The results are in-line with figures reported by transport authorities in the press (around 97% of coverage). The overestimation in coverage can be explained by the simpler approach used by the authorities (i.e., straight line buffer areas) compared to the more precise approach proposed in this work based on service areas. Additionally, results showed that the walking accessibility is unequal when considering gender and age, with young citizens (0 to 14 years old) and men showing lower levels of coverage compared to their counterparts.

The main lines of future work include incorporating line schedules in order to analyze how accessibility indicators and coverage vary throughout the day. Also, we propose to compare the computed indicators against the results from a household mobility survey conducted in 2016. Finally, the results of this study could be used as input to address many different optimization problems, such as, bus stop (re)location, network redesign, and expanding the catchment areas of current bus stops by including facilities for other active modes (e.g., shared bikes) to be used as a feeding method for the public transport system.

Acknowledgements. This work was partly funded by CSIC-Udelar and Intendencia de Montevideo. The work of R. Massobrio was funded by European Union-NextGenerationEU.

References

1. Abrantes, P.A., Wardman, M.R.: Meta-analysis of UK values of travel time: an update. Transp. Res. Part A: Policy Pract. **45**(1), 1–17 (2011)
2. Audirac, I.: Accessing transit as universal design. J. Plan. Lit. **23**(1), 4–16 (2008)
3. Brand, J., Hoogendoorn, S., van Oort, N., Schalkwijk, B.: Modelling multimodal transit networks integration of bus networks with walking and cycling. In: 2017 5th IEEE International Conference on Models and Technologies for Intelligent Transportation Systems (MT-ITS). pp. 750–755 (2017)
4. Daniels, R., Mulley, C.: Explaining walking distance to public transport: the dominance of public transport supply. J. Transp. Land Use **6**(2), 5–20 (2013)
5. García-Palomares, J.C., Gutiérrez, J., Cardozo, O.D.: Walking accessibility to public transport: an analysis based on microdata and GIS. Environ. Plann. B. Plann. Des. **40**(6), 1087–1102 (2013)
6. Hansen, W.G.: How accessibility shapes land use. J. Am. Inst. Plann. **25**(2), 73–76 (1959)
7. Hernandez, D.: Uneven mobilities, uneven opportunities: social distribution of public transport accessibility to jobs and education in montevideo. J. Transp. Geogr. **67**, 119–125 (2018)
8. Hernandez, D., Hansz, M., Massobrio, R.: Job accessibility through public transport and unemployment in Latin America: The case of Montevideo (Uruguay). J. Transp. Geogr. **85**, 102742 (2020)
9. Hernández, D., Rossel, C.: Unraveling social inequalities in urban health care accessibility in montevideo: a space-time approach. J. Urban Aff. 1–16 (2022)
10. Langford, M., Fry, R., Higgs, G.: Measuring transit system accessibility using a modified two-step floating catchment technique. Int. J. Geogr. Inf. Sci. **26**(2), 193–214 (2012)
11. Mauttone, A., Hernández, D.: Encuesta de movilidad del área metropolitana de Montevideo. principales resultados e indicadores (2017)

12. Pablo, M.: LadoB - ¿Cómo se transporta Montevideo? Entrevista a Pablo Menoni. TV Ciudad (2022). https://www.youtube.com/watch?v=nU6gZKqi_k8. Accessed 03 Oct 2022
13. Rijsman, L., van Oort, N., Ton, D., Hoogendoorn, S., Molin, E., Teijl, T.: Walking and bicycle catchment areas of tram stops: factors and insights. In: 2019 6th International Conference on Models and Technologies for Intelligent Transportation Systems (MT-ITS), pp. 1–5 (2019)
14. van Soest, D., Tight, M.R., Rogers, C.D.: Exploring the distances people walk to access public transport. Transp. Rev. **40**(2), 160–182 (2020)

Artificial Intelligence for Automatic Building Extraction from Urban Aerial Images

Lucas González[1] , Jamal Toutouh[2(✉)] , and Sergio Nesmachnow[1]

[1] Universidad de la República, Montevideo, Uruguay
{lucas.gonzalez.petti,sergion}@fing.edu.uy
[2] Universidad de Málaga, Málaga, Spain
jamal@uma.es

Abstract. Cartographic information is key in urban city planning and management. Deep neural networks allow detecting/extracting buildings from aerial images to gather this cartographic information. This article explores the application of deep neural networks architectures to address automatic building extraction. The results reported that UNet-based architectures provide the most accurate predictions.

Keywords: building detection · artificial neural networks · deep learning

1 Introduction

Cartographic information is an essential tool for urban decision-makers. It plays a key role in urban city planning, citizen welfare, and resources management [5]. High-resolution remote sensing images are now easier and cheaper to acquire using satellites and unmanned aerial vehicles. Thus, cartographic information can be obtained from aerial and satellite images by applying computer vision and artificial intelligence, at limited costs [22].

Land cover and land use classification is a fundamental task in remote sensing. The main goal of land cover and land use classification is to assign a category label to each pixel of an image [9]. It provides the opportunity to get cartographic information and to monitor the evolution of the regions easily [2]. New applications have emerged using this technology, such as precision agriculture [21] and population density estimation [4]. This article focuses on a specific application, the automatic building detection/extraction from optical remote sensing images.

For more than two decades, significant research has been carried out on automatic building extraction. However, incomplete cue extraction, sensor dependency of data, and scene complexity are hindering the success of automatic building extraction and modeling [9]. Nowadays, the most popular methods to address automatic building detection are based on deep learning (DL) using deep neural networks (DNN). DL allows DNNs to learn representations of data samples with several levels of abstraction [6]. DL overcomes the main challenges in the literature on automatic building detection.

© The Author(s), under exclusive license to Springer Nature Switzerland AG 2023
S. Nesmachnow and L. Hernández Callejo (Eds.): ICSC-CITIES 2022, CCIS 1706, pp. 31–45, 2023.
https://doi.org/10.1007/978-3-031-28454-0_3

This article focuses on DL for automatic building extraction (or detection). Three different DNNs are evaluated: fully convolutional neural networks (FCNs), residual neural networks (ResNet), and UNet. Specifically, the `FCN-ResNet50`, `UNet-ResNet101`, and `UNet-ResNeXt50` architectures are evaluated over the Inria Aerial Image Labeling Dataset (IAD) [14]. The IAD dataset includes aerial images from different regions representing various types of urban areas.

The main results of the research indicate that the proposed models were able to learn building extraction tasks in different building composition contexts. Additionally, better performance was observed in models that were trained with larger image cutouts. Overall, this article contributes to the proposal of a methodology for building identification using FCN and the evaluation of the proposed methodology in a real case study. The research was developed in the context of the SaniBID project, from the Inter-American Development Bank.

The article is organized as follows. Next section describes the problem solved and reviews relevant related works. Section 3 introduces the network architectures analyzed applied to address building extraction. The experimental evaluation is reported in Sect. 5. Finally, Sect. 6 presents the conclusions and formulates the main lines for future work.

2 Problem Definition and Literature Review

This section describes the addressed problem and reviews relevant related works.

2.1 The Automatic Building Detection Problem

The easy acquisition of high-resolution remote sensing images has promoted the emergence of remote sensing studies and applications. Remote sensing methods apply classification at the pixel level to extract/detect artificial objects, such as buildings, roads, and vehicles, to perform mapping and to build cartographic data. One of the most salient applications is automatic building extraction.

Given an aerial/satellite source image, the general idea behind the automatic building extraction is to obtain a 2D labeling output matrix (i.e., a binary image) with the same scale in which the pixels represent whether the corresponding pixel in the source image belongs to a building or not. In general, the 2D labeling output is obtained according to a 2D building class probability matrix. Figure 1 illustrates an example of the workflow of how a CNN is applied to automatic building extraction. The white pixels in the output indicate that the corresponding pixel in the input image belongs to a building.

In some locations, the shapes and colors of buildings and the objects in their surrounding (such as tanks, lakes, and plants) are very similar, making the automatic building extraction task extremely challenging. As the sensors are able to retrieve more accurate data with higher resolution (such as multispectral images), the applied models get more clues for recognizing the building regions. These models require higher computational resources to deal with such higher information.

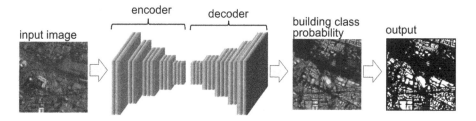

Fig. 1. CNN architecture with encoder and decoder networks applied to automatic building extraction.

The progress of DL has motivated several authors to address the computer vision problem behind automatic building extraction using DNNs. At the same time, machine learning (ML) methods were adopted to deal with the same problem by principally applying feature learning methods.

2.2 Related Work

DNNs have shown they are able to learn features describing buildings and map them onto output layers. The output layers of the DNNs represent the probability that a given pixel in an image belongs to a building. The learning methods applied by DNNs are improving their efficacy and efficiency thanks to the development of modern parallel computing processors and graphics processing units. Different annotated aerial high-resolution image datasets have been collected, contributing to the continuous improvement of the accuracy and quality of the results because the training process may use more data.

Variations of convolutional neural networks (CNNs) are the most commonly applied DNNs in building extraction literature. CNNs have been shown to be highly competitive in computer vision tasks, such as large-scale image recognition, object detection, and semantic segmentation [23]. A representative set of these DNNs are FCNs, DeepLab, Pyramid Scene Parsing Network or Pyramid Scene Parsing Network, LinkNet, ResNets, ResNetXt, and UNet [15].

UNet-based DNNs have been the most promising models for building extraction. Two comparative studies [8,10] evaluated UNet against LinkNet on building extraction over the Planet dataset, which covers different areas of Russia. Both studies concluded that UNet provides more competitive results than LinkNet. UNet was also applied over the SpaceNet dataset by Khryashchev et al. [11]. The authors modified the original UNet architecture by including two separate encoders to accept two separate inputs from the same geographical area: an RGB image and an infrared (IR) image. The proposed approach improved the results provided by the original UNet for the regions studied. The same approach (using two separate UNet encoders) was used over Inria Aerial Image Labeling Dataset (IAD) [20]. In this case, the authors evaluated this approach by applying different loss functions during the training process. The experimental analysis did not provide statistical results on which loss function provided the best performance.

A general problem when dealing with building extraction is that the buildings can be located close to each other and be merged into one single object after segmentation (extraction). A variation of UNet was proposed by Pasquali et al. [18] to deal with this problem. The authors proposed using two encoders, one specialized in detecting the buildings and the other in detecting the separation between buildings. The experimental results show that the proposed approach was able to extract the buildings while detecting their boundaries.

Li et al. [12] analyzed five modifications to the UNet architecture (adding and removing layers) to check which modifications showed the best accuracy and were the most computationally efficient. Besides, UNet has been studied over several types of imagery databases, for example, a combination of aerial imagery with data from geographic information systems [17], a high-resolution imagery dataset [1], and a very ultra-high-resolution imagery dataset captured by unmanned aerial vehicles.

This article analyzes different DNNs whose architectures combine UNet and ResNet. In literature, an approach based on this combination, a UNet-ResNet architecture, adapted the UNet to jointly accept different data types such as IR imagery, RGB satellite imagery, and others. Xu et al. [25] proposed this approach to extract buildings on multispectral imagery from Vaihingen and Potsdam, Germany. The method was compared with other remote sensing algorithms, a FCN and a CNN combined with Random Forest. Experimental results showed that UNet-ResNet was better than the other methods in terms of accuracy and F1 score.

The main contribution of the research reported in this article over the previous approach is that the proposed models only use as input RGB images because the other type of data used to address the analyzed problem, e.g., IR imagery or normalized differential vegetation index, is not always available.

3   Deep Neural Networks Considered in the Study

This section describes the three main DNNs architectures applied for the automatic building detection problem.

3.1   Residual Neural Networks

The depth of DNNs is an important factor for their performance and it has proven to be one of the main parameters that allows learning of increasingly complex functions. However, increasing the number of layers brings the main problem of vanishing gradient, which prevents the network weights to be updated, i.e., no learning is being performed [15]. ResNet was developed to mitigate the gradient vanishing problem shown by very dense CNNs. The main idea of ResNet is to introduce skip connections among residual units, which bypass one or more layers (see Fig. 2). Skip connections allow the gradient to flow backward through the shortcut created between layers, from later layers to initial filters [7].

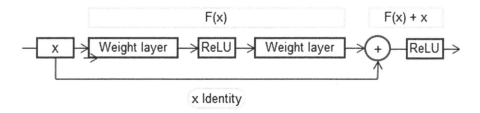

Fig. 2. Basic diagram of a residual unit.

Several variants of ResNet have been proposed, e.g., ResNet34, ResNet50, and ResNet101. The number in the name, i.e., 34, 50, and 101, indicate the number of layers of the network. These CNNs have one MaxPool layer at the beginning and one AveragePool layer at the end, and convolution layers.

Subsequently, the ResNeXt architecture [24] was proposed as an extension to ResNet. ResNeXt applies the "split-transform-merge" paradigm to replace the standard residual blocks. Instead of performing convolutions on the entire input mapping (i.e., using a unique convolution block), the block input is projected onto a set of lower-dimensional representations (channels) to which convolutional filters are applied separately to finally merge the results (i.e., generating multiple convolution paths to different convolution blocks, which outputs are merged by adding them together). In ResNetXt, all the convolution paths have the same topology. The number of paths is a hyperparameter itself called cardinality (C).

Figure 3 compares a residual block of ResNet50 and one of ResNeXt with $C=32$. The input of the ResNeXt block is divided into 32 channels of dimension 4 ("split"). Then, the convolutions are performed in each of the paths separately ("transform"). Finally, the channels are added together ("merge"). ResNeXt applies skip connections as in the case of ResNet.

3.2 Fully Convolutional Neural Networks

CNNs perform well in addressing image classification, i.e., labeling input images with a unique category. However, CNNs lack the notion of locality mainly because they use fully connected layers in the output. FCNs were proposed to keep the locality concept in learning, required to deal with image segmentation (i.e., the task of labeling individually each pixel of the input image) [13].

FCNs replace fully connected layers in the output with 1×1 convolutional layers. After performing the CNN downsampling operations to the input image, adding the new 1×1 convolutional layers allows upsampling to calculate the pixelwise output (label map). Thus, the classification output and the input image have a one-to-one correspondence at the pixel level: the channel dimension at any output pixel holds the classification results for the input pixel at the same spatial position.

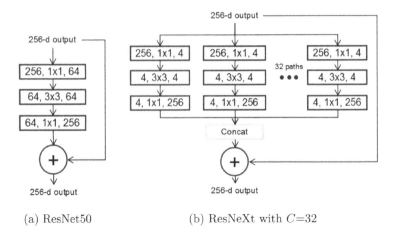

(a) ResNet50   (b) ResNeXt with $C=32$

Fig. 3. ResNet50 residual block and ResNeXt block ($C=32$). Each layer is represented as (number of input channels, kernel size, number of output channels).

The main advantages of using FCN over CNN are: a) FCNs are better suited to perform image segmentation, and b) FCNs do not necessarily have to receive inputs whose dimensions are of a fixed size.

3.3   UNet

The UNet architecture is based on FCN and it was introduced to address image segmentation task in the field of bio-medicine [19]. The main idea is to have a new ANN trained with few images (and making use of data augmentation) able to be used for image segmentation.

The UNet architecture consists of a contraction path (encoder) and an expansive path (decoder). The encoder is similar to that of FCN architecture and its objective is to capture the context in the image, while the decoder has the function of specifying the location of the elements. The contracting path is more or less symmetric to the expansive path, which yields a U-shaped architecture.

The main benefits of UNet over other ANNs architectures are: a) it has a simple structure built by using convolutional, ReLu activation function, and max pooling layers, and b) it exhibits very competitive performance in segmentation tasks by requiring a little amount of training data (i.e., labeled images).

4   Experimental Setup

This section introduces the ANN architectures analyzed, the dataset used to define the problem instances, the evaluation metrics, the hardware platform used to run the experiments, and the software libraries to develop the code.

4.1   Evaluated ANNs Architectures

The experimental analysis performed in this study considered more than one single ANN architecture. The idea is to find the best-suited architecture for the building segmentation problem. Among an initial list of candidate architectures and after performing preliminary experiments, three architectures performed better than the other ones and they were selected to address the problem. These architectures are defined by combining the architectures introduced in Sect. 3 (i.e., ResNet, ResNeXt, FCN, and UNet). These architectures are:

- FCN-ResNet50, a FCN with a ResNet50 as the backbone (i.e., encoder);
- UNet-ResNet101, a UNet with a ResNet101 as the backbone;
- and UNet-ResNeXt50, a UNet with a ResNeXt50 as the backbone.

The three models were trained by using the same main hyper-parameters: 40 training epochs, learning rate of 8×10^{-5} and Dice Loss as the loss function.

4.2   Problem Instance

The experimental evaluation was carried out over the IAD dataset [14]. IAD includes color aerial imagery covering a total area of $810 \, km^2$, divided into $405 \, km^2$ for the training set and $405 \, km^2$ for the testing set. The data covers different regions in the USA and Austria: San Francisco, Chicago, Kitsap County, Bellingham, and Bloomington in the USA; Vienna and Innsbruck in Austria. These regions represent different types of urban areas, from small cities to megacities.

The dataset was constructed by combining public domain images and the official location of public domain buildings from the cadaster. The dataset contains three color bands (Red, Green, and Blue) orthorectified images with a resolution of 1000×1000 pixels and a spatial resolution of $0.3 \, m$ per pixel.

As the ultimate goal of the IAD dataset is to evaluate building remote sensing techniques, the semantic segmentation of the images considers two different labels: building and no-building. Including data (images) from several types of cities allows this dataset to evaluate the generalization capabilities of the segmentation algorithms. Thus, the training and test sets do not overlap, i.e., include images from different cities. For example, the images of Chicago are included in the training set (and not in the test set), and the images of San Francisco are included in the test set (and not in the training set).

The training dataset contains 180 color image frames of size 5000×5000 pixels, covering an area of 1500×1500 m each. The regions included are Austin, Chicago, Kitsap County, West Tyrol, and Vienna. The test dataset has also 180 images and covers Bellingham, Bloomington, Innsbruck, San Francisco, and East Tyrol.

In the proposed experimental evaluation, the automatic building extraction was addressed over IAD (defining an instance named IAD). In order to evaluate the impact of the size of the dataset images on the accuracy of the evaluated methods, four additional datasets (instances) were defined by cropping the original IAD images. Four derived instances were defined:

- IAD1000: including 1000×1000 pixels images,
- IAD1250: including 1250×1250 pixels images,
- IAD1666: including 1666×1666 pixels images,
- and IAD2500: including 2500×2500 pixels. images.

4.3   Performance Metric

The metric used to evaluate the proposed models is Intersection over Union (IoU). IoU is a standard performance metric used for comparing the similarity between two arbitrary shapes, which is useful for image segmentation problems. Given an input image, IoU provides a measure of the similarity between the predicted region by using an ANN and the input image ground truth.

IoU is defined as the size of the intersection divided by the size of the union of the two regions (Eq. 1, where X is the actual class mapping of an image (given by the ground truth) and Y is the predicted map by the ANN). IoU is a normalized measure, invariant to the scale of the problem under consideration.

$$IoU = \frac{|X \cap Y|}{|X \cup Y|} \qquad (1)$$

4.4   Development and Execution Platform

The proposed approach was developed in Python using PyTorch and Segmentation Models PyTorch libraries. OpenCV and Albumentation [3] were used for image manipulation and data augmentation. The experimental evaluation was performed on the high performance computing infrastructure of National Supercomputing Center (Cluster-UY), Uruguay [16].

5   Experimental Evaluation and Discussion

This section describes the main results by reporting IoU and discussing the quality of the predictions.

5.1   Quantitative Analysis: IoU Results

Table 1, summarizes the IoU results for the three evaluated architectures (i.e., FCN-ResNet50 UNet-ResNet101, and UNet-ResNeXt50) and the five instances (i.e., IAD1000, IAD1250, IAD1666, IAD2500, and IAD). Besides, the table presents the

Table 1. IoU values obtained for each dataset derived from IAD.

Dataset	Architecture			Mean	Std
	FCN-ResNet50	UNet-ResNet101	UNet-ResNeXt50		
IAD1000	0.8469	0.8802	0.8694	0.8694	0.0139
IAD1250	0.8666	0.8611	0.8771	0.8683	0.0066
IAD1666	0.8782	0.8534	0.8816	0.8711	0.0126
IAD2500	0.9181	0.9057	0.9102	**0.9113**	0.0051
IAD	0.8965	0.9177	0.8965	0.9036	0.0100
mean	0.8813	0.8836	**0.8869**		
std	0.0245	0.0248	0.0146		

mean and standard deviation (std) values for all the architectures and all the instances. When evaluating the IoU metric, the higher values the better the results.

Results of the evaluated models depend on the size of the images in the instances. According to the results in Table 1, UNet-ResNeXt50 is the most competitive ANN architecture taking into account the mean and the standard deviation IoU values. The mean IoU achieved by UNet-ResNeXt50 is the highest one (i.e., it was the model that has best learned to identify buildings from aerial images). Besides, its standard deviation is the lowest, meaning that it was the most robust method. Even though, UNet-ResNeXt50 provided the best IoU values only for two instances, the IAD1250 and IAD1666.

The second most competitive architecture was UNet-ResNet101, which provided the second-best mean IoU value. UNet-ResNet101 got the best results for the IAD1000 and IAD instances, i.e., for the instances that have the smallest and the biggest images, respectively. FCN-ResNet50 was able to provide the most competitive results only for the IAD2500.

Thus, the results in Table 1 show that in general the ANN architectures that are based on UNet provide better results than the one based on FCN. This is because UNet is an evolution of FCN that provides enhancements that make it better suited for image segmentation tasks such as in the building extraction from aerial images. Likewise, the results show that the use of ResNeXt as a backbone yields to results that improve over the results compared to the use of the basic ResNet.

5.2 Qualitative Results Analysis: Output Labeling Map Results

In order to perform a qualitative analysis, four aerial images from the testing dataset of IAD were selected to compute the labeling map by using the three

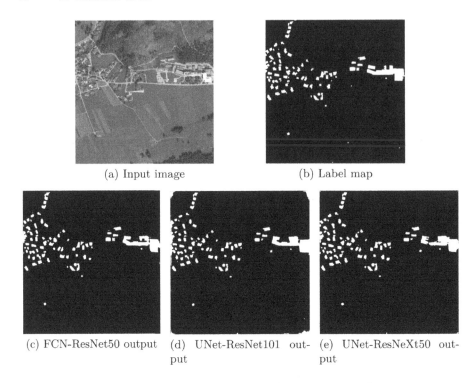

(a) Input image   (b) Label map

(c) FCN-ResNet50 output   (d) UNet-ResNet101 out-   (e) UNet-ResNeXt50 out-
                           put   put

Fig. 4. Image `tyrol-w322500_2500` from `IAD2500` results.

studied architectures. Figures 4–7 present the areal image, the ground truth (i.e., true labeling map), and the output labeling maps for each one of the models.

Figure 4 corresponds to an areal image from a rural area where there are just a few small buildings. In general, the three models provided similar results. They were able to extract the buildings, differentiating them from the vegetation and the roads. Focusing on `UNet-ResNeXt50`, the right side of the image in Fig. 4e that the model was able to extract different buildings that were not found by the other models. These different buildings are seen on the original aerial image in Fig. 4a, but the map in Fig. 4a labels all of them as one unique building.

Figures 5 and 6 represent areas with an increasing number of buildings in the suburbs of Chicago. In the results shown in Fig. 5, `FCN-ResNet50` provided the least competitive results because the output labeling map includes several false positives (i.e., several white shapes in the output labeling map that in the real image do not correspond to any building). The other two models got pretty similar results. However, the shapes of the buildings extracted by `UNet-ResNet101` match better with the ground truth shapes than the shapes

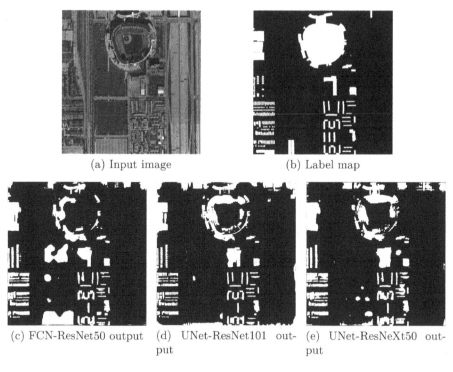

(a) Input image   (b) Label map

(c) FCN-ResNet50 output   (d) UNet-ResNet101 out-   (e) UNet-ResNeXt50 out-
                           put   put

Fig. 5. Image `chicago312500_2500` from `IAD2500` results.

computed by `UNet-ResNeXt50`. It is remarkable that the three models were able to extract buildings with special shapes like the baseball stadium, where the predictions were able to distinguish the playing field from the stands.

The area represented in Fig. 6 includes buildings of different shapes, including cross-shaped buildings. In general, all the evaluated models were able to predict all the buildings, regardless of the shape. The results show that `UNet-ResNet101` provided the best results. `UNet-ResNet101` was able to extract all the buildings while getting a negligible number of false positives. `FCN-ResNet50` and `UNet-ResNeXt50` were able to extract almost all buildings, but the shapes do not fit the ground truth in Fig. 6b as well as the shapes extracted by the `UNet-ResNet101`.

The aerial image in Fig. 7 is taken from an urban area with a high density of buildings and several roads in Vienna. In turn, it includes buildings of different sizes (ranging from small houses to big condos). The results provided by the three models show that they were able to extract the buildings distinguishing them from other types of infrastructures included in the image and the roads.

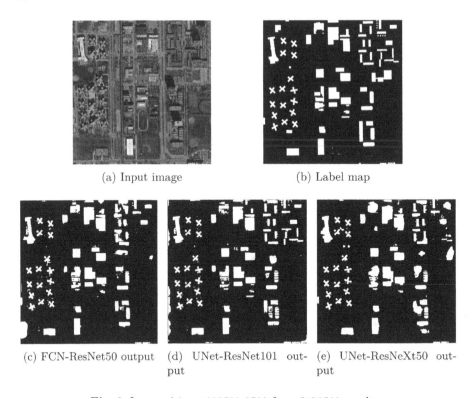

(a) Input image

(b) Label map

(c) FCN-ResNet50 output

(d) UNet-ResNet101 output

(e) UNet-ResNeXt50 output

Fig. 6. Image `chicago322500_2500` from `IAD2500` results.

Besides, the three models correctly labeled buildings of any size. In this case, it is pretty difficult to select which architecture got the most competitive results because the output labeling maps are close.

Summarizing, the qualitative results are in line with the quantitative results discussed in Sect. 5.1. The accuracy of the results of the networks build using a UNet architecture (i.e., `UNet-ResNet101` and `UNet-ResNeXt50`) is better than the network based on FCN.

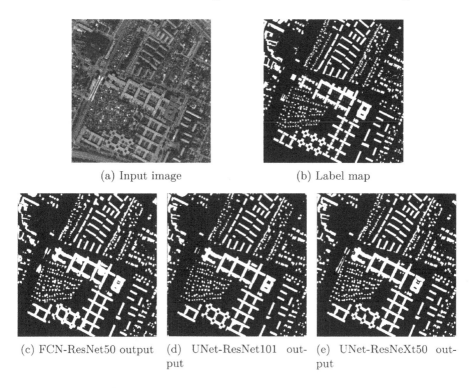

(a) Input image   (b) Label map

(c) FCN-ResNet50 output   (d) UNet-ResNet101 out-   (e) UNet-ResNeXt50 out-
                           put   put

Fig. 7. Image `vienna32250_0` from `IAD2500` results.

6   Conclusions and Future Work

This article presented a study of different architectures of deep neural networks
in the task of buildings extraction.

Based on the related works, the FCN, ResNet, UNet architectures and their
combinations were selected for the analysis. Special emphasis was placed on
exploring the network encoder, using the ResNet architecture and its variants
for that purpose. Besides the experiments made for the mentioned architectures,
the effect of different image sizes in training was explored. Four datasets were
constructed from the standard IAD dataset, and for each of them the three
candidate models were trained if the size of training images had an impact on
performance.

From the considered architectures, a better performance from those based on
UNet was computed, compared to the FCN variants. Regarding the size of the
training images, for the studied dataset a tendency to better performance was
detected over the models trained with larger images.

The results obtained in the experimental evaluation suggest that it is feasible developing automatic strategies for building detection using deep neural
networks. Results from these strategies are valuable inputs for addressing more

complex tasks such as population estimation or planning wastewater treatment in urban areas.

The main lines for future work are related to extending this study to datasets constructed from cities with dissimilar characteristics, e.g., to model scenarios with a poor urban development where buildings patterns are not regular, and introducing automatic methods for the calibration of certain hyperparameters of the studied neural networks, such as the learning rate and the cost function.

References

1. Ahmed, N., Mahbub, R.B., Rahman, R.M.: Learning to extract buildings from ultra-high-resolution drone images and noisy labels. Int. J. Remote Sens. **41**(21), 8216–8237 (2020)
2. Asokan, A., Anitha, J.: Change detection techniques for remote sensing applications: a survey. Earth Sci. Inf. **12**(2), 143–160 (2019). https://doi.org/10.1007/s12145-019-00380-5
3. Buslaev, A., Iglovikov, V., Khvedchenya, E., Parinov, A., Druzhinin, M., Kalinin, A.: Albumentations: fast and flexible image augmentations. Information **11**(2), 125 (2020)
4. Doda, S., Wang, Y., Kahl, M., Hoffmann, E., Taubenböck, H., Zhu, X.: So2sat pop-a curated benchmark data set for population estimation from space on a continental scale. arXiv preprint arXiv:2204.08524 (2022)
5. Donnay, J., Barnsley, M., Longley, P.: Remote Sensing and Urban Analysis: GIS-DATA 9. CRC Press, Boca Raton (2000)
6. Goodfellow, I., Bengio, Y., Courville, A.: Deep Learning. MIT Press, Cambridge (2016)
7. He, K., Zhang, X., Ren, S., Sun, J.: Deep residual learning for image recognition. In: IEEE Conference on Computer Vision and Pattern Recognition, pp. 770–778 (2016)
8. Ivanovsky, L., Khryashchev, V., Pavlov, V., Ostrovskaya, A.: Building detection on aerial images using u-net neural networks. In: 24th Conference of Open Innovations Association, pp. 116–122 (2019)
9. Jahan, F., Zhou, J., Awrangjeb, M., Gao, Y.: Fusion of hyperspectral and lidar data using discriminant correlation analysis for land cover classification. IEEE J. Sel. Top. Appl. Earth Observations Remote Sens. **11**(10), 3905–3917 (2018)
10. Khryaschev, V., Ivanovsky, L.: Urban areas analysis using satellite image segmentation and deep neural network. In: E3S Web of Conferences, vol. 135, p. 01064. EDP Sciences (2019)
11. Khryashchev, V., Larionov, R., Ostrovskaya, A., Semenov, A.: Modification of u-net neural network in the task of multichannel satellite images segmentation. In: East-West Design & Test Symposium, pp. 1–4 (2019)
12. Li, W., He, C., Fang, J., Zheng, J., Fu, H., Yu, L.: Semantic segmentation-based building footprint extraction using very high-resolution satellite images and multi-source gis data. Remote Sens. **11**(4), 403 (2019)
13. Long, J., Shelhamer, E., Darrell, T.: Fully convolutional networks for semantic segmentation. In: Proceedings of the IEEE Conference on Computer Vision and Pattern Recognition (CVPR) (2015)

14. Maggiori, E., Tarabalka, Y., Charpiat, G., Alliez, P.: Can semantic labeling methods generalize to any city? the inria aerial image labeling benchmark. In: IEEE International Geoscience and Remote Sensing Symposium, pp. 3226–3229 (2017)
15. Minaee, S., Boykov, Y., Porikli, F., Plaza, A., Kehtarnavaz, N., Terzopoulos, D.: Image segmentation using deep learning: a survey. IEEE Trans. Pattern Anal. Mach. Intell. **44**(7), 3523–3542 (2022)
16. Nesmachnow, S., Iturriaga, S.: Cluster-UY: collaborative scientific high performance computing in uruguay. In: Torres, M., Klapp, J. (eds.) ISUM 2019. CCIS, vol. 1151, pp. 188–202. Springer, Cham (2019). https://doi.org/10.1007/978-3-030-38043-4_16
17. Pan, Z., Xu, J., Guo, Y., Hu, Y., Wang, G.: Deep learning segmentation and classification for urban village using a worldview satellite image based on u-net. Remote Sens. **12**(10), 1574 (2020)
18. Pasquali, G., Iannelli, G., Dell'Acqua, F.: Building footprint extraction from multispectral, spaceborne earth observation datasets using a structurally optimized u-net convolutional neural network. Remote Sens. **11**(23), 2803 (2019)
19. Ronneberger, O., Fischer, P., Brox, T.: U-Net: convolutional networks for biomedical image segmentation. In: Navab, N., Hornegger, J., Wells, W.M., Frangi, A.F. (eds.) MICCAI 2015. LNCS, vol. 9351, pp. 234–241. Springer, Cham (2015). https://doi.org/10.1007/978-3-319-24574-4_28
20. Sedov, A., Khryashchev, V., Larionov, R., Ostrovskaya, A.: Loss function selection in a problem of satellite image segmentation using convolutional neural network. In: Systems of Signal Synchronization, Generating and Processing in Telecommunications, pp. 1–4 (2019)
21. Sishodia, R., Ray, R., Singh, S.: Applications of remote sensing in precision agriculture: a review. Remote Sens. **12**(19), 3136 (2020)
22. Weng, Q., Quattrochi, D.A.: Urban Remote Sensing. CRC Press, Boca Raton (2018)
23. Wurm, M., Stark, T., Zhu, X., Weigand, M., Taubenböck, H.: Semantic segmentation of slums in satellite images using transfer learning on fully convolutional neural networks. ISPRS J. Photogramm. Remote. Sens. **150**, 59–69 (2019)
24. Xie, S., Girshick, R., Dollár, P., Tu, Z., He, K.: Aggregated residual transformations for deep neural networks. In: 2017 IEEE Conference on Computer Vision and Pattern Recognition (CVPR), pp. 5987–5995 (2017)
25. Xu, Y., Wu, L., Xie, Z., Chen, Z.: Building extraction in very high resolution remote sensing imagery using deep learning and guided filters. Remote Sens. **10**(1), 144 (2018)

Distribution of Police Patrols as a Covering Problem in Smart Cities: Fuengirola Use Case

Jamal Toutouh[1], Francisco Chicano[1(✉)], and Rodrigo Gil-Merino[2]

[1] Universidad de Málaga, Málaga, Spain
{jamal,chicano}@uma.es
[2] Universidad de León, León, Spain
rgilmerino@unileon.es

Abstract. Security and emergency services are among the biggest concerns for both authorities and citizens. Better adapting those services to inhabitants is a key goal for smart cities. All emergency services have their own peculiarities, and in particular, the control of police patrols in urban areas is a complex problem connected to the dynamic vehicle routing and traveling salesman problems. We propose in this paper two bi-objective integer linear programming formulations for the police patrol routing problem, which differs from the vehicle routing and travelling salesman problems in which not all the nodes in the city must be served, and there is no "depot". The first formulation is more precise but computationally costly, and the second one is a relaxation that standard integer linear programming solvers can easily solve. The experimental analysis shows that the complete Pareto front can be computed for the relaxed formulation, providing valuable information to solve the precise formulation in future work. In particular, we analyze the number of patrols and the length of the routes they traverse.

1 Introduction

Smart cities try to improve their functioning using information and communication technologies [2]. Consequently, there are many ways of making a city smart [4]. In general terms, the smartness of a city should translate into more and better-personalized services for its inhabitants. Among these services, security in cities is probably one of the biggest concerns for both authorities and citizens. To increase security and how the urban population perceives security, emergency services must be well coordinated in order to prevent crime, minimize arrival times to crime spots, and effectively attend to emergencies and disasters. The most visible corp in terms of security in cities is the fleet of police patrols, and optimizing the use of these police resources to serve citizens better is one of the ways of making a city smarter.

The control of police patrols in urban areas is a complex problem of increasing difficulty with cities' growth. Two main issues must be considered in patrol

© The Author(s), under exclusive license to Springer Nature Switzerland AG 2023
S. Nesmachnow and L. Hernández Callejo (Eds.): ICSC-CITIES 2022, CCIS 1706, pp. 46–60, 2023.
https://doi.org/10.1007/978-3-031-28454-0_4

routes: on the one hand, effective positioning of patrols might prevent crime in conflicting areas and assist communities more efficiently; on the other hand, emergencies stochastically appear and must be responded to on real-time bases, leaving unattended areas during certain periods. Strategies to solve these issues are included in the concept of the police patrol routing problem (PPRP) [10].

Studies on the PPRP are very limited. The PPRP has many similarities with the vehicle routing problem (VRP) [9], which is a generalization of the traveling salesman problem (TSP) [8]. There exist many variants of the VRP [5,14,19], and it is usual to find in the literature a treatment of the PPRP as a dynamical vehicle routing problem (DVRP) [13], a VRP that evolves in time. Nevertheless, the police patrol problem has its own characteristics, making it a significantly different problem by itself. In particular, the existence of stochastic events, in the form of emergencies and disasters, forces the police patrols to be reactive, suspend current tasks, minimize their reaction times towards demanding spots and resume daily tasks once the emergency finishes.

Police patrol emergencies are conceptually different from emergency calls received by other emergency services, such as ambulances and fire-trucks. In these last services, vehicles attend the emergencies from their depots and return when they are over without altering prefixed routes. Some authors have tried to solve these kinds of problems by treating them as the maximal expected coverage relocation problem [12], where the aim is to maximize the coverage of an urban area by allocating waiting sites for emergency vehicles. In this scheme, the city is divided into blocks in which waiting emergency vehicles have a driving time until the emergency spot to be minimized.

This work aims to propose PPRP as a covering problem in the context of smart cities: a fixed number of police patrols are distributed in an urban region in such a way that they cover the maximum possible conflicting areas and, at the same time, the total cost of deploying the patrols is minimized. We use the total length of the routes traversed by the patrols as a proxy for the cost since this length is directly related to fuel consumption and greenhouse gas emissions. Thus, PPRP is addressed as a multi-objective optimization problem by using mathematical programming. Specifically, a variant of the ε-constraint method, called *hybrid method* by Ehrgott [11], is used to compute the set of *efficient* solutions that represent different trade-offs between the objectives. The problem is addressed over three instances defined using real data from the city of Fuengirola (Spain).

The main contributions of this paper are: *a)* providing two new formulations of the PPRP problem as a covering problem, *b)* using a multi-objective exact method to address one of the formulations of PPRP, and *c)* solving the PPRP problem on a real-world instance.

This paper is organized as follows: the next section mathematically describes the police patrol routing problem as a covering problem; Sect. 3 reviews related work in the context of smart city problems; Sect. 4 details the proposed methodology, algorithm and experimental setup used to solve the problem; Sect. 5 discusses the results and the solutions found; and finally, Sect. 6 draws the main conclusions and ideas for future work.

2   The Police Patrol Routing Problem

We model a city with a graph $G = (V, E)$, where V is the set of nodes, representing junctions of streets, and $E \in V \times V$ is the set of edges of the graph representing the streets. The graph is vertex- and edge-weighted. The weights associated with the nodes, denoted with w_i with $i \in V$, represent the number of events associated with the node. These weights are computed based on the historical data recorded in the city. In particular, historical data provides events that occurred at different streets (edges), and the events are assigned to the closest node. The weight w_i is the number of events for which i is the closest node in the map. The weights associated with the edges (streets), denoted with c_e with $e \in E$, represent the length of the street. The *successor* and *predecessor* functions of G, denoted with $N^+ : V \mapsto 2^V$ and $N^- : V \mapsto 2^V$, are defined as follows:

$$N^+(i) = \{j \in V | (i, j) \in E\} \tag{1}$$

$$N^-(i) = \{j \in V | (j, i) \in E\} \tag{2}$$

A solution x to the PPRP is a set of cycles in graph G with each cycle representing the route of one patrol. We will assume a maximum of P patrols that will be denoted with numbers 1 to P. We will use the notation $[n]$ to denote the integer numbers from 1 to n. Thus, the patrols will have labels in the set $[P]$. The goals of PPRP are to maximize the sum of the weights of the visited nodes and minimize the distance traveled by all the patrols to visit those nodes. By maximizing the sum of weights, we are providing a better service quality; while minimizing the length of the routes, we reduce the cost of the solution and the pollution due to police vehicles. Since we have a limited number P of patrols, reducing the lengths of the routes and covering all the nodes of the graph are conflicting objectives. Thus, we formulate the problem as a bi-objective problem.

In the following, we propose two formulations for the problem. The first is more precise but also more complex, and solving it requires more computational power. The second is a relaxation of the first formulation and can be solved efficiently using exact methods but assumes an unlimited number of patrols.

2.1   Precise Formulation

Before presenting the formulation we will present the variables used in it. Let $x_{p,e}$ be a binary variable that is 1 when patrol p traverses edge e and zero otherwise, and let y_j be a variable that is 1 when node j is covered by at least one route and 0 otherwise. We will use variables l and u to represent the lower and upper bounds for the length of the routes. We will also introduce variables $z_{p,j}$ and $d_{p,j}$ to avoid several cycles associated with the same patrol. We can formalize the PPRP with the following bi-objective mixed integer linear program:

$$\min \sum_{e \in E} c_e \sum_{p=1}^{P} x_{p,e}, \quad \max \sum_{i \in V} w_i y_i, \tag{3}$$

subject to:

$$\sum_{i \in N^-(j)} x_{p,(i,j)} = \sum_{k \in N^+(j)} x_{p,(j,k)} \quad \forall j \in V, \forall p \in [P], \tag{4}$$

$$\sum_{i \in N^-(j)} x_{p,(i,j)} \leq 1 \quad \forall j \in V, \forall p \in [P], \tag{5}$$

$$\sum_{i \in V} d_{p,i} = 1 \quad \forall p \in [P], \tag{6}$$

$$z_{p,j} \geq z_{p,i} + 1 + |V|(x_{p,(i,j)} - d_{p,j} - 1) \quad \forall (i,j) \in E, \forall p \in [P], \tag{7}$$

$$y_j \leq \sum_{i \in N^-(j)} \sum_{p=1}^{P} x_{p,(i,j)} \quad \forall j \in V, \tag{8}$$

$$l \leq \sum_{e \in E} c_e x_{p,e} \quad \forall p \in [P], \tag{9}$$

$$\sum_{e \in E} c_e x_{p,e} \leq u \quad \forall p \in [P], \tag{10}$$

$$u - l \leq \alpha u, \tag{11}$$

$$x_{p,e} \in \{0,1\} \quad \forall e \in E, \forall p \in [P], \tag{12}$$

$$d_{p,j} \in \{0,1\} \quad \forall j \in V, \forall p \in [P], \tag{13}$$

$$0 \leq y_j \leq 1 \quad \forall j \in V, \tag{14}$$

$$z_{p,j} \geq 0 \quad \forall j \in V \; \forall p \in [P], \tag{15}$$

$$u, l \geq 0. \tag{16}$$

Equation (3) expresses the two objectives, which is minimizing the sum of the lengths of the routes and maximizing the sum of the weights of the nodes covered by the routes. Observe that even if y_j is continuous, it can only take values 0 or 1 due to constraint (8) and the second objective in (3). The family of constraints (4) force the patrols to pass through a node and not stop on it. Equations (5) prevents a patrol from visiting the same node twice. Together, Eqs. (4) and (5) force the patrols to follow cycles in the graph. But there could be more than one cycle associated to one patrol, which is not realistic. To solve this issue we add Equations (6) and (7). We adapted here the sub-tour elimination equations traditionally used in the ILP formulation of the Vehicle Routing Problem (VRP) formulation [1]. In this case, the main difference is that we do not have a designated depot (as it happens in VRP). Thus, we add a new variable $d_{p,j}$ that is 1 when patrol p uses node j as a depot and is 0 otherwise. Equation (6) ensures that only one depot per patrol exists. Equations (7) ensure that the cycle associated with each patrol is connected. One criticism of the adopted approach is that routes in real life do not need to be cycles in the city. There can be nodes visited more than once in a route because it could be convenient due to the existing road graph. In that case, our model is still valid, but we need to pre-process the underlying graph. Instead of using the real roads in the city as edges, we produce a complete graph where the nodes are those with nonzero weights, and the edges represent the shortest path from one node to another. That is, each edge in this second graph corresponds to a complete path in the original road graph. We defer to future work the analysis of this approach.

Equation (8) ensures that y_j is zero if there is no route visiting node j. Otherwise, y_j will be 1 due to the second objective, as pointed out above. Equations (9) and (10) introduce the constraints for the lower and upper bound variables l and u, respectively. These variables are used in Equation (11) to put some limits to the difference between the lengths of the patrol routes. With this constraint, we want to allow the decision-maker to fix the maximum difference in the length of the routes followed by the different patrols. The parameter α provides a convenient parameter to tune this difference. If $\alpha = 0$, all routes should have the same length, which could be impossible for some graphs. If $\alpha = 1$, the routes can have any length. A value between 0 and 1 for α will set the difference between the longest and the shortest route to a fraction of the longest route. The decision-maker can use low values for α, if it is important that the routes do not differ too much in length. This parameter is related to "fairness". Finally, Equations (12), to (16) establish the domain of the variables.

2.2   Relaxed Formulation

The precise formulation is equivalent to solving several VRPs simultaneously. We ran out of computational resources when performing preliminary experiments on this formulation. Since VRP is NP-hard, solving precise formulation will require using heuristics when the instances are medium to large. In this section, we propose a relaxed ILP formulation that can be solved exactly using ILP solvers in a reasonable time and can provide valuable information to guide the use of heuristics and the precise formulation. In this relaxed formulation, we assume that $\alpha = 1$ and omit the corresponding constraints for the lower and upper bounds, Equation (11).

Let x_e be a binary variable that is 1 when one of the patrols traverses edge e and 0 otherwise. The relaxed formulation of the PPRP is as follows:

$$\min \sum_{e \in E} c_e x_e, \quad \max \sum_{i \in V} w_i y_i, \tag{17}$$

subject to:

$$\sum_{i \in N^-(j)} x_{(i,j)} = \sum_{k \in N^+(j)} x_{(j,k)} \quad \forall j \in V \tag{18}$$

$$y_j \leq \sum_{i \in N^-(j)} x_{(i,j)} \quad \forall j \in V \tag{19}$$

$$x_e \in \{0,1\} \quad \forall e \in E \tag{20}$$

$$0 \leq y_j \leq 1 \quad \forall j \in V \tag{21}$$

In this relaxed formulation, the number of patrols is unbounded. One solution provided by this formulation will be composed of a set of cycles covering nodes in the graph, which will be given by the variables x_e. We use again variables y_j to represent the visit of at least one patrol to node j. Given the values of x in one solution, it will be possible to provide a lower bound to the number of patrols required to implement that solution. The minimum number of patrols will be the number of connected components in the subgraph induced by the set of edges $E' = \{e \in E | x_e = 1\}$. We can also compute some statistics regarding the lengths of the routes associated with those patrols. The computation of the Pareto front for this relaxed model will provide an "optimistic" Pareto front; that is, no solution to the precise formulation can dominate any solution in the Pareto front of the relaxed formulation. The solutions in the front also represent real solutions for the case in which the number of patrols is not bounded, and there is no constraint related to the lengths of the routes.

3   Related Work

Literature on smart cities includes many research studies on addressing optimization problems with the aim of improving inhabitants' life. These optimization problems deal with real-world environments, and, in general, their objective functions are noisy and/or are based on simulations. Besides, these optimization problems comprise substantial search spaces and/or consider several (not easy to meet) constraints. These specific characteristics make these problems hard to solve (most of them are NP-hard problems) [17,18]. Therefore, heuristics and metaheuristics (e.g., evolutionary computation, EC) emerged as effective and efficient tools to compute good solutions requiring bounded computational resources. Besides, mathematical programming techniques (e.g., integer linear programming, ILP) have become very popular in addressing such problems in the last few years.

Many studies in the literature focus on the use of heuristics and metaheuristics to address smart city problems. For example, different EC methods were coupled with machine learning approaches to build accurate models for road traffic mobility [21] and car parking availability [3] prediction. The first study applied EC to address feature selection, and the second used EC to optimize the hyperparameters and architecture of a neural network. A heuristic algorithm was designed to address communication among vehicles and road infrastructure elements to improve security and efficiency in urban road transportation [20]. The authors proposed a communication algorithm based on swarm intelligence in which each node in the network takes the routing decisions in order to optimize its own and the neighborhood nodes' throughput.

Many real-world smart city problems are multi-objective because they consider several (often conflicting) objectives (e.g., when dealing with public transportation: the quality-of-service and economic cost). For example, multi-objective EC algorithms were analyzed for the efficient design of the vehicle charging infrastructure [6]. The authors considered two conflicting objectives:

the quality-of-service regarding charging time and distance to the charging station and the economical cost of the charging station installation [7].

In recent years, mathematical programming methods are gaining prominence. Thus, several studies in the literature apply mathematical programming techniques to solve problems in the domain of smart cities. A mono-objective variant of the problem of designing the vehicle charging infrastructure was addressed by using ILP [17]. The exact approach improved the results provided by a genetic algorithm (GA). Other authors applied ILP to find the best location for parking lots [15]. This research aimed to minimize the vehicles' travel time for finding a parking lot near the users' destination. Multi-objective mixed-ILP was proposed to deal with the problem of rescheduling trains to serve passengers from delayed high-speed railway trains [23]. The objectives of this problem were to maximize the number of expected transported passengers and minimize the number of extra trains and operation-ending time of all extra trains.

PPRP problem is a variant of VRP. Some studies use mathematical programming to address VRP (and variants) in smart cities literature. The ε-constraint method was applied to optimize the delivery service provided by unmanned aerial vehicles (UAV) [24]. The problem was addressed as a multi-objective nonlinear programming problem established by taking the minimum total flight distance and the highest average customer satisfaction as the objective functions. The proposed method improved the results computed by a GA. A combination of the ε-constraint method and the modified column-and-constraint generation algorithm was proposed to deal with the efficient urban waste collection [25]. The authors defined a bi-objective problem to minimize the worst-case total collection cost and the environmental disutility, considering service demands uncertainty and traversing costs uncertainty on roads. Another variation of the urban waste collection problem was proposed by considering three objectives: minimizing the average required collection frequency of the containers, minimizing the installation cost of bins, and minimizing the average distance between the users and the bins [18]. The authors applied the augmented ε-constraint method and the Page-Rank heuristic. The results show the proposed approaches' competitiveness for constructing a set of candidate solutions that considers the different trade-offs between the optimization criteria.

4   Methodology

In multi-objective optimization problems, there is usually no single solution that optimizes all the objectives at the same time. Instead, we are interested in finding a set of the so-called *efficient solutions*, with the property that it is not possible to improve one objective without worsening another one. Let d be the number of objectives in our multi-objective problem, we say that a solution x is *efficient* if there is no solution y such that $f_i(y) \leq f_i(x)$ for all $i \in [d]$ and $f_j(y) < f_j(x)$ for at least one $j \in [d]$. The set of all efficient solutions of a multi-objective problem is called *efficient set*, and the image of that set is called *Pareto front*. Each d-dimensional point in the Pareto front is called *non-dominated point*. There can be more than one efficient solution mapped to a single non-dominated point. In those cases, we are interested in finding only one of those efficient solutions. In the following subsections, we first present the algorithm used to find the Pareto front (and one efficient solution per non-dominated point). We also explain the experimental setup used in this work to illustrate how the problem can be solved in a real scenario. To the best of our knowledge, the formulation of the problems used here is novel, and thus, there are no algorithms to compare in the literature. Furthermore, since we use an exact algorithm, the optimality of the solutions is ensured, and the only comparison we can do with potential previous algorithms is related to the time required to solve the problem.

4.1   Algorithm

In this work, we are interested in finding the complete Pareto front of the relaxed formulation of the PPRP. In order to compute the front, we use a variant of the ε-constraint method, called the *hybrid method* by Ehrgott [11, p. 101], that optimizes a weighted sum of the objectives to ensure that the solutions found by the ILP solver are always efficient. Algorithm 1 shows the Hybrid method adapted to the bi-objective case we face. We assume that f_1 and f_2 are to be minimized. If one of the objectives is to be maximized (as it happens with the second objective in Eq. (17)) we can multiply it by -1. The method transforms the bi-objective problem into a set of single-objective problems where the goal is to minimize $f_2(x) + \lambda f_1(x)$, with λ a constant. The value of λ must be small enough not to lose any non-dominated point in the Pareto front, but large enough to ensure that all the solutions found are efficient[1]. In addition to the constraints of the problem, that we represent with the expression $x \in X$, the method adds a new constraint on f_1: $f_1(x) \leq \varepsilon$. This constraint is the key to obtaining all the efficient solutions even if the Pareto front is concave. The value ε is reduced by an amount δ along the search to find all the non-dominated points. In the beginning, ε must be large enough to find the non-dominated point with a minimum at f_2 value (and maximum at f_1 value). The value of δ should be small enough not to jump over any solution in the Pareto front. The algorithm ends when the problem is unfeasible, or ε reaches a minimum value ε_s. We use this limit in ε to be able to compute only one part of the Pareto front. This is useful when the decision maker has a clear idea of the range of values to consider. It is also especially useful to parallelize the computation of the whole Pareto front.

In our case, we use $\lambda = 0.0001$, since we computed the two lexicographic optimal solutions of the Pareto front and found that this value is small enough not to lose any efficient solution. Our first objective, f_1, is the sum of the weights of the visited nodes multiplied by -1, and f_2 is the sum of the lengths of the routes traversed by the patrols. We use the sum of weights as f_1 because the weights are integers and, thus, a value of $\delta = 1$ ensures that we do not miss any efficient solution. The length of the routes traversed by the patrols take, in

---

[1] In theory, for any value of $\lambda > 0$ the solution found is efficient, but in practice numerical errors in floating point operations can result in non-efficient solutions.

Algorithm 1: Hybrid method [11, p. 101]

Data: $\lambda, \delta, \varepsilon_0, \varepsilon_s$
Result: Pareto front, PF
1 $\varepsilon \leftarrow \varepsilon_0$;
2 $PF \leftarrow \emptyset$;
3 **while** $\exists x \in X$ *with* $f_1(x) \leq \varepsilon$ *and* $\varepsilon > \varepsilon_s$ **do**
4      $\quad x^* \leftarrow \underset{x \in X, f_1(x) \leq \varepsilon}{\arg\min} \; f_2(x) + \lambda f_1(x)$;
5      $\quad PF \leftarrow PF \cup \{(f_1(x^*), f_2(x^*))\}$;
6      $\quad \varepsilon \leftarrow f_1(x^*) - \delta$;
7 **return** PF

---

general, fractional values. If we would choose the length of routes as f_1, then finding the appropriate value for δ would have been more involved.

4.2 Experimental Setup

The experimentation was performed over three instances based on a realistic scenario defined in Fuengirola, a low-medium-sized city in the south of Spain. Fuengirola covers an area of 10.37 square kilometers and nowadays it has more than 82 000 inhabitants. The information about the events was provided by Fuengirola's City Police and the geographical data was obtained from Open Street Maps [16].

The instances have been defined as connected graphs in which the edges represent the roads, and the nodes encapsulate the number of events that occurred in their immediate area. During the period considered in our study (from January 1st, 2017 to December 31st, 2017), there were 2764 events that are distributed in 948 different nodes in the graph. We call this instance real. Due to data privacy issues, we cannot publish more details of the real instance, and for this reason, we generated two synthetic additional problem instances based on the real one. In one of them, called shuffled, the weights of the nodes are randomly shuffled and then re-assigned to different nodes; the set of events is the same, but not their node in the graph. This instance contains 2764 events distributed in 473 different nodes. In the third instance, called sampled, we recover the original empirical distribution and generate a new set of weights according to this statistical distribution; the set of events is different, and so the place where they took place, but the statistical properties remain the same. This last instance has 2329 events distributed in 469 different nodes. Figure 1 illustrates the map of the shuffled instance. The size of the nodes represents the number of events that occurred at that node in the considered period. The weight of an edge is the distance between the two nodes connected by that edge.

The experiments were run in the Picasso supercomputing facility of the University of Málaga with 126 SD530 servers with Intel Xeon Gold 6230R (26 cores each) at 2.10GHz, 200 GB of RAM and an InfiniBand HDR100 network. In order to speed up the execution, we run several instances of the hybrid method, each computing in one part of the Pareto front. In order to speed up the computation of the whole Pareto front, we split the whole range of values for f_1 in the Pareto front in 30 intervals and run 30 instances of Algorithm 1 in parallel per problem instance. Each algorithm instance used different values for ε_0 and ε_s to avoid overlapping the computed solutions. The range of values for f_1 was computed based on the objective values of lexicographic optima (efficient solutions with minimum f_1 and minimum f_2 values).

The source code was written in Python using the Pyomo 6.2 library[2] to create the ILP model and Gurobi 9.5.1 as ILP solver. All the source code, data (except for the real instance) and results can be found in Zenodo [22].

5 Results and Discussion

In this Section, we present the results of the application of the hybrid method described in Subsect. 4.1 to the three instances considered: `real`, `shuffled` and `sampled`. Since we are using a deterministic exact algorithm, we only performed one run of it. Different runs could differ in runtime, but we are not interested here in the analysis of runtime. However, we can say that the computation in parallel of the 30 algorithm instances to get the whole Pareto in front of the three problem instances took no more than 4 min in the Picasso supercomputing facility. This means that computing the whole Pareto front using one single machine with a sequential approach should not require more than 120 min (2 h). This time is considered small compared to the lifetime of the solution, which is in the order of days. The Pareto front could be computed during the night because the routes have to be planned daily. We defer to future work on applying *anytime muti-objective algorithms*, which are specially designed to find a set of well-spread solutions in the objective space at any point during the search. These algorithms are especially useful when the runtime is an important parameter.

Figure 2 shows the Pareto fronts of the three instances of PPRP. Table 1 presents the main metrics of the computed Pareto fronts: the normalized hypervolume and the number of solutions in the front. Focusing on Fig. 2, we observe that there are no big gaps in the front in any instance, in spite of the fact that the problem is combinatorial. For the `real` and `shuffled` instances, the front is wider in the x axis because these instances contain more events. However, we noticed that not all the events can be covered. In particular, for the `real` instance, the maximum number of events covered was 2756 (out of 2764). In the case of the instances `shuffled` and `sampled`, the maximum number of events covered were 2692 and 2292, respectively, out of 2764 and 2329. The reason for not covering some of the events has to do with the connectivity of the graph. The uncovered events must be in nodes that form isolated, strongly connected components of the graph, and it is not possible to form a cycle. There can be two reasons for this to happen. First, the node is really disconnected from the traffic network (for example, a fire in the countryside), and it makes no sense to visit

---

[2] https://pyomo.readthedocs.io/en/stable/.

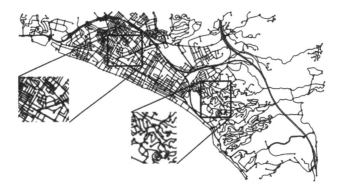

Fig. 1. Graph representing an efficient solution for the shuffled instance with 1900 events covered.

that node with a police car. Second, it could also be an artifact due to errors in the map used for the computations or a cut of a road at an extreme of the map. In this case, we could fix the problem by correcting the map and adding the missing edges. We defer to future work a detailed analysis of the uncovered events and their potential solution.

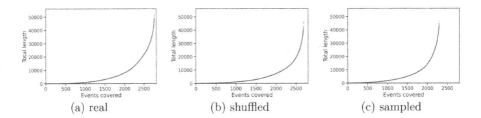

Fig. 2. Pareto fronts of the instances.

Table 1. Hypervolume and number of solutions of the computed Pareto fronts.

Metric	real	shuffled	sampled
Normalized hypervolume	0.874	0.879	0.872
Number of solutions	2038	2345	2148

Now we will analyze in more detail the features of the efficient solutions found by the hybrid method. In all the cases, we will use the number of events covered as an index of the efficient solution (we could also use the length of the routes). Figure 3 illustrates the minimum number of patrols required to implement the efficient solution. We should say that efficient solutions could exist with fewer patrols than the ones plotted in the figure because we are not minimizing the number of routes in our relaxed formulation of the problem. Furthermore, it is always possible in a real situation to cover several routes with one single patrol by asking the patrol to alternate between the different routes (increasing the length of the routes). Thus, what we see in the figure is the minimum number of patrols required to implement *the* particular efficient solution found by the solver assuming that patrols are not allowed to alternate between routes. This number is related to the effort in personnel and vehicles required by the municipality to provide a good service to the citizens. We see that for a city like Fuengirola, this number could be as high as 300.

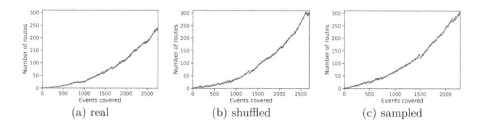

(a) real   (b) shuffled   (c) sampled

Fig. 3. Number of routes computed according to the number of covered events.

Figure 4 shows statistics about the length of the routes followed by the different patrols. We plot the quartiles 1, 2 (median) and 3 of the set of routes corresponding to each efficient solution. This information is again indexed by the number of events (x axis). Ideally, these routes should be as short as possible to visit the conflicting points more frequently. We can see that for the efficient solutions found, these distances do not exceed 100 m in the median. We can also appreciate these short routes in the representation of a solution in Fig. 1. These short routes explain the high number of vehicles required by the efficient solutions. In a real scenario, with a limited number of vehicles (around tens), this number should be much higher. Considering this more realistic scenario implies solving the precise formulation of PPRP, which we defer to future work.

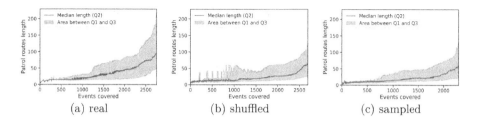

(a) real   (b) shuffled   (c) sampled

Fig. 4. Length of the routes given the events covered.

We are also interested in analyzing the difference between the length of the routes. In the precise formulation, we can limit this difference using the α parameter, but in the relaxed formulation, there is no limit to the difference. Thus, we want to analyze how different these routes are. This is a measure of "fairness" for the patrols. Ideally, all the patrols should have routes with the same length since the length of the route is directly related to the cost of covering the routes (fuel consumption and greenhouse gas emissions). We plot in Fig. 5 the interquartile range (IQR) of the length of the routes divided (normalized) by the median length. We can see that this measure of fairness has no clear trend (as it happens with the previous features). An interesting observation in the three instances is that the normalized IQR has a peak between 1000 and 1500 events covered (depending on the instance). Definitely, the underlying graph has an influence on the routes that are possible and could explain part of the behaviour that the normalized IQR exhibit for the efficient solutions. We defer to future work a detailed analysis and the optimization of the distance between route lengths.

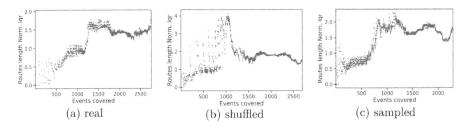

(a) real   (b) shuffled   (c) sampled

Fig. 5. Normalized interquartile range of the routes length given the events covered.

6   Conclusions

This paper presents two bi-objective formulations for the PPRP problem. One is precise but computationally costly to solve, while the second is a relaxed formulation that is easy to solve using standard exact methods. The problem has been formulated as a covering problem in the road graph of a city. The edges of the graph describe the streets, and the weight of the nodes represents the number of events. Thus, the police patrols have to visit (cover) the areas (nodes) with the highest number of events. Three instances of the problem have been generated based on real data from the city of Fuengirola (Spain). The relaxed formulation has been solved over the three instances to analyze the feature of the solutions that can be obtained for the problem. The results obtained show that the complete Pareto front of the relaxed formulation can be obtained in a few minutes. The analysis of this relaxed formulation provides valuable information to solve the precise formulation in a future work. In particular, we have an "optimistic" Pareto front, which informs about the range of values expected in the precise formulation. We also have an idea of the minimum number of patrols required to reach the minimum length of the routes. The analysis of the lengths of the proposed routes provides information regarding the difference between the proposed routes. This will be useful to set the values for parameter α in the precise model.

Future work can focus on solving the precise formulation. This will probably require the use of a combination of exact methods (like ILP solvers) and heuristics (the so-called *matheuristics*). The information gained from solving the relaxed formulation in this paper will be very valuable in selecting the algorithms and parameters to solve the precise formulation. We also plan to do a deeper analysis of the difference in the lengths of the routes traversed by the patrols. We can consider dynamism as part of the problem formulation. In this case, one patrol must cover emergencies, and the other ones have to re-schedule their routes to maximize the coverage of the conflicting points. Another future line of research is the design of specific algorithms and operators to solve this problem.

Acknowledgements. This research is partially funded by the Universidad de Málaga, Andalucía Tech, Consejería de Economía y Conocimiento de la Junta de Andaluía and FEDER under grant numbers UMA18-FEDERJA-003 (PRECOG) and UMA-CEIATECH-07 (DataPol). It was also funded by MCIN/AEI/ 10.13039/501100011033 under grant number PID 2020-116727RB-I00 (HUmove) and TAILOR ICT-48 Network (No 952215) funded by EU Horizon 2020 research and innovation programme. Thanks to the Supercomputing and Bioinnovation Center (SCBI) of the University of Málaga for their provision of computational resources and support.

References

1. Achuthan, N., Caccetta, L.: Integer linear programming formulation for a vehicle routing problem. Eur. J. Oper. Res. **52**(1), 86–89 (1991). https://doi.org/10.1016/0377-2217(91)90338-V
2. Batty, M., et al.: Portugali: smart cities of the future. Eur. Phys. J. Spec. Top. **214**(1), 481–518 (2012). https://doi.org/10.1140/epjst/e2012-01703-3
3. Camero, A., Toutouh, J., Stolfi, D.H., Alba, E.: Evolutionary deep learning for car park occupancy prediction in smart cities. In: Battiti, R., Brunato, M., Kotsireas, I., Pardalos, P.M. (eds.) LION 12 2018. LNCS, vol. 11353, pp. 386–401. Springer, Cham (2019). https://doi.org/10.1007/978-3-030-05348-2_32
4. Camero, A., Alba, E.: Smart city and information technology: a review. Cities **93**, 84–94 (2019). https://doi.org/10.1016/j.cities.2019.04.014
5. Christofides, N.: Vehicle routing. Traveling Salesman Probl. (1985)
6. Cintrano, C., Toutouh, J.: Multiobjective electric vehicle charging station locations in a city scale area: malaga study case. In: Jiménez Laredo, J.L., Hidalgo, J.I., Babaagba, K.O. (eds.) EvoApplications 2022. LNCS, vol. 13224, pp. 584–600. Springer, Cham (2022). https://doi.org/10.1007/978-3-031-02462-7_37
7. Cintrano, C., Toutouh, J., Alba, E.: Citizen centric optimal electric vehicle charging stations locations in a full city: case of malaga. In: Alba, E., et al. (eds.) CAEPIA 2021. LNCS (LNAI), vol. 12882, pp. 247–257. Springer, Cham (2021). https://doi.org/10.1007/978-3-030-85713-4_24
8. Dantzig, G., Fulkerson, R., Johnson, S.: Solution of a large-scale traveling-salesman problem. J. Oper. Res. Soc. Am. **2**(4), 393–410 (1954). https://doi.org/10.1287/opre.2.4.393

9. Dantzig, G.B., Ramser, J.H.: The truck dispatching problem. Manag. Sci. **6**(1), 80–91 (1959)

10. Dewinter, M., Vandeviver, C., Vander Beken, T., Witlox, F.: Analysing the police patrol routing problem: a review. ISPRS Int. J. Geo-Inf. **9**(3), 157 (2020). https://doi.org/10.3390/ijgi9030157

11. Ehrgott, M.: Multicriteria Optimization, 2nd edn. Springer, Cham (2005). https://doi.org/10.1007/3-540-27659-9

12. Gendreau, M., Laporte, G., Semet, F.: The maximal expected coverage relocation problem for emergency vehicles. J. Oper. Res. Soc. **57**, 22–28 (2006)

13. Khouadjia, M.R., Sarasola, B., Alba, E., Talbi, E.G., Jourdan, L.: Metaheuristics for dynamic vehicle routing. In: Alba, E., Nakib, A., Siarry, P. (eds.) Metaheuristics for Dynamic Optimization, pp. 265–289. Springer, Heidelberg (2013). https://doi.org/10.1007/978-3-642-30665-5_12

14. Laporte, G.: The vehicle routing problem: An overview of exact and approximate algorithms. Eur. J. Oper. Res. **59**(3), 345–358 (1992). https://doi.org/10.1016/0377-2217(92)90192-C

15. Mukherjee, T., Gupta, S., Sen, P., Pandey, V., Karmakar, K.: Go-park: a parking lot allocation system in smart cities. In: Singh, M., Gupta, P.K., Tyagi, V., Flusser, J., Ören, T. (eds.) Advances in Computing and Data Sciences, pp. 158–166. Springer, Singapore (2018). https://doi.org/10.1007/978-981-13-1813-9_16

16. OpenStreetMap contributors: Planet dump retrieved from OpenStreetMap. https://www.openstreetmap.org (2017). Accessed 20 Dec 2021

17. Risso, C., Cintrano, C., Toutouh, J., Nesmachnow, S.: Exact approach for electric vehicle charging infrastructure location: a real case study in málaga, spain. In: Nesmachnow, S., Hernández Callejo, L. (eds) Ibero-American Congress of Smart Cities, pp. 42–57. Springer, Cham (2021). https://doi.org/10.1007/978-3-030-96753-6_4

18. Rossit, D.G., Toutouh, J., Nesmachnow, S.: Exact and heuristic approaches for multi-objective garbage accumulation points location in real scenarios. Waste Manag. **105**, 467–481 (2020)

19. Toth, P., Vigo, D.: Vehicle Routing. Society for Industrial and Applied Mathematics, Philadelphia (2014). https://doi.org/10.1137/1.9781611973594

20. Toutouh, J., Alba, E.: A swarm algorithm for collaborative traffic in vehicular networks. Veh. Commun. **12**, 127–137 (2018)

21. Toutouh, J., Arellano, J., Alba, E.: Bipred: a bilevel evolutionary algorithm for prediction in smart mobility. Sensors **18**(12), 4123 (2018)

22. Toutouh, J., Chicano, F., Gil-Merino, R.: Code and datasets for the paper "distribution of police patrols as a covering problem in smart cities: fuengirola (spain) use case". Zenodo. https://doi.org/10.5281/zenodo.7153528

23. Wang, W., Bao, Y., Long, S.: Rescheduling urban rail transit trains to serve passengers from uncertain delayed high-speed railway trains. Sustainability **14**(9), 5718 (2022)

24. Xiong, M., Fei, H., Yan, W.: Research on distribution path of multi-target urban UAV (unmanned aerial vehicle) based on epsilon-constraint method. In: 2021 International Conference CISAI, pp. 632–637 (2021). https://doi.org/10.1109/CISAI54367.2021.00127

25. Xu, K., Zheng, M.M., Liu, X.: A two-stage robust model for urban food waste collection network under uncertainty. In: 2021 IEEE International Conference on Industrial Engineering and Engineering Management (IEEM), pp. 824–828 (2021). https://doi.org/10.1109/IEEM50564.2021.9672895

Super Resolution Generative Adversarial Network for Velocity Fields in Large Eddy Simulations

Maximiliano Bove$^{(\boxtimes)}$ ⓘ, Sergio Nesmachnow ⓘ, and Martín Draper

Universidad de la República, Montevideo, Uruguay
{mbove,sergion,mdraper}@fing.edu.uy

Abstract. This article presents an approach for generating synthetic velocity fields in Large Eddy Simulations. This is a relevant problem, considering the high computational effort required to simulate turbulent flows with fine resolution. The proposed approach applies a Generative Adversarial Network, considering relevant information about horizontal slices of turbulent velocity fields. The approach is evaluated on a real-world case study: augmenting the resolution of horizontal velocity fields downstream of a wind turbine. The main results indicate that the proposed approach is able to generate high resolution images of horizontal velocity fields given a low resolution counterpart, without the need for explicitly performing computationally expensive Large Eddy Simulations.

Keywords: velocity fields · superresolution · Large Eddy Simulations · GANs

1 Introduction

Several well-known methods have been proposed for modeling turbulent flows, within the area of Computational Fluid Dynamics (CFD) [19]. Although turbulent flows respond to Navier-Stokes equations, there is no general analytical solution for them so far. Numerical methods allow approximating solutions to Navier-Stokes equations applied to turbulent flows, but the computational resources needed for realistic engineering applications are usually excessively large, especially for very turbulent flows [30]. Methods like Large Eddy Simulation (LES) are responsible for solving only the low-frequency turbulent scales (large vortices) and evaluating the effects of small scales without having to solve them explicitly [5,20]. LES provides a compromise between the computational cost and the resolution accuracy of the turbulent scales in the studied phenomenon [2].

A viable alternative to solve the turbulent flows problem using less computational resources consists in augmenting the resolution of CFD simulations using synthetic data. Synthetic data generation refers to the process of creating new

© The Author(s), under exclusive license to Springer Nature Switzerland AG 2023
S. Nesmachnow and L. Hernández Callejo (Eds.): ICSC-CITIES 2022, CCIS 1706, pp. 61–76, 2023.
https://doi.org/10.1007/978-3-031-28454-0_5

data by applying a systematic and programmatic method [3]. The main idea is to use both real and synthetic data when obtaining new data is not practical or even not possible. The (new) synthetic data must approximate accurately the distribution of real data, and even incorporate realistic features to the datasets.

The super resolution problem refers to reconstructing or recovering high resolution details from low resolution data, usually to overcome the limitations of physical systems. This is a very important problem in image processing [13,14] but it is also applied in signal and multimedia processing, astronomy, privacy and security, remote sensing, etc. Obtaining such super resolution dataset from low-resolution samples is a challenging problem, for which several computational algorithms have been proposed. Among them, Generative Adversarial Networks (GANs) have shown very good problem solving capabilities, computing accurate results, especially in image generation and recovery tasks [26].

In this line of work, this article presents an approach for the generation of synthetic velocity fields in LES. A specific GAN is applied to generate high fidelity (resolution) horizontal velocity fields slices (images) of a portion of the flow downstream of a wind turbine. The applied GAN is trained with low and high fidelity single channel images of velocity fields horizontal planes at hub height of a wind turbine. The main goal is learning to generate new synthetic high resolution slices, using as input a low resolution slice computed using LES simulations. The main results of the research is the acquired capability of the trained GAN to generate high resolution turbulent flow images. In turn, the generated images have good similarity metrics, when compared with the original images from LES simulations. Overall, the article contributes with a methodology for generating synthetic velocity fields in LES and the evaluation of the proposed methodology in a real case study, relevant for the study of renewable energies.

The article is organized as follows. Next Section presents the main concepts about GANs and a description of the problem solved. Section 3 reviews relevant related works. Section 4 presents the applied methodology and implementation details. The experimental evaluation of the proposed resolution approach is described in Sect. 5. Finally, Sect. 6 presents the conclusions of the research and formulates the main lines for future work.

2   Generative Adversarial Networks

A generative model is a statistical tool that allows modeling the joint probability distribution $p(X, Y)$ relating a given observable variable X (input or data instance) and a target variable Y (output) [16]. Generative machine learning is a branch of computational intelligence including methods that are able to generate new instances of data, by learning the joint probability $p(X, Y)$ to describe the process of generating new datasets [4].

GANs use adversarial artificial neural networks (ANNs) for generating new data [7]. A GAN consists of two ANNs competing and cooperating: the *generator* and the *discriminator*. Both ANNs apply an adversarial learning approach to optimize their parameters in order to generate accurate synthetic data.

The generator ANN (g) specializes on learning how to create synthetic data samples x', taking as input random vectors from a latent space z. The generator is characterized by the equation $g(z) = x'$. The main goal of the generator is to approximate the distribution of true data, by considering the information about the problem provided by the discriminator. The discriminator ANN specializes on learning how to distinguish real data samples x (from a training dataset) from the synthetic samples x' created by the generator. Both ANNs are trained simultaneously and following an adversarial approach: the discriminator tries to learn the real data distribution for a proper evaluation of new synthetic data and the generator seeks to generate images that deceive the discriminator, by generating data samples that the discriminator cannot label as real or synthetic. A well-designed training process converges to a generator ANN that approximates the real data distribution, thus generating high-quality synthetic data samples.

Recent articles have demonstrated that GANs are useful tools for many applications that require generating synthetic data, especially in multimedia processing, healthcare, time series analysis, and other areas [11,17,23,24]. This article applies a GAN-based approach for generating synthetic velocity fields in LES. The generator learns to upsample an image while maintaining its quality, applying several transformations via specific ANN layers (residual and convolutional networks). Instead of taking random noise as input, the GAN takes an image and increases its resolution. The discriminator evaluates both the original high resolution image and the synthetic image created by the generator. Through a succession of convolutional layers, the discriminator outputs a binary result that indicates whether the input image is real or synthetic. The discriminator is trained by comparing its output with the ground truth. In the resulting adversarial game, the generator tries to create super resolution images indistinguishable from the original image and the discriminator attempts to discriminate the high resolution image from the super resolution image.

3   Related Work

The super resolution problem has been successfully addressed using GAN in many application areas, including computer vision, image synthesis and translation, video generation, and also fluid dynamic problems [26].

Ledig et al. [9] proposed Super Resolution GAN (SRGAN) for the super resolution problem on images. SRGAN included a supervised training method, applying a generator conditioned on a low resolution image. In turn, new components were included to complement the adversarial loss used for training: a perceptual loss from a pre-trained classifier and a regularization loss to promote the creation of spatially coherent images. SRGAN was able to create photorealistic images, upscaling four times the input image.

Xie et al. [29] applied a generative model to synthesize multi dimensional physics fields. A conditional GAN was proposed to infer 3D volumetric data and generate realistic high-resolution flow data. A data augmentation phase was included, guided by physics information to avoid overfitting. The approach was validated over a 3D plume scenario and simulations augmented with additional turbulence. The GAN generated stable and realistic details, properly benefiting from coherent, physical information. The method was robust for realistic models of physical phenomena, but required a moderate execution time for training in 2D and a large execution time (many days) for the full 3D models.

Werhahn et al. [28] proposed Multi-Pass GAN, a method for sampling volumetric functions using GANs. A decomposition was applied to divide the problem into simpler subproblems. Two GANs were applied: one for upscaling and the other for refining the volume, using two-dimensional slices. Two components are included in the loss function for spatial and temporal supervision. The method was validated on realistic buoyant smoke motion scenarios, including colliding smoke plumes. The approach was able to compute significant upscaling factors for volume, while showing a better computing performance than the models proposed by Xie et al., i.e., five days using a single GPU.

Subramaniam et al. [22] proposed Turbulence Enrichment residual block neural network (TEResNet) and Turbulence Enrichment GAN (TEGAN) applying physics-based data-driven and the SRGAN approach, for studying turbulent phenomena. TEResNet is formed by the residual network generator of TEGAN, trained without the adversarial approach. The validation of the proposed methods was performed on an incompressible forced isotropic homogeneous turbulence problem in a 3D periodic domain, considering as input data a low resolution turbulent flow. The evaluation studied different loss functions and physics-based terms. TEGAN obtained the best results, being able to enrich low resolution fields and recover a large portion of the missing finer scales.

Li and McComb [10] applied Physics-Informed Generative Adversarial Networks (PIGANs) for super resolution multiphase fluid simulations. A variant of the adversarial generative approach in SRGAN was proposed to reconstruct fluid phase fraction at a higher resolution. The proposed model incorporates a physics-informed term in the loss function. Accurate results were reported, outperforming other non-learning upsampling approaches in terms of accuracy and detail preservation. Even though the proposed model computed accurate results, a comparison with a traditional SRGAN suggested that using physic information does not allow to significantly improve the results.

The analysis of related works indicates that there is still room to contribute in this line of research, by proposing and studying generative models for super resolution in the context of CFD.

4   Super Resolution GAN for Velocity Fields in LES

This section describes the methodology applied for the generation of velocity fields in LES using GANs.

4.1   Resolution Approach

Overall description. The strategy for solving the problem consists of taking high-resolution images and applying a random image cropping of a defined size (96

$\times$ 96 for images from the DIV2K dataset and 32 $\times$ 32 for the UxLES dataset). Each image is flipped horizontally and rotated an angle of 90° (clockwise), with a probability of 0.5. Then, images are scaled down using a bicubic kernel in order to have low resolution images 4$\times$ smaller (i.e., 24 $\times$ 24 or 8 $\times$ 8 depending on the dataset). After that, the high resolution image is normalized with a mean of 0.5 and a standard deviation of 0.5 ($[0, 1]$ range) on each channel. Similarly, the low resolution image is normalized with a mean of 0 and a standard deviation of 1 ($[0.5, 0.5]$ range). The resulting images stored in a tensor are then used to define the training and validation sets for the proposed GAN.

Both the generator and the discriminator in the proposed GAN are trained with the goal of obtaining super resolution images that the discriminator is not able to distinguish from the original high resolution images. The details of the applied generator and the discriminator are presented in the next subsection.

4.2   Architecture of the Applied ANNs

The proposed GAN is based on deep residual networks (ResNet) [8], which have shown very good capabilities for image recognition and image processing tasks. The main details of the architectures are described next.

Residual Networks. The decision of using the ResNet structure is based on the need of properly dealing with the information degradation. ResNet is able to handle the difficulties of propagating the information from the superficial layers to the deepest layers of the model. Additional features are included, namely skip-connections and batch normalization, to mitigate the effect of internal covariate shift, i.e., the change in the distribution of network activations due to the change in network parameters during training.

Generator. Instead of using a random latent space, as usually applied in GANs, the generator receives a low resolution image as input and processes it using a Convolutional Neural Network (CNN). The CNN architecture consists of a single convolutional layer with kernel size $k = 9$, number of feature maps $n = 64$, and stride $s = 1$ (k9n64s1). The activation function is a channel-wise Parametric ReLU (PReLU), which overcomes the shortcomings of the traditional ReLU activation function and considers different slopes for each exit channel. Then, $B = 16$ residual blocks are defined. Each block consists of a CNN, followed by batch normalization (BN) to standardize the inputs of a layer for each mini-batch, to stabilize the learning process and reduce the required number of training epochs. The final components of each block are a PReLU activation, a CNN, BN, and the sum of the input of the block (using the skip connection). Following the B residual blocks, a new CNN, BN, and a skip-connection from the start of the block series is applied to avoid loss information during the B blocks. The scale up is performed in two successive 2$\times$ factor increases after applying a CNN having a number of output channels four times greater than the input, and then performing a PixelShuffler. PixelShuffler is used to convert the depth (channel) into the 2D space (height and width), to upsample the images, i.e., distributing the increase in the width and height of the image $(C \cdot 4 \times H \times W \rightarrow C \cdot H \times 2 \times W \times 2)$. This step is performed twice, to obtain an increase of four times of the original resolution. Finally, a CNN with 3 output channels corresponding to the RGB colors is added. A diagram of the generator is presented in Fig. 1(a).

Discriminator. The discriminator receives a high resolution image (either real or synthetic) as input. The architecture of the discriminator includes a CNN with LeakyReLU activation, followed by seven blocks composed by a CNN, BN, and LeakyReLU, with successive increases in kernel size and alternating with stride 1 or 2. After that, the discriminator applies a linear ANN with LeakyReLU and finally another linear ANN with sigmoid activation. The discriminator returns the probability that the two input images are identical, according to the learned criteria. A diagram of the discriminator is presented in Fig. 1(b).

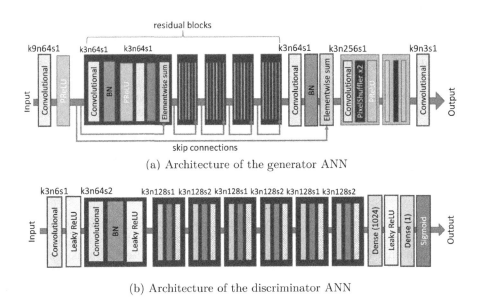

(a) Architecture of the generator ANN

(b) Architecture of the discriminator ANN

Fig. 1. Architecture of generator and discriminator (based on Ledig et al. [9])

4.3   Loss Functions

Commonly used loss functions for GAN training (Mean Squared Error (MSE) or Peak Signal-to-Noise Ratio (PSNR)) do not capture relevant differences in velocity fields per se, because they are defined as a mere pixel difference [9].

The loss function for training the generator is the sum of two components: the content and the adversarial terms. For the content term, the loss function based on MSE is replaced by a specific loss function computed from the feature maps of a VGG network ($l^{SR}_{VGG/i.j}$). The content term is defined in Eq. 1, where $W_{i,j}$ and $H_{i,j}$ are the dimensions of the fetaure maps defined by the VGG network.

$$l^{SR}_{VGG/i.j} = \frac{1}{W_{i,j}H_{i,j}} \sum_{x=1}^{W_{i,j}} \sum_{y=1}^{H_{i,j}} (\phi_{i,j}(I^{HR})_{x,y} - \phi_{i,j}(G_{\theta_G}(I^{LR}))_{x,y})^2 \qquad (1)$$

The proposed content term evaluates the differences between the features of the super resolution image generated by VGG and the features of the original high resolution image. Specifically, the proposed VGG loss is based on the ReLU activation layers of the VGG19 ANN.

Regarding the adversarial term of the loss function, the following ideas are applied. The main goal of the generator is to deceive the discriminator, trying to generate synthetic super resolution images indistinguishable from real high resolution images. Thus, the output of the discriminator of the synthetic super resolution image is maximized, since the main goal is for the discriminator to output the value one for synthetic super resolution images. For a better convergence, the opposite value of the discriminator output is minimized (Eq. 2).

$$l^{SR}_{GEN} = \sum_{n=1}^{N} -\log D_{\theta_D}(G_{\theta_G}(I^{LR})) \qquad (2)$$

Despite MSE not being fully adequate to evaluate the differences of the synthetic and the real image, an empirical evaluation demonstrated that the best training results are obtained when adding the MSE loss, defined in Eq. 3.

$$l^{SR}_{MSE} = \frac{1}{r^2\,WH} \sum_{x=1}^{rW} \sum_{y=1}^{rH} (I^{HR}_{x,y} - G_{\theta_G}(I^{LR})_{x,y})^2 \qquad (3)$$

Then, terms are added to define the global loss function, applying a suitable rescaling of the content loss and the adversarial loss, for the three considered functions to have the same order of magnitude. The content loss is rescaled by a factor of 6×10^{-3} and the adversarial term is rescaled by a factor of 1×10^{-3}.

5   Experimental Analysis and Discussion

This section reports the experimental analysis of the proposed GAN for the generation of velocity fields in LES.

5.1   Methodology

Development and Execution Platform. The proposed GAN was developed in Python using the open source machine learning framework PyTorch [18], and the albumentations and matplotlib libraries. The developed code is publicly available at https://github.com/maxibove13/SRGAN. The experimental analysis was performed on the high performance computing platform of National Supercomputing Center (Cluster-UY), Uruguay [15].

GAN Training and Validation. A k-fold cross validation was applied for validating the proposed method, for efficiently using the available data. k-fold cross validation [6] overcomes the reduction of data samples when using training, validation, and testing datasets, to lowering the risk of overfitting. It does not require a test dataset, since the model is evaluated on a subset of the training set.

The applied k-fold cross validation first divided the dataset in 89% of the samples for training and 11% for validation. Then, the training set was divided in k subsets (folds). Subsequently, the model was trained k times, leaving out from the training a different subset of the k folds each time. Thus, the evaluation metrics were computed for the k training instances, averaged, and considered for hyperparameter tuning. After determining suitable values for the hyperparameters, the final version of the model was trained with all the training set, including all folds. The performance of the model on unseen data was evaluated with the (previously separated) testing set.

The Adam optimizer was used for training the ANNs, with learning rate 1 $\times 10^{-4}$ and $\beta \in \{0.9, 0.999\}$. A batch size of 16 was selected, and the training was stopped after 160 epochs. A parallel implementation was developed, using four worker processes to generate and process batches in parallel.

Evaluation metrics. PSNR and Structural Similarity Index Measure (SSIM) [27] are used to assess the quality of the generated images. PSNR is an expression for the ratio between the maximum possible signal power and the power of the distorting noise. This ratio is computed in decibel form and it tends to infinity when the images are identical. SSIM is a perception based model, in which image degradation is considered as the change of perception in structural information. This metric extracts three key features of an image: luminescence, contrast and structure. SSIM ranges from 0 to 1; two identical images have an SSIM of 1. [21]. Both metrics were calculated on the first channel over the entire image.

5.2 Problem Instances

The problem instances used in this research consider data from two repositories. The first repository is the DIVerse 2K (DIV2K) dataset [1], including high quality resolution images used in image super resolution challenges. The dataset includes 900 generic photographs with resolution 462×510 pixels. Low resolution images from DIV2K (i.e., Train Data Track 1) were used for training and validation of the proposed approach. DIV2K is publicly available at https://data.vision.ee. ethz.ch/cvl/DIV2K. A $4\times$ bicubic downscaling was applied.

The second repository is the UxLES dataset, consisting of 1609 images of a real CFD problem. Images correspond to the first component (Ux) of the velocity field of an LES simulation around a wind turbine (dimension 64×64) obtained using the heterogeneous computing CFD-LES code caffa3d [12,25]. Figure 2a shows the entire horizontal domain of the simulation with the selected plane indicated as a black dashed line and the wind turbine in the thick black line. A close up is shown in Fig. 2b. Images in the UxLES dataset were obtained from the velocity vector using colormap jet and adjusting the color scale to cover all the Ux velocity changes throughout the dataset. The applied color scale is defined within the range 2 to 12 m/s. Points with a speed of 2 m/s are represented with a color with RGB encoding [0,0,1] and points with a speed of 12 m/s are represented with a color with RGB encoding [1,0,0]. Despite having the same number of points, the data points are not equally spaced. Thus, the image is not square (Fig. 2c). Therefore, images were resized to a 64 × 64 pixel size to use usual ANN architectures. A 4× downscaling was applied.

The UxLES dataset is publicly available at shorturl.at/hjsv1. Figure 3 presents two sample images in the UxLES dataset.

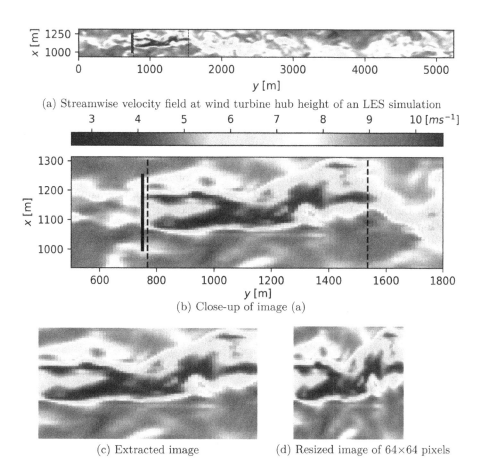

(a) Streamwise velocity field at wind turbine hub height of an LES simulation

(b) Close-up of image (a)

(c) Extracted image   (d) Resized image of 64×64 pixels

Fig. 2. Data from the UxLES dataset

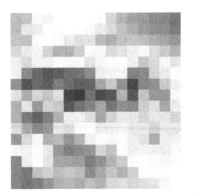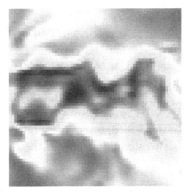

(a) Low resolution image (16×16 pixels) (b) High resolution image (64×64 pixels)

Fig. 3. Two sample images in the UxLES data set.

5.3   Results and Discussion

This section reports the results of training and validation experiments.

Training Stage. Figure 4 presents the evolution of the adversarial losses (the generator loss, the discriminator loss for real images and the discriminator loss for synthetic images) over epochs for the UxLES dataset. The adversarial loss evolution shows an stable training despite the large variance of the losses, specially of the generator. This variance represents the *minmax* adversarial game of alternated gradient reductions.

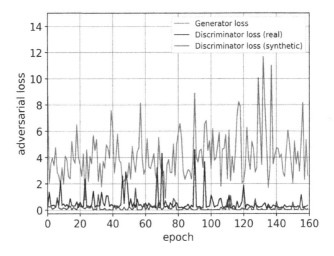

Fig. 4. Adversarial loss for the generator and discriminator through epochs.

Figure 5 reports the MSE and VGG losses evolution for training. They behave in a similar way, with a sharp decreasing slope for the first 40 epochs, and then reach an asymptote that caps the reduction of these losses.

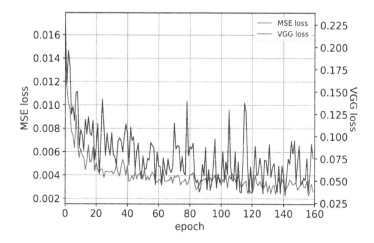

Fig. 5. Generator losses: MSE and VGG through epochs.

As expected, both the MSE and VGG components of the generator loss diminish considerably as the epochs pass. MGE and VGG are associated with the similarity between the original and the generated image, and particularly help to achieve better PSNR results (i.e., greater dB).

Figure 6 reports the evolution of the PSNR and SSIM metrics along epochs during training. Both PSNR and SSIM metrics increase along the epochs, showing an improvement of the quality of the synthetic image over learning iterations. Both improve fast on the first 20 epochs, but then the learning pace slows down up to a point on which more iterations do not improve the quality of the generated images or the improvement is marginal; this occurs after 100 epochs.

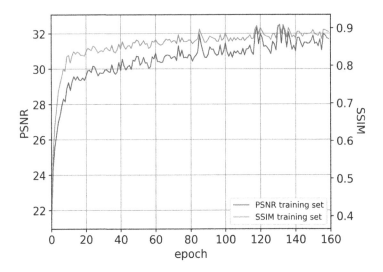

Fig. 6. PSNR and SSIM metrics on training data through epochs.

Validation Stage. Regarding the considered performance metrics, the model reached a mean of 32.50 db for PSNR and 0.93 for SSIM, with a relatively low variance of 0.73 and 0.01 respectively.

Figure 7(a) compares four random samples of the testing dataset of the LR, SR and HR images. The coordinate axes on each image are expressed as a ratio between the position and the diameter of the wind turbine. Figure 7(b) depicts the error (difference) between the synthetic (SR) and the real (HR) velocity fields (images) in ms^{-1} for the same random testing samples.

The obtained results proved to be satisfactory, by judging not only the objective metrics PSNR and SSIM, but also applying a subjective visual inspection of the quality of the generated images. It is noteworthy that the lack of diversity of the considered UxLES dataset helps the model to improve its performance. However, this property is not necessarily an indication of a poor quality dataset, because for many specific applications the dataset is still useful.

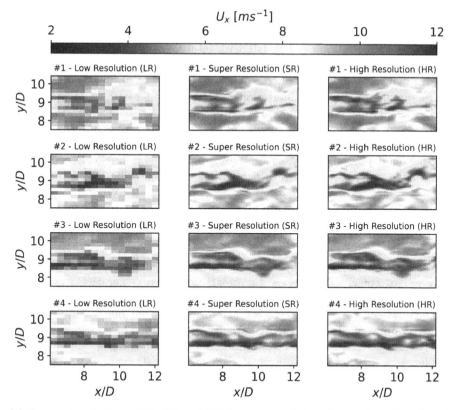

(a) Comparison between LR, SR and HR images rescaled and resized to the original value of the velocity planes.

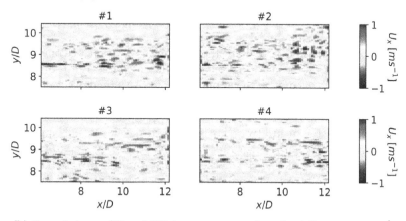

(b) Error between SR and HR images measured as the difference in ms^{-1}.

Fig. 7. Visual comparison of a 4× upscale using the trained SRGAN. From left to right: low resolution image, super resolution image and high resolution image. The images are scaled to the original velocity values, and the coordinates are expressed as a ratio of the wind turbine diameter.

Computational Efficiency Analysis. A LES simulation like the one used to trained and validate the proposed GAN approach demands five days of computing time in a HP ProLiant DL380 G9, with Intel Xeon Gold 6138 processors (18 cores), to simulate a 1.1 h period. Considering that a coarse (LR) LES simulation requires half the computational cost of a fine (HR) one, the proposed approach implies a reduction of the computational cost by 2.5 d for each horizontal plane of a fine simulation. This reduction is most beneficial for some applications, like micrositing of wind turbines or analysis of operating wind farms, where tenths or even hundreds of fine grid simulations are needed. In these applications, using a surrogate model based on GANs might imply a potential reduction in computing times in the order of weeks, thus highlighting the importance of the proposed approach.

6   Conclusions and Future Work

This article presented an approach for the generation of synthetic velocity fields in LES. Particularly, the proposed approach applies a Generative Adversarial Network to increase the resolution of horizontal slices of turbulent velocity fields.

The proposed GAN learned structural information from high resolution velocity fields and applied the learned knowledge to infer (generate) new high resolution velocity slices when a low resolution one is given as input.

The proposed approach was evaluated on a real-world case study: augmenting the resolution of horizontal velocity fields downstream of a wind turbine. Results showed an stable and converging training process of the proposed GAN. In turn, the objective metrics PSNR and SSIM considered in the evaluation exhibited a relatively good similarity between the super resolution generated image (slice of horizontal velocity field) and the high resolution used as a reference baseline. Besides, a subjective visual inspection showed a strong similarity between the synthetic and the real images.

The reported research is a first step on the application of computational intelligence methods for generating velocity fields in Large Eddy Simulations. The obtained results encourage the application of GANs (and other deep Learning techniques) as surrogate models in order to reduce the cost of performing complex CFD simulations.

The main lines for future work are related to develop a full approach for generating images to characterize the three velocity components of turbulent velocity fields and generalizing the methodology for a more diverse dataset that includes other type of flows. The proposed approach can also be integrated with the formalism of Physics-Informed Neural Networks, in order to give the model the ability to evaluate if the generated image is physically possible.

References

1. Agustsson, E., Timofte, R.: NTIRE 2017 challenge on single image super-resolution: dataset and study. In: The IEEE Conference on Computer Vision and Pattern Recognition Workshops (2017)
2. Breton, S., Sumner, J., Sørensen, J., Hansen, K., Sarmast, S., Ivanell, S.: A survey of modelling methods for high-fidelity wind farm simulations using large eddy simulation. Philos. Trans. R. Soc. A: Math. Phys. Eng. Sci. **375**(2091), 20160097 (2017)
3. El Emam, K., Mosquera, L., Hoptroff, R.: Practical Synthetic Data Generation. O'Reilly Media Inc., Sebastopol (2020)
4. Foster, D.: Generative Deep Learning. O'Reilly Media Inc., Sebastopol (2019)
5. Fröhlich, J., Rodi, W.: Introduction to large eddy simulation of turbulent flows (2002)
6. Fushiki, T.: Estimation of prediction error by using k-fold cross-validation. Stat. Comput. **21**(2), 137–146 (2011)
7. Goodfellow, I., et al.: Generative adversarial nets. In: Advances in Neural Information Processing Systems, pp. 2672–2680 (2014)
8. He, K., Zhang, X., Ren, S., Sun, J.: Deep residual learning for image recognition. In: IEEE Conference on Computer Vision and Pattern Recognition (2016)
9. Ledig, C., et al.: Photo-realistic single image super-resolution using a generative adversarial network. In: IEEE Conference on Computer Vision and Pattern Recognition (2017)
10. Li, M., McComb, C.: Using physics-informed generative adversarial networks to perform super-resolution for multiphase fluid simulations. J. Comput. Inf. Sci. Eng. **22**(4), 044501 (2022)
11. Machín, B., Nesmachnow, S., Toutouh, J.: Multi-target evolutionary latent space search of a generative adversarial network for human face generation. In: Genetic and Evolutionary Computation Conference (2022)
12. Mendina, M., Draper, M., Kelm, A., Narancio, G., Usera, G.: A general purpose parallel block structured open source incompressible flow solver. Clust. Comput. **17**(2), 231–241 (2014)
13. Milanfar, P.: Super-resolution imaging. CRC Press, Boca Raton (2017)
14. Nasrollahi, K., Moeslund, T.B.: Super-resolution: a comprehensive survey. Mach. Vis. Appl. **25**(6), 1423–1468 (2014). https://doi.org/10.1007/s00138-014-0623-4
15. Nesmachnow, S., Iturriaga, S.: Cluster-UY: collaborative scientific high performance computing in uruguay. In: Torres, M., Klapp, J. (eds.) ISUM 2019. CCIS, vol. 1151, pp. 188–202. Springer, Cham (2019). https://doi.org/10.1007/978-3-030-38043-4_16
16. Ng, A., Jordan, M.: On discriminative vs. generative classifiers: a comparison of logistic regression and naive Bayes. In: Conference on Neural Information Processing Systems (2002)
17. Pan, Z., Yu, W., Yi, X., Khan, A., Yuan, F., Zheng, Y.: Recent progress on generative adversarial networks (GANs): a survey. IEEE Access **7**, 36322–36333 (2019)
18. Paszke, A., et al.: Pytorch: an imperative style, high-performance deep learning library. In: Advances in Neural Information Processing Systems, vol. 32 (2019)
19. Pope, S.: Turbulent Flows. Cambridge University Press, Cambridge (2000)
20. Sagaut, P.: Large Eddy Simulation for Incompressible Flows: An Introduction. Springer Science & Business Media, Cham (2006)

21. Sara, U., Akter, M., Uddin, M.: Image quality assessment through FSIM, SSIM, MSE and PSNR-a comparative study. J. Comput. Commun. **7**(3), 8–18 (2019)

22. Subramaniam, A., Wong, M.L., Borker, R.D., Nimmagadda, S., Lele, S.K.: Turbulence enrichment using physics-informed generative adversarial networks (2020). https://arxiv.org/abs/2003.01907 [June 2022]

23. Toutouh, J., Esteban, M., Nesmachnow, S.: Parallel/Distributed generative adversarial neural networks for data augmentation of COVID-19 training images. In: Nesmachnow, S., Castro, H., Tchernykh, A. (eds.) CARLA 2020. CCIS, vol. 1327, pp. 162–177. Springer, Cham (2021). https://doi.org/10.1007/978-3-030-68035-0_12

24. Toutouh, J., Nesmachnow, S., Rossit, D.G.: Generative adversarial networks to model air pollution under uncertainty. In: International Workshop on Advanced Information and Computation Technologies and Systems, CEUR Workshop Proceedings, vol. 2858, pp. 169–174. CEUR (2020)

25. Usera, G., Vernet, A., Ferré, J.: A parallel block-structured finite volume method for flows in complex geometry with sliding interfaces. Flow Turbul. Combust. **81**(3), 471–495 (2008)

26. Wang, L., Chen, W., Yang, W., Bi, F., Yu, F.R.: A state-of-the-art review on image synthesis with generative adversarial networks. IEEE Access **8**, 63514–63537 (2020)

27. Wang, Z., Bovik, A.C., Sheikh, H.R., Simoncelli, E.P.: Image quality assessment: from error visibility to structural similarity. IEEE Trans. Image Process. **13**(4), 600–612 (2004)

28. Werhahn, M., Xie, Y., Chu, M., Thuerey, N.: A multi-pass GAN for fluid flow super-resolution. Proc. ACM Comput. Graph. Interact. Tech. **2**(2), 1–21 (2019)

29. Xie, Y., Franz, E., Chu, M., Thuerey, N.: tempoGAN. ACM Trans. Graph. **37**(4), 1–15 (2018)

30. Zhiyin, Y.: Large-eddy simulation: past, present and the future. Chin. J. Aeronaut. **28**(1), 11–24 (2015)

Deep Neural Networks for Global Horizontal Irradiation Forecasting: A Comparative Study

Cristian Arbeláez-Duque⬛, Alejandro Duque-Ciro⬛, Walter Villa-Acevedo⬛, and Álvaro Jaramillo-Duque(✉)

Universidad de Antioquia, Calle 67 #53-108, CP 050010 Medellín, Colombia
{cristiand.arbelaez,alejandro.duque2,walter.villa, alvaro.jaramillod}@udea.edu.co

Abstract. In order to contribute to the integration of photovoltaic renewable energy into power system, this paper addresses the problem of forecasting solar irradiance or Global Horizontal Irradiation (GHI). The collection, adjustment and processing of meteorological data used as input is carried out, in addition various Deep Neural Networks (DNN) models are implemented and analyzed, among which are the Artificial Neural Networks (ANN) of type as Transformer, LSTM, GRU, and mixed between Convolutional ANN (CNN)-LSTM, and CNN-GRU. These ANN variants are implemented, and a comparative study are made. Finally, the results obtained show that the ANN transformer has less error in the GHI forecasting.

Keywords: Deep Neural Networks · Artificial Neural Network · Global Horizontal Irradiation Forecasting · Transformer · LSTM · GRU · Convolution

1 Introduction

Electrical energy has become a fundamental support for modern society that uses technology powered by it, constituting itself as the essential hub in the development of daily activities worldwide. Electricity is used in sectors such as industrial, agricultural, domestic and many others, making it a primary and fundamental service for the global economy. Due to aforementioned, electricity consumption worldwide maintains a constant growth; therefore, technologies focused on energy efficiency and the management of the renewable resources for electricity generation have been developed in the last decades [1].

1.1 Background

As the consumption of electricity increases globally, it is a challenge to supply this demand without generating additional environmental impacts. In addition, the infrastructure of electricity systems and conventional technologies of electricity generation must be adapted to achieve an energy transition towards sustainable and more environmentally friendly technologies. Due to the above, the energy sector has been driven to develop and to integrate alternatives of non-conventional technologies for electricity generation such as renewable energies, which allow diversifying the energy matrix and energy transition. This without neglecting environmental responsibility and guaranteeing competitive and accessible prices in the electricity market [2].

In the many countries, there has been an increase in the use of non-conventional technology for electrical energy generation, whose availability of natural resources is intermittent, for example, photovoltaic solar energy or wind energy. Also the implementing costs of these technologies have been greatly reduced in the last decades, making those options cost-effective electricity sources. In addition, these reduce greenhouse gas emissions and have lower environmental impacts [2]. Unlike of the conventional technologies, one of the biggest challenges presented by intermittent technologies are to determine exactly how much energy will be generated at each moment of the day [3].

One of the tasks in the power system operation, is to dispatch of power plants, in order to meet the electricity demand. For conventional power plants, it can be quantified very precisely how much energy can be generated in the future, considering the amount of fuel available in a thermal power plant, or from the water stored in the case of a hydroelectric power plant [3]. On the other hand, the electricity production from photovoltaic and wind power plants may be affected by weather conditions, such as solar radiation, wind speed, geographical location, temperature, humidity, atmospheric pressure, among other weather factors. These factors cannot be controlled and do not allow to forecast with precise accuracy how much energy will be available in the future. Therefore, a challenge arises when it make planning of energy dispatch in power systems that includes intermittent energy sources electricity generation [4].

For photovoltaic (PV) power plants, the challenge is to determine the availability of the solar irradiance or Global Horizontal Irradiation resource (GHI) to estimate the energy production. There exist several forecasting models for solar irradiance are classified into physical models, statistical and Machine Learning (ML) models.

1.2   Literature Review

Physical models, such as numerical weather prediction (NWP), are computationally expensive because they consider several environmental aspects to calculate the future irradiance. Statistical models, such as the autoregressive integrated and moving average model (ARIMA) perform temporal mappings over past data and produce forecasts and have been used in several irradiance forecasting applications [5].

Machine Learning (ML) models are one of the most promising computational methods for forecasting GHI and energy production, because they are more suitable for mapping nonlinear patterns [5]. ML models are not only capable of performing nonlinear mappings in the data but also present some flexibility regarding noisy data [5].

A ML model can be described as a group of mathematical expression to find patterns or make predictions. Once a ML model is built to forecast the GHI, a training process is carried out from a set of historical data, called a training set. After the training process is completed, the performance of the model is evaluated with another set of data, called test set. If the performance metrics have adequate values, it moves on to the stage of forecasting the future values of the variable of interest with new data. Otherwise, to improve performance models a hyperparameters tuning process or a architecture modification of the ML model is carried out. This process is made until reaching adequate performance metrics according to the nature of the problem.

Predictions problems can be divided into two types of tasks: classification and regression tasks. The intermittent renewable resource forecasting or the power generated from intermittent renewable technologies is classified as a regression task, in which the time series of future values is forecasted from data from the past. For example, to calculate the forecast of GHI for the next day, with an hourly resolution, radiation data from previous days are used [6].

For the time series forecasting problem there is a type of ANN, which has characteristics suitable for the management of temporal sequences and the temporal dependence of the data that make up the time series. This advantage makes it suitable for GHI time series forecasting. This ANN is known as Recurrent Neural Network (RNN), it has the particularity of having connections between neurons, which propagate information forward and backward (recurrent connection), so RNN present a good response processing data sequences as is the case of time series, without this affecting the size or number of layers that make up the RNN [7].

According to [7–12], a type of RNN is Long Short Term Memory (LSTM) that has the ability to process long time series sequences, allowing to handle short and long term dependencies on the data stream. Due to the recurrence in LSTM structure, those models can remember previous states and from them forecast which will be the next state [6]. The LSTM models are capable by predicting variables that have trend and seasonal behaviors, and in general long term dependencies into data [6].

In [13], a simple RNN and an LSTM are proposed to make the next day of solar irradiance forecasting. To reduce the error into forecasting and given the high dependence that the climate state has on solar irradiance, four different states are proposed to make the forecast, which are sunny, cloudy, rainy and intense rainy states. The proposed model is composed of three main parts which are: 1) Preprocessing of the solar irradiance data using Discrete Wavelet Transformation (DWT), 2) Extraction of the local features based on a Convolutional layer, and 3) the processing of the sequence using an LSTM layer. The results presented according to the performance metrics obtained less error for sunny days. On the other hand, in [9], an LSTM is also used, to make the forecasting of the GHI in Atlanta, New York and Hawaii. To do the prediction, three classifications of the weather are proposed, which are: sunny, cloudy and mixed. The presented model has a hidden single layer structure with a Relu activation function. The dropout is added to the hidden layer allowing some connections to be discarded randomly during training process; which allows to reduce the overfitting problem in the LSTM response. The proposed LSTM has less forecasting error on cloudy and mixed days.

In [14] is present a LSTM network used to predict the power produced from a photovoltaic power plan, and compares it to a simple RNN, a Generalized Regression Neural Network (GRNN), and an Extreme Learning Machine (ELM). The LSTM network consists of an input layers, hidden layers, and an output layer in sequential manner. The results show that the performance of the LSTM for the four seasons of the year is superior with respect to the others ANN since it presents a lower forecasting error due to the LSTM cells, which allows to maintain the long-term temporal dependencies.

In [15] the authors perform a forecasting task for which, in training different ANN models, then combine their results to solve the same problem. The same data is entered simultaneously to the ANN, and then averaging the forecasts given by each one. In this case, two types of ANN were used: MultiLayer Perceptron (MLP) and LSTM. After training the ANN with four different databases, the results of the combined forecasting have less error compared to the results of MLP and LSTM individually.

In [16] a forecast combiner is proposed in which the outputs generated individually by LSTM and GRU models are used to finally deliver a combined forecast. These two RNNs are used because they allow long term information to be retained and thus maintain correlations between the values of the time series. The results show that LSTM and GRU individually delivered values of performance metrics with higher errors compared to the proposed forecast combination process showing a significant improvement in the forecasting of the variables.

A forecast model based on Deep Neural Networks (DNN) combined with self-attention mechanisms, known as Transformers, which are characterized by parallelizing computational processes, have shown great potential in natural language and image processing; so they are shown as promising candidates to make forecasts in time series [15].

In this work, different ANN are implemented to the task of short-term forecasting of GHI, with a horizon of 24 h and a temporal resolution of 15 min. This forecast will serve as an input to establish the future generation of photovoltaic power plants. Among the ANN to be considered are LSTM, GRU, CNN-LSTM, CNN-GRU and Transformer, architectures and hyperparameters based on those found in the technical literature such as those obtained by hyperparameter tuning tools will be considered. A database of meteorological variables of two years that are used for the experiments. The performance evaluation of each ANN model is done with metrics for both training and validation data [7].

The contribution of this work focuses on determining from an evaluation and comparison of different ANN models, what is the best model configuration for the GHI forecast of a full day using historical data. Different architectures, scaling types, and data inputs were used for ANN types, including the Transformer model. A one-day time window with a resolution of fifteen minutes between each measurement was used for all experiments [18].

2   Background

This section presents the basic concepts for the implementation of ANN models for the GHI forecast.

2.1   Factors Influencing GHI Forecast

In [6, 8, 9, 15, 19] were found that, in order to forecast GHI and electrical energy from a solar power plant, it is vitally important to consider these important aspects: 1) Forecast time horizons, 2) Data preparation and model inputs, 3) Artificial intelligence (AI) tools, and 4) Model performance evaluation metrics.

Forecast Time Horizons

For the development of a prediction model, aspects such as: prediction horizon and temporal resolution must be considered in the model design. The prediction horizon of the data corresponds to the period towards the future in which the forecast is made, starting from a given moment in which the prediction is made. Depending on the forecast horizon of the GHI, the following classification is available: very short term (ranging from one hour to three hours); short term (comprises up to 24 h); medium term (includes up to a week) and long term (includes up to weeks). For the temporal resolution of the data, each horizon must be considered. They must be fractions of the prediction horizon, which adjust to the nature of the problem and the user needs. For example, for very short term it must be 1, 5, 10, 15 or 30 min are handled. The horizon and resolution must be considered in the forecast task so that the data is prepared according to the available information and the type of forecast will be implemented.

Data Preparation and Model Inputs

Input data is critical in any ML model, as these are what feed the models. Based on [8, 9] and [17], a cleaning and preparation of the data is performed, replacing the missing data with the closest previous value in the time series, not zero. A resampling of the data is also carried out, to avoid missing values, if the missing values do not exceed the new resolution of the resampling time. Subsequently, the normalization and standardization of the set of data obtained is used. It is worth highlighting the importance of the selection of the input variables of the model, in [7] and [9] the most important variables are selected and with more correlation with the generated power of the PV power plant, making use of a correlation map. It is found that the most important variables for the data set are irradiance, global irradiance and direct irradiance. Likewise, other variables that can be useful are air temperature and hour.

2.2   Artificial Intelligence Models

In [14, 16] the methods that were used for the forecasting of the solar resource are based on AI techniques, especially machine learning models. The term AI adheres to systems that have the ability to mimic human intelligence to perform tasks and improve according to the information that they collect.

   ANN are a broad family of algorithms that form the basis of the so-called AI, which has been called Deep Learning (DL). These types of AI techniques have been very well accepted, getting satisfactory results forecasting natural resources, such as solar irradiance and wind speed. ANN has become a very popular AI technique, due to their high degree of application in multiple tasks. ANN creates an interconnection system between layers and artificial neurons that processes a set of data and generates an output. Likewise, other types of neural networks have been developed that have had great acceptance in forecasting applications, which are mainly used in others works [6].

MultiLayer Perceptron - MLP

It is a feedforward approach since the information present in the inputs flows in just one direction, from the input layer to the output layer. The general principle of MLP consists of a set of artificial neurons that are connected to each other with the aim of transmitting the signals forward. Each output value of the previous neuron is multiplied by a weight, then to the output of the neuron is applied a limiting function or activation function which is responsible for modifying or limiting the output value that will be propagated to the other neurons.

In addition, the values assigned to the weights are updated in the training process, through the minimization of a loss function; known as back propagation algorithm [6]. The MLP is a universal function approximator because it can map any continuous, nonlinear, limited, and differentiable function with a predetermined error threshold [5].

Recurrent Neural Networks - RNN
It is an ANN that has a greater capacity to handle and learn different computational structures. Which in practical terms means that it can learn the trend and seasonal behaviors into the time series as the solar irradiance. RNN not only includes feedforward connections like an MLP, but also backward connections; thus, having a kind of feedback with the other neurons that are in the layers [6]. RNN has different variants to handle the recurrence connections into architecture such as the LSTM and Gated Recurrent Unit (GRU).

Long Short-Term Memory - LSTM
RNN has a problem due to the form of time sequence information propagation within its architecture, since it propagates not only forward, but also backward. Sometimes an accumulated error into the neural network response is produced, commonly this problem appears when RNN handles time series with long-term dependencies; called long-term memory problems. LSTM solves the problem of long-term memory in simply RNNs, since these have as their main characteristic that information can persist by introducing loops in the flow of information from the network. So, basically, LSTM can remember previous states and use this information to decide what the next state will be. This feature makes them very suitable for handling long time series. Therefore, it can be stated that LSTM can learn long dependencies and thanks to this they have a long-term memory [7].

Gated Recurrent Unit - GRU
GRU is a new generation of RNN and is like the LSTM network but has less complex architecture and allows you to control the flow of information to capture time series dependencies without using an internal memory cell. This characteristic solves the problems that arise from local minimums and gradient descent. In addition, as it is a less complex network, it uses less computational resources, therefore it spends less time to carry out its training [7].

Convolutional Neural Networks - CNN
This is a type of network that integrates the convolution mathematical operator, which transforms the input data, reducing its dimensions and computational complexity when processing it. These networks instead of neurons have filters, kernels and the amount of them is determined according to the needs of the problem [7]. For the forecast of time

series, a CNN with a layer of one dimension is used, which allows it to process temporal sequences instead of images that have information structures in two dimensions, for which the CNNs were created.

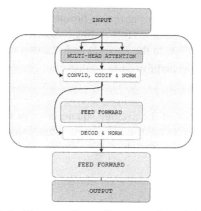

Fig. 1. Transformer ANN Architecture shows the structuring of the Attention function, normalization, the final layer of with convolution, in addition to simple ANNs, also called Feed Forward.

Transformer Model

As presented in [20] and Fig. 1, Transformer deep learning model is based on the combination of two stages (Encoder and Decoder). The Encoder stage starts with a positional coding block, a Multi-Head Attention block, a block of simple neurons, and finally Decoder stage that is the output of the model.

As presented in [21], an Attention function can be described as assigning a query (encoding) and a set of key-value pairs as output. Where the query, keys, values, and output are all vectors. The output is calculated as a weighted sum of the values, where the weight assigned to each value is calculated using a query compatibility function with the corresponding key.

Next with the development of the study of the Attention functions, in [21] it was found that better performances were produced in the models by linearly projecting the queries, keys and values a certain number of times with different linear projections in three-dimensional space. For each projection, an Attention function is applied in parallel to the others, then a concatenation is performed that is projected and results in the output of the model. The Multi-Head Attention function allows the model to process information as a set. This function is included in the structure of the Transformer model [17]. The Transformer network used in this work is presented in Fig. 1. Its main features are that in the encoder block it uses a one-dimensional convolutional layer after the Multi-head Attention block and in the decoding stage it uses a layer of an MLP feed forward network.

2.3 Evaluation of Model Performance

Usually, the most used metrics to measure the error of DL forecasting models are: 1) MSE (Mean Square Error), 2) RMSE (Root Mean Square Error), 3) MAE (Mean Absolute Error), 4) MAPE (Mean Absolute Percentage Error). These metrics are used for the evaluation of the models in regression problems, these metrics are appropriate to evaluate performance in time series forecasting contexts such as the one addressed in this work. As is showed below, in the Eqs. (1) and (2), two values are required for the calculations, the real value y_i and forecasted value $\breve{y}_i$.

RMSE

This index measures the root of the average square error of the forecasts made, using the expression shown in Eq. (1). For each sample what it does is calculate the square difference between the forecasts and the target outputs, and then average these values [7].

$$RMSE = \sqrt{\frac{1}{n} \sum_{i=1}^{n} \left(y_i - \breve{y}_i \right)^2} \tag{1}$$

MAE

In this metric the error is calculated as the average of absolute differences between the target values and the forecasts, as presented in Eq. (2). The MAE is a linear score, which means that all individual differences are weighted equally in the average. An advantage of this metric is that it penalizes huge errors, therefore, it is not as sensitive to outliers [6].

$$MAE = \frac{1}{n} \sum_{i=1}^{n} \left| y_i - \breve{y}_i \right| \tag{2}$$

In [14, 16], the most used metrics to evaluate the performance of the implemented models are RMSE and MAE. In [8, 11, 14] and [22], it is observed that the chosen metric is RMSE. Unlike [6, 10, 12, 15, 16, 23, 24], where the metric used is MAE.

3 Implementation of ANN

This section will explain the general structure carried out for the assembly and realization of the experiments. It is important to note that the same programming and organization structure was maintained for each of the models that were implemented. The structure and development of the models is available at [18].

3.1 Problem Definition

It seeks to make a forecast of GHI or solar irradiance using various ML models. Where at the model inputs are historical data of a full day taken from zero hour to twenty-fourth hour are entered, with a resolution of fifteen minutes between each data. Each model will deliver the forecast of a forecasting horizon or time window with the same amount of data and the same input resolution, which corresponds to the forecasts of the solar irradiance of the day immediately following the one entered.

3.2 Dataset

To carry out the experiment, freely accessible historical data, never used before for this propose, recorded by a weather station located in Kenya, were used. With the following measurements: GHI, wind speed, humidity and air temperature, Zenith, and Azimuth angles. The data has a measurement resolution of one minute for a full year. The database was separated into two sets, one with 80% of the data to train the models and a second set with the other 20% of data to validate models performance [25].

3.3 Data Preparation

A preparation of the data was carried out that would allow an objective and global analysis of the data. The first adjustment was to change the headings and indexes with the appropriate names and order that in the case of the index was converted to date format. Then the resolution of the measures was changed from one minute to fifteen minutes. Finally, the missing data were filled in using arithmetic means to avoid altering the statistical measures of the data.

Data Preprocessing
This step is performed in order to adjust the data with the sequence and dimensions required by the ML models. The first step is to scale the data using normalization or standardization. For the different models, the two types were used to analyze the differences in the results. The second step is to segment the data into time windows, with 96 data, equivalents to a full last day with a resolution of 15 min, that will be the input of the model as illustrated in (3).

$$Datos = \begin{bmatrix} \begin{bmatrix} x_{1,1} \ x_{1,2} \ x_{1,3} \ \dots \ x_{1,96} \\ x_{2,1} \ x_{2,2} \ x_{2,3} \ \dots \ x_{2,96} \\ \vdots \quad \vdots \quad \vdots \quad \ddots \quad \vdots \\ [x_{n,1} \ x_{n.2} \ x_{n,3} \ \dots \ x_{n,96}] \end{bmatrix} \end{bmatrix} \tag{3}$$

where the first subscript refers to the day on which the data was taken, and the second subscript refers to the data number of the day the measurement was taken. It is also important to note that x can be in addition a number or a data vector. For example, it can contain GHI, humidity, temperature, as data of an instant of time for the case of multivariate models.

3.4 Definition of Models

In this step, the ML models with an architecture and hyperparameters that correspond to a particular model under study were defined. The Python programming language, Keras and TensorFlow libraries were used to implement the ML models. The models implemented are those presented in Table 1, which also includes the main characteristics of these.

3.5 Model Performance Measures

The RMSE and MAE, shown in Eqs. (1) and (2), were taken as global performance measures for the models. The training process of the models with a learning curve was also monitored. Finally, random forecasting was taken from the dataset to graphically analyze the behavior of the forecasts compared to the actual results.

4 Results and Analysis

Table 1 presents the results obtained for the different models implemented in this work. It considers performance metrics, architecture and the scaling type used in the input data. It is important to note that these work results can be replicated using the scripts hosted in the public repository in [18]. All scripts are available with the implemented models, their parameters, hyperparameters, the structuring of the data, and all the specific information needed.

4.1 Forecast Errors

As shown in Table 1, architectures are shown, and number of neurons in each layer for the LSTM, CNN-LSTM, GRU, CNN-GRU models. For the Transformer model are shown number of heads, blocks, and units in each block. The best performing models, based on MAE metric, were marked in bold. For the LSTM, CNN-LSTM, GRU and CNN-GRU models, a fixed structure was used, varying the way of scaling the data in addition to entering one or more variables (univariate or multivariable) as the case may be. In the case of multivariate models, the variables used were GHI, rainfall, relative air humidity, time of day and wind speed.

Table 1. Implemented ANN Models

ANN type	Architecture	Input	Scaling	MAE	RMSE
LSTM	100/150	Univariable	Standard	40,54	77,41
LSTM	100/150	Univariable	MinMax	38,91	74,92
LSTM	100/150	Multivariable	Standard	39,46	74,88

(continued)

Table 1. (*continued*)

ANN type	Architecture	Input	Scaling	MAE	RMSE
LSTM	**100/150**	**Multivariable**	**MinMax**	**39,94**	**76,53**
CNN-LSTM	32/100/150	Univariable	Standard	41,05	77,06
CNN-LSTM	32/100/150	Univariable	MinMax	39,14	75,46
CNN-LSTM	32/100/150	Multivariable	Standard	40,17	76,94
CNN-LSTM	**32/100/150**	**Multivariable**	**MinMax**	**39,24**	**75,12**
GRU	100/150	Univariable	Standard	43,79	77,04
GRU	100/150	Univariable	MinMax	52,97	83,78
GRU	100/150	Multivariable	Standard	41,12	76,46
GRU	**100/150**	**Multivariable**	**MinMax**	**38,63**	**74,34**
CNN-GRU	32/100/150	Univariable	Standard	46,47	80,87
CNN-GRU	32/100/150	Univariable	MinMax	75,57	104,0
CNN-GRU	32/100/150	Multivariable	Standard	44,06	78,38
CNN-GRU	**32/100/150**	**Multivariable**	**MinMax**	**39,07**	**74,50**
Transformer	**24 h/ 4 b/ 200 u**	**Univariable**	**MinMax**	**37,85**	**72,24**

The performance metrics presented in Table 1 were calculated by forecasting the complete validation dataset and then the MAE and RMSE, described in equitation (2) and (1), were computed for each model. After executing each script multiple times, no significant change was found in the errors shown, so the last result obtained was presented. It should be noted that in other studies MAPE is commonly used, which is like MAE, but is presented in a relative percentage way. However, its use was ruled out because when the values to be estimated are close to zero, the error tends to very high values, although the forecast is correct.

Considering the 24 h forecast horizon with a resolution of 15 min, resulting in a total of 96 total data for one day. The results obtained, compared to those presented in [20], are similar. However, the maximum forecast horizon proposed in this study was 12 h with a resolution of 1 h, being a smaller and less complex problem.

In [20], the model that yields the best performance is the Transformer as found in this work and observed in Table 1. It is also relevant to mention the results of [10], which makes forecasts with a maximum horizon of 9 h and a resolution of one hour; where their lowest error was 2.82 W/m^2 with an LSTM model, in addition to that, authors use the clear sky index as input data for their implemented models.

In [16] as in this work, they predicted 24 h of solar irradiance, however, values with a resolution of 1 h between each data were used, obtaining as a minimum error of 5.78 W/m^2 unlike this work, where the time resolution used it is 15 min, four times longer. Another aspect that influences in [16], is the maximum irradiance values recorded in its database, is in the order of 600 W/m^2, while the database used in this study records values that are around 1200 W/m^2. This is reasoning the performances of both models are not directly comparable, but in proportion to this analysis, the Transformer model yields similar results in the error, even minor.

4.2 Forecasts

Figure 2 shows the forecast on the same day with clear weather conditions (sunny day). These cases were randomly taken from the validation dataset, for the Transformer, LSTM, CNN-LSTM, GRU and CNN-GRU models, respectively. In the face of clear sky conditions, all models make good forecasts with low errors. The forecast in the hours of sunrise and sunset have low error, as well as in the peak value of irradiance. In general, the models are adjusted almost superimposing the real data, as it also happens in [9, 16] and [19].

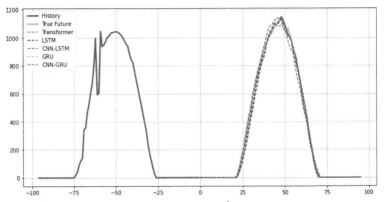

Fig. 2. Forecast of a full day of irradiance given in W/m^2, made by the Transformer, LSTM, GRU and CNN models, compared to the actual values for a sunny day.

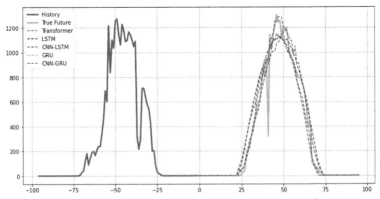

Fig. 3. Forecast of a full day of irradiance given in units performed W/m^2 by the Transformer, LSTM, GRU and CNN models, compared to the actual values for a cloudy day.

Figure 3 shows the forecast for the same day, with cloudy conditions for a few hours during it. These cases were randomly taken from the validation dataset, for the

Transformer, LSTM, CNN-LSTM, GRU and CNN-GRU models respectively. The best forecast is made by the Transformer model, and it is also worth highlighting the behavior of the CNN-LSTM, since they correctly forecast the time of sunrise and sunset. The Transformer model, in this case, is the only one capable of correctly forecasting the peak irradiance value of the day. However, like the other models, it cannot adequately predict sudden changes in the behavior of the variable. Finally, it is important to note that the overall performance of the models is quite accurate, since they all manage to adjust tendentially to the real behavior they intend to forecast. When deviations in the results occur, the responses are not distant. All the above considering that no variables were entered that could provide information for the forecasting regarding cloudiness and therefore solar irradiance.

5 Conclusions

In the proposed work, different ML models were proposed, implemented, and evaluated, currently used for the solution of similar problems, obtaining forecasts with lower errors compared to those analyzed from other previously published works.

Transformer model gives outstanding results for the problem of GHI forecasting. For this reason, and due to the few findings in the literature, it is highly recommended to further investigate the behavior of this type of neural network.

The clear sky index is an input variable that provides valuable information, which enriches the models to generate good estimates of GHI. Therefore, it becomes convenient for subsequent work, to obtain a historical dataset with this index or information to calculate it.

Finally, all models performed in a good way, but considering the results obtained, the model with the best performance in the development of this work was the Transformer model and the lowest performance was the Univariable CNN-GRU model with MinMax scaling.

Funding. This research was funded by the Colombia Scientific Program within the framework of the so-called Ecosistema Científico (Contract No. FP44842-218-2018).

References

1. Morales Ramírez, D., Luyando Cuevas, J.R.: Analisis del Consumo de Energia Electrica Residencial en el Area Metropolitana de Monterrey, vol. 31, no. 62, Art. n.º 62
2. REN21, Renewables Global Status Report, Paris, France, 22 March 2022. https://www.ren21.net/reports/global-status-report/. Accessed 22 Mar 2022
3. Demanda de energía eléctrica en tiempo real, estructura de generación y emisiones de CO2, REE, 22 March 2022. https://demanda.ree.es/visiona/seleccionar-sistema. Accessed 22 Mar 2022
4. Robledo Quintero, Á.: Predicción de la radiación global utilizando redes de neuronas artificiales, July 2018). https://e-archivo.uc3m.es/handle/10016/29002. Accessed 22 Mar 2022
5. de Santos Jr, D.S.O., et al.: Solar irradiance forecasting using dynamic ensemble selection. Appl. Sci. **12**(7), 3510 (2022)

6. Aliberti, A., Fucini, D., Bottaccioli, L., Macii, E., Acquaviva, A., Patti, E.: Comparative analysis of neural networks techniques to forecast global horizontal irradiance. IEEE Access **9**, 122829–122846 (2021). https://doi.org/10.1109/ACCESS.2021.3110167

7. Géron, A.: Hands-On Machine Learning with Scikit-Learn, Keras, and TensorFlow: Concepts, Tools, and Techniques to Build Intelligent Systems. O'Reilly Media, Inc., Sebastopol (2019)

8. Liu, C.-H., Gu, J.-C., Yang, M.-T.: A simplified LSTM neural networks for one day-ahead solar power forecasting. IEEE Access **9**, 17174–17195 (2021). https://doi.org/10.1109/ACCESS.2021.3053638

9. Aslam, M., Lee, S.J., Khang, S.H., Hong, S.: Two-stage attention over LSTM with Bayesian optimization for day-ahead solar power forecasting. IEEE Access **9**, 107387–107398 (2021). https://doi.org/10.1109/ACCESS.2021.3100105

10. Yu, Y., Cao, J., Zhu, J.: An LSTM short-term solar irradiance forecasting under complicated weather conditions. IEEE Access **7**, 145651–145666 (2019). https://doi.org/10.1109/ACCESS.2019.2946057

11. Konstantinou, M., Peratikou, S., Charalambides, A.G.: Solar photovoltaic forecasting of power output using LSTM networks. Atmosphere **12**(1), Art. n.º 1 (2021). https://doi.org/10.3390/atmos12010124

12. Jalali, S.M.J., Ahmadian, S., Kavousi-Fard, A., Khosravi, A., Nahavandi, S.: Automated Deep CNN-LSTM architecture design for solar irradiance forecasting. IEEE Trans. Syst. Man Cybern. Syst. **52**(1), Art. n.º 1 (2022). https://doi.org/10.1109/TSMC.2021.3093519

13. Wang, F., Yu, Y., Zhang, Z., Li, J., Zhen, Z., Li, K.: Wavelet decomposition and convolutional LSTM networks based improved deep learning model for solar irradiance forecasting. Appl. Sci. **8**(8), Art. n.º 8 (2018). https://doi.org/10.3390/app8081286

14. Prado-Rujas, I.-I., García-Dopico, A., Serrano, E., Pérez, M.S.: A flexible and robust deep learning-based system for solar irradiance forecasting. IEEE Access **9**, 12348–12361(2021). https://doi.org/10.1109/ACCESS.2021.3051839

15. Khan, W., Walker, S., Zeiler, W.: Improved solar photovoltaic energy generation forecast using deep learning-based ensemble stacking approach. Energy **240**, 122812 (2022). https://doi.org/10.1016/j.energy.2021.122812

16. Abdel-Nasser, M., Mahmoud, K., Lehtonen, M.: HIFA: promising heterogeneous solar irradiance forecasting approach based on kernel mapping. IEEE Access **9**, 144906–144915 (2021). https://doi.org/10.1109/ACCESS.2021.3122826

17. Katrompas, A., Ntakouris, T., Metsis, V.: Recurrence and self-attention vs the transformer for time-series classification: a comparative study. In: International Conference on Artificial Intelligence in Medicine, 2022, pp. 99–109 (2022)

18. Cristian Arbelaez-Duque, A.D.: Solar Forecasting Elec Eng UdeA. Medellin, 25 July 2022. https://github.com/cdarbelaez/SolarForecastingElecEngUdeA. Accessed 23 Sep 2022

19. Romero Rodríguez, J.M.: Modelo para predicción de potencia de paneles fotovoltaicos utilizando técnicas de clasificación no supervisada y redes neuronales artificiales (2020). https://manglar.uninorte.edu.co/handle/10584/9049. Accessed 22 Mar 2022

20. Sharda, S., Singh, M., Sharma, K.: RSAM: robust self-attention based multi-horizon model for solar irradiance forecasting. IEEE Trans. Sustain. Energy **12**(2), 1394–1405 (2021). https://doi.org/10.1109/TSTE.2020.3046098

21. Vaswani, A., et al.: Attention is all you need. In: Advances in Neural Information Processing Systems, vol. 30 (2017). https://proceedings.neurips.cc/paper/2017/file/3f5ee243547dee91fbd053c1c4a845aa-Paper.pdf

22. Huang, X., Zhang, C., Li, Q., Tai, Y., Gao, B., Shi, J.: A comparison of hour-ahead solar irradiance forecasting models based on LSTM network. Math. Probl. Eng. **2020**, e4251517 (2020). https://doi.org/10.1155/2020/4251517

23. Ashfaq, Q., Ulasyar, A., Zad, H.S., Nisar, S., Khattak, A., Imran, K.: Multi-step forecasting of global horizontal irradiance using long short-term memory network for solving economic dispatch problem. In: 2021 International Conference on Innovative Computing (ICIC), pp. 1–9 (2021). https://doi.org/10.1109/ICIC53490.2021.9693031
24. Vakitbilir, N., Hilal, A., Direkoğlu, C.: Hybrid deep learning models for multivariate forecasting of global horizontal irradiation. Neural Comput. Appl. ene. (2022). https://doi.org/10.1007/s00521-022-06907-0
25. GeoSUN Africa: Kenya - Solar Radiation Measurement Data, EnergyData.info (2020). https://energydata.info/dataset/kenya-solar-radiation-measurement-data. Accessed 23 Sep 2022

Internet of things

IoT Platform for Monitoring Nutritional and Weather Conditions of Avocado Production

Pedro Moreno-Bernal[1,2(✉)] ⓘ, Paris Arizmendi-Peralta[2],
José Alberto Hernández-Aguilar[2] ⓘ, Jesús del Carmen Peralta-Abarca[1] ⓘ,
and J. Guadalupe Velásquez-Aguilar[1] ⓘ

[1] Facultad de Ciencias Químicas e Ingeniería, Universidad Autónoma del Estado
de Morelos, Cuernavaca, Mexico
{pmoreno,carmen.peralta,jgpeva}@uaem.mx
[2] Facultad de Contaduría, Administración e Informática, Universidad Autónoma
del Estado de Morelos, Cuernavaca, Mexico
paul.arizmendi@uaem.edu.mx, jose_hernandez@uaem.mx

Abstract. Agricultural productivity is crucial to supply the current food demand. However, food production requires facing technological challenges to achieve the level of demand production. In this context, Internet of Things technology is used for efficient farming processes. This article proposes an Internet of Things platform for collecting and processing soil nutrients and weather data of crop avocados in an orchard. Data were collected every 300 s for 24-h monitoring of the avocado trees. Experimental validation recorded 8 832 data for monitoring soil nutrients and weather variables of an avocado orchard in the Northeast of Morelos, Mexico. Results demonstrate that the proposed IoT platform can effectively monitor agriculture information in the context of smart farming.

Keywords: Smart farming · Avocado production · Internet of Things

1 Introduction

The world population is growing with considerable acceleration, i.e., it is expected to increase from 7.7 billion in 2020 to 9.7 billion people in 2050 [21]. The demographic growth implies an increase in food consumption in the following years. Therefore, food consumption will demand an increment in agricultural productivity. Food productivity requires technological challenges to achieve the level of production needed to satisfy the predicted world food demand [8]. However, excessive crop production implies a deterioration of soil by chemical nutrients and pesticides, water dearth, terrain deforestation, greenhouse gas emissions producing scarceness of natural resources and contamination.

Recently, the Industry 4.0 revolution has extended as an integral part of social and technological changes under the paradigm of smart cities [15,22]. In this context, agriculture must provide practical solutions to benefit food consumption

© The Author(s), under exclusive license to Springer Nature Switzerland AG 2023
S. Nesmachnow and L. Hernández Callejo (Eds.): ICSC-CITIES 2022, CCIS 1706, pp. 95–109, 2023.
https://doi.org/10.1007/978-3-031-28454-0_7

demand by incorporating technology based on Industry 4.0. in a sustainable manner. Sustainable agriculture refers to the cycle of producing, harvesting, and distributing all related to farming without waste. Today, agriculture uses advanced technology to increase productivity by optimizing resources in a controlled and measurable way [1]. This way, smart farming combines sustainable agriculture and the Information and Communication Technologies [14]. In particular, the Internet of Things (IoT) and sensor technology are vital for increasing productivity in smart farming. IoT technologies permit the migration from traditional agriculture to smart farming, i.e., automatization, control systems, supervision, and monitoring of farming performance. Furthermore, the combination of IoT with artificial intelligence and big data approaches helps estimating future production and increase crop productivity for immediate human needs [7].

This article proposes an IoT platform for collecting and processing data of soil nutrients and weather conditions in the context of smart farming. The proposed approach applies the Message Queue Telemetry Transport (MQTT) protocol-based smart farming solution to send data of soil nutrients and weather variables from an orchard of avocado trees to a cloud MQTT server by an IoT device. Furthermore, a specific design of the proposed IoT platform is presented for monitoring avocado tree nutrients using soil NPK RS485 sensors and Arduino Mega 2560 microcontroller hardware. The proposed IoT platform sends data to a remote MQTT server through 4G LTE band support using a GSM/GPRS module (SIM808) hardware. Experimental evaluation is performed by collecting data every 300 s for 24-hour monitoring. Results demonstrate that the proposed IoT platform can monitor farming information in the considered scenario in the Northeast of the State of Morelos, Mexico.

The article is structured as follows. Section 2 describes the application of IoT in agriculture and smart farming. Section 3 describes the proposed IoT platform for the studied orchard of avocado trees. Section 4 reports and discusses the evaluation results. Finally, Sect. 5 presents the conclusions and formulates the main lines for future work.

2   Agriculture and Smart Farming

This section describes agriculture production and the model of smart farming. The section also reviews the related works about relevant technologies applied in the context of smart farming.

2.1   Agriculture Production

Food production and supply systems are categorized into primary agriculture, i.e., cropping, livestock, horticulture, and fisheries; food processing and packing; commerce and transportation; and household consumption [16]. Nevertheless, food production depends on the sustainability of farming production systems and natural resources. This way, agricultural production includes all farming operations from land preparation to land development, e.g., tillage, sowing, fertilizing, pest control, and harvest, continuing with transportation and trade. However, increasing agricultural production involves land wear by the excessive application of agrochemicals, e.g., fertilizers, soil ameliorants, and pesticides [10]. In this sense, automatization and technological control systems based on IoT, computational intelligence, and sensors are necessary to improve and optimize agricultural production and supply procedures. Post-hoc optimization methods take advantage of data collected using IoT and sensors, to design improved plans to assist production [5, 6]

2.2 Smart Farming

Smart farming applies computational intelligence, Information and Communication Technologies, and sensor technologies to agriculture. The most relevant technologies applied in smart farming involve satellite and aerial imagery, agricultural robots, IoT devices with sensor nodes, and Unmanned Aerial Vehicles [4, 9]. As a result, smart farming scales agricultural production, reducing the workforce and enabling overcoming challenges in food production demands [12]. Technological resources in farms are applied in the diverse phases of the production process, i.e., nutrient and soil monitoring, growing plants monitoring, irrigation, fertilizer, pest control, and harvesting. This way, relevant data to collect are soil nutrients, soil PH, electrical conductivity, temperature, luminosity, moisture, and pressure for better farm production management. Essentially, the main objective of smart farming is to reduce agricultural cost production, minimizing crop waste while still maintaining end product quality.

2.3 Related Works

Producers, governments, and academia are exploring innovative manners to increase farming production. Recent related works propose different methodologies using IoT technologies for efficient farming processes. A brief review of related works is presented next.

Gomes et al. [3] proposed a system to gather data from the soil probe using an IoT platform for farm water management. The IoT device collected data and displayed information in a dashboard monitoring. Several sensor nodes were connected to the IoT platform, including the temperature and humidity DHT22 sensor, ambient light BH1750 sensor, geospatial position Venus GPS device, the ground temperature DS18B20 sensor, and the soil moisture CSMv1.2 sensor. A Raspberry Pi-2 module received signals from sensor nodes through the I2C interface and GPIO serial bus. Cloud Applications used were Fiware IoT, Fiware Orion, MongoDB, Draco, MySQL, and Grafana. Results showed that the IoT platform analyzed data in the cloud. Then, processed data were sent as input in a physical system based on a Programmable Logic Controller for the irrigation system, decreasing the impact on water management.

Serikul et al. [17] proposed a smart capsule prototype to monitor humidity in paddy bags stored on a warehouse. The prototype used an ESP8266 microcontroller and an SHT21 humidity sensor. Data collected was sent to a Blynk server through a Wi-Fi network and a mobile application. The investment in the hardware prototype was 300 USD. Results showed effective monitoring of humidity at each smart capsule in real-time. Smart capsules application was suitable for humidity controlling in paddy bags helping to prevent excessive humidity.

Trilles et al. [20] proposed an IoT platform for monitoring wine production in a smart farming context. The studied IoT platform was evaluated for scalability, stability, interoperability, and reusability. Computer paradigms used were microservices and serverless computing. The technological architecture proposed (SEnviro Connect) was validated for wine production in Spain. Experimental results showed that concerning scalability, the microservices architecture evaluated requires only a single server to ensure scalability and stability with 0% losses of throughput rates upper than 2400 msg/sec. The CPU and memory consumption were lower and stable. The proposed architecture based on Docker containers offered horizontal scalability and reusability. Platform validation was carried out over 140 days during vineyard season in 2018, monitoring five *SEnviro* nodes.

Ahmed et al. [2] proposed an IoT-based control system for advancement in the agriculture and farming of rural areas. The proposed architecture connected rural farms using IoT of low cost. The architecture combined one WiLD network and a set of 6LoWPAN to enable Wireless Sensor Network (WSN). The 6LoWPAN-based wireless sensor and actuator network were used in the farm domain for sensing and actuating multiple operations. The performance of the proposed approach was analyzed in two phases. First, the individual performance of the proposed WSN and WiLD network were studied, and second, the performance of the overall framework using results achieved in the first phase was evaluated. The cross-layer-based MAC and routing solution for IoT achieved better energy, delay, and throughput performance. The proposed solution, combined with the WiLD network, reduced delay and improved throughput performance for end-mile connectivity concerning connected rural farms by IoT devices.

Muangprathub et al., [11] proposed the design and development of a control system based on WSN to manage crops grown by monitoring data via smartphone and a web application. The proposed control system included IoT hardware, a web application, and a mobile application. An IoT hardware device was used as a control box connected to WSN to collect data on the crop. Soil moisture sensors were used to monitor the field. The web application was designed and implemented to analyze the details of crop data, i.e., temperature, humidity, and soil moisture. The control of crop watering was managed through a smartphone application. The control crop system was implemented and tested in Makhamtia District, Thailand. The results showed that the appropriate temperature for increased productivity of homegrown vegetables and lemons was between 29 °C and 32 °C. Moreover, suitable humidity for high productivity of lemons was within 72–81%. Also, the soil moisture content was maintained appropriately for vegetable growth, reducing costs and increasing agricultural productivity.

Suhag et al. [19] proposed a framework for IoT-based soil nutrition. The proposed approach used several sensors to collect plant-related data through the proximal soil sensor. Data collected were sent by the IoT device to a mobile application. The hardware component was included in polyhouse farming. Results showed that the appropriate temperature for increased productivity of sugar cane was between 20 °C and 35 °C, for rice was between 15 °C and 25 °C, and for wheat between 11 °C and 25 °C.

The related works allowed identifying a growing interest in IoT-based platforms for increasing agriculture productivity in the context of smart farming. In this line of work, this article contributes to smart farming with an IoT platform for monitoring soil nutrients and weather conditions for avocado production in the Northeast of the state of Morelos, Mexico. Next section describes the implementation of the proposed IoT platform to monitor soil nutrients and weather conditions is described.

3 IoT Platform for Monitoring Avocado Production

This section describes the proposed IoT platform for monitoring avocado production.

3.1 Internet of Things

The IoT paradigm has developed as an essential component of the transformative era of technological changes in smart and rural cities. IoT is defined as the interaction of the physical and digital worlds through various sensors and actuators [23]. IoT is a paradigm of embedded computing and networking capabilities in any conceivable object with capacities to modify its state [13]. In this context, IoT refers to devices and appliances connected to a network collaboratively to execute a task with high intelligence through embedded sensors, actuators, processors, and transceivers [18].

The basic architecture for IoT considers three layers: perception layer, network layer, and application layer. However, additional layers are required to properly consider all the aspects involved in realistic and research applications [18]. The five-layer architecture includes additional layers: the network layer is separated into transport and processing layers, and a new business layer is included to manage the deployed the IoT platform. The five layers are:

1. *Perception Layer.* The perception layer is the physical layer, and it provides the function of converting analog signals into digital form and vice versa. In addition, this layer is responsible for sensing and gathering information about the environment through sensors and actuators. Sensors are used to detect environmental changes by physical parameters such as humidity or temperature to transform them into electric signals. Actuators allow the transforming of an electrical signal into physical actions through a machine or device.

2. *Transport Layer.* The transport layer is responsible for transport communications between smart components of the IoT network, including network devices and computers. This layer transmits sensor data collected from the perception layer to the processing layer through wireless sensor networks such as 3G/4G/5G, LAN, Bluetooth, RFID, and NFC.
3. *Processing Layer.* The processing layer stores, analyses, and processes a large volume of data from the transport layer. Technologies used in the processing layer are cloud computing, distributed computing, databases, and big data.
4. *Application Layer.* The application layer provides services to the end-user. IoT applications are deployed in smart cities, smart homes, smart health, and smart farming.
5. *Business Layer.* The business layer manages service applications based on IoT through business and profit models.

3.2   The Proposed IoT Platform for Monitoring Crop Avocado Information

Overall Structure of the System. Based on the first three layers of the five layer architecture for IoT, the proposed IoT architecture is divided into three stages. The first stage corresponds to collecting data from soil nutrient sensors and weather conditions through the IoT device as a monitoring station. The collected information contains the following data: date/hour, soil temperature, area temperature, soil moisture, lumens, nitrogen (N), phosphorus (P), and potassium (K) of two avocado trees. One avocado tree is fertilized, and the other consumes natural soil nutrients. The second stage sends information collected from the IoT device every 300 s to an MQTT server. A local storage device is used to record data as backup. In the last stage, data cleaning is performed using a Python script for future analysis.

Hardware Components. The hardware components of the proposed IoT platform include:

- *Main board*: Arduino MEGA 2560 board (voltage: 5 V)
- *4G LTE Network*: GSM/GPRS/SIM808 module (voltage: 3.4 V~4.4 V)
- *Soil nutrients*: Soil NPK generic sensor (voltage: 12 V)
- *Communication* RS-485 to TTL module (voltage: 3.4 V~4.4 V)
- *Temperature sensor*: DS18B20 (voltage: 3 V~5.5 V)
- *Soil moisture*: HD–38 sensor (voltage: 3.3 V~12 V)
- *Lumens*: Photoresistor sensor (voltage: 5 V)

All these components are integrated in an easy-to-deploy platform, adapted to be used in any agricultural facility. The proposed IoT platform is energy efficient: the estimated overall power consumption of the deployed infrastructure is just ~365 mA (0.0438kWh). The overall cost of the built platform is approximately 250 USD.

Software Components. The proposed IoT platform for monitoring crop avocado information is implemented using MQTT and Arduino libraries. The MQTT broker is available by a Mosquitto server on a cloud host with a public IP address. The main function of the MQTT broker is filtering incoming messages from the IoT device client into the MQTT topic `huitzilac`. Then, a Python script is executed to save data in a CSV file on a local storage disk. Once the data are saved, a data cleansing process is performed to process the gathered data, in order to verify the coherency and redundancy of the stored information, for future analysis.

Figure 1 describes the proposed IoT architecture for monitoring the nutrients and weather conditions of avocado production. The main hardware components and software products are identified.

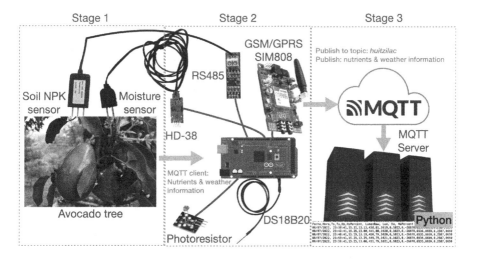

Fig. 1. Diagram of the proposed IoT platform for monitoring crop avocado information

Figure 2 presents photographs of the real deployment (in production) of the proposed IoT platform for monitoring crop avocado information in Huitzilac, Morelos. The photograph in Fig. 2(a) shows the Soil NPK sensor in one of the avocado trees being monitored. The photograph in Fig. 2(b) presents the IoT device. The photograph in Fig. 2(c) shows the metal shield protection of the IoT device placed on the avocado orchard. Finally, the photograph in Fig. 2(d) shows the Soil NPK sensor wrapped into a plastic shield to protect it from rodents and external factors. The deployed IoT platform allowed gathering relevant data about the avocado crop.

The proposed IoT platform aims to collect and generate a database of avocado crops comparing nutrients by fertilization and without fertilization to study machine learning techniques to predict avocado production.

(a) Avocado tree with Soil NPK sensor (b) IoT device

(c) Shield protection of the IoT device (d) Soil NPK sensor

Fig. 2. IoT platform for monitoring crop avocado information

The following section analyzes the experimental results of the proposed IoT platform for monitoring avocado information.

4 Experimental Validation and Discussion

This section describes the experimental validation of the proposed IoT platform and the specific data processing methods. The main results from the collected information are reported and discussed.

4.1   Development and Execution Platform

The control and processing software of the IoT device was coded in Arduino employing TinyGSMClient, PubSubClient, ArduinoRS485, ThreeWire, RtcDS1302, OneWire, DallasTemperature, Wire, SPI, and SD libraries.

The experimental evaluation was performed using an Intel Xeon E5-2650 (16 cores, 32 threads) processor at 2.0 GHz, 32 GB of RAM, and the Debian 4.19 Linux operating system.

4.2   Studied Area

The area considered for the case study is described next.

The avocado orchard "La Ceiba" is located in the municipality of Huitzilac, in the Northeast of the state of Morelos, México (UTM coordinates 19.008174,-99.268800).

The terrain has an altitude of 2 273 MSL. The weather has an average temperature between 14 °C and 22 °C throughout the year. The avocado orchard is divided into four zones, and the zone in production was used for the validation of the proposed IoT platform.

The production zone contains ten-year-old avocado trees. The other zones have young trees without production. The study area is fertilized every four months. This way, two avocado trees are studied through the soil nutrients. One avocado tree is fertilized with an average of 21.77 g per tree (g/t) of N, 4.7 g/t of P, and 39.16 g/t of K. The other avocado tree studied is not fertilized.

Figure 3 shows the geographic location of the avocado orchard studied. The image was taken from Google Earth, and used only for academic purposes, according to the "fair use" copyright.

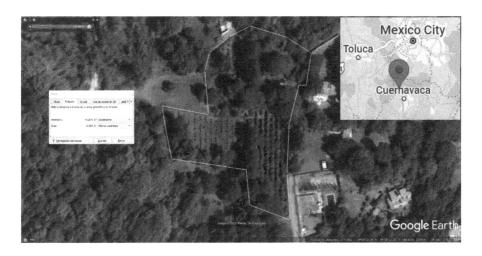

Fig. 3. Geographic location of the avocado orchard

For the case study presented in this article, the proposed IoT platform for monitoring crop avocado information was set to collect, process, and store soil nutrients and weather data every 300 s during 58 days, from August 05 to September 30, 2022.

4.3   Data Cleaning Process

The cleaning process prepares the data gathered by the proposed IoT device for analysis by removing or modifying erroneous records.

Raw data are emitted by the Arduino control program of the IoT device. These data are an ASCII-encoded, stored in a file, with fields delimited by commas (CSV format). Data cleaning involves identifying duplicate data, correcting spelling and syntax errors, and correcting empty fields and negative or null values. Data errors occur when the IoT device has a power supply interruption by an external factor in the rural area or when environmental conditions affect the sensors producing a piece of erroneous lecture information.

Figure 4 shows collected data by the IoT device in raw format.

```
Fecha,Hora,Ts,Ta,Hs,HsPercent, LumenRaw, Lux, Ha, HaPercent, NSA, PSA, KSA, NSB, PSB, KSB
08/05/2022, 11:11:53,13.44,17.50,392,87,44,1113,1022,0,28673,16158,8703,151,2050,8703
08/05/2022, 11:11:59,13.44,17.50,418,83,44,1230,1017,0,28673,16158,8703,151,2050,8703
08/05/2022, 11:12:06,13.44,17.50,408,85,43,1140,1020,0,28673,16158,8703,151,2050,8703
08/05/2022, 11:12:13,13.38,17.56,424,83,43,1140,1020,0,28673,16158,8703,151,2050,8703

Fecha,Hora,Ts,Ta,Hs,HsPercent, LumenRaw, Lux, Ha, HaPercent, NSA, PSA, KSA, NSB, PSB, KSB
08/05/2022, 11:12:31,13.44,17.69,324,96,42,1169,1019,0,28673,16158,8703,151,2050,8703

Fecha,Hora,Ts,Ta,Hs,HsPercent, LumenRaw, Lux, Ha, HaPercent, NSA, PSA, KSA, NSB, PSB, KSB
08/05/2022, 11:12:41,13.44,17.69,367,90,42,1169,1019,0,28673,16158,8703,151,2050,8703
08/05/2022, 11:12:47,13.50,17.75,422,83,42,1169,1019,0,28673,16158,8703,151,2050,8703
08/05/2022, 11:12:54,13.50,17.75,412,84,42,1169,1019,0,28673,16158,8703,151,2050,8703
Fecha,Hora,Ts,Ta,Hs,HsPercent, LumenRaw, Lux, Ha, HaPercent, NSA, PSA, KSA, NSB, PSB, KSB
Fecha,Hora,Ts,Ta,Hs,HsPercent, LumenRaw, Lux, Ha, HaPercent, NSA, PSA, KSA, NSB, PSB, KSB
08/05/2022, 11:15:42,13.50,17.44,412,84,40,1230,1017,0,-26870,6535,8659,0,2566,8659

Fecha,Hora,Ts,Ta,Hs,HsPercent, LumenRaw, Lux, Ha, HaPercent, NSA, PSA, KSA, NSB, PSB, KSB
08/05/2022, 11:25:44,13.63,17.87,421,83,40,1230,1019,0,-28918,28744,8659,0,2567,8659
08/05/2022, 11:30:44,13.63,17.31,419,83,40,1230,1017,0,-28918,28744,8659,0,2567,8659
08/05/2022, 11:35:44,13.63,16.94,435,81,41,1198,1021,0,-28918,28744,8659,0,2567,8659
08/05/2022, 11:40:44,13.69,17.37,438,81,42,1169,1020,0,-28918,28744,8659,0,2567,8659
```

Fig. 4. Data in raw format

Then, the data cleaning process verifies the coherence and redundancy of data. Several options for actions are performed if there is missing data, e.g., normalize by scaling to a range by approximating upper and lower bounds on data or approximate uniformly in a range. The previous data can be copied if there is no considerable variation in values. The missing value can be omitted, but having different information for subsequent models is preferable. Figure 5 shows the data after the cleaning process.

4.4   Results and Discussion

This subsection presents and discusses the results of the proposed IoT platform for monitoring crop avocados. Figure 6 shows the information collected and sent

Fecha	Hora	Ts	Ta	Hs	HsPercent	LumenRaw	Lux	Ha	HaPercent	Nitrum	Kalium	Phosphorus	Nitrum	Kalium	Phosphorus
05/08/2022	11:11:07	13.38	17.44	317	97	41	1198	1019	0	28673	16158	8703	151	2050	8703
05/08/2022	11:11:13	13.44	17.44	350	93	44	1113	1020	0	28673	16158	8703	151	2050	8703
05/08/2022	11:11:20	13.44	17.37	359	92	40	1230	1020	0	28673	16158	8703	151	2050	8703
05/08/2022	11:11:27	13.38	17.37	367	90	40	1230	1020	0	28673	16158	8703	151	2050	8703
05/08/2022	11:11:33	13.44	17.44	342	94	42	1169	1022	0	28673	16158	8703	151	2050	8703
05/08/2022	11:11:40	13.38	17.44	362	91	42	1169	1020	0	28673	16158	8703	151	2050	8703
05/08/2022	11:11:46	13.38	17.44	364	91	41	1198	1019	0	28673	16158	8703	151	2050	8703
05/08/2022	11:11:53	13.44	17.5	392	87	44	1113	1022	0	28673	16158	8703	151	2050	8703
05/08/2022	11:11:59	13.44	17.5	418	83	40	1230	1017	0	28673	16158	8703	151	2050	8703
05/08/2022	11:12:06	13.44	17.5	408	85	43	1140	1020	0	28673	16158	8703	151	2050	8703
05/08/2022	11:12:13	13.38	17.56	424	83	43	1140	1020	0	28673	16158	8703	151	2050	8703
05/08/2022	11:12:31	13.44	17.69	324	96	42	1169	1019	0	28673	16158	8703	151	2050	8703
05/08/2022	11:12:41	13.44	17.69	367	90	42	1169	1019	0	28673	16158	8703	151	2050	8703
05/08/2022	11:12:47	13.5	17.75	422	83	42	1169	1019	0	28673	16158	8703	151	2050	8703
05/08/2022	11:12:54	13.5	17.75	412	84	42	1169	1019	0	28673	16158	8703	151	2050	8703
05/08/2022	11:15:42	13.5	17.44	412	84	40	1230	1017	0	28673	6535	8659	0	2566	8659
05/08/2022	11:25:44	13.63	17.87	421	83	40	1230	1019	0	28673	28744	8659	0	2567	8659

Fig. 5. Data after cleaning process

to the cloud by the IoT device. The notification of data stored locally in a storage device is presented in Fig. 6a. In turn, Fig. 6b shows the notification of information sent through the data network received by the MQTT server.

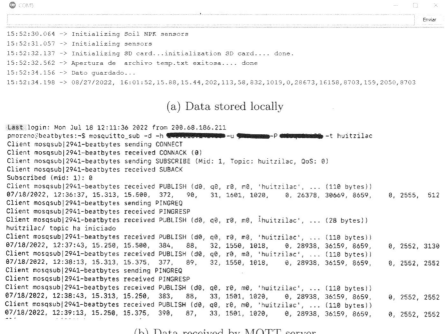

(a) Data stored locally

(b) Data received by MQTT server

Fig. 6. Information collected by the IoT device

The IoT device for monitoring crop avocado trees collects data on soil temperature, weather temperature, soil moisture, and lumens. Also, it collects the soil NPK data of two avocado trees. Table 1 reports the maximum, minimum, and

average values of data collected by the IoT platform. The average soil temperature value was 15.57 °C, and the weather temperature was 14.57 °C, considering
an average temperature in the zone between 14 °C and 22 °C during the year,
helping maintain healthy roots and flowering. The average soil moisture value
was 75% (scale from 0 to 100) during the rainy season. The average amount
of visible light collected by a photoresistor sensor was 980 lumens during the
rainy season. From the two monitoring avocado trees, the average N value of
the fertilized tree (Sensor A) was 18405 mg/kg compared with the non-fertilized
tree (Sensor B), which had an average value of 129 mg/kg. The average K value
for sensor A was 14394 mg/kg compared with sensor B was 2150 mg/kg. Finally,
the average P value for both sensors was 8694 mg/kg.

Table 1. Maximum, minimum and average values of data collected by the IoT platform

#	Variable	minimum	Maximum	average
1	Soil temperature	12.88 °C	17.69 °C	15.57 °C
2	Weather temperature	8.63 °C	20 °C	14.69 °C
3	Soil moisture	21%	100%	75%
4	Lumens	0	25 550	980
5	N sensor A	26 870 mg/kg	28 673 mg/kg	18 405 mg/kg
6	K sensor A	6 535 mg/kg	28 744 mg/kg	14 394 mg/kg
7	P sensor A	8 659 mg/kg	8 703 mg/kg	8 694 mg/kg
8	N sensor B	0 mg/kg	159 mg/kg	129 mg/kg
9	K sensor B	2 050 mg/kg	2 587 mg/kg	2 150 mg/kg
10	P sensor B	8 659 mg/kg	8 703 mg/kg	8 694 mg/kg

The graphics in Fig. 7 show the maximum, minimum, and average values of
soil temperature, weather temperature, soil moisture, lumens, and soil nutrients
of two avocado trees.

Regarding soil temperature and weather temperature, both showed a steady
behavior. The average value was 15 °C for both temperatures. Soil moisture sensors returned raw values that must be appropriately calibrated by establishing
a range for dry and wet values. The Arduino-based soil moisture sensor ranges
from 0 to 1023; therefore, collected data were converted into a percentage output, to get values from 0 to 100. Figure 7c shows the normalized values for soil
moisture behavior. The graphic reporting lumens shows an incorrect behavior
during two days, when the photoresistor sensor did not collect data.

Finally, Fig. 7e shows the differences in the behavior of NPK nutrients for
sensor A (SA) and sensor B (SB). The average N value for sensor B represents
0.7% of the average N value of sensor A, and the average K value for sensor B
represents 14.9% of the average of nutrient K for sensor A. However, both sensors
have the same average value for the nutrient P; probably due to the properties
of the soil in the studied area.

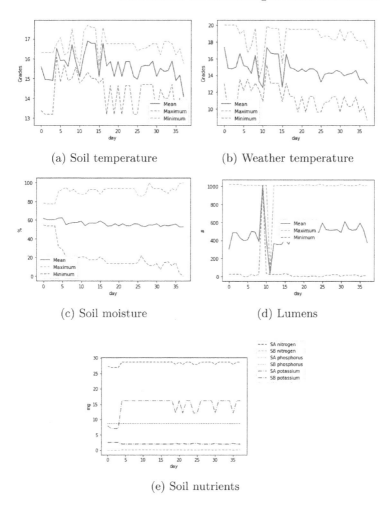

(a) Soil temperature

(b) Weather temperature

(c) Soil moisture

(d) Lumens

(e) Soil nutrients

Fig. 7. Soil nutrients and weather variables

Summarizing, the experimental validation results demonstrate that the information collected by the proposed IoT platform was coherent and valid for monitoring crop avocado orchards. The system showed a correct stability and robustness, collecting and processing significant information every 300 s.

5   Conclusions and Future Work

This article presented an IoT platform for monitoring the nutritional and weather conditions of crop avocados in an orchard in the context of smart cities, particularly for smart farming applications.

The proposed IoT platform combines cloud computing and open hardware using sensors to collect and clean data for relevant analysis in smart farming.

First, the platform collects nutritional and weather conditions from an IoT device over the MQTT protocol to the Mosquitto broker; then, data is saved in a CSV file to be cleaned using a spreadsheet reader.

The experimental validation recorded 8832 data from August 05 to September 30, 2022. The main results indicate that the proposed IoT platform effectively collects and processes nutritional and weather data every 300 s.

The main lines for future work are oriented to extend the proposed system to compute essential indicators and statistics of smart farming applications, i.e., vegetables, citrus, fruits, and exotic plants. Also, the data collected by the proposed IoT platform will be used to study machine learning techniques to predict avocado production in the studied orchard. In turn, the data collected by the IoT platform can be used for analysis through computational intelligence techniques to improve farming production and supply systems for increasing agriculture productivity in the context of smart farming.

Acknowledgements. This work acknowledges Salomon Paul Arizmendi Muñoz, owner of the orchard "La Ceiba", for the attention and facilities provided in the development of the work.

References

1. Acharya, B., Garikapati, K., Yarlagadda, A., Dash, S.: Internet of things (IoT) and data analytics in smart agriculture: benefits and challenges. In: Abraham, A., Dash, S., Rodrigues, J., Acharya, B., Pani, S. (eds.) AI, Edge and IoT-based Smart Agriculture, pp. 3–16. Academic Press, Intelligent Data-Centric Systems (2022)
2. Ahmed, N., De, D., Hussain, I.: Internet of things (IoT) for smart precision agriculture and farming in rural areas. IEEE Internet Things J. **5**(6), 4890–4899 (2018)
3. Alves, R., et al.: A digital twin for smart farming. In: IEEE Global Humanitarian Technology Conference, pp. 1–4 (2019)
4. Bacco, M., Barsocchi, P., Ferro, E., Gotta, A., Ruggeri, M.: The digitisation of agriculture: a survey of research activities on smart farming. Array **3–4**, 100009 (2019)
5. Bayá, G., Canale, E., Nesmachnow, S., Robledo, F., Sartor, P.: Production optimization in a grain facility through mixed-integer linear programming. Appl. Sci. **12**(16), 8212 (2022)
6. Bayá, G., Sartor, P., Robledo, F., Canale, E., Nesmachnow, S.: A case study of smart industry in Uruguay: Grain production facility optimization. In: Nesmachnow, S., Hernandez Callejo, L. (eds.) Smart Cities. ICSC-Cities 2021. CCIS, vol. 1555, pp. 101–115. Springer, Cham (2022). https://doi.org/10.1007/978-3-030-96753-6_8
7. Bhardwaj, H., Pradeep, T., Aditi, S., Uttam, S.: Artificial intelligence and its applications in agriculture with the future of smart agriculture techniques. In: Pradeep, T., Kaur, G. (eds.) Artificial Intelligence and IoT-Based Technologies for Sustainable Farming and Smart Agriculture, pp. 25–39. IGI Global (2021)
8. Colizzi, L., et al.: Introduction to agricultural IoT. In: Castrignano, A., Buttafuoco, G., Khosla, R., Mouazen, A., Moshou, D., Naud, O. (eds.) Agricultural Internet of Things and Decision Support for Precision Smart Farming, pp. 1–33. Academic Press (2020)

9. Garate, B., Díaz, S., Iturriaga, S., Nesmachnow, S., Shepelev, V., Tchernykh, A.: Autonomous swarm of low-cost commercial unmanned aerial vehicles for surveillance. Program. Comput. Softw. **47**(8), 558–577 (2021)

10. Maraseni, T., Cockfield, G.: Including the costs of water and greenhouse gas emissions in a reassessment of the profitability of irrigation. Agric. Water Manag. **103**, 25–32 (2012)

11. Muangprathub, J., Boonnam, N., Kajornkasirat, S., Lekbangpong, N., Wanichsombat, A., Nillaor, P.: IoT and agriculture data analysis for smart farm. Comput. Electron. Agric. **156**, 467–474 (2019)

12. Navarro, E., Costa, N., Pereira, A.: A systematic review of IoT solutions for smart farming. Sensors **20**(15), 4231 (2020)

13. Peña-López, I.: The Internet of things. Technical report, ITU Internet Reports (2005)

14. Pretty, J.: Agricultural sustainability: concepts, principles and evidence. Philos. Trans. R. Soc. Lond. **363**, 447–465 (2008)

15. Rossit, D.A., Toncovich, A., Rossit, D.G., Nesmachnow, S.: Flow shop scheduling problems in industry 4.0 production environments: missing operation case. In: Hussain, C.M., Di Sia, P. (eds.) Handbook of Smart Materials, Technologies, and Devices, pp. 1–23. Springer, Cham (2022). https://doi.org/10.1007/978-3-030-84205-5_71

16. Safa, M.: Measuring and auditing on-farm energy use. In: Sims, R.E. (ed.) Energy-Smart Farming: Efficiency, Renewable Energy and Sustainability, pp. 8–35. Burleigh Dodds Science Publishing (2022)

17. Serikul, P., Nakpong, N., Nakjuatong, N.: Smart farm monitoring via the Blynk IoT platform: case study: humidity monitoring and data recording. In: 16th International Conference on ICT and Knowledge Engineering, pp. 1–6 (2018)

18. Sethi, P., Sarangi, S.: Internet of things: architectures, protocols, and applications. J. Electr. Comput. Eng. **2017**, 25–32 (2017)

19. Suhag, S., Singh, N., Jadaun, S., Johri, P., Shukla, A., Parashar, N.: IoT based soil nutrition and plant disease detection system for smart agriculture. In: 10th IEEE International Conference on Communication Systems and Network Technologies, pp. 478–483 (2021)

20. Trilles, S., González-Pérez, A., Huerta, J.: An IoT platform based on microservices and serverless paradigms for smart farming purposes. Sensors **20**(8), 2418 (2020)

21. United Nations Department of Economic and Social Affairs, Population Division: World population prospects 2022: Summary of results (2022)

22. Ustundag, A., Cevikcan, E.: Industry 4.0: Managing The Digital Transformation. SSAM, Springer, Cham (2018). https://doi.org/10.1007/978-3-319-57870-5

23. Vermesan, O., et al.: Internet of things strategic research roadmap. In: Internet of Things - Global Technological and Societal Trends, vol. 1, pp. 9–52 (2011)

IoT System for Thermographic Data Acquisition of Photovoltaic Installations

Leonardo Cardinale-Villalobos[1]([⊠])(ID), Luis Antonio Solís-García[1](ID),
and Luis Alonso Araya-Solano[2](ID)

[1] Costa Rica Institute of Technology, San Carlos, Costa Rica
lcardinale@tec.ac.cr, antsolis04@estudiantec.cr
[2] Costa Rica Institute of Technology, Cartago, Costa Rica
luaraya@tec.ac.cr
https://www.tec.ac.cr/

Abstract. Infrared thermography (IRT) has been widely used to diagnose photovoltaic installations, however, its effectiveness needs to be improved to contribute to greater energy efficiency in Smart Cities. This research shows a solution that creates a database (DB) of IRT information, through an IoT solution that allows the process to be automated and accessed remotely. The functionality and accuracy of the system was validated in a real PV plant through an experiment inducing conditions that generate hot spots obtaining a temperature measurement error of less than $4°C$. During the investigation, 1.777 thermograms were generated and the ability to detect hot spots due to soiling, partial shading and short circuits in the module was verified. The DB generated by this solution will be used to establish better fault detection criteria for IRT, which is of high interest to thermographers and will benefit the users of distributed PV installations in Smart Cities around the world.

Keywords: IoT Applications · Photovoltaic · Infrared Thermography · Image Acquisition Systems

1 Introduction

For several years there has been a common trend that seeks the maximum possible use of renewable energy sources. Because of this, smart cities are characterized by the approach of strategies that incorporate distributed generation schemes that also consider an efficient use of energy and maximum exploitation over time. Solar photovoltaic (PV) energy is an option that adapts very well to the requirements of smart cities, making that in recent years it is being adopted in an accelerated way both at residential and industrial level, accompanied by Internet of Things (IoT) solutions that automate and optimize their activities [1].

Supported by Costa Rica Institute of Technology (TEC).

S. Nesmachnow and L. Hernández Callejo (Eds.): ICSC-CITIES 2022, CCIS 1706, pp. 110–122, 2023.
https://doi.org/10.1007/978-3-031-28454-0_8

A PV installation will be exposed to a variety of factors that could slightly or significantly affect its performance during its lifetime. When a solar PV module experiences a suboptimal condition due to some external or internal factor, a reduction in delivered power occurs that manifests itself as a localized temperature gradient known as a *hot spot* [2]; this has been extensively verified, for example, several hot spots were analyzed in [3] causing a reduction in power greater than 11.9% in the cases analyzed. For the detection of hot spots in PV modules it is required to meet several conditions, in [4] a protocol is shown that is validated by a case study, however, a strict definition of the minimum delta temperature (DT) that exists in a hot spot is still pending, for example, in [5] it is defined in 10°C with an irradiance of 700 W/m^2, while in [6] it is defined in 20°C for an irradiance of 600 W/m^2.

The transformation to smart cities that exploit PV technology is extending all over the world, even in cities with varying climatic conditions. Considering that a minimum irradiance of 700 W/m^2 is required for an infrared thermography (IRT) inspection and that the irradiance may vary abruptly, there is a risk that an IRT inspection may have to be suspended even after it has started, which implies an increase in costs for the users of this type of services. This research originates from the identification of the problem that the criterion of hot spot detection with IRT in PV modules requires environmental conditions that may be difficult to achieve for the users of distributed PV systems and that are a requirement for a correct application of the technique.

In order to create a new fault detection criterion, a large volume of thermographic information is required, including modules with hot spots and healthy modules, unfortunately there is no open database (DB) with this information. To contribute in the solution of this problem, the objective of this research was to create an IoT data acquisition system for the analysis of hot spots with IRT. The high volume of IRT information that will be generated with this system will allow future research to the establishment of new criteria for the detection of hot spots in PV generation systems under irradiances less than 700 W/m2.

The research was developed in a distributed generation PV installation that has been in operation since 2018 at the Tecnológico de Costa Rica in Santa Clara of San Carlos. An IoT-based system was developed that periodically captures images and environmental variables that are useful in the analysis of IRT. The reading of temperatures in the thermal images is done automatically by means of digital image processing. To validate the performance of the system, 1,777 thermograms were taken and a fault-inducing experiment was developed by inducing hot spots through faults based on previous experience evaluated by [7].

This research has as its contribution: 1) The presentation of an IoT system for the acquisition of thermal information and 2) The under development generation of a large volume of thermographic information of modules under suboptimal and normal conditions. The mentioned DB its been used by a currently second stage of this research, that is processing the hot spot information for the definition of a new criterion using artificial intelligence for irradiances greater than 300 W/m^2. This is an aspect of great interest for the managers of photovoltaic installations and thermographers, since it will facilitate the implementation of the technique and will contribute to improve its efficiency, as has been pointed out in [3] as an aspect to be solved. The DB creat by this system will later be accessible to all those who can contribute to this objective.

2   Related Work

Works on IoT based solar module analysis using thermography are emerging, for example, [8] presents an analysis at normal and some faulty conditions using equipment like PV analyser, Solar Power Meter and thermal camera to compare PV performance for the monitoring of a generation plant. In regards to fault detection, hotspot detection using IRT has proven a effective technique to be used, see [9], where thermograms were analyzed by a hotspot detection algorithm called K-means clustering. Moreover, in a broader context, papers published on a special issue [10] have demonstrated that the autonomous monitoring and analysis approach is highly crucial in the performance monitoring, operation, and maintenance of PV systems. In [11] a summary of types and available fault detection techniques in photovoltaic installations is presented, visual inspection, IRT and analysis of electrical variables are among those techniques. In [12] several visual defects were detected in visual RGB and thermal orthomosaics, such as cracks, soiling, and *hotspots*. In addition, a procedure of semi-automatic *hotspots* extraction was also developed and is presented therein. Unmanned aerial vehicles were concluded as advantageous tools within the thematic of fault detection. The work on [13] identifies the main faults in PV arrays and correlates detection techniques that can detect them. In the study of [14] a metric to compare fault detection techniques is established. This metric takes into account detection capabilities like detection and classification, real-time detection, localization and fault isolation. The paper [15] compares fault detection techniques considering aspects such as: faults detected, level of diagnosis provided by the technique, on-line or off-line use, integration complexity and cost.

More pertinently, [7] establishes a comparison between multiple techniques to detect sub-optimal conditions in photovoltaic systems. The results showed that the visual inspection technique was the best at detecting soiling and partial shading with 100% of effectiveness. IRT and electrical analysis had an effectiveness of 78% and 73%, respectively, detecting the three types of conditions under study. Additionally, it's important to have a criterion over what is to be considered a fault. In regard to hotspots, [16] says hotspots temperature gradients larger than $20°C$, in any case, and even larger than $10°C$ in certain conditions, are proposed as rejecting conditions for routine inspections under contractual frameworks. Also, hotspots can be considered failures if power variation goes over 4% [17].

3   Materials and Methods

The development of the solution started with the identification of the IRT requirements and the characteristics that the IoT system should have according to the conditions of the PV installation and the user.

The system was placed in a fixed location to maintain the conditions between thermograms following the requirements for this technique established in [4].

The photovoltaic installation used is located in the northern part of Costa Rica, 10°32' latitude and 84°31' longitude. According to the Köppen-Geiger system, the climate in this location is classified as tropical rainforest climate. The PV plant is located at the San Carlos Local Technological Campus in Santa Clara, Costa Rica. The PV panels model used is the Canadian Solar CS6k-280M tilted an angle of 15° and with an azimuth of 150° with respect to the North. Regarding the system instrumentation, a radiometric thermographic camera specialized for PV module inspection was used, and also sensors for irradiance, ambient temperature, relative humidity and cell temperature. The specifications are shown in Table 1 and Table 2. Due to the possibility of remote and on-site access to the system, the results obtained were validated from the beginning of the project.

Table 1. Characteristics of the FLIR VUE PRO R 336. Thermal camera used for the system.

Parameter	Value	Parameter	Value
HFOV x VFOV	25° x 19°	Weight	4 oz
Sensor (width x height)	5.764 mm x 4.351 mm	Accuracy	$\mp$ 5°C
Focal length	13.00 mm	Spectral band	7.5μ m -13.5 μ m
Image width x height	336×256	Thermal sensitivity	40 mK
Frequency	9 Hz	Power dissipation	2.1 W

Table 2. Characteristics of the components used for the sensing process

Component	Parameter	Value
DHT11 Sensor	Temperature range	0°C to 50°C
	Humidity Range	20% to 90%
	Accuracy	±1°C and ±1%
DS18B20 Sensor	Temperature range	-55°C to +125°C
	Accuracy	±0.5°C for range -10°C to +85°C
Spektron 210	Irradiation range	0 to 1500 W/m^2
	Accuracy	78.88 mV for each 1000 W/m^2

3.1   System Validation

Temperature measurements were taken in a specific cell with IRT and with contact measurement at the back of the cell using the DS18B20 sensor, in order to compare them and evaluate the accuracy of the system measurements.

To evaluate its performance under hot spot conditions, an experiment were developed inducing failure conditions on the array. The test considerations are described below:

– Soiling, partial shadows and short-circuit conditions were induced in the cell.
– Each measurement was taken 10 min after inducing the fault condition and the next fault was induced by waiting at least 10 min after the previous measurement; this was done to eliminate residual effects between tests (to ensure inter-sample independence).
– All measurements were made applying only one fault condition at a time (no interaction).

The types of tests applied are described in Table 3.

Table 3. Description of faults considered for the system evaluation.

Induced fault condition	Number of failures	Description
Shor circuit (SC)	11	Short-circuit through PV switch on module 8
Partial shading (PS)	6	Applied on modules 3, 6, 9 and 12 varying the shading area
Soiling (S)	9	Transparent plastic sheets with drawings of leaves and bird's dropping were randomly distributed in the array
Control module	26	In each test, module 2 was assigned as a non- faulty module to take its temperature as a reference

The experiment was carried out on March 2 and 9, 2022, starting at 07:30:00 and ending at 17:00:00. The system analyzes only the modules that are completely observed in the thermograms (see Fig. 1), therefore, modules 1, 4, 7 and 10 were not considered.

4   Automated Fault Detection in PV Modules Using IRT

This section describes in detail the data acquisition system developed for IRT analysis. It is subdivided into a) System requirements, b) General schematics, c) Position of the system with respect to the array, d) Thermographic image acquisition and processing, e) Data management.

Fig. 1. Segmentation of the solar array used by the system. Module 2 serves as a reference for the calculation of temperature gradients.

4.1   System Requirements

The following requirements were identified for the design of the system:

a) Automatic and synchronous acquisition of thermal images and environmental variables. In order to create a high volume of data, the system had to be able to activate a IRT camera automatically on a periodic interval. In addition, to improve the accuracy of a thermogram, it is necessary to know the relative humidity and ambient temperature of the site [18], therefore, the system had to measure both variables in real time. As the main future objective is to detect hot spots at irradiances below 700 W/m2, this variable had to be measured. Finally, all variables had to be acquired synchronously.
b) Automatic processing of IRT information. The technique allows indirectly measuring the temperature of the PV modules through a mathematical model that had to be applied automatically to each acquisition. Additionally, for each image the system had to be able to extract the specific IRT information for each module, discarding the information of the image that is not required (background).
c) Information management and remote access. The system had to be able to store the information in a cloud storage unit, with the possibility of accessing it from anywhere via the Internet. Additionally, all control of the system had to be able to be done remotely.

4.2   General Schematics

Figure 2 shows a general schematic of the developed system. The main control unit (Raspberry Pi) combines wired and wireless links to access the measurement devices. All the IRT processing is done by the control unit and the information is stored in a DB. The measurement of irradiance and cell temperature is done through wireless communication with another Raspberry Pi. Finally, like any IoT solution, the system can be accessed remotely by the user.

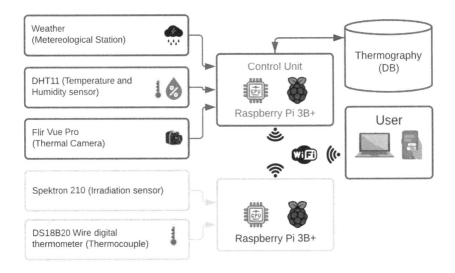

Fig. 2. General scheme of the IoT system developed for IRT analysis.

4.3   Positioning of the System with Respect to the PV Array

The final system was installed at a height of 7.05 m with respect to the ground, at an angle of 50° to the plane of the array at a distance of 9.2 m from the center of the array; in this way the thermograms meet the criteria established in [4] for correct temperature measurement at a resolution of PV cells. Since the system would be outdoors, the implementation considered that all electronic equipment be protected from rain. Figure 3 shows the solution installed on site in detail.

4.4   Thermographic Image Acquisition and Processing

The algorithm of acquisition and processing of IRT information is represented in Fig. 4. The system was configured to generate radiometric .rjpg images, so each thermogram generates 86.016 specific temperature measurements. To obtain temperature measurements of each particular PV module, the system segments the array and identifies each PV module with a specific identifier (see Fig. 1).

Each image taken is calibrated to obtain thermograms with an adequate level of accuracy. This is done automatically with the package *thermimage* [19], which applies the principles of Plank's law and the Stephan Boltzmann relationship. The Table 4 shows the parameters used to obtain the temperature of each thermogram, in addition to the ambient temperature and relative humidity, which are updated in real time by the system's sensor, which in case of not obtaining such value, the value determined as default would be used.

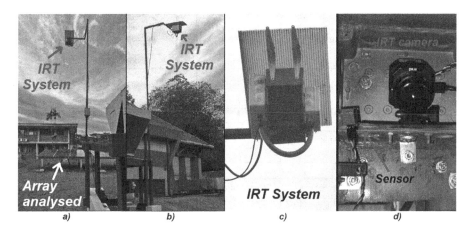

Fig. 3. a) Rear view of the system, b) side view of the system, c) front view of the system, d) IRT camera and temperature/humidity sensor.

Table 4. Parameters used to generate the thermogram of thermography.

Parameter	Value	Parameter	Value
Subject distance	10.41 m	Emissivity	0.9
Atmospheric temp (default)	28°C	Humidity (default)	60%
Ir window transmission	1	Ir window temp	None

After acquiring the thermogram, a statistical analysis of the temperature values of each module is performed to obtain the maximum, minimum, average, mode and delta temperature (DT). DT is calculate with Eq. (1); where, $T_{max,SM}$ corresponds to the maximum temperature of the module of interest and $T_{ave,REF}$ is the average temperature of the reference module (module 2). Finally, a color thermogram is generated to facilitate qualitative analysis (see Fig. 5). All the information is stored in the DB automatically.

$$DT = T_{max,SM} - T_{ave,REF} \tag{1}$$

4.5 Data Management

The main control unit manages a DB with the processed IRT information. The Table 5 shows in detail the main DB information that is stored for each PV module of each captured thermogram. The DB is backed up in the cloud and can be accessed remotely.

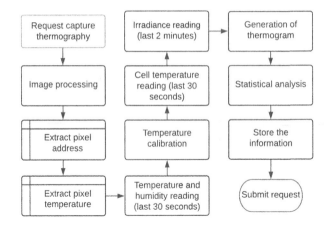

Fig. 4. Process implemented for the acquisition of thermal information, including external request sub-processes.

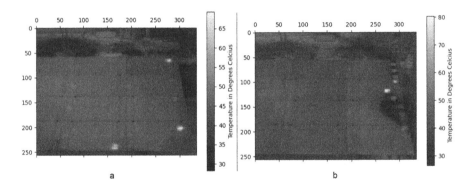

Fig. 5. a) color termogram of soiling test with hotspot of $DT = 23.7°C$ with a irradiance of $224\ W/m^2$, b) Color termogram of partial shading test with hotspot of $DT = 37°C$ with a irradiance of $529\ W/m^2$.

5   Results and Discussion

This section describes, validates and analyzes the main results obtained by the developed system.

5.1   Temperature Measurements

From 12 measurements between 08:09 am and 2:27 pm with values ranging between 36.7°C and 55.25°C, a variation of less than 4°C was found between the measurements of the IRT camera and contact sensor. Considering that proportionality was found in the range of temperatures evaluated, and that the

Table 5. Structure used for storing information in the experimentation DB. Temperature information is stored for each PV module.

Identifier			Electrical		Meteorological			Module temperature ($°C$)		
Date	Hour	ID	Power (W)	Irradiance (W/m^2)	State	HR (%)	Ta ($°C$)	T_{max}	T_{min}	DT

State: Clear, cloudy, rainy
HR: Relative humidity
Ta: Ambient temperature

thermography is an indirect measurement on the front face and the contact measurement is on the back face, it is determined that the temperature measurements of the system are correctly taken with an accuracy of $\pm 4°C$.

5.2   System Evaluation Under Induced Faults

During the time the system was under test, 1,777 thermographs were captured, allowing to verify the continuous operation of the system.

With the experiment described in Sect. 3.1, the relationship between the maximum DT value and irradiance was plotted (see Fig. 6). We can observe that the DT of the hot spots increased with respect to the irradiance for SC and S type faults, which agrees with what was observed by [20]. On the other hand, for PS a decreasing trend was observed, which could be related to the activation or not of the by-pass diodes [21,22], however, this requires a more detailed study by analyzing a larger amount of data. There were 26% and 8% of cases in areas C and D ($DT \geq 10°C$) of Fig. 6, respectively, however, it is known that in all cases a fault condition was being induced to the array and that for other irradiance conditions a $DT \geq 10°C$ was reached for the same fault, therefore, new criteria should be generated to identify these faults for all possible range of irradiances. In area A, 42% of cases with a $DT < 10°C$ were identified, however, with the premise that at least $700\ W/m^2$ are required to perform the IRT analysis, these cases could not have been analyzed until the required irradiance conditions were reached, which represents a possible delay to be able to make the diagnosis in an agile way. Finally, it should be noted that for all types of induced faults there were cases that did not meet the minimum value of DT for failure, therefore, this suggests that faults of different types could be identified with $DT < 10°C$; but for this new criteria need to be established.

From a qualitative analysis of the Fig. 5, it is possible to observe that the thermograms are taken correctly, since it has a good focus of the PV array, it is possible to identify cases where a single cell is hotter than the neighboring cells and that by means of the color scales the user can easily identify the hot spots.

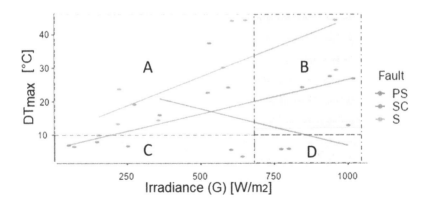

Fig. 6. Plot of the maximum DT(DT_{max}) found in each test with respect to the irradiance (G) present during each measurement. Shaded areas A and C correspond to $G < 700W/m^2$ and shaded areas C and D correspond to measurements with a $DT_{max} < 10°$C.

6   Conclusions

The developed system shows a viable alternative to automate the process of collecting IRT information continuously in photovoltaic installations for the creation of a high volume of IRT data of PV modules under suboptimal conditions. The temperature measurements obtained had an error of less than 4°C. The system validation process showed that under hotspot conditions, the developed system extracts information that is consistent with the theory, generating qualitative and quantitative information that is valuable for diagnosing faults in PV systems. The characteristics of the DB designed will allow to contribute to the improvement of the detection of hotspots through IRT analysis for a greater range of irradiance conditions than those currently established. The platform developed is an example of an innovative IoT solution for the optimization of energy sources usage in smart cities, which can be used by managers and inspectors of PV installations. It remains for future research to use the platform to perform an exhaustive analysis of the behavior of hot spot temperature with respect to irradiance for different types of faults, in order to establish better fault detection criteria.

Acknowledgement. This paper is part of the project 1360051 "Identificación de Fallas en Sistemas Fotovoltaicos" financed by the Costa Rica Institute of Technology.

References

1. Ghadami, N., et al.: Implementation of solar energy in smart cities using an integration of artificial neural network, photovoltaic system and classical delphi methods. Sustain. Urban Areas **74**, 103149 (2021)

2. Tsanakas, J.A., Ha, L., Buerhop, C.: Faults and infrared thermographic diagnosis in operating c-Si photovoltaic modules: a review of research and future challenges (2016)
3. Cardinale-Villalobos, L., Meza, C., Murillo-Soto, L.D.: Experimental comparison of visual inspection and infrared thermography for the detection of soling and partial shading in photovoltaic arrays. In: Nesmachnow, S., Hernández Callejo, L. (eds.) ICSC-CITIES 2020. CCIS, vol. 1359, pp. 302–321. Springer, Cham (2021). https://doi.org/10.1007/978-3-030-69136-3_21
4. Cardinale-Villalobos, L., Rimolo-Donadio, R., Meza, C.: Solar panel failure detection by infrared UAS digital photogrammetry: a case study. Int. J. Renew. Energy Res. (IJRER) **10**(3), 1154–1164 (2020)
5. International Energy Agency. Review on Infrared and Electroluminescence Imaging for PV Field Applications. Technical report, Photovoltaic Power Systems Programme
6. International Energy Agency. Review of Failures of Photovoltaic Modules. Technical Report July, International Energy Agency
7. Cardinale-Villalobos, L., Meza, C., Méndez-Porras, A., Murillo-Soto, L.D.: Quantitative comparison of infrared thermography, visual inspection, and electrical analysis techniques on photovoltaic modules: a case study. Energies **15**(5), 1841 (2022)
8. Phoolwani, U.K., Sharma, T., Singh, A., Gawre, S.K.: IoT based solar panel analysis using thermal imaging. In: 2020 IEEE International Students' Conference on Electrical, Electronics and Computer Science (SCEECS), pp. 1–5 (2020)
9. Salazar, A., Macabebe, E.Q.: Hotspots detection in photovoltaic modules using infrared thermography. In: MATEC Web of Conferences, vol. 70, p. 10015 (2016)
10. Aghaei, M.: Autonomous monitoring and analysis of photovoltaic systems. Energies **15**(14), 1–6 (2022)
11. Madeti, S.R., Singh, S.N.: A comprehensive study on different types of faults and detection techniques for solar photovoltaic system. Sol. Energy **158**, 161–185 (2017)
12. Zefri, Y., ElKettani, A., Sebari, I., Ait Lamallam, S.: Thermal infrared and visual inspection of photovoltaic installations by UAV photogrammetry-application case: Morocco. Drones **2**(4), 41 (2018)
13. Alam, M.K., Khan, F., Johnson, J., Flicker, J.: A comprehensive review of catastrophic faults in PV arrays: types, detection, and mitigation techniques. IEEE J. Photovoltaics **5**(3), 982–997 (2015)
14. Appiah, A., Zhang, X., Ayawli, B., Kyeremeh, F.: Review and performance evaluation of photovoltaic array fault detection and diagnosis techniques. Int. J. Photoenergy **1–19**(02), 2019 (2019)
15. Mellit, A., Tina, G.M., Kalogirou, S.A.: Fault detection and diagnosis methods for photovoltaic systems: a review. Renew. Sustain. Energy Rev. **91**, 1–17 (2018)
16. Moretón, R., Lorenzo, E., Narvarte, L.: Experimental observations on hot-spots and derived acceptance/rejection criteria. Sol. Energy **118**, 28–40 (2015)
17. Köntges, M., et al.: Review of failures of photovoltaic modules. Technical report (2014)
18. Roca, D., Lagüela, S., Díaz-Vilariño, L.: Infrared thermography: fundamentals and applications. In: Riveiro, B., Solla, M., (ed.), Non-Destructive Techniques for the Evaluation of Structures and Infrastructure, Chapter 6, p. 26. CRC Press
19. Tattersall, G.J.: Thermimage: Thermal image analysis. R package version 4.1.3 (2021)
20. Cubukcu, M., Akanalci, A.: Real-time inspection and determination methods of faults on photovoltaic power systems by thermal imaging in Turkey. Renew. Energy **147**, 1231–1238 (2020)

21. Satpathy, P.R., Sharma, R., Panigrahi, S.K., Panda, S.: Bypass diodes configurations for mismatch and hotspot reduction in PV modules. In: 2020 International Conference on Computational Intelligence for Smart Power System and Sustainable Energy (CISPSSE), pp. 1–6. IEEE (2020)
22. Guerriero, P., Daliento, S.: Toward a hot spot free PV module. IEEE J. Photovoltaics **9**(3), 796–802 (2019)

A New Approach to Automate the Connectivity of Electronic Devices with an IoT Platform

Juan José Flores-Sedano, Hugo Estrada-Esquivel[(✉)], Alicia Martínez Rebollar, and Juan José Jassón Flores Prieto

TecNM/Centro Nacional de Investigación y Desarrollo Tecnológico CENIDET, C.P. 62470 Cuernavaca, Morelos, Mexico
{m20ce084,hugo.ee,alicia.mr,jose.fp}@cenidet.tecnm.mx

Abstract. At present, the Internet of Things is one of the most promising technologies considering a large number of applications domains. The IoT solutions imply the integration of electronic devices, communication protocols, the cloud as data storage and smart software systems to process the data. The complexity of current IoT solutions has given rise to the creation of IoT platforms to manage the implementation of the solutions, however, one of the most complicated tasks is the configuration of the electronic devices to send information to the cloud through a specific protocol and a specific IoT agent. Currently, this process is done manually and it represents a challenge for novel developers. In this paper a novel approach is presented to automate the connection of IoT devices with a specific Platform using IoT Agents. The evaluation of the proposed approach with users with different development knowledge levels is also presented in the paper.

Keywords: Internet of Things · IoT Platform · FIWARE

1 Introduction

The Internet of Things (IoT) is a network of devices that are embedded with software, sensors, and network connectivity that collect and exchange data. The Internet of Things enables everyday objects to be "intelligent" by allowing data transmission and automates tasks, without requiring any manual intervention. IoT offers different opportunities and improvements in people's lives, being smart cities a concept that allows multiple technologies of this paradigm to be combined to generate solutions. Smart cities provide several digital services to sensorize and to automate different aspects of the city, such as the use of electricity, garbage management, city water management, pollution in different areas of the city, noise in the streets, etc. The proliferation of smart services based on IoT is largely due to the lower price of sensors and communication services. This cheapening of electronic devices has popularized the creation of applications that use sensor data to understand the context in which an object operates and the development of applications that capture and analyze this context data for decision making. The creation of IoT applications implies a great responsibility in software development, because the objects need to be in constant communication with the IoT platforms, which implies that

S. Nesmachnow and L. Hernández Callejo (Eds.): ICSC-CITIES 2022, CCIS 1706, pp. 123–139, 2023.
https://doi.org/10.1007/978-3-031-28454-0_9

the objects remain connected to the Internet all time. This situation causes the information produced by the sensors to be exposed to computer threats, which must be addressed immediately in order to guarantee the integrity of the systems. As a consequence of this situation, intelligent agents were created as an intermediary between the information coming from the sensors and the software platforms and to also manage the security aspects produced.

This paper is organized as follows. Section 2 shows main concepts involved in the research. Section 3 presents the related work. Section 4 presents the proposed approach to automate the connection of electronic devices with an IoT Platform. Section 5 shows the experimentation, and finally, Sect. 6 details the conclusions and future work.

2   Background

This section presents the fundamental concepts involved in this research work.

2.1   Internet of Things in the Cloud

The constant growth in the number of "things" connected to the Internet and the large number of applications that require collecting and analyzing data from devices for decision-making was the origin of the Internet of Things (IoT). The Internet of Things considers the services and standards necessary to connect, manage and protect different IoT devices and applications. These devices can be sensors, actuators, mobile devices, etc. All the data collected by these devices is stored in the cloud, in order to have easy access to them, in addition to providing greater security in the event of a mishap [1].

2.2   Internet of Things Platform

The emergence of the Internet of Things gave rise to a set of solutions to manage all the interactions between hardware and application layers. These solutions, called IoT Platforms, must be able to manage the huge amount of data that smart devices collect. Today there are a large number of IoT platforms, some examples are Amazon Web Services, Google, Microsoft Azure, IBM and FIWARE [2].

2.3   FIWARE

FIWARE is one of the emerging IoT Platforms for the development and deployment of Future Internet applications. FIWARE provides a completely open architecture which allows developers, service providers, companies and other organizations to develop products that meet their needs. FIWARE comprises a set of technologies called generic enablers which provide open interfaces for APIs and support interoperability with other generic enablers, these enablers arise as a proposal to respond to the need for approaches for smart cities solutions [2].

2.4   Orion Context Broker of the FIWARE Platform

This component of the FIWARE Platform, which allows the publication of context information by entities, is a server that implements an application programming interface based on an NGSI information model. This component allows to execute the following operations [3]:

- Register context applications.
- Update context information.
- Be notified when changes to context information arise.
- Consult background information.

2.5   Internet of Things Agent

The connection of objects to the internet implies overcoming a set of problems that arise in the different layers of the communication model. The lack of globally accepted standards for communication between objects has caused a heterogeneous environment to be required for devices using different protocols. For this reason, the IoT agents were created together with the FIWARE platform, so that the devices can send their data to the Context Broker using their own native protocols. Internet of Things Agents are intermediaries, a so-called bridge between IoT devices and platforms. In this context, the protocols used by the sensors are very relevant to select an appropriate IoT agent. Figure 1 shows the relationship between communication protocols, IoT agents and the Orion Context Broker [4].

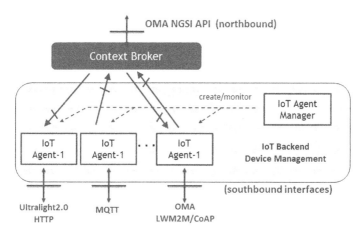

Fig. 1. Interaction between the Orion Context Broker, IoT agents and communication protocols.

The following are examples of IoT agents provided by the FIWARE Platform for communication between objects (Table 1):

Table 1. IoT Agent list

IoTAgent-JSON.	IoTAgent loRanWAN
IoTAgent-LWM2M	IoTAgent OPC-UA
IoTAgent-Utralight	IoTAgent sigfox

3 Related Work

This section presents the main research works related to the solution proposed in this paper.

In [5], the authors propose a model that allows the connection of services based on FIWARE OAuth 2.0 with the eID authentication provided by the eIDAS reference. With this model and its services that are already connected with an OAuth 2.0 identity provider can automatically connect with eIDAS nodes to provide eID authentication. To validate the proposed model, the authors have deployed an instance of the FIWARE identity manager connected to the eIDAS node. Later they registered 2 services; a private video conference system and a smart city deployment, in addition to expanding the functionalities to improve the user experience by taking advantage of. The authors conclude that the proposed solution facilitates the integration of FIWARE based generic OAuth 2.0 services for the eIDAS infrastructure, making the connection transparent for developers.

In [6], the authors demonstrate that the use of cloud services in the agronomic industry could be considered beneficial. In particular FIWARE, because it provides free and open-source development modules. The authors developed an application using the FIWARE components, and it has been validated in real crops located in a semi-arid area of southern Spain with the aim of reducing the amount of water needed for irrigation tasks.

In [7], the authors propose an authentication and identity management (IdM) method called YubiAuthIoT integrated with the FIWARE platform, as a way to provision and authenticate IoT devices. There are several benefits for IoT device authentication such as: device identity, scalability, offline crypto assets, revocation, and broadcast. YubiAuthIoT enables more decentralized device provisioning and management using subCAs, reducing the need for a discrete IdM service to manage devices. This approach provides more efficient and robust authentication and communication than the default on the FIWARE platform, which is based on HTTPS over HTTP/1.1 with JSON bodies, where authentication is provided by access tokens requested by each device/user and provided by the centralized IdM service.

In [8], the authors deal with the adoption of FIWARE for RPM development and, in general, for telehealth projects with the aim of supporting clinical centers interested in adopting cloud computing technology. Specifically, the authors presented a step-by-step approach to developing an RPM solution, investigating how the FIWARE platform and Generic Enablers (GE) could be adopted and integrated.

In [9], the authors present a customizable open source IoT platform setup using FIWARE. For the integration of existing building automation networks, this work extends an OpenMUC gateway with BACnet functionality and connects it to their platform via

MQTT. The authors have successfully demonstrated the general setup with a website, by visualizing high resolution energy monitoring and control loop as basic requirements for the integration of more advanced control algorithms in future building energy management systems.

4 The Proposed Approach to Automate the Connection of Electronic Devices with an IoT Platform

One of the current challenges in the Internet of Things is the current connection between IoT devices and the FIWARE platform. This connection, which is currently done manually, involves configuring the physical devices to be able to link them with the appropriate IoT Agent. The selected IoT agent needs to be configured for each protocol, which implies in-depth knowledge of the operation of the protocol and the IoT agent. In case of request for a communication protocol that does not yet have a standard for the IoT agent, it is necessary to create a specific IoT agent. This involves encoding the necessary commands and attributes for the IoT agent to function properly. With the appropriate IoT agent, the connection between sensors and the Orion Context Broker can be made. This connection implies knowledge of the physical device, knowledge of the IoT agents and the Orion Context Broker. The difficulty of making this manual configuration has caused this connection to be made directly between the devices and the Orion Context Broker, completely omitting the use of IoT agents, which breaks with the ideal scheme and allows unauthorized access to the data read from the sensors [10].

The architecture of the solution proposed in this work aims to automate the device connection processes using a specific communication protocol towards an IoT agent and the automatic connection of the agents to the FIWARE Internet of Things platform. The proposed architecture uses the components of the FIWARE platform for the development of the application with the aim of generating a totally open-source system, which adapts to the standards provided by this IoT platform and also uses the concept of IoT agents that was developed by FIWARE to improve the security between the connection of devices and the cloud. The FIWARE components used in this work are: the Orion Context Broker, CrateDB and Grafana. The interaction between FIWARE and the created web system is done through a RESTful API. RESTful APIs are services with which we can exchange information through established protocols and standards such as HTTP. Figure 2 shows the proposed architecture, which is made up of the following layers: Application Layer, Services Layer and FIWARE services.

The application layer contains the system developed in this research work, which is responsible for receiving, storing, processing and sending data from IoT devices. The services layer uses RESTful services to enable the interaction between the application layer and the FIWARE ecosystem, through requests to send data. The FIWARE service is responsible for receiving the data sent through the web system, in order to handle the data received by the Orion Context Broker. This layer makes a connection with the CrateDB module to create a database where all historical data sent to FIWARE is stored. This in order to connect to the Grafana module to display the data from the sensors graphically. The proposed system is made up of a series of modules that allow the automation of the

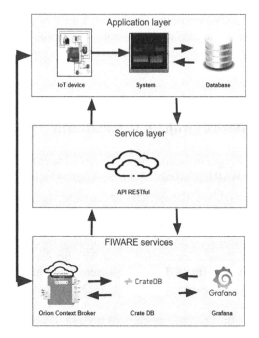

Fig. 2. Architecture of the proposed solution.

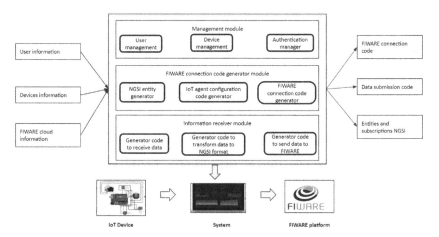

Fig. 3. Specific architecture of the proposed system

connection process of IoT devices to the cloud of the FIWARE platform. These modules are presented in Fig. 3.

In following sections, the explanation of each module of the architecture is presented in detail:

4.1 Manager Module

The manager module allows the system to manage user information (name, email and password), devices (name, readings, units, protocols) and FIWARE cloud details (Orion Context Broker address and IoT agent), as well as to take care of the authentication of the users who register in the system. This module connects to a database to store all the information it receives, this information is used to create the connection codes and data reception code of the device.

On the device registration screen (Fig. 4) the user must fill in the form with the name of the device, units, maximum and minimum value of the device reading, the address of the Orion Context Broker server, the communication protocol and the Internet of Things agent that the device use and the readings of the device.

Fig. 4. Device registration form

4.2 FIWARE Platform Connection Module

The purpose of this module is to generate the necessary code to define the FIWARE entities corresponding to the devices that will provide data to the IoT system. The creation of NGSI entities and the generation of code in order to make the connection with FIWARE. The approach is based on the concept of entities that relate and entities with attributes and metadata. All communication between the different components of the OCB architecture is done through the NGSI v2 RESTful API. The context information in FIWARE is represented through generic data structures referred to as context elements, the context elements are composed of an identifier, a type associated with its entity, in addition to having attributes which contain a name, type and attribute value, these attributes in turn have metadata given which have a name, type and value, the metadata is optional when building the context elements. The values that are captured from the sensors must be represented using the concept of entities. Users must use the code generator to create the NGSI entities to define the map between the various sensors defined in the system and the various entities predefined by FIWARE, with the NGSI entities being JSON-type data formats that represent an object or thing in the system. Real world with tangible attributes or characteristics. These entities help to send information to FIWARE, more specifically to the Orion Context Broker component, which uses a mongo database to store the current status of the entities, it does not store historical information of its changes. With the entities created, the users must select a specific IoT agent using the submodule's code generator to configure an IoT agent according to the protocol defined in the sensor.

Figure 5 shows an example of the code generated to launch the FIWARE services. This code is composed of the following elements: the version of FIWARE cloud, the Orion Context Broker service, the dependencies such as mongodb, the ports it uses, in addition to including the configuration of the IoT agent. The information is obtained from the data that the user registers when adding a new device in the system, with the generated code the user can compile the code on the server where he wishes to host the FIWARE services.

4.3 Information Receptor Module

This module aims to produce the necessary code so that the IoT system can obtain data from previously registered devices. In addition, it also aims to generate the code that allows the transformation of sensor data to the NGSI format (NGSI REST API) to be sent to the Orion Context Broker through a specific IoT agent. This code, which is compiled later, allows the IoT system to take data from each sensor and pass it to the sub-module in charge of transforming it into the NGSI format for subsequent sending to the Orion Context Broker. To load the Arduino code to send data, in the Arduino code screen (Fig. 6) the Arduino file is loaded so that the system inserts the code with the necessary data to send data, the code is made up of the id and the reading variables of the device, the address of the system, as well as the necessary libraries for the operation of the code which the user downloads and compiles to send data to the system.

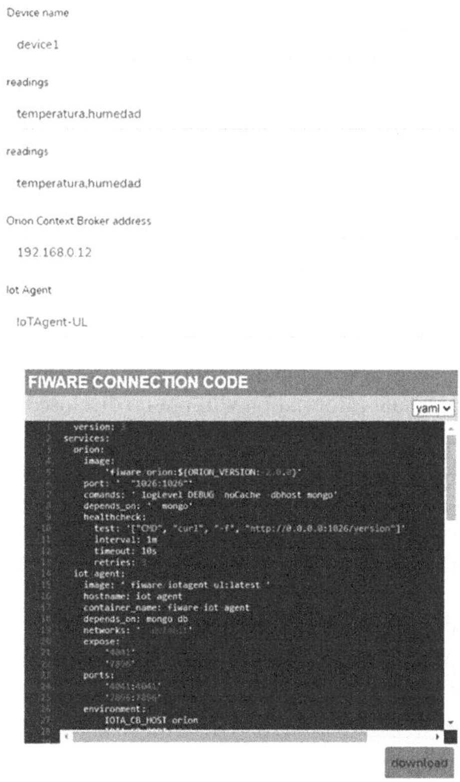
Device name
device1
readings
temperatura,humedad
readings
temperatura,humedad
Orion Context Broker address
192.168.0.12
Iot Agent
IoTAgent-UL
FIWARE CONNECTION CODE
yaml
download

Fig. 5. FIWARE connection code.

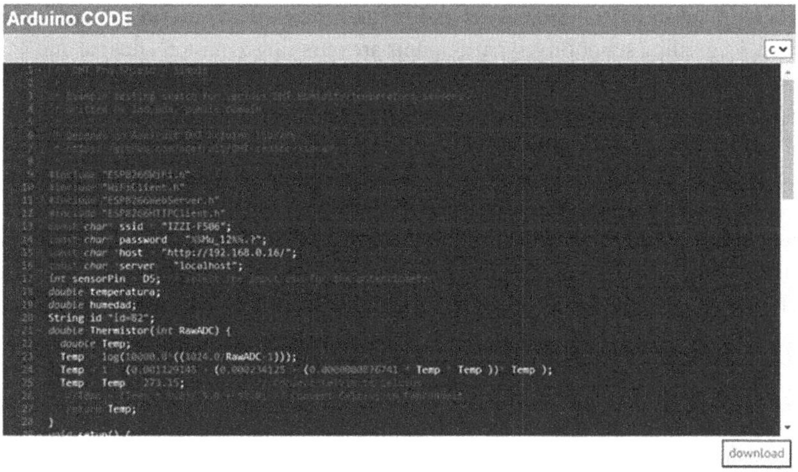
Arduino CODE
C
download

Fig. 6. Arduino code.

5 Experimentation

In order to validate the proposed approach, experimentation was carried out with developers with different levels of knowledge about sensors, cloud computing and the Internet of Things.

5.1 Phases of Experimentation

The experimentation was carried out in three phases:

Phase 1. In this phase, participants were given an informed consent document explaining the objective of the experimentation, the procedures followed during the tests, and establishing that their personal information will not be disclosed. The participants read the consent document and signed it stating their agreement with the test plan.

Phase 2. In this phase, the functionality of the developed system is evaluated. The evaluation requires the development of 7 tasks. Each of the tasks must be evaluated with a questionnaire that allows knowing the functionality of the system and the times used for the participant to develop each of the tasks.

Phase 3. In this stage, the preliminary evaluation of the graphical interface of the system is carried out. The evaluation consists of a Likert-type questionnaire of 12 questions related to the interaction of the participants with the interfaces of the Web system in order to evaluate the usability of the system.

5.2 Experimentation Participants

To carry out the experimentation of the new approach presented in this article, 8 male subjects (with ages ranging from 23 to 26 years) with different knowledge regarding the development in IoT environments and in the assembly and use of IoT devices were recruited. Regarding schooling, 4 participants are pursuing a master's degree and 4 of the participants are pursuing a computer science degree. The participants were summoned to a space where the computer with the developed system and the Arduino devices used to send data were located. In this environment, the 3 phases of experimentation were carried out continuously, ending with the preliminary evaluation of the graphical interface. The participants were divided into three groups (group 1: No IoT experience, group 2: Average experience in IoT, group 3: Advanced IoT expertise) according to their experience with devices, managing IoT agents and sending data to the cloud, whether from FIWARE or from another cloud service provider. The division was carried out through a brief questionnaire where the participants were asked about their experience using IoT devices, the management and configuration of Internet of Things agents, programming with Arduino and the configuration of the FIWARE cloud.

Table 2 presents the organization of the groups of participants according to their experience in the use of IoT or sending data to the cloud.

Table 2. Table of participants.

Participant	Age	Academic level	Experience
1	23	Master	Advance
2	23	Master	Average
3	26	Master	Advance
4	23	Master	Advance
5	24	Engineering	No experience
6	22	Engineering	Average
7	21	Engineering	No experience
8	24	Engineering	Average
9	21	Engineering	No experience
10	24	Engineering	Average
11	23	Engineering	Average
12	22	Engineering	Average
13	25	Engineering	No experience
14	23	Engineering	No experience
15	23	Engineering	No experience
16	24	Engineering	Advance

5.3   Resources Used in Experimentation

The resources used for the experimentation were the electronic devices, the informed consent document and the questionnaires to obtain feedback from the participants. Electronic devices: in order to reduce the problem in the availability of devices for the test, a set of devices that were used in the test sessions were made available to the participants. The devices that were made available to the participants during the test sessions are as follows:

- 3 generic Wemos D1 boards.
- 1 water sensor -SL067
- 1 Propane Gas Sensor – MQ-5
- 1 pulse sensor - MLM604362783
- 1 temperature and humidity sensor - Dht11A
- 1 accelerometer -MPU6050
- 1 Lenovo laptop with Windows 10, Arduino IDE in its latest version. The System was installed on this device.

Informed consent: the informed consent document has the purpose of informing the participants about the objectives of the testing phase, the procedure for the execution of the experimentation, and, above all, to make explicit the approval of the subjects to participate in the study. Test plan and to record that the personal data of the participants will be anonymous. Evaluation questionnaires: the evaluation questionnaire was carried out after completing each of the tasks where the participant expressed the complexity of performing the task. The test plan considers that the participants of the experiment can perform a series of tasks with the system in order to send data generated by sensors to the FIWARE cloud, but using the concept of Internet of Things agents as intermediaries. The questionnaires developed for this test plan have the objective of evaluating the ease of use of the system's functionalities, the time used to perform each of the tasks and the usability of each of the modules.

5.4 Experimentation Procedure

The main idea of carrying out the experimentation tasks is to make the connection between IoT devices and the FIWARE platform using the system. For this part, the system automatically performs the tasks of transforming the data read from the sensors into FIWARE entities in NGSI format and in accordance with a specific data model. In turn, the system automatically sends data to the FIWARE platform.

Phase 1 Start of experimentation

In this phase, participants were given an informed consent document explaining the objective of the experimentation, the procedures followed during the tests, and establishing that their personal information will not be disclosed. The participants read the consent document and signed it stating their agreement with the test plan.
Phase 2 Execution of tasks using the system

In this phase, the evaluation of the functionality of the developed system is carried out. The evaluation requires the development of 7 tasks which are:

- Task 1 User registration
- Task 2 Login
- Task 3 Device registration
- Task 4 Upload the Arduino code to the IoT device
- Task 5 Upload connection code with FIWARE
- Task 6 Reception of sensor data
- Task 7 Data visualization with Grafana

The objective of the tasks is to allow the participant to connect an IoT device to the system, and subsequently perform the configuration tasks that allow him to read the data from the device's sensors and send the standardized data to the FIWARE cloud. Each of the tasks must be evaluated with a questionnaire that allows knowing the usability of the system and the times used for the participant to develop each of the tasks.
Phase 3 Evaluation of the graphical interface

Once the 7 tasks were carried out using the Web system, the preliminary evaluation of the graphical interface of the web system was carried out in order to evaluate the usability of the system. The evaluation consists of a Likert-type questionnaire of 12 questions. Once the tasks and the questionnaires were completed, the evaluation was considered finished, which lasted an average of 15 min.

5.5 Functionality Results

In order to have a first approximation to measure the ease of use of each functionality of the system, a functionality questionnaire was applied, which aimed to evaluate the complexity at the time of performing the tasks of the experimentation. The result of this evaluation made it possible to determine that all users were able to complete all the expected functionalities. The difficulty level of the average tasks is shown below:

- Task 1 User registration. Difficulty level (Easy 15 participants, Medium 1 participants and Difficult 0 participants).
- Task 2 Login. Difficulty level (Easy 16 participants, Medium 0 participants and Difficult 0 participants).
- Task 3 Device registration. Difficulty level (Easy 10 participants, Medium 5 participants and Difficult 1 participant).
- Task 4 Upload the Arduino code to the IoT device. Difficulty level (Easy 13 participants, Medium 2 participants and Difficult participants).
- Task 5 Upload connection code with FIWARE. Difficulty level (Easy 16 participants, Medium 0 participants and Difficult 0 participants).
- Task 6 Reception of sensor data. Difficulty level (Easy 12 participants, Medium 3 participants and Difficult 1 participants).
- Task 7 Data visualization with Grafana. Difficulty level (Easy 14 participants, Medium 2 participants and Difficult 0 participants).

The results of this evaluation allow us to establish that the system not only performs the tasks successfully, but also establishes that the functions are easy to follow and perform even for less experienced users in the Internet of Things area.

5.6   Results of the Evaluation of the Time Used for Each of the Tasks

This section presents the results of the time that participants spent to perform each one of the tasks needed to operate the proposed system. Figure 7 shows the expected time (in minutes) that is expected to be used by the participant to perform the functionalities of the system. It is important to mention that expected time is based on the average time that an expert takes to use the functionalities of the system.

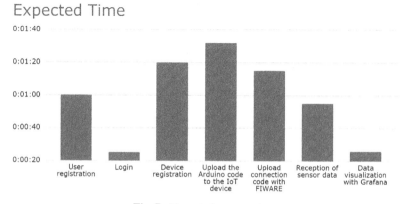

Fig. 7. Expected average time

The average time the user actually used to perform the evaluated activities is shown in Fig. 8. The average time considers the time spent by the three groups of the evaluation: Advanced Participant, Average Experience Participant and Inexperienced Participant.

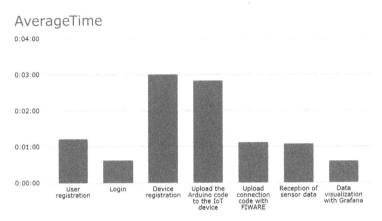

Fig. 8. Average time.

The analysis of the time used allowed us to detect that the times used in practice by the participants of the experiment were less than expected. In addition to the overall average time for all participants, the average time it took for each of the groups mentioned in the participants section of this document is also shown. The results for each of the participant groups are shown below.

5.7 Group C Results

Figure 9 shows the average time it took group C (Advanced Participant) to perform the tasks. The tasks that required the longest time were task 3 "device registration" and task 4 "upload Arduino code". It is important to mention that the participants in the advanced group used more sensors than the other two groups, which led to the participants to take more time to register the devices that they were using and it also took more time to upload the Arduino code because it need it more processing resources because of the more sensor in the devices than the other group.

5.8 Group B Results

Figure 10 shows the average time it took group B (Average Experience Participant) to perform the tasks and, as well as the results of Group C. In this group, the tasks that also required the longest time were task 3 "device registration" and task 4 "upload Arduino code".

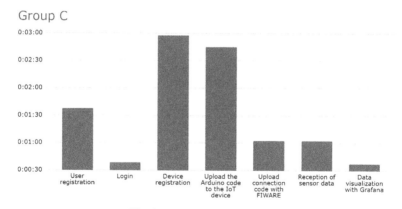

Fig. 9. Average time in group C.

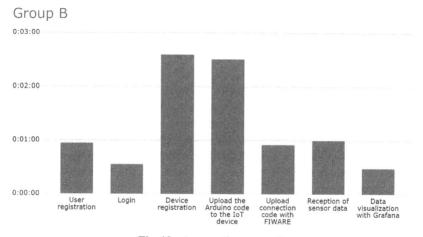

Fig. 10. Average time group B.

5.9 Group a Results

Figure 11 shows the average time it took for group A (Inexperienced Participant) to perform the tasks and, as well as the results of groups C and B. Task 3 and 4 also required more time to be completed with times slightly higher than the other two groups.

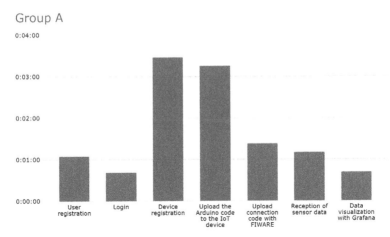

Fig. 11. Average time group A.

6 Conclusions

The research work presented in this paper has demonstrated that it is possible to automate the process to connect sensors to FIWARE Platform using the concept of IoT Agent. This paper presents the development of a software system that allows data to be sent automatically to the FIWARE platform using the CoAP and MQTT protocols in conjunction with Internet agents of Things. The proposed software system is responsible to obtain the needed information for registering the sensors of an IoT device and also to produce the code for a software module that obtains the data from sensors and establishes the connection with the FIWRE Cloud. The system was evaluated with a series of tests with young software developers, resulting in an effectiveness of 100% in all the functionalities of the proposed software system. The evaluation also considers the time that developers spent in developing each one of the tasks that compose the evaluation questionnaires. The results demonstrated that proposed solution fulfill the goal of automating the connection of IoT devices with the FIWARE Platform.

The developed system allows the user to save a significant amount of time when performing the connection and sending of data to the FIWARE platform. This type of system drives the transformation of traditional cities to smart cities, which have as obtained improve the quality of life of its inhabitants. The system presented in this work, being an intermediary between the devices and the platform FIWARE, allows you to safely manage the data collected by the sensors of the devices, to later send them securely and automatically to the Orion Context Broker.

References

1. Bliznakoff del Valle, D.J.: IoT: Tecnologías, usos, tendencias y desarrollo future (2014). http://openaccess.uoc.edu/webapps/o2/bitstream/10609/40044/6/dbliznakoffTFM0115memoria.pdf
2. FIWARE-ABOUT US, ABOUT US FIWARE (2016). https://www.fiware.org/about-us/

3. APRENDE FIWARE EN ESPAÑO, Orion Context Broker (2016). https://fiwaretraining.rea dthedocs.io/es_MX/latest/ecosistemaFIWARE/ocb/
4. FIWARE, Tuturial time series data (2018). https://github.com/FIWARE/tutorials.IoT-Agent
5. Alonso, Á., et al.: An identity framework for providing access to FIWARE OAuth 2.0 based services according to the eIDAS European regulation. IEEE Access **7**, 88435–88449 (2019). https://doi.org/10.1109/ACCESS.2019.2926556
6. López-Riquelme, J.A., Pavón-Pulido, N., Navarro-Hellín, H., Soto-Valles, F., TorresSánchez, R.: A software architecture based on FIWARE cloud for precision agriculture. Agric. Water Manag. **183**, 123–135 (2017). https://doi.org/10.1016/j.agwat.2016.10.020
7. Sousa, P.R., Magalhães, L., Resende, J.S., Martins, R., Antunes, L.: Provisioning, authentication and secure communications for IoT devices on FIWARE. Sensors **21**(17), 5898 (2021)
8. Celesti, A., et al.: How to develop IoT cloud e-health systems based on FIWARE: a lesson learnt. J. Sens. Actuator Netw. **8**(1), 7 (2019)
9. Storek, T., Lohmöller, J., Kümpel, A., Baranski, M., Müller, D.: Application of the open-source cloud platform FIWARE for future building energy management systems. In: J. Phys. Conf. Ser. **1343**(1), 012063. IOP Publishing (2019)
10. APRENDE FIWARE EN ESPAÑO, Plataforma FIWARE (2016). https://fiware-training.rea dthedocs.io/es_MX/latest/ecosistemaFIWARE/plataformaFIWARE/

Optimization, Smart Production, and Smart Public Services

Lean Office Approach for *muda* Identification in the Admission Process of University Students

Jesús del Carmen Peralta-Abarca[1]([✉]) [iD], Pedro Moreno-Bernal[1,2] [iD],
and Viridiana Aydeé León-Hernández[1] [iD]

[1] Facultad de Ciencias Químicas e Ingeniería,
Universidad Autónoma del Estado de Morelos, Cuernavaca, Mexico
{carmen.peralta,pmoreno,vleon}@uaem.mx
[2] Facultad de Contaduría, Administración e Informática,
Universidad Autónoma del Estado de Morelos, Cuernavaca, Mexico

Abstract. The new model of industry 4.0 boosts productivity in modern life, as an essential part of social and technological changes under the paradigm of smart cities. As a part of social changes, universities restructured their ability to trace internal processes through smart campuses, using Information and Communication Technologies and industrial improvement methodologies. Lean principles are used for process improvement through *muda* elimination and value generation in office tasks. This article introduces a Lean Office methodology for the admission process of incoming students in a public university in Mexico. Ishikawa and Pareto diagrams are applied to analyze and identify *muda* in the admission procedure, reducing the time delays in the admission form exchange subprocess.

Keywords: Lean office · Process improvement · Industry 4.0 · University

1 Introduction

In recent years, the Industry 4.0 revolution has advanced as an essential part of social and technological changes under the paradigm of smart cities [10,13]. As part of the social changes, universities have restructured their ability to track their internal processes on smart campuses, to the benefit of students and their community. A smart campus is related to internal communications, Internet of Things (IoT), Big Data, and data governance [3]. Local communications networks are used to provide connectivity and services, impacting daily user experience [14].

Universities are essential in civil societies for learning and higher education. Nonetheless, universities worldwide needed to restructure their internal processes after the COVID-19 pandemic, complementing the smart campus digitalization. In this context, a smart campus must provide practical digital applications

S. Nesmachnow and L. Hernández Callejo (Eds.): ICSC-CITIES 2022, CCIS 1706, pp. 143–157, 2023.
https://doi.org/10.1007/978-3-031-28454-0_10

based on information and communication technologies and process improvement methodologies for better school services management.

Methodologies for process improvement in engineering increase productivity and help boosting business goals. Several process improvement methodologies, including Six Sigma, Total Quality Management, Toyota Production System (TPS), Kanban, Kaizen, Lean Manufacturing, have been proposed as decision-making methodologies for industrial processes, and selecting the best approach for a particular process is essential to improve its productivity and efficiency. Each methodology assists the process improvement step by step, to deliver better products and services. Methodologies use tools like diagrams, flowcharts, etc., to detect and evaluate defects or inconsistencies in a particular process. Particularly, Lean Manufacturing principles have been extended to non-manufacturing areas, e.g., services and offices, receiving the Lean Office (LO) name [15,18]. The lean concept emerged from TPS, based on making work more satisfying by eliminating *muda* or converting it into value [6]. Muda represents all waste created by human activities absorbing resources without creating value [16]. Everything a client refers to, in terms of satisfying his needs at any specific moment, generates value for the product or service. The LO concept comprises the application of lean thinking principles in administrative areas to eliminate muda in processes and information flows [4,12]. In this context, information management identifies opportunities for improving the management of information sources and information systems infrastructure, adding value to the information provided to the customer [5].

This article proposes the application of a LO methodology to the admission process for incoming students in a public university, particularly for the admission token. Admission form exchange subprocess. A specific case study is analyzed, for the 2019–2020 admission process to Universidad Autónoma del Estado de Morelos (UAEM), Mexico. The annual admission process for new students requires carrying out a series of personal procedures in the admission services offices of the institution. However, during the COVID-19 pandemic, the subprocess for exchanging the admission form could not be performed in person, and a migration to web forms based on LO principles was adopted.

The main contribution of this article is the implementation of LO tools to identify muda by ranking the significant non-value added activities in the admission process. Several muda are detected, including redundant activities that are performed in different subprocesses, causing waiting times to applicant; low efficiency in customer service tasks due to limited computer equipment resources; and error-prone office and support activities because of the lack of trained personnel. The causes identified in each stage are integrated into an optimization plan to conduct a standardized process. Results demonstrate that LO tools identified the major waste that impacts waiting times in the different stages of the admission form exchange subprocess.

The article is structured as follows. Section 2 describes the admission process for incoming students and reviews related works. Sect. 3 describes the proposed methodology for the admission form exchange subprocess and the LO tools used. Section 4 presents and discusses the results for the case study. Finally, Sect. 5 presents the conclusions and formulates the main lines for future work.

2   The Admission Process of University Students

This section describes the admission process for incoming students to UAEM. Also, the section reviews the related works about LO principles applied for processes that require substantial time improvements and waste elimination.

2.1   Admission Process Before the COVID-19 Pandemic

Every year, UAEM calls for the admission of new students interested in joining middle and higher education educational programs. According to the Quality Plan of the Department of Admission and Revalidation, the admission process starts with the planning. Later, the call for admission Then, an admission deadline is established for the applicants to exchange the pre-registering admission form for an official admission sheet.

The institutional admission process is carried out by the admission services area of the school services offices of UAEM. Usually, the admission process presents contretemps due to failures in personnel management, the digital database system, and the lack of communication and visual support instructions. These deficiencies generate inconveniences and complaints from applicants, who expect the process to be carried out as efficiently as possible. Besides, the current admission process represents a problem for the organization because UAEM has the ISO 9001 certification; therefore, the admission process must maintain a quality standard as a part of the organizational processes.

The admission form exchange subprocess comprises seven stages. First, the call for admission is published in local media. Second, the pre-register stage permits candidates to fill out a form to provide personal information, i.e., identity card (INE) and a certificate of high school studies. Third, the registration fee is published for applicants to pay the admission charges before the fifth stage. Fourth, applicants proceed to the admission services office to validate the information on the pre-register form by presenting authentic documents. Then, the admissions services office takes a photo of the applicant to include on the pre-register form. Fifth, the admission form exchange process is carried out by the admission services office, to exchange the pre-register form for an admission sheet. Sixth, applicant are appointed on a date to take the admission exam. Finally, the results are published in local media to show the lists of accepted candidates for the different educational programs, in accordance with the procedure established in the Manual of Processes and Operating Procedures of UAEM.

2.2   Related Works

Research in smart campuses uses ICT to provide intelligent process systems that support digital applications for better management. Smart campus applications use Big Data, IoT, and mobile devices as tools for managing internal processes. Current works propose different methodologies for better and more efficient processes in the context of the smart industry, smart campus, and smart cities. A review of related works is presented next.

Chen and Cox [2] applied Lean Manufacturing concepts in an office environment. The authors proposed a systematic procedure for Lean practitioners to conduct Lean events in their office environment. The proposed LO method incorporates the knowledge of several articles, books, and successful Lean events for many study cases. The proposed systematic procedure transforms the office environment into Lean Office customer-triggered working processes. As a result, results were faster and more systematic tasks, tracking-reducing costs due to reduced non-value-added activities.

Sabur and Simatupang [11] applied Lean principles in the service support of a manufacturing company to increase customer satisfaction on order acceptance to achieve the targeted customer response time. Lean tools were applied on the office floor of the company, particularly in handling the administration of customer order acceptance. The causes of the treated problem were the lack of practical business orientation and an integrated system for information and data sharing. Value stream mapping (VSM) was used to identify waste using solution maps. Also, the standardization of processes was applied for better time response. The solutions were based on analyzing future VSM by changing the priorities. The proposed solution point targeted 40-hour customer response may be achieved in 37 h 22.2 min.

Monteiro et al. [9] applied LO tools to improve opportunities for raw materials management of a logistics department in shop-floor operations. Lean tools identified waste by lacking information integration and visibility on managing raw materials, producing low data processing efficiency. 5S, Poka-Yoke mechanism, standard work, and visual management were used as Lean tools to identify waste and generate value opportunities. Results obtained were transparency on processes, better task definition of priorities to perform, better organization and work management. The *open points* and *production losses*, and both reduced their processing time by 84% and 66%, respectively. Also, standardization and a clear definition of stakeholders responsibilities allowed significant reductions in process lead time equivalent to $645/year of saving for the company.

Magalhães et al. [8] applied LO tools, i.e., electronic standardization and critical performance indicators, in the administrative processes of an undergraduate/postgraduate office of the Department of Production and Systems at the University of Minho, Portugal. Lean techniques were applied in an administrative environment allowing the development of skills at a professional level and professional teamwork. Electronic standardization was applied to six educational projects and it was implemented successfully. Personal computers and network drives reorganization reduced 84% of the file search time, impacting students registration and project management. Also, student searching was reduced by 69% of search time, impacting input times and information handling, equivalent to 12 h/year of saving for the Department of Production and Systems.

The related works allowed identifying several proposals showing a growing interest in LO tools. The optimization of the design of administrative processes is part of strategic management toward a productive process. In this sense, organizations seek to improve their operations in an efficient and productive way.

Organizations review their administrative processes through the identification of waste in workflows to eliminate them. This work contributes to a LO methodology for the admission process of incoming students in UAEM. The benefits of the proposed methodology include significant reductions in time delays in the admission form exchange subprocess. Next, the implementation of LO tools to identify *muda* by ranking the significant non-value added activities in the admission process is described.

3   Lean Office for the Admission Process of Incoming Students

This section describes the proposed LO methodology of the admission form exchange subprocess and the LO tools used.

3.1   Lean Office

The LO concept came from TPS, which originated in the Japanese automotive industry after World War II. Japan started to work in automobile production, but the lack of resources prevented efficient and dynamic production models. The need to have a production model adapted to the Japanese requirements generated the Just in Time (JIT) concept. The main goal of JIT is to increase production efficiency through waste disposal within the production environment [6]. Womack et al. [17] called this production system Lean Thinking. The word Lean becomes a way to define TPS in practice. The starting point of the lean principle is to recognize a small fraction of time and effort in an organization to eliminate waste from activities that do not generate value, e.g., customer satisfaction is achieved by offering a service at an acceptable price and quality, as defined in each case by the customer. It applies to everything the client refers to in terms of satisfying their needs; at that moment, value is generated for the product or service given value to the different processes in a company. Currently, the Lean philosophy is applied through its different aspects defined by the organizations: Lean Manufacturing for the productive sector, LO for office and service environments, Lean Construction for environments and sectors related to construction, and Lean Health for the health sector. The Lean aspects share the mentality of quality principles to optimize work, improve results and establish continuous improvement within the organization [1].

   In practice, the significant waste of LO is the time of activities, lack of standardization, generating batch and unorganized documents, careful data entry and information, and document report unstructured correctly. Once waste is identified, it is necessary to implement LO tools to analyses the value in the office to eliminate or reduce wastes. Likewise, root-cause Ishikawa diagrams help to create and classify ideas or hypotheses concerning the root causes of a problem in a graphical manner. Another useful technique is Pareto analysis. Pareto diagrams help to prioritize tasks highlighting which actions are proposed to solve each problem. In addition, VSM and programs like 5S are used to standardize the new value achieved to stabilize the new process. Finally, it is necessary to stimulate continuous cycle improvements in the LO deployment process for higher performance.

3.2   LO Tools for Admission Form Exchange Subprocess

Locher [7] recommended performing an observation of the current process to identify, differentiate and detect opportunities for improvement that allow an objective evaluation from the perspective of the LO. Therefore, in the proposed approach the admission process is analyzed in two stages. The first stage follows the four basic steps [stabilize, standardize, make visible, and continuous improvement] to apply the lean methodology. If a process is unstable, the focus on adopting the methodology depends on the starting point, e.g., an unstable, irregular, and unacceptable process must be stabilized. Then, the stabilized process is initialized in the standardization stage. Later, a standardized process must be visible inside the organization for a correct following. Finally, the process improvement must be in continuous way. In this context, the first action is searching for instability or unacceptable activities in the admission process. The implementation of the four phases for the stabilizing stage is described in the following paragraphs.

Identification of Essential Activities. Critical activities and procedures of the admission process are used to identify possible *muda*. The Quality Plan of the Department of Admission and Revalidation defines five essential activities for the support staff. However, the process quality manual does not identify the specific activities, so they are not considered standardized elements. Table 1 shows the essential activities and the corresponding procedures related to the admission form exchange subprocess.

Table 1. Procedures carried out during each activity of the admission process

	Activity	Procedure
1	Reception of documents	Gathering documents from applicants
2	Detailed data review	Careful review of data in documents of the applicant
3	Photography	Save applicant photograph in a digital database
4	Applicant registration	Store applicant information in a local database
5	Print	Print and deliver admission form

Process Organization. The applicant goes to the admission services office to deliver the admission form. Subsequently, the documents of the applicant are collected and reviewed according to the activities in Table 1. If all the documents are correct, the applicants can exchange their admission form for an admission sheet that endorses them as candidates.

Table 2 describes the activities developed at the admission form exchange subprocess phases to identify possible *muda* in practice, according to the Quality Plan of the Department of Admission and Revalidation.

Table 2. Admission form exchange subprocess activities performed in a module

#	Phase	Activity
1	Applicants reception	Arrange and review documentation (INE, admission token and charge voucher)
2	Documents preparation	Staple the admission form and fee voucher
3	Documents reception	Review personal information, i.e., INE, admission form, and charge voucher. If there is a mistake in personal information, the staff comments on the mistake to alert and be corrected in phase 4
4	Detailed revision	Inspect carefully the personal information to identify any mistakes from the receptionist staff. The difference from the past module is careful verification. Also, this phase prepares the applicant for a photo in phase 3
5	Take a photo	Take a photo if the personal information is valid. Subsequently, the photo is uploaded to the Documentation Management and Scholar Control System (SADCE)
6	Assignment	Staff assigns and sends the applicant to the data capture phase
7	Data capture	Data capturer staff collate personal documents with data captured in SADCE. Then, two filters are applied to find any mistake notifying the applicant if it is necessary to make any correction or continue the process. If the information is correct, the applicant signs a printed admission sheet
8	Deliver admission sheet	Applicant collects its print admission sheet. The printed admission sheet indicates the date, place, campus location, and degree bachelor of interest
9	Critical information	The staff in this phase explains to the applicant important information about campus location, exam date and provides a study guide for the admission exam

Muda is identified in phases one, two, six, and nine of Table 2. The phases are not standardized processes yet. Phase nine is an activity recently implemented in the admission form exchange subprocess. In practice, the staff roles are not clearly defined, impacting the development of the admission process and generating possible *muda*.

Muda Identification. *Muda* detected in the admission process includes redundant activities that are performed in different subprocesses, causing waiting times to applicants; suitable communication and collaboration of personnel; bottleneck by cross information; low efficiency in service attention by limited computer equipment resources; and error-prone office and support activities because of the lack of trained personnel. Table 3 summarizes the detected *muda* for admission form exchange subprocess.

Table 3. Detected activities do not generate value

Muda	Identification	Problems
Waiting times: time delays at previously activities for next step	A document preparation bottleneck in phase 2 A prolonged recess times in activities A failure of computer system	Unoptimized activities in phase 2 generate time delays Lack of trained personnel Lack of computer system support and maintenance
Unused talent: do not exploit the experience, knowledge, and creativity of the staff	Limited collaboration between support staff The lack of cross-training in support staff	The coordinator does not take advantage of the support staff ideas to implement them Lack of training for job roles
Movements: unnecessary movements by staff	Unnecessary movement generated in activities	Lack of communication when the applicant makes a mistake in registering personal information on the admission form or when the applicant decides to switch from the initial academic program selected during the admission form exchange subprocess

Identification of Opportunities for Improvement. The improvements allow redesigning the current process, considering the information presented in Tables 2 and 3. The improvement activities proposed for the admission form exchange subprocess are described in Table 4. Those activities identified as *muda* and the not standardized phases are merged or eliminated to achieve a better efficiency in the admission process.

Once the unacceptable activities for stabilizing stage are identified, a problem cause-effect analysis based on Ishikawa diagram was carried out to define possible

Table 4. Improvement activities proposed for the admission form exchange subprocess

Activities	Improvement
Documents reception	Provide precise and simplified instructions about the admission form exchange Improve the delivery of documents in phase 2: prepare the stapling documents by cropping the admission form by half Allow student access in blocks of 16 individuals to avoid congestion
Documents review and validation	Provide the first filter to detect mistakes or inconsistencies in record information Documents detailed review; personal information must coincide with the admission form recorded Specify and comment as mistake correction the error of the registration form or when the applicant decides to switch from the initial academic program selected Provide precise instructions to the applicant or clarify doubts for next steps
Detailed review information	Delete this module The labor of this module must be reassigned as an duty for instructors
Photo	Increase the number of photographic equipment and personnel
Data capture registration	Implement a visual control system for applicants can identify which data capture staff was assigned Reduce the number of applicant teams by 15%; there is an excess
Print	Assign trays to classify admission forms by venue and incoming exam date; give recommendations by blocks of applicants

causes of the problem. The criteria considered for the cause-effect analysis based on 'why questions' about the possible causes of the problem:

1. Why is this a factor that causes the problem?
2. Why does that factor directly produce the problem?
3. If it is a direct cause, why has it not been eliminated to correct the problem?
4. Why is it not considered a feasible solution?
5. Why can not it assess if the solution worked?
6. Why is the solution a lower-cost solution?

Figure 1 presents a qualitative analysis applying an Ishikawa diagram. The analysis shows that continuous and frequent complaints are generated by time delays in activities at each phase impacting the value flow of the admission form exchange subprocess.

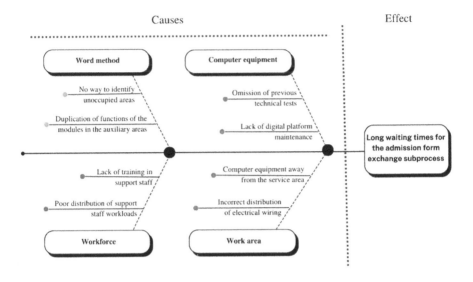

Fig. 1. Ishikawa diagram for the admission form exchange subprocess

Once the main problems that affect the admission form exchange subprocess have been identified, an improvement analysis was applied through Lean tools. LO tools helps to develop ideas that can be implemented to increase the value flow through continuous improvement of the admission process. Next section describes and discusses the results of the improvement analysis using LO for admission form exchange subprocess.

4   Results and Discussion

This section describes the results of the LO approach to identify *muda* for the admission form exchange subprocess, and a specific case study is described for the 2019–2020 admission process of UAEM.

4.1   Studied Case

The analysis of the admission was carried out in person, to learn about the current procedures of the admission form exchange subprocess operated during the 2019–2020 period. UAEM carried out the admission process simultaneously in four locations (campuses). Information from the North campus, located in Cuernavaca, Morelos, was considered, since this campus has a higher demand for admission (12 395 applicants in 2020). The college tuition in the North campus is 5 075 new students to be accepted into the university for the 2020–2021 term.

4.2   Results and Discussion

The admission form exchange subprocess was analyzed using the *muda* identification method, and Ishikawa and Pareto diagrams. These tools help understanding processes failures and the relations between the facts and the possible causes. Lean tools provide a perspective on the analyzed process that will propose improvements to deploy for process higher performance. The score to qualify each cause considers a scale between 1 and 3. Value 3 is equivalent to a more significant benefit, and value 1 to a lower benefit. The evaluated criteria and their respective solutions are listed on Table 5.

Table 5. Evaluated criteria and their respective solutions

#	Causes	Solution
1	Lack of activities distribution of the process	Merge phase 2 with the documents reception
2	Lack of visual support communication	Apply Kanban to the LO process
3	Lack of maintenance to the computer system	Provide technical support and maintenance to the computer system
4	Omission of previous computer system technical tests	Carry out preliminary simulations of the process
5	Poor planning of personnel management	Implement Heinjunka to level the LO process
6	Poor management of staff during the process	Implement cross-training based on the Pull LO System
7	Distribution of communication network by cable	Restructure the communication network installation
8	Poor distribution of computer equipment	Redistribution of the computer equipment for data capturer staff

Table 6 shows the assessment analysis of the criteria evaluated: problem factor (*PF*), direct cause (*DC*), solution (*SL*), feasible (*FE*), measurable (*ME*), and low cost (*LC*). The causes with the most benefit score are "Poor planning of personnel management" and "Poor management of staff during the process", and the cause with the lower benefit score is "Distribution of communication network by cable". The number of failures was measured during the in-person evaluation, and the number of events was counted.

Table 6. Assessment analysis of the criteria evaluated

# Cause	Criteria						Total
	PF	DC	SL	FE	ME	LC	
1	3	2	3	2	1	3	**13**
2	3	2	3	3	2	2	**14**
3	3	3	3	1	3	1	**14**
4	3	2	2	3	1	2	**12**
5	2	3	3	3	1	3	**15**
6	2	3	3	3	1	3	**15**
7	1	1	3	1	1	1	**8**
8	2	2	3	2	1	3	**13**

Figure 2 shows the critical phases of the admission form exchange subprocess reported by the admission services area. Critical phases presented failures in the activities developed in the admission process. The main failures identified are:

1. Staff carelessness when receiving documents
2. Reception staff carelessness due to lack of care in receiving documents
3. Reception staff carelessness in comparing the recorded admission form with information of the applicant
4. Photo equipment failure to take the photo
5. Printer failure

Fig. 2. Critical phases of the admission form exchange subprocess

The main failures detected in the admission process were not consecutive and occasionally a failure occurs due to factors unrelated to the process. The failures in sectors such as offices are not continuous, unlike failures in the manufacturing sector, which are consecutive. In this way, failures were measured to prioritize tasks that could assist in solving the main failures. In addition, Pareto analysis was performed to identify the frequency that a failure occurs in the admission process. Table 7 shows the frequency of failures in the admission form exchange subprocess.

Table 7. Frequency of failures that occurs in the admission form exchange subprocess

#	Failure	Frequency	Sum	Share	Sum
1	Digital database failure	135	135	34.09%	34.09%
2	Reception carelessness	99	234	25.00%	59.09%
3	Detail review careless	72	306	18.18%	77.27%
4	Printer failure	60	366	15.15%	92.42%
5	Entrance carelessness	30	396	7.57%	100.00%
	Total	**396**		**N/A**	**100.00**

Figure 3 shows the Pareto chart of the frequency of failures in the admission form exchange subprocess.

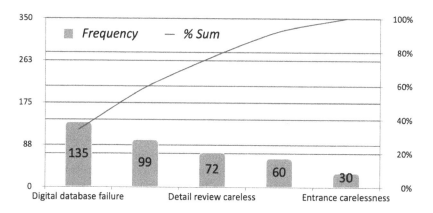

Fig. 3. Pareto chart of failures frequency in the admission process

Figure 3 shows that failures #1, #2, and #3 in Table 7 produce 80% of the problems in the admission form exchange subprocess. The analysis carried out using the Ishikawa diagram (Fig. 1) identifies that there is *i)* excess of time in the detailed review of the applicant information, *ii)* the phase does not have a sufficient number of cameras to satisfy all the demand in a reasonable time, *iii)* the Data Capture phase is deficient and confusing for applicants, and *iv)* the digital database usually has problems accessing concurrently, generating access time delays in next activities.

5   Conclusions and Future Work

This article presented a Lean methodology for *muda* identification in the admission form exchange subprocess of new university students in the smart campus context. The proposed Lean methodology combines Lean tools to identify mistakes generated in the admission process of UAEM, a case study in Mexico. The Lean methodology employed analysis tools, i.e., Ishikawa and Pareto diagrams.

The Lean tools helped understand process failures to improve the admission process. The main failures detected in the admission form exchange subprocess are: *i)* time excess on document detailed review activities, *ii)* high demand on photo taking in function with the number of photo equipment, *iii)* confusion by applicants to find the data capture staff location, and *iv)* concurrent access problems to the computer system. Also, the admission form exchange subprocess lacks standardization of subprocesses. Even though there is a standardized operation manual, the subprocesses are neglected. The methodology validation focused on evaluating the time saving of the admission form exchange subprocess by employing *muda* identification. The college tuition offered was of 5 075 new students to be accepted into the university for the 2020–2021 term. The number of applicants was 12 395 in 2020. The computed results indicate that the proposed Lean methodology is efficient for *muda* identification and for agile improvements for the admission form exchange subprocess in reasonable time.

The main lines for future work are oriented to extend the proposed Lean methodology to apply essential indicators, statistics, and Lean tools such as Failure Mode and Effect Analysis and Andon. In addition, those tools would be valuable for relevant research, such as standardizing processes through Digital Lean Manufacturing and Industry 4.0. Also, the proposed Lean methodology must be extended for the income educational offer for new students on all university campuses.

Acknowledgements. This work acknowledges Carlos Salvador Hernández Anzúrez of the Facultad de Ciencias Químicas e Ingeniería of Universidad Autónoma del Estado de Morelos (UAEM) for his participation in the development of the work.

References

1. Bhamu, J., Singh, K.: Lean manufacturing: literature review and research issues. Int. J. Oper. Prod. Manage. **34**(7), 876–940 (2014)
2. Chen, J., Cox, R.: Value stream management for lean office-a case study. Am. J. Ind. Bus. Manag. **2**, 17–29 (2012)
3. Cheong, P., Nyaupane, P.: Smart campus communication, internet of things, and data governance: understanding student tensions and imaginaries. Big Data Soc. **9**(1) (2022). https://journals.sagepub.com/doi/pdf/10.1177/20539517221092656
4. Greef, A., Romanel, F., Do Carmo, M.: Lean Office: Operação, Gerenciamento e Tecnologias. Atlas Editora (2012)
5. Hicks, B.: Lean information management: understanding and eliminating waste. Int. J. Inf. Manage. **27**(4), 233–249 (2007)
6. Liker, J.: The Toyota Way: 14 Management Principles From the World's Greatest Manufacturer. McGraw-Hill Education (2003)
7. Locher, D., Benavent, E.: Lean office: Metodología Lean en servicios generales, comerciales y administrativos. Profit Editorial (2017)

8. Magalhães, J., Alves, A., Costa, N., Rodrigues, A.: Improving processes in a post-graduate office of a university through lean office tools. Int. J. Qual. Res. **13**, 797–810 (2019)
9. Monteiro, J., Alves, A., Carvalho, M.: Processes improvement applying lean office tools in a logistic department of a car multimedia components company. Proc. Manuf. **13**, 995–1002 (2017)
10. Rossit, D.A., Toncovich, A., Rossit, D.G., Nesmachnow, S.: Flow shop scheduling problems in industry 4.0 production environments: missing operation case. In: Hussain, C.M., Di Sia, P. (eds.) Handbook of Smart Materials, Technologies, and Devices, pp. 1–23. Springer, Cham (2021). https://doi.org/10.1007/978-3-030-58675-1_71-1
11. Sabur, V., Simatupang, T.: Improvement of customer response time using lean office. Int. J. Serv. Oper. Manage. **20**(1), 59–85 (2015)
12. Tapping, D., Shuker, T.: Value Stream Management for the Lean Office: Eight Steps to Planning, Mapping, & Sustaining Lean Improvements in Administrative Areas. Taylor & Francis (2018)
13. Ustundag, A., Cevikcan, E.: Industry 4.0: Managing the Digital Transformation (2018)
14. Van Deursen, A., Mossberger, K.: Any thing for anyone? A new digital divide in internet-of-things skills. Policy Internet **10**(2), 122–140 (2018)
15. Wang, J.: Lean Manufacturing: Business Bottom-Line Based, 1st edn. CRC Press, Boca Raton (2010)
16. Womack, J., Jones, D.: Lean Thinking: Banish Waste and Create Wealth in Your Corporation. Simon & Schuster, UK (2013)
17. Womack, J., Jones, D., Roos, D.: La máquina que cambió el mundo: La historia de la Producción Lean, el arma secreta de Toyota que revolucióno la industria mundial del automóvil. Profit Editorial (2017)
18. Yokoyama, T., Oliveira, M., Futami, A.: A systematic literature review on lean office. Industr. Eng. Manage. Syst. **18**, 67–77 (2019)

Smart Mobility for Public Transportation Systems: Improved Bus Timetabling for Synchronizing Transfers

Claudio Risso[1], Sergio Nesmachnow[1], and Diego Rossit[2]

[1] Universidad de la República, Montevideo, Uruguay
{crisso,sergion}@fing.edu.uy
[2] Department of Engineering, INMABB, Universidad Nacional del Sur-CONICET, Bahía Blanca, Argentina
diego.rossit@uns.edu.uy

Abstract. Providing an efficient public transportation system is a key issue to increase the livability and sustainability of modern cities. This article addresses the bus timetabling problem for enhancing multi-leg trips or transfers. For this purpose, a mixed-integer programming model is proposed, aimed at maximizing the amount of transfers while considering budgetary and quality of service constraints. The proposed model is evaluated on real scenarios from the case study of the public transportation system in Montevideo, Uruguay. Results indicate that the solutions of the proposed model outperforms the current timetable used in the city in terms of number of transfers, cost, and number of required buses.

Keywords: Public transportation · Timetable synchronization · Transfers · Quality of service · MILP model

1 Introduction

Smart mobility is a key component of smart cities [7]. Smart mobility is based on the design and operation of intelligent transportation networks, by applying innovative technologies and planning/management methods.

A crucial problem for administrations is the increasing number of automobiles and other private non-sustainable transportation modes, which prevent a correct preservation of the environment [19,27]. For addressing this problem, the smart mobility paradigm heavily relies on public transportation systems, using efficient motor vehicles, electric vehicles, and other innovative transportation modes. The main goal is to promote a behavioral change of citizens, towards lowering private car ownership, reducing pollution, traffic congestion, and other related issues.

Public transportation is recognized as one of the key services for smart mobility in smart cities [9,18]. A proper design and operation of public transportation systems is crucial to guarantee efficient mobility. Important related problems include route design, timetabling and planning, drivers scheduling, etc., whose

S. Nesmachnow and L. Hernández Callejo (Eds.): ICSC-CITIES 2022, CCIS 1706, pp. 158–172, 2023.
https://doi.org/10.1007/978-3-031-28454-0_11

main goals are providing citizens a proper travel experience [3] and promoting sustainability [10]. The problem of designing timetables for public transportation systems is a crucial issue within the transit planning process. Timetable definition involves determining bus trip frequencies for a given operation period. An important subproblem of the timetabling problem is synchronizing multi-leg trips or *transfers*, which allows providing passengers adequate waiting times for transfers from one bus route to another.

Synchronizing timetables has been identified as a very difficult problem within public transportation planning and optimization [2]. Usually, experienced bus operators and planners define ad-hoc intuitive solutions that provide reasonable quality of service (QoS) to citizens. Our previous articles proposed exact and metaheuristic methods for an extended variant of the timetable synchronization problem, considering extended transfer zones [15,21,22].

In this line of work, this article presents a mathematical formulation of the timetable synchronization problem with the main goal of maximizing the number of transfers, while considering specific constraints for the minimal QoS and the available budget. The proposed model improves over our previous works [21,22] by including specific models for the cost of each bus trip, considering vehicle-time and vehicle-distance variables, and a model to assess the QoS provided by the public transportation system to users that perform direct trips (no transfers). A Mixed-Integer Linear Programming (MILP) model is proposed for solving realistic problems by taking advantage of modern high performance computing infrastructures.

The proposed problem formulation is evaluated on a real case study, considering 25 scenarios defined with real data of the public transportation system in Montevideo, Uruguay. The main results demonstrate that the proposed model is able to compute accurate solutions, significantly improving over the current timetable in Montevideo regarding synchronized transfers, while guaranteeing a proper cost and QoS for directs trips.

This article is organized as follows. Section 2 describes the Bus Synchronization Problem (BSP), its mathematical formulation, and reviews relevant related works. The case study is described in Sect. 3. Section 4 reports the experimental evaluation performed on a set of real-world instances. Finally, the conclusions and main lines for future work lines are outlined in Sect. 5.

2 The Bus Synchronization Problem

This section describes the BSP model and reviews related work. The problem data, the mathematical formulation, and the cost model are also described.

2.1 Conceptual Problem Model

The problem proposes finding the best configuration of headways (i.e., intervals between consecutive trips of the same line) for each line to optimize the number of transfers. Transfers are only effective when two trips are synchronized. A synchronization is achieved when not only the passenger has enough time to walk from the bus stop in which he has got off the first trip to the stop in which he has to take the second trip, but also when the waiting time at the bus stop for the second trip is not larger than a certain threshold that guarantees a minimum QoS for passengers. The schedule is defined over a reference interval, within which, relevant data for the problem –such as buses traveling times between points and the number of passengers per unit of time– is steady and has a uniform distribution. Considering reference intervals within which certain parameters are constant is common in the related literature [8,11] and allows making the complex timetabling problem more tractable and, thus, to obtain (near) optimal plannings in a period of interest (e.g., peak hours of the system).

The problem does not assume a prefixed number of trips per line. It only considers that headways must be within minimum and maximum values that are pre-established for each bus line. Additionally, the estimated cost of the bus schedule is limited by a maximum budget that the decision makers are willing to spend. The cost of the bus schedules is affected by the working times of drivers and the distances traveled by buses, as explained in Sect. 2.5.

The reference QoS model combines random boarding with deterministic alighting. The Poisson process is the de-facto reference for independent and identically distributed random arrivals. Due to the regularity hypothesis along the planning period, the Poisson process is assumed of fixed rate. Thus, given the per-line average daily number of tickets ts_i sold by line i within the planning period $[0, T]$, $\Lambda_i = ts_i/T$ is the rate of boardings to the whole set of running buses of that line. The process actually alludes to the number of passengers arriving to some bus stop in order to be picked up, but the number of stops is large enough to refer to both processes as equivalent. Per-line descents are assumed fixed in this model. Let L_i be the traveling distance of passengers of line i. The average speed V_i of buses of line i is also known. Therefore, the time each passenger rides a bus before alighting is simply $td_i = L_i/V_i$. All the buses of each line i start their trips empty and they receive passengers along the route. Since the alighting time is fixed, buses only load new passengers along the interval $[0, td_i]$ (the ramp-up period). The end-to-end travel time $T2E_i$ for buses of line i is also known, i.e., it is computed from Global Positioning System (GPS) records on each bus. For consistency, the model assumes that there is also a ramp-down period at the end $[T2E_i - td_i, T2E_i]$ where no passengers board. Finally, the QoS model assumes fixed headways F^i for every line i. If the passengers of that line arrived along the entire end-to-end travel time, the arrival rate of each bus is $\Lambda_i \cdot F^i/T2E_i$. However, to preserve the expected number of tickets sold, the rate must be adjusted to $\overline{\Lambda_i} = \Lambda_i \cdot F^i/(T2E_i - td_i)$, because of the ramp-down period.

The previous model was implemented by means of an ad-hoc discrete event simulator. A sample distribution of passengers over a bus is sketched in Fig. 1.

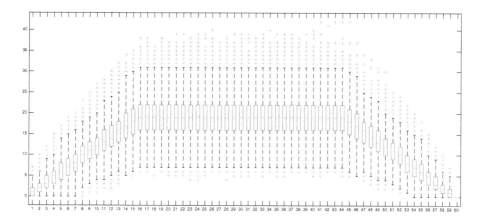

Fig. 1. Sample boxplot of a bus occupation along a 60 min end-to-end travel with $td_i = 16\,\text{min}$ and $\overline{\Lambda_i} = \frac{9}{8}\,\text{min}^{-1}$, after 10,000 simulations. (Color figure online)

In Fig. 1, red crosses are samples identified as outliers. Regarding occupation, higher outliers (those placed above upper whiskers) were discarded. The considered QoS objective is that the whiskers are at most in the capacity of the buses, which is 65 passengers for the considered case study. So, for each line i, higher F^i values are explored until an upper whisker attains the limit of passengers. Let $\overline{F^i}$ be the maximum headway complying the target QoS for line i.

2.2   Related Work

Bus timetabling has been addressed in the related literature under different criteria [11]. The most common optimization criteria are: minimizing the waiting time of users, minimizing the fleet size and travel time of buses, and maximizing the load factor of buses. However, few works considered setting frequencies to optimize the synchronization between buses or with other mobility means [11]. Moreover, being a problem which is recognized as computationally complex problem, works which use exact approaches to solve BSP are quite scarce.

Synchronizations improve as trips schedules promote buses with relaying passengers to arrive at times that allow convenient transfers to other buses. A convenient transfer simultaneously satisfies having waiting times short enough to provide good QoS for passengers but also long enough to allow passengers to move from one line to another [8]. Thus, the Synchronization Bus Problem consists in determining the departure time of every bus trip to maximize the synchronization of different bus lines of a network.

Ibarra and Rios [12] presented a MILP formulation for solving small instances. Due to the NP-hard of the problem, large instances are intractable with this model. Fouilhoux et al. [8] presented a plain MILP formulation with the addition of valid inequalities to solve a problem in which the number of trips per bus line is fixed. They proved that the valid inequalities are able to provide a stronger formulation of the problem allowing to address practical instances that cannot be solved with the plain MILP without these inequalities. Chu et al. [6] presented a more comprehensive model in which the primary objective is to reduce the travel time of the passengers from the origin to the destination and the bus synchronization is performed as a subordinated consequence in order to reduce the travel time. They proposed two mathematical formulations: a direct formulation like others in the literature and set-partitioning formulation. The set-partitioning formulation computed better results. Our previous article [22] addressed two different variants of the BSP for peak hours. In the first variant, regularly spaced departures of buses of the same line are considered (thus only the offset –departure of the first bus– has to be determined). In the second variant, the headways of consecutive departures of buses of the same bus line can vary within certain limits. Both variants were solved with an exact MILP formulation for real instances of the city of Montevideo, proposing buses schedules that clearly overcome in terms of number of synchronizations and average waiting times for transfers the real schedules used in the city.

This article contributes with a mathematical formulation for the timetable synchronization problem to maximize the number of transfers for users that are willing to perform multi-leg trips, while considering specific constraints regarding the QoS and the available budget. Thus, the proposed model improves over previous works [21, 22] through the inclusion of a specific cost model, which takes into account the distance and travel time of the buses, and a model to estimate the QoS that is provided to users that perform direct trips. Moreover, this problem is applied to realistic instances using an exact resolution approach.

2.3   Problem Data

The formulation of the studied problem considers the following datasets:

- The planning period $[0, T]$, expressed in minutes. It corresponds to a reference interval within which relevant data for the problem (traveling times, number of passengers. etc.) are steady and has a uniform distribution.
- A set of bus lines $I = \{i_1, \ldots, i_n\}$, whose routes are fixed and known beforehand. Each trip of a line has an also known end-to-end cost, c_i.
- This problem does not assume a prefixed number of trips per line. Instead, headways and offset values are to be determined within a range of minimum (h_i) and maximum (H_i) values for each line i. The upper bound for the number of trips of any line within the planning period is $f_i = \lceil \frac{T}{h_i} \rceil$.
- A set of *synchronization nodes*, or *transfer zones*, $B = \{b_1, \ldots, b_m\}$. Each transfer zone $b \in B$ has three elements $<i, j, d_b^{ij}>$: i and j are the lines to synchronize, whereas d_b^{ij} is the distance that separates the bus stops for lines

i and j in b. Each b considers two bus stops with registered transfer demand between lines i and j. The distance d_b^{ij} is expressed in time-units rather than distance, accounting for the time a passenger must walk to transfer from the bus stop of line i to the bus stop of line j in the considered transfer zone.

- A *traveling time function* $TT : I \times B \rightarrow \mathbf{Z}$. $TT_b^i = TT(i,b)$ defining the time that buses of line i need to travel to reach the transfer zone b. The time is measured from the departure of the line. The traveling time depends on the studied scenario and is affected by several factors such as the maximum allowed speed, the traffic in the city, the travel demands, etc., but it is considered fixed within the planning period.

- A *demand function* $P : I \times I \times B \rightarrow \mathbf{Z}$. $P_b^{ij} = P(i,j,b)$ defines how many passengers perform a transfer from line i to line j at transfer zone b along the entire $[0, T]$ period. As described previously in this subsection, a hypothesis of uniformity is assumed. Hence, the potential number of transfers between any two trips of lines i and j are proportional to the time between two consecutive trips of buses in line i, i.e., to headways of the line from whom passengers alight. As we see next, not every potential transfer is considered successful, among other conditions, because of the quality-of-service expectations of passengers. The uniform demand hypothesis is realistic for short periods, such as in the problem instances studied.

- The maximum time that passengers are willing to wait to board to line j, after alighting from line i and walking to the corresponding stop of line j at the transfer zone b, W_b^{ij}. Two trips of line i and j are synchronized for transfers if, and only if: i) passengers alighting from i get to the second bus stop in time to board the trip from line j; ii) waiting time of those passengers standing there to transfer between lines is lower or equal to W_b^{ij}; and iii) all of these events happen within the planning period.

- The number of trips for line i to fulfill the QoS occupation goal, $N_i = \lceil T/\overline{F^i} \rceil$.

2.4   Problem Formulation

Control variables in this problem are those in the set of departing times X_r^i of each trip r of every line i. Given any line i, the *headways* of the line are the times between consecutive trips. They can be easily derived from control variables using the expression $F_r^i = (X_r^i - X_{r-1}^i)$. Without losing generality, the model assumes $X_0^i = 0$, so the *offset* of a line i (departure time of the first trip of that line) is F_1^i, which matches X_1^i. Headway values must be within a range of minimum (h_i) and maximum (H_i) values for that line.

Since the number of trips of a line is a-priori unknown, control variables for trips are indexed from 1 to the upper bound $f_i = \lceil \frac{T}{h_i} \rceil$. Trips whose departing time are greater than T are not scheduled in the solution.

The mathematical model of the considered BSP variant as MILP problem is formulated in Eq. 1.

$$\max \quad \sum_{b \in B} (\sum_{r=1}^{f_i} \sum_{s=1}^{f_j} Z_{rsb}^{ij}) \cdot \frac{P_b^{ij} \times (X_r^i - X_{r-1}^i)}{T} \tag{1a}$$

$$\text{s.t.} \quad Z_{rsb}^{ij} \leq 1 + \frac{(A_{rb}^i + d_b^{ij} + W_b^{ij}) - A_{sb}^j}{M}, \qquad \begin{array}{l} \forall b = <i,j,d_b^{ij}> \in B, \\ 1 \leq r \leq f_i, 1 \leq s \leq f_j, \end{array} \tag{1b}$$

$$Z_{rsb}^{ij} \leq 1 + \frac{A_{sb}^j - (A_{rb}^i + d_b^{ij})}{M}, \qquad \begin{array}{l} \forall b = <i,j,d_b^{ij}> \in B, \\ 1 \leq r \leq f_i, 1 \leq s \leq f_j, \end{array} \tag{1c}$$

with $A_{rb}^i = X_r^i + TT_b^i$, $A_{sb}^j = X_s^j + TT_b^j$

$$\sum_{s=1}^{f_j} Z_{rsb}^{ij} \leq 1, \forall i,j \in I, 1 \leq r \leq f_i \tag{1d}$$

$$Q_r^i \leq 1 + \frac{T - X_r^i}{N}, \qquad \forall 1 \leq r \leq f_i, \tag{1e}$$

$$\frac{T + 1 - X_r^i}{T + 1} \leq Q_r^i, \qquad \forall 1 \leq r \leq f_i, \tag{1f}$$

$$Z_{rsb}^{ij} \leq Q_s^j, \qquad \begin{array}{l} \forall b = <i,j,d_b^{ij}> \in B, \\ 1 \leq r \leq f_i, 1 \leq s \leq f_j, \end{array} \tag{1g}$$

$$h_i \leq X_r^i - X_{r-1}^i, \qquad \forall r \in 2, .., f_i \tag{1h}$$

$$X_r^i - X_{r-1}^i \leq H_i, \qquad \forall r \in 2, .., f_i \tag{1i}$$

$$\sum_{r=1}^{f_i} Q_r^i \geq N_i, \qquad \forall i, 1 \leq i \leq n \tag{1j}$$

$$\sum_{i=1}^{n} c_i \cdot (\sum_{r=1}^{f_i} Q_r^i) \leq C \tag{1k}$$

$$0 \leq X_1^i \leq H_i \tag{1l}$$

$$Z_{rsb}^{ij}, Q_r^i \in \{0, 1\} \tag{1m}$$

The objective function (Eq. 1a) aims upon maximizing the total number of successful transfers along the planning period, which is accounted by adding up effective transfers between any combination of lines at every transfer zone. Because of the uniformity hypothesis, $P_b^{ij} \cdot (X_r^i - X_{r-1}^i)/T$ is the number of potential transfers from the r-th trip of line i to some trip of line j at zone b. passengers can only board into one of those trips, and not every passenger succeeds to board the next trip of a line j before awaiting its maximum tolerance W_b^{ij} at the relaying bus stop. These additional conditions are captured through Z_{rsb}^{ij} auxiliary binary variables that take the value 1 whenever the r-th trip of line i and the s-th trip of line j are synchronized at node b. Thus, $Z_{rsb}^{ij} \cdot P_b^{ij} \cdot (X_r^i - X_{r-1}^i)/T$ matches the number of successful transfers between trips r and s at b. Note that an active Z_{rsb}^{ij} increases the number of nonzero terms in the objective function, thus improving the overall result. In other words, the more variables where $Z_{rsb}^{ij} = 1$, the better. So, constraints are to be added in order to preserve consistency, i.e., to only account for successful transfers.

Equation 1b prevents Z_{rsb}^{ij} from taking the value 1 whenever passengers should wait longer than W_b^{ij} at zone b before the next trip of line j arrives. The expression A_{rb}^i corresponds to the alighting time to the zone b of passengers coming from line-i/trip-r, while A_{sb}^j is the time at which the s-th trip of line j arrives to this zone. So, $A_{rb}^i + d_b^{ij}$ is the time at which relaying passengers get to the next stop after walking, and that time should not exceed W_b^{ij} before the s-th trip reaches that point (i.e. A_{sb}^j). Whenever that does not hold, Z_{rsb}^{ij} must be lower than 1, ergo 0. The constant M is large enough to prevent the right-hand side to be lower than 0, what would make equations inconsistent. Complementarily, Eq. 1c inhibits Z_{rsb}^{ij} to be 1 if passengers of trip-r/line-i cannot reach the next bus stop at b in time to take the s-th line of j. In addition, Eq. 1d prevents from transfers to be accounted more than once.

It is not mandatory using all the available trips of each bus line. Unused trips are represented by a departing time beyond the planning horizon T. Considering that binary variable Q_r^i indicates whether trip r of line i is to be scheduled, Eq. 1e deactivates Q_r^i variables whose departure times X_r^i are greater than T, and Eq. 1f forces $Q_r^i = 1$ for those where $X_r^i \leq T$. Furthermore, transfers to unused trips are not accounted as synchronizations. This is guaranteed by Eq. 1g, which enforces variable Z_{rsb}^{ij} to be deactivated in line with the decision taken on variable Q_r^i.

Equation 1h and Eq. 1i force headways F_r^i to be within limits h_i and H_i, while Eq. 1l does the proper for offsets X_1^i. Equation 1m simply states the integrity of Z_{rsb}^{ij} and Q_r^i variables. Since the more trips scheduled, the higher the number of possible successful transfers, the number of trips is controlled through the operational cost. $\sum_{r=1}^{f_i} Q_r^i$ is the total number of trips scheduled for line i. Besides, the cost of each one of these trips is c_i. Therefore, the left-hand side of Eq. 1k matches the operational cost of the fleet, which must be limited to a parameter C. Consequently, the problem seeks for the maximum number of successful transfers within a reference period for a given operational budget. Conversely, lower bounds for the number of effective trips of each line are forced to prevent saturation of the capacity of buses, as it is described in Sect. 2.1. Equation 1j guarantees that the necessary minimum number of trips N_i is achieved.

Products $Z_{rsb}^{ij}(X_r^i - X_{r-1}^i)$ in the objective function make the formulation as that of a Mixed-Integer Quadratic Programming, what is nomerically undesirable. This issue is tackled by a change of variables and additional constraints. Let $y_{rsb}^{ij} = Z_{rsb}^{ij}(X_r^i - X_{r-1}^i)$, so the objective is $\frac{1}{T}\sum_{b\in B}\sum_{r=1}^{f_i}\sum_{s=1}^{f_j} y_{rsb}^{ij} \cdot P_b^{ij}$, which is linear. To guarantee both objective functions match after this change, two equations are added per-each y_{rsb}^{ij} variable: i) $y_{rsb}^{ij} \leq (X_r^i - X_{r-1}^i)$ and ii) $y_{rsb}^{ij} \leq H_i \cdot Z_{rsb}^{ij}$. Within a maximization problem, variables y_{rsb}^{ij} will take a value as high as possible. H_i is an upper bound for $(X_r^i - X_{r-1}^i)$ because of Eq. 1i, so, whenever $Z_{rsb}^{ij} = 1$, the second equation results $y_{rsb}^{ij} \leq H_i$ and it is the first equation that guarantees y's value to be $(X_r^i - X_{r-1}^i)$ at most, which is then exactly the value variable y_{rsb}^{ij} will take. Conversely, when $Z_{rsb}^{ij} = 0$, the second equation forces y_{rsb}^{ij} to be 0. This behavior replicates that of $Z_{rsb}^{ij}(X_r^i - X_{r-1}^i)$ product, so the change of variables turns the problem into a linear one.

2.5 Cost Model

The complexity of the cost models considered in public transportation systems varies significantly, depending on the specific purposes of the model [1]. This article focuses on the tactical problem of defining the headways of the bus schedule. Thus, the layout of the bus lines is not affected. For cases in which the layout of the bus lines is fixed, costs functions that are composed by the linear aggregation of different unitary costs per key parameters, such as the time the buses on road or the distance they travel have been extensively used in the related literature [16,17,26]. Moreover, these linear functions are usually used by practitioners [25]. Thus, a cost function related to vehicle-time and vehicle-distance variables is applied.

Vehicle-Time. Some operating costs such as the salaries of the drivers, which usually represents a large proportion of the total operating cost, and hours of administrative supervision are directly linked to the amount of vehicle hours. Thus, these expenses are appropriately allocated to vehicle hours. Moreover, the use of vehicle hours is usually a surrogate for working hours of employees in cost allocation models since it is much easier to compute [5].

Vehicle-Distance. Among the several operating costs which are related directly to the distance traveled by buses are the fuel, oil, tires and other vehicle maintenance expenses. These models are so-called allocation cost models, where key operating expense items are allocated to a specific operating statistic, such as vehicle-time or vehicle-distance [4]. Several linear costs models also consider the number of buses or the fleet size [17] or, more specifically, the number of buses required to cover the demand on peak hours (generally different to off-peak hours) [5]. The model considered in this article aims at analyzing short time windows in peak hours and, thus, the size of the fleet is considered as fixed. Furthermore, the case study solved is also an example of a public transportation system that operates with a rather fixed-size fleet, since the acquisition of new buses occurs each five years or more. The cost function used in this article is $Cost = U_{VH}VH + U_{VKM}VKM$ where VH and VM are the hours and distance that buses are used, respectively. U_{VH} and U_{VKM} are the unitary costs per hour and kilometer respectively.

Operating Costs in the Public Transportation System of Montevideo. The different expenses of the bus system in Montevideo are regularly analyzed by the local authorities to estimate the tariff per kilometer, which is used as input information for defining the amount of the state subsidies that are received by the system. In Montevideo, there are different types of subsidies. Two of the most important subsidies are the reduced price of fuel for the bus system and the reduced ticket for specific target users (students, pensioners, frequent commuters, etc.). Subsidies strongly influence the impact of each cost item in the cost structure of the system. For example, the reduced price of fuel provokes that the impact of this item in the cost structure is remarkably lower than it is in other bus systems just explaining 5% of the total estimated cost in Montevideo [13] against 13% in other similar systems [1]. However, the reduced price for fuel represents a large expense for the Uruguayan state. In the last years, the city of Montevideo has started to replace diesel buses with electric buses (e-buses) [10]. Shifting to electric buses is an environmentally friendly policy which involves the reduction of fossil fuels consumption [24] and greenhouse gases emission of the system [28].

Two of the main costs in the system are the salary of drivers and the fuel and/or electricity (if the system uses e-buses). Thus, these two costs are considered associated with the vehicles-hours in the case of salary of drivers and vehicle-distance in the case of fuel and/or electricity (parameters U_{VH} and U_{VKM}) The salary of the drivers is approximately 9.2 USD per hour (8 USD of the basic wage and 1.2 USD of social charges). Regarding the fuel, the average consumption of fuel for a typical diesel bus in the system of Montevideo is 0.396 liters per km [13] and the cost per liter of fuel in the city is about 1.6 USD per liter.

3   Case Study: The Public Transportation System in Montevideo, Uruguay

In Montevideo, Uruguay, the public transportation system is under the Metropolitan Transportation System (STM) [23]. The STM was proposed to integrate in a common system all the public transportation of Montevideo and its metropolitan area, including all urban agglomerations around Montevideo located in nearby departments of Canelones and San José.

STM introduced new technologies that allow a more efficient public transportation. One of the most significant technologies introduced by the STM was the use of a smart card to pay for trips [14]. The smart card allows gathering relevant data and also extracting useful knowledge about the mobility patterns of citizens of Montevideo [22].

STM provides two main alternatives for passengers to get to their destination. On the one hand, the traditional *direct* (i.e., end-to-end) trips. On the other hand, multi-leg trips (*transfers*) either under the 'one hour' or 'two hours' tickets, are enabled by the STM card. The system stores historical data about both direct and transfer trips, tickets sold, and also several other relevant data, including GPS records for each bus [14]. Using these data, official and third-party apps have been designed to provide accurate information and interact with users.

Overall, the STM comprises 145 main lines, more than one thousand line variants, and approximately five thousand bus stops in three departments. This numbers are remarkable large for a city like Montevideo, and highlights the importance of a proper planning for providing a good QoS for citizens that use public transportation.

4   Experimental Evaluation

This section presents the computational experimentation performed over real-world instances of the city of Montevideo is presented, including the implementation details, a description of the set of instances, and the report and analysis of the results obtained.

4.1   Methodology

The main details of the methodology applied in the experimental evaluation are presented next.

Implementation Details. The proposed MILP formulation for the BSP was implemented in IBM ILOG CPLEX Interactive Optimizer 12.6.3.0. A C program was developed to convert problem instances (in .csv format) to the LP-format used by CPLEX. Matlab version R2015a-8.5.0 was used for the pre-processing, analysis, and post-processing of the computed solutions. The ad-hoc discrete event simulator used for the reference QoS model was also developed in Matlab.

Problem Instances. The computational experimentation was performed over 25 instances built using real information of the city of Montevideo. For building the problem instances several sources of information were used. The bus lines description, routes, timetables, and bus stop locations in the city were retrieved from the National Open Catalog of Uruguay. The information regarding transfers was provided by Intendencia de Montevideo and processed applying a urban data analysis approach [14]. The considered period is the rush hour at midday (12:00 to 14:00) [19]. The demand function is computed from transfers information registered by smart cards used to sell tickets. The synchronization points are chosen according to their demand, i.e., the pairs of bus stops with the largest number of registered transfers for the period are selected; the bus lines correspond to the lines passing by the synchronization points.

The instances include 30 synchronization points, randomly selected from the most demanded transfer zones for the considered period in the city (a total number of 170 zones). The time traveling function TT for each line is computed empirically by using GPS data. The walking time function is the estimated walking speed of a person (6 km/h) multiplied by the distance between bus stops in each transfer zone computed using geospatial information about stops. The maximum waiting time is equal to λH, with $\lambda \in [0.3, 0.5, 0.7, 0.9, 1]$, to configure instances with different levels of tolerance/QoS.

The name of the problem instances is NL.λ.id. NL is the number of bus lines, λ is the coefficient applied to the waiting time of the line in percentage, and *id* is a relative identifier for instances with the same NL and λ.

Execution Platform. The computational experimentation was performed in an HP ProLiant DL380 G9 high end server with two Intel Xeon Gold 6138 processors (20 cores each) and 128 GB RAM, from the high performance computing infrastructure of National Supercomputing Center, Uruguay (Cluster-UY) [20].

Comparison with Current Real Situation. A relevant baseline for comparison is the current timetable (CT) applied in the transportation system of Montevideo (the real timetable). The metrics for comparing the MILP solutions and the CT are: i) the number of transfers, as is proposed in the objective function ii) the cost of the bus schedule, and iii) the number of buses required for the solution.

4.2   Numerical Results

Results of the MILP model and the comparison to the baseline CT in Montevideo are presented in Table 1. The Table reports three metrics: from left to right, the number of successful transfers, the cost of the bus schedule in monetary units and the number of buses required for operation of the computed schedule. For each metric, the value computed by the MILP model, the CT of the city and the percentage of improvement of MILP over CT (*impr.*) are reported.

Table 1. Results of the MILP model and comparison to CT in Montevideo.

Instance	Successful transfers			Cost			Number of buses		
	MILP	CT	impr.	MILP	CT	impr.	MILP	CT	impr.
37.30.1	298.99	110.40	170.82%	8,711.71	8,721.80	−0.12%	442	439	0.68%
37.50.1	308.88	175.67	75.83%	8,713.82	8,721.80	−0.09%	435	439	−0.91%
37.70.1	310.22	236.18	31.35%	8,679.70	8,721.80	−0.48%	437	439	−0.46%
37.90.1	310.55	263.41	17.90%	8,687.76	8,721.80	−0.39%	433	439	−1.37%
37.100.1	311.37	263.41	18.21%	8,697.71	8,721.80	−0.28%	436	439	−0.68%
40.30.0	239.38	92.19	159.66%	8,566.40	8,592.64	−0.31%	423	419	0.95%
40.30.4	262.24	106.48	146.28%	7,943.69	8,717.53	−8.88%	388	428	−9.35%
40.50.0	243.73	136.12	79.06%	8,387.31	8,592.64	−2.39%	399	419	−4.77%
40.50.4	264.65	134.54	96.71%	8,706.01	8,717.53	−0.13%	427	428	−0.23%
40.70.0	244.37	184.56	32.41%	8,546.13	8,592.64	−0.54%	431	419	2.86%
40.70.4	268.98	198.87	35.25%	8,717.16	8,717.53	0.00%	429	428	0.23%
40.90.0	245.36	209.02	17.39%	8,529.95	8,592.64	−0.73%	420	419	0.24%
40.90.4	270.98	224.82	20.53%	8,103.04	8,717.53	−7.05%	403	428	−5.84%
40.100.0	243.83	209.02	16.65%	8,568.87	8,592.64	−0.28%	426	419	1.67%
40.100.4	270.57	226.72	19.34%	7,634.73	8,717.53	−12.42%	374	428	−12.62%
41.30.2	280.97	102.65	173.72%	9,173.49	10,056.59	−8.78%	421	471	−10.62%
41.50.2	287.73	158.69	81.32%	9,924.92	10,056.59	−1.31%	468	471	−0.64%
41.70.2	286.14	213.11	34.27%	9,997.24	10,056.59	−0.59%	470	471	−0.21%
41.90.2	288.25	243.96	18.15%	9,155.90	10,056.59	−8.96%	426	471	−9.55%
41.100.2	289.41	244.42	18.41%	10,054.34	10,056.59	−0.02%	477	471	1.27%
42.30.3	271.61	98.26	176.42%	10,384.46	10,410.35	−0.25%	479	485	−1.24%
42.50.3	274.48	150.73	82.10%	10,392.92	10,410.35	−0.17%	490	485	1.03%
42.70.3	276.15	203.04	36.01%	10,397.22	10,410.35	−0.13%	496	485	2.27%
42.90.3	271.53	227.72	19.24%	10,376.56	10,410.35	−0.32%	483	485	−0.41%
42.100.3	277.68	228.30	21.63%	10,351.95	10,410.35	−0.56%	499	485	2.89%

Results in Table 1 report that the MILP model was able to outperform the CT in all the studied instances, in terms of number of transfers. In average, the MILP model computed solutions with 63.95% more transfers than CT, and up to 176.42% for instance 42.30.3. Regarding the budgetary expenses, the MILP model managed to make a proper use of the resources. Schedules obtained with the MILP model have a smaller cost in 24 out of 25 instances (obtaining an average cost reduction of 2.21% and a maximum reduction of 12.42% for instance 40.100.4). In terms of the required number of buses, the solutions computed by the MILP model required 1.79% less buses on average and up to 12.62% less buses (for instance 40.100.4) than the current timetables applied in the city. These results confirm that the MILP model computed accurate and efficient schedules, both form the QoS and economic/resource utilization points of view.

Table 2 reports the average values of the three considered metrics. Instances are grouped by the values of λ used to model different tolerance levels regarding the considered maximum waiting time W_b. This is a useful analysis to determine the capabilities of the proposed model to compute accurate solutions under tighter QoS thresholds for transfers.

Table 2. Average improvements of MILP solutions over CT for each value of λ

λ	Transfers	Cost	Number of buses
0.3	165.38%	−3.67%	−3.91%
0.5	83.00%	−0.82%	−1.10%
0.7	33.86%	−0.35%	0.94%
0.9	18.64%	−3.49%	−3.39%
1	18.85%	−2.71%	−1.49%

Results in Table 2 indicate that, in terms of transfers, the MILP model was able to compute significantly better solutions than CT with smaller values of λ. The reason for this result is that the current timetables are not designed to promote or offer a better QoS to transfers. In addition, instances with a tighter threshold for waiting times pose a significantly more difficult challenge to practitioners to obtain manual solutions to the problem. The reason for this is that a smaller number of synchronizations will be considered successful since the time spent at the bus stop by the user waiting for the second bus exceeds the tolerance of the user. In this context, computer aided decision-making support tools, as the proposed MILP, contribute to successfully explore the solution space and obtain better solutions in these restricted instances.

Overall, results show that the computed solutions allow improving the QoS provided to passengers that perform transfers in the public transportation system of Montevideo. The QoS improvements are computed without increasing the overall operation cost of using additional resources.

5   Conclusions and Future Work

This article presented a MILP approach for bus timetabling to enhance multi-leg trips. The optimization proposes maximizing the number of successful transfers, while considering constraints on the QoS and the deployment cost.

The model was evaluated over a set of 25 real-world instances from the public transportation system in Montevideo, Uruguay, considering different numbers of bus lines and different threshold values for the maximum waiting time of users that transfer. The results evince that numerical solutions outperformed the current timetables used in Montevideo in terms of the number of effective transfers (up to 176.42%), the total cost necessary to implement those schedules (up to 12.42%) and the number of buses to be used (up to 12.62%). Regarding transfers, the improvement of the numerically aided solutions over the manually crafted timetables increases as the problem becomes more restricted (smaller threshold value for the maximum allowable waiting time of users).

Overall, results show that schedules computed with the MIP model can efficiently use the available resources, since they have a larger number of successful transfers with similar budgets and a lesser number of running buses than the current–manually crafted–timetable.

The main lines for future work are related to include the cost to deploy the bus fleet as an optimization objective in a multi-objective approach, and including new technologies (i.e., electric buses) in the proposed model, with corresponding control variables to assess the convenience of using electric buses for some lines.

References

1. Avenali, A., Boitani, A., Catalano, G., D'Alfonso, T., Matteucci, G.: Assessing standard costs in local public bus transport: a hybrid cost model. Transp. Policy **62**, 48–57 (2018)
2. Ceder, A., Tal, O.: Timetable synchronization for buses. In: Wilson, N.H.M. (ed.) Computer-Aided Transit Scheduling. Lecture Notes in Economics and Mathematical Systems, vol. 471, pp. 245–258. Springer, Heidelberg (1999). https://doi.org/10.1007/978-3-642-85970-0_12
3. Ceder, A., Wilson, N.: Bus network design. Transp. Rese. Part B: Methodol. **20**(4), 331–344 (1986)
4. Cherwony, W., Gleichman, G., Porter, B., Hamilton, B.: Bus route costing procedures: a review. Urban Mass Transportation Administration (1981)
5. Cherwony, W., Mundle, S.: Peak-base cost allocation models. Transp. Res. Rec. **663**(663), 52–56 (1978)
6. Chu, J., Korsesthakarn, K., Hsu, Y., Wu, H.: Models and a solution algorithm for planning transfer synchronization of bus timetables. Transp. Res. Part E: Logist. Transp. Rev. **131**, 247–266 (2019)
7. Deakin, M., Al Waer, H.: From intelligent to smart cities. Intell. Build. Int. **3**(3), 140–152 (2011)
8. Fouilhoux, P., Ibarra, O., Kedad, S., Rios, Y.: Valid inequalities for the synchronization bus timetabling problem. Eur. J. Oper. Res. **251**(2), 442–450 (2016)
9. Grava, S.: Urban Transportation Systems: Choices for Communities. McGraw-Hill (2002)
10. Hipogrosso, S., Nesmachnow, S.: Analysis of sustainable public transportation and mobility recommendations for Montevideo and Parque Rodó neighborhood. Smart Cities **3**(2), 479–510 (2020)
11. Ibarra, O., Delgado, F., Giesen, R., Muñoz, J.: Planning, operation, and control of bus transport systems: a literature review. Transp. Res. Part B: Methodol. **77**, 38–75 (2015)

12. Ibarra, O., Rios, Y.: Synchronization of bus timetabling. Transp. Res. Part B: Methodol. **46**(5), 599–614 (2012)
13. Marquez, G.: Informe sobre tarifas y subsidios a usuarios del sistema de transporte público de pasajeros de Montevideo (2019)
14. Massobrio, R., Nesmachnow, S.: Urban mobility data analysis for public transportation systems: a case study in Montevideo, Uruguay. Appl. Sci. **10**(16), 5400 (2020)
15. Massobrio, R., Nesmachnow, S., Muraña, J., Dorronsoro, B.: Learning to optimize timetables for efficient transfers in public transportation systems. Appl. Soft Comput. **119**, 108616 (2022)
16. Mehran, B., Yang, Y., Mishra, S.: Analytical models for comparing operational costs of regular bus and semi-flexible transit services. Public Transp. **12**(1), 147–169 (2020). https://doi.org/10.1007/s12469-019-00222-z
17. Mishra, S., Mehran, B., Sahu, P.: Assessment of delivery models for semi-flexible transit operation in low-demand conditions. Transp. Policy **99**, 275–287 (2020)
18. Nesmachnow, S., Baña, S., Massobrio, R.: A distributed platform for big data analysis in smart cities: combining intelligent transportation systems and socioeconomic data for Montevideo, Uruguay. EAI Endors. Trans. Smart Cities **2**(5), 1–18 (2017)
19. Nesmachnow, S., Hipogrosso, S.: Transit oriented development analysis of Parque Rodó neighborhood, Montevideo, Uruguay. World Dev. Sustain. **1**, 100017 (2022)
20. Nesmachnow, S., Iturriaga, S.: Cluster-UY: collaborative scientific high performance computing in Uruguay. In: Torres, M., Klapp, J. (eds.) ISUM 2019. CCIS, vol. 1151, pp. 188–202. Springer, Cham (2019). https://doi.org/10.1007/978-3-030-38043-4_16
21. Nesmachnow, S., Muraña, J., Goñi, G., Massobrio, R., Tchernykh, A.: Evolutionary approach for bus synchronization. In: Crespo-Mariño, J.L., Meneses-Rojas, E. (eds.) CARLA 2019. CCIS, vol. 1087, pp. 320–336. Springer, Cham (2020). https://doi.org/10.1007/978-3-030-41005-6_22
22. Nesmachnow, S., Risso, C.: Exact and evolutionary algorithms for synchronization of public transportation timetables considering extended transfer zones. Appl. Sci. **11**(15), 7138 (2021)
23. Risso, C., Nesmachnow, S.: Designing a backbone trunk for the public transportation network in Montevideo, Uruguay. In: Nesmachnow, S., Hernández Callejo, L. (eds.) ICSC-CITIES 2019. CCIS, vol. 1152, pp. 228–243. Springer, Cham (2020). https://doi.org/10.1007/978-3-030-38889-8_18
24. Rossit, D., Nesmachnow, S., Toutouh, J.: Multiobjective design of sustainable public transportation systems. In: CEUR Workshop Proceedings, vol. 2858, pp. 152–159 (2021)
25. Sinner, M., Weidmann, U., Nash, A.: Application of a cost-allocation model to swiss bus and train lines. Transp. Res. Rec. **2672**(8), 431–442 (2018)
26. Taylor, B., Garrett, M., Iseki, H.: Measuring cost variability in provision of transit service. Transp. Res. Rec. **1735**(1), 101–112 (2000)
27. Tolley, R. (ed.): Sustainable Transport. Elsevier, Amsterdam (2003)
28. Toutouh, J., Nesmachnow, S., Rossit, D.: Generative adversarial networks to model air pollution under uncertainty. In: CEUR Workshop Proceedings, vol. 2858, pp. 169–174 (2021)

Classification of Polyethylene Terephthalate Bottles in a Recycling Plant

Diego Alberto Godoy[1](✉) ⓘ, Enrique Marcelo Albornoz[2] ⓘ, Ricardo Selva[1] ⓘ,
Nicolas Ibarra[1] ⓘ, and Cesar Gallardo[1] ⓘ

[1] Centro de Investigación en Tecnologías de la Información y Comunicaciones (CITIC),
Universidad Gastón Dachary, Av. López y Planes 6519, 3300 Posadas, Argentina
diegodoy@citic.ugd.edu.ar

[2] Instituto de Investigación en Señales, Sistemas e Inteligencia Artificial - Sinc(i),
CONICET-UNL, Santa Fe City, Santa Fe, Argentina
emalbornoz@sinc.unl.edu.ar

Abstract. One of the more serious problems that the planet faces is the pollution, which exposes its integrity and the living beings that inhabit it at risk. Pollution is a constantly growing problem due to the increase in population and large companies, and it contributes to the detriment of people's health and the environment. The advancement of technologies, and in particular of intelligent systems, allows automating and optimizing many processes that are usually carried out manually and very expensive. The artificial intelligence systems allow the redistribution of efforts and resources, increasing productivity. In this work, an approach to the detection of different types of recyclable plastic waste that arrive at a recycling plant using a convolutional neural network is presented. Several models were evaluated for this task and the YOLOv5 achieved the best results. Preliminar results show a confidence of up to 65% on images taken from the recycling plant in the city of Posadas, Misiones (Argentina).

Keywords: Convolutional Neural Networks · Waste Classification · Computer Vision

1 Introduction

For many years now, the world has been challenged by problems that compromise the environment, such as the deterioration of the ozone layer [1], massive deforestation of trees, poaching of animals, or environmental pollution. The latter has several classes such as contamination of the soil, water, air, radioactive, acoustic, or chemical contamination. In addition to the environmental pollution, this causes dangerous and serious illnesses, and also in the worst cases, death [2]. Recycling is the method through which it is possible to reuse raw materials and one of its most relevant impacts is to help curb exploitation of natural resources. For example, recycling paper and cardboard helps reduce deforestation and chemical pollution of the air and rivers, and consequently helps preserve the environment [3]. In this sense, garbage recycling is of vital importance for

S. Nesmachnow and L. Hernández Callejo (Eds.): ICSC-CITIES 2022, CCIS 1706, pp. 173–184, 2023.
https://doi.org/10.1007/978-3-031-28454-0_12

our environment. However, some aspects must be taken into account before thinking of a solution. According to studies carried out by the organization Natural Resources Defense Council (NRDC) [4] in Latin America, if the garbage were properly separated before reaching the municipal dump, an average of almost 92% could be recycled, but since citizens do not usually differentiate their waste, it is only possible to recycle 30%. In 2020, the city of Posadas produced an average of 8,000 tons of waste per month [5] which is equivalent to approximately 266 tons per day. Taking into account the mentioned percentage, it is probably that less than 80 tons were processed per day. This number is constantly growing due to the trend of increasing population and large companies in recent years in Posadas. The recycling process is carried out through a waste collection plant located in the municipal green center in the City of Posadas, being a part of the Integral Management of Urban Solid Waste (GIRSU).

The main problem is social, although there is a city ordinance corresponding to the proper separation of waste in the city of Posadas [6], people are not used to making an adequate differentiation of garbage and usually mix organic and inorganic waste. This is the reason why most of the daily garbage cannot be recycled, since organic waste decomposes and makes waste that could be recycled useless. This has a direct impact on GIRSU, since before the classification process of a particular type of waste (such as plastic, cardboard, etc.), a manual pre-sorting process is needed to assess which waste can be recycled.

To automate the classification process, it is necessary to emulate the complex human task of image recognition. In addition, for the GIRSU scene, the system is immersed in a fast and continuous process where the elements are presented in different positions, sizes, colors, and overlap with other elements. In order to simplify the processing, some mechanical systems could be used to isolate the elements avoiding irregularities and classify them. It is important to note that the conveyor belt does not stop and large volumes of waste must be processed in a very fast manner.

The computer vision techniques, that include digital image processing and neural networks, can support the identification of waste automatically. However, it is necessary to establish a set of restrictions and conditions on certain waste classification operations, considering how waste arrives at GIRSU today. The approach presented in this work focuses on the classification of polyethylene terephthalate (PET) bottles (crystal, green and light blue).

2 Related Works

In [7] the classification of waste is addressed using Machine Learning using Google Cloud Platform, Microsoft Azure, and a model designed by the authors. The main described problem is the lack of any treatment or management process for the inevitable massive generation of garbage by people in cities. The objective was to develop an API based on computer vision techniques supported by Cloud services that allows the recognition of waste and determines the belonging of an element to the group of recyclable waste. Two approaches are taken for the waste sorting process. The first is based on Auto Machine Learning, which together with cloud services allows automatically designing of a Machine Learning model for a given dataset. Specifically, Cloud Vision API and

AutoML (which are Google Cloud Platform products), and Custom Vision (which is a Microsoft Azure product) were used. The second is based on the manual design of a computer vision model using convolutional neural networks and Transfer Learning, which allows taking a previously trained model and adapting it to a particular problem. Various experiments were performed combining architectures such as VGG16, VGG19, and MobileNet while tuning hyperparameters such as the number of epochs and batch size.

The used dataset has 2527 waste images and it is freely available online at [8]. This dataset is made up of 501 images of glass, 594 of paper, 403 of cardboard, 482 of plastic, 401 of metal, and 137 of non-recyclable waste. For the tests, the images were taken on a white background with both artificial and natural light. The size of each image is 512 × 384 pixels. The devices used to take the images were: Apple iPhone 7 Plus, Apple iPhone 5S, and an Apple iPhone SE. The results obtained were 76% correct for the model designed by the authors, while 93% and 98% correct with cloud tools. Both the source code of the experiments carried out as well as the complete results can be found at [9].

Different from the aforementioned work, Deep Learning was used to identify recycled waste in the Municipal Green Center. For the training of the neural network, 300 images of each type of residue will be used, while for the tests, 100 images of each one. In both training and testing processes, photographs will be taken with a GoPro camera.

In [10], authors propose the automatic classification of plastics, glass bottles, and cans using the SSD-Mobilenet [11] convolutional neural network. The motivation of this work was the great generation of waste on the beaches, where most of the waste is recyclable but people have no interest or knowledge to throw the waste in the corresponding container. The corpus contains 317 images of 3 types of waste: plastic bottles, glass bottles, and metal cans; including a wide variety of brands for each type. For plastic bottles, 31 different brands were used; 19 brands for glass bottles, and 18 for cans. The labeling of the dataset and the training of the model was carried out in a computer: Intel Core i7-6700 CPU, 8 GB RAM, with a GEFORCE GTX 1070 TI 8 GB GDDR5 GPU. In the test phase, a Raspberry Pi with a camera was used. For each type of waste, 5 experiments with 20 images in each were done. The results show for metal cans a success rate of 86%, a success rate of 95% for plastic bottles, and a success rate of 82% for glass bottles.

In this case, the waste includes plastic bottles, glass bottles, and metal cans, while in our approach different types of plastics will be identified: green PET, crystal PET, light blue PET, and blown plastic. In addition, they used an average of 300 images per type of waste, while in our work 400 images per type of waste are used and the classes are more similar between them. In our approach, the labeling phase is also done.

3 Methodology

In this section the Crisp-DM methodology is introduced, and it was selected because it is widely used in data mining projects in multiple industries [12].

3.1 Data Model Analysis

In the first phase, the aim was to understand and determine what types of images were the best input to reach a suitable prototype. These images should be as realistic as possible and appropriately reflect the scenario and conditions where the prototype will work. For this purpose, the authors captured and labeled photos in the GIRSU plant. Additionally, images from other available waste datasets were used, as Bottles and cans images [13], and Garbage Classifications [14] datasets.

Available Datasets

Two available datasets were used to perform the image survey: Bottles and Cans Images [13] and Garbage Classification [14]. On these, there is a great variety of PET crystal, light blue, green, and blown arranged on white backgrounds that serve as a starting point to provide the network with knowledge about the data that must be identified. Some examples can be found in Fig. 1.

Fig. 1. Examples of images from Garbage database [14].

Acquired Data

Our own database is formed by images captured in the municipal green center, and images taken at the author's homes where the PETs were set in situations that simulate the application scenario. Some examples are shown in Fig. 2.

3.2 Data Preparation

At this point, the available datasets were ready to use but our own database needed to be labeled. After that, the sets for experiments were defined.

Images Labeling

In this process, each image is associated with a label that represents it. In this way, all the data will be suitable to perform the training or test phase. Here, Roboflow [15] was used as a labeling tool.

Datasets Definition

In this phase, with uniform labeled images, different subsets of images were formed that will have different purposes: training, validation, and test. The validation set is very useful to avoid overtraining [16]. The training and validation sets were randomly selected while the test set contains only examples of the real scenario.

Fig. 2. Examples of images taken at home and in the GIRSU plant.

Table 1. Distribution of image sets. An image can have more than one object.

	Number of images	%	Labels	Labels per class	% of each class in the dataset
Training	635	69	Light blue	357	43.97
			Crystal	393	48.4
			Green	62	7.64
Validation	257	28	Light blue	107	33.75
			Crystal	182	57.41
			Green	28	8.83
Test	25	3	Light blue	4	11.76
			Crystal	27	79.41
			Green	3	8.82
Total	917	100			

3.3 Model Exploration

In this stage, different CNN approaches were evaluated in order to obtain the best implementation for the prototype. It is important to note that all the CNN were pre-trained and here, the transfer learning technique was used. In this scheme, the weights of the CNN are set and it is not necessary to train the network from scratch. In Table 1 is possible to observe an important unbalance of the data with respect to the classes. In this sense, it appropriated the use of metrics that consider the unbalanced among classes, and thus avoid an erroneous interpretation of the performance of the system. This means that the global metric must take into account the performance of the system for each class. To achieve this, the unweighted average recall (UAR) is used and it is computed as the average of all recalls per class (see Eqs. 1 to 4).

$$recall_{light\ blue} = \frac{number\ of\ hits\ in\ detecting\ a\ light\ blue\ class}{total\ number\ of\ images\ of\ light\ blue\ class} \quad (1)$$

$$recall_{crystal} = \frac{number\ of\ hits\ in\ detecting\ a\ crystal\ class}{total\ number\ of\ images\ of\ crystal\ class} \quad (2)$$

$$recall_{green} = \frac{number\ of\ hits\ in\ detecting\ a\ green\ class}{total\ number\ of\ images\ of\ green\ class} \quad (3)$$

$$UAR = \frac{recall_{light\ blue} + recall_{crystal}recall_{green}}{3} \quad (4)$$

The analyses were performed checking the UAR obtained on the validation set in order to select the best model for this domain. The results can be seen in Table 2, while in Fig. 3, the evolution of the metrics with respect to the number of epochs is presented.

Table 2. Best results using 25 training epochs as maximum.

CNN	Execution time (min)	Best Epoch	UAR (val)	UAR (test)
ALEXNET	3.0	6	0.87	0.71
GOOGLENE	3.3	13	0.56	0.30
INCEPTION	3.0	3	0.33	0.34
RESNET18	3.0	15	0.87	0.79
VGG16	9.6	6	0.87	0.79
YOLO V5	6.2	18	0.84	**0.85**

4 Prototype Architecture

The proposed prototype was implemented in Python using PyTorch, and includes the best trained model obtained in the previous stage. In Fig. 4, the prototype workflow can be seen. The input images are taken from a database or from the camera, and feed the CNN which gives as a result the class to which the PET belongs.

4.1 Input Data

The prototype can take images from different sources, such as video or surveillance cameras, where snapshots are taken at certain pre-established time intervals; or from stored images in jpg, jpeg, or png format. These images are transformed into Pytorch Tensors [16] for further processing in the next stage.

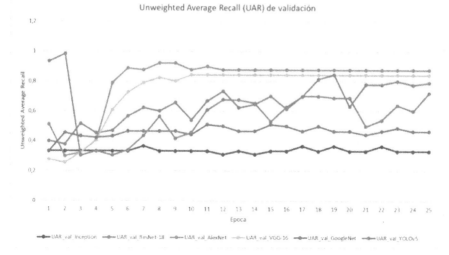

Fig. 3. Validation accuracy progress over 25 epochs (training phase).

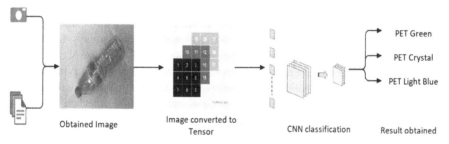

Fig. 4. Prototype workflow

4.2 Inference

It is done through the Python programming language using the Pytorch library and the YOLOv5 convolutional neural network. The model is already trained, and the inference is the operation that allows to classify the test images taken from the application scenario.

5 Testing Scenarios

5.1 Bottles Classification: Lab Test

In initial laboratory tests, the different PET (crystal, green and light blue) were used. These were put on clean surfaces, with a white background and the photos were captured close to the PET (see Fig. 5). This was done to evaluate the feasibility of the project. The results demonstrate a very appropriate initial approach evaluating the metrics obtained.

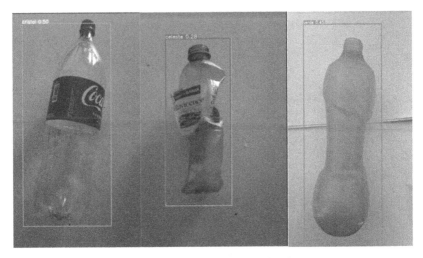

Fig. 5. Examples of images used in lab test.

5.2 Bottles Classification: Clean Environment

In a second instance, different scenarios presented in Figs. 6 and 7 have been evaluated, where it is evident that the prototype is capable of identifying the elements. In the figure on the left, confidence is relatively low and it could be attributed to the size of the element, although it can be observed empirically that the model is capable of identifying the glass PET bottles that were on the floor and the tabletop. In the figure on the right, the network recognizes the element with a confidence of 51% and it could be reached because of the orientation of the element. These results show that it is possible to recognize the recyclable waste on remote surfaces and with a computationally complex scenario.

Fig. 6. Distant bottles with no close or overlapped objects.

Fig. 7. Distant bottles with waste around them.

5.3 Bottles Classification: Complex Scenario

We defined the complex scenario when the images are as those show in Figs. 8 and 9, where the bottles are not only scattered on the green floor, but can be confused with the green glass and glass PET bottles, can be overlapped and occluded, even with other waste. Taking into account the metrics in the Fig. 8 and 9, where the average confidence is about 23%, it is possible to say that the results are promising to identify waste in noisy environments.

It is important to highlight these results because the used images have similar characteristics as the goal scenario where the waste is scattered on a surface with other elements around it, for example, other waste that is not within the scope of this project. On the other hand, in some cases the obtained confidences are relatively low with respect to the previous proofs. Therefore, even though the metrics are not high enough to think about implementation, they could be a starting point to the future work due to the feasibility of the prototype.

5.4 Bottles Classification: Goal Scenario

The images presented in Fig. 10 were taken on the conveyor belt of the recyclable waste plant. These show some confidence results and indicate that it is possible to recognize the desired elements with a good rate. The best results are associated with different PETs bottles forms. It would be possible to take advantage of this by using a hierarchical classification scheme in future work, where in a first step a coarse classification is performed and then, a specific PET classification is done.

6 Conclusion and Future Works

An approach to PET classification in a conveyor belt at a recyclable waste plant was designed and implemented. Pre-trained CNNs were used to reduce time and resources to

Fig. 8. Complex scenario for green and crystal PET. (Color figure online)

Fig. 9. Distant bottles with waste around them in a complex scenario.

Fig. 10. Bottles at closer distance, in a conveyor belt with waste around.

build the image classification prototype. After the experiments, the YOLOv5 was chosen because it achieved the best results, as can be seen in Table 2. It also has the advantage of being able to detect and classify different class objects in the same image. However, like any prediction model, it can be affected by factors such as the brightness of the environment, the partial or complete capture of the object, the overlap between bodies, or the focus and distance from them. These circumstances can confuse the model generating erroneous results, such as false positives, wrong classes, or low success percentages. At the same time, the prototype presents the possibility of improving the outcomes by providing, exhaustively, inputs that reflect all the conditions and circumstances that could be found when carrying out an evaluation. In addition, this prototype is a first step in the development of a fully automated waste classification system, which would mean a reduction in the time of exposure of workers to harmful substances and an increase in the productivity of the beneficiary entity.

As future work the real photo set and the augmented data need to be emphasized to get a better trained model, as well as to allow a bigger number of epochs in the training. An issue to analyze in future works is to apply image processing techniques to improve the learning performance of the network, even super-resolution techniques. Also, a new design of the model, maybe using hierarchical structures in order to reach better results, is contemplated. In addition, the implementation of the prototype in a real environment, such as the recycling plant in the Municipal Green Center is agreed.

References

1. Romo-Gómez, C.: Actividades antrópicas: deterioro de la capa de ozono estratosférico. Bol. Científico Cien. Básicas Ingenierías ICBI 7(13), 1–5 (2019)
2. Arcos Medina, G., Arcos, A., Oñate Andino, M., Danilo, P., Jerves Cobo, R.: Simulación para estimación de muertes por cáncer de pulmón por contaminación ambiental de PM2.5 (2018)
3. Citlalic Gonzales Martinez, A.: Costos y beneficios ambientales del reciclaje en México. Una aproximación monetaria (2001)
4. Moyer, E.: Día del Reciclaje: ¿Qué tanto se recicla en América Latina? In: NRDC. https://www.nrdc.org/es/experts/erika-moyer/dia-reciclaje-tanto-recicla-america-latina.   Accessed 2018
5. Municipalidad de Posadas: Servicio de Recolección general de Residuos Sólidos Urbanos. In: Desarrollo Sustentable. https://posadas.gov.ar/sustentable/servicio-de-recoleccion-general-de-residuos-solidos-urbanos/. Accessed 2018
6. Honorable Concejo Deliberante de la Ciudad de Posadas: Ordenanza VI - N 29., Posadas (2021)
7. Castrillon Medina, M.: REDO: Sistema de reconocimiento de desechos reciclables (2019)
8. Thung, G., Yang, M.: Dataset of images of trash; Torch-based CNN for garbage image classification. In: Github. https://github.com/garythung/trashnet. Accessed 2017
9. Castrillon Medina, M.: Sistema de reconocimiento de desechos reciclables. https://github.com/ManuCastrillonM/redo. Accessed 2019
10. Sorawit, T., Kittiya, T., Prajaks, J.: Valuable waste classification modeling based on SSD-MobileNet (2021)
11. Howard, A., et al.: MobileNets: efficient convolutional neural networks for mobile vision (2017)
12. Schröer, C., Kruse, F., MarxGómez, J.: A systematic literature review on applying CRISP-DM process model (2021)
13. Kaggle: Starter: Bottles and Cans Images. In: Kaggle. https://www.kaggle.com/code/kerneler/starter-bottles-and-cans-images-aa8808c7-4. Accessed 14 July 2020
14. cchangcs: Garbage Classification. In: Kaggle. https://www.kaggle.com/datasets/asdasdasasdas/garbage-classification. Accessed 2018
15. Roboflow: Roboflow - Give your projects the power to see objects in images and videos. https://roboflow.com/. Accessed 2022
16. Bishop, C.M., Nasrabadi, N.M.: Pattern Recognition and Machine Learning, vol. 4, no. 4, p. 738. Springer, New York (2006)

Synthesized Data Generation for Public Transportation Systems

Federico Gómez$^{(\boxtimes)}$ and Sergio Nesmachnow ⓘ

Universidad de la República, Montevideo, Uruguay
{fgomez,sergion}@fing.edu.uy

Abstract. This article presents a proposal for generating synthesized data for public transportation systems. This is a relevant problem whose solution assists the planning and operation of Intelligent Transportation Systems. The proposed methodology applies a conditional Generative Adversarial Network approach, considering relevant real information about trips performed by citizens. A practical validation is presented for a real case study in the public transportation in Montevideo, Uruguay. The main results indicate that the proposed approach is able to generate accurate synthesized data.

1 Introduction

Mobility and urban transportation are fundamental components of the functional dimension of a city, which together with other relevant factors (land use, urban planning, etc.) determines the way in which citizens perform their daily activities [1].

The analysis of urban mobility data is crucial to help public administrations and policy makers to improve public transportation systems [15]. The emergence of data-driven approaches led to an improved transportation paradigm, known as Intelligent Transportation Systems (ITS). ITS are innovative systems that, by integrating synergistic technologies, allows providing services to both traffic management operators and citizens. Their main goal is to develop coordinated and integrated mobility means that in turn are smarter, safer, efficient, and provide a better user experience [24].

Synthesized data generation refers to the process of creating a repository of data by applying a systematic and programmatic method [3]. Synthesized data complement real data in those situation where real-life or experimental gathering is not practical or even not possible. Synthesized data allows performing more accurate analysis to better understand underlying processes, a critical component for self-driven data science [8]. The most desired properties of synthesized data are they must follow or accurate approximate the distribution of real data, have the same type of features than real data, randomness should be controlled and noise must be injected if needed. In particular, synthesized data are crucial for developing computational intelligence and machine learning methods to solve complex problems.

S. Nesmachnow and L. Hernández Callejo (Eds.): ICSC-CITIES 2022, CCIS 1706, pp. 185–199, 2023.
https://doi.org/10.1007/978-3-031-28454-0_13

Synthesized mobility data are very useful for planning and operation within ITS. Retrieving real high-quality mobility data is a hard task, mainly due to privacy issues related to gathering and managing sensitive data about citizens. In addition, the real mobility time series gathered by ITS usually have missing data due to several reasons, including missing, malfunctioning, and low maintenance of the gathering devices/sensors and intermittent communications between devices/sensors and the central server. Thus, synthesized mobility data are useful for characterizing mobility patterns, detecting anomalies and unusual mobility patterns, and also for performing simulations of different realistic scenarios. Some interesting studies that benefit from the availability of both real and synthesized mobility data are public transportation network design, analysis and improvement of the quality of service and user experience, determining stress conditions and other traffic-related situations such as predicting traffic jams, analyzing speed of vehicles, detecting special incidents, and performing traffic engineering and traffic operation tasks [17]. Overall, accurate (real and synthesized) mobility data provide useful insights about traffic and citizens movement patterns, which are important inputs for nowadays ITS.

In this line of work, this article presents an approach applying Generative Adversarial Networks (GANs) for the generation of synthesized mobility data for ITS. A specific conditional network architecture is studied and implemented and a practical validation is presented for a real case study, the ITS for public transportation in Montevideo, Uruguay. The main results of the research indicate that the proposed conditional GAN is able to generate accurate synthesized mobility data, according to the statistical analysis and metrics studied.

Overall, this article contributes with the proposal of a methodology for synthesized public transportation data generation based on GANs and the evaluation of the proposed methodology in a real case study, considering real data from the public transportation system in Montevideo, Uruguay.

The article is organized as follows. Next section presents the main concepts about GANs. Section 3 presents a description of the problem solved and reviews relevant related works. Section 4 describes the case study, the public ITS in Montevideo, Uruguay. The applied methodology and implementation details is presented in Sect. 5. The experimental evaluation of the proposed generative approach is reported in Sect. 6. Finally, Sect. 7 presents the conclusions of the research and formulates the main lines for future work.

2   Generative Adversarial Networks

A generative model is a statistical tool that allows modeling the joint probability distribution $p(X, Y)$ relating a given observable variable X (input or data instance) and a target variable Y (output) [20]. Generative machine learning is a branch of computational intelligence including methods that are able to generate new instances of data, by learning the joint probability $p(X, Y)$ to describe the process of generating new datasets [5].

GANs are a type of generative machine learning methods that use adversarial artificial neural networks (ANNs) for generating new data [6]. A GAN consists of two ANNs working in competition and cooperation: the *generator* and the *discriminator*. Both ANNs apply and adversarial learning approach to optimize their parameters in order to generate accurate synthesized data.

The generator ANN (g) specializes on learning the way of creating synthesized data samples x', taking as input random vectors from a latent space z. The generator can be characterized by the equation $g(z) = x'$. The main goal of the generator is to approximate the distribution of true data, by considering the information about the problem provided by the discriminator. In turn, the discriminator ANN specializes on learning how to distinguish real data samples x (taken from a training dataset) from the synthesized samples x' created by the generator. Both ANNs are trained simultaneously and following an adversarial approach: the discriminator tries to learn the real data distribution for a proper evaluation of new synthesized data and the generator seeks to generate images that deceive the discriminator, by generating data samples that the discriminator cannot label as real or synthesized. A well-designed training process converges to a generator ANN that approximates the real data distribution, thus generating high-quality synthesized data samples.

Recent articles have demonstrated that GANs are very useful tools for many applications that propose/require generating synthesized data, especially in multimedia processing, healthcare, time series analysis, and other areas [12, 21, 25, 26]. Figure 1 presents a schema of a GAN.

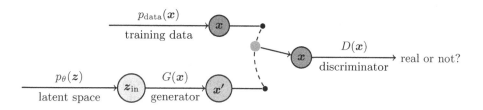

Fig. 1. Schema of a GAN

3   Problem Definition and Literature Review

This section describes the addressed problem and reviews relevant related works.

3.1   Problem Description

The addressed problem concerns the generation of synthesized data for mobility and transportation systems. Passenger mobility information is very relevant for management and quality of service assessment of public transportation, infrastructure planning, and other relevant issues to provide an enhanced and smart mobility [23].

In the real world, it is very common that the available data are not enough for a proper analysis, mainly because they are incomplete (e.g., the time series has gaps due to logging errors), they are obtained from different sources that are not always directly combinable (e.g., GPS traces, ticket sales, mobility data from third parties such as the applications from Google or Waze, mobile phones location data, etc.), or even because relevant information is not recorded (such as alighting points for trips performed in bus). Therefore, the generation of synthesized mobility data is an important line of research.

Special care must be taken to apply systematic methodologies that allow generating good quality data, which capture with the greatest possible precision the distributions and characteristics of the real data.

3.2   Related Work

Several recent articles from Jauhri et al. have studied the problem of generating mobility data in urban areas. In 2020, Jauhri et al. [10] applied GANs for creating a model to generate synthesized mobility data for real world cases considering ride-sharing/hailing services from four cities in the USA (San Francisco, Los Angeles, New York, and Chicago) considering different temporal and spatial quantization of raw ride request data. The proposed GAN was able to learn the spatial and temporal variability of mobility patterns, according to the validation analysis performed considering the fractal dimensionality and the densification power law quantitative characterizations. A specific application of the generated data was also presented, namely the dynamic vehicle placement problem, to place in real time idle vehicles near possible future pickup locations. Results using the synthesized dataset maintained the same pattern than when using the real dataset. After that, Jauhri and Shen [9] applied the analysis for the characterization of human mobility considering data from twelve cities. The authors proposed a framework including a stochastic graph model and GANs for data augmentation to preserve the geographical and temporal characteristics observed in real data. The analysis included a formal characterizations of mobility applications (ride pooling and vehicle placement) and how to apply augmented datasets to analyze different mobility scenarios to be applied in real cities.

Saxena and Cao [22] propose a model based on a deep GAN for learning feature representations on spatio-temporal urban mobility data. Two computational intelligence models were applied: i) a deep GAN for feature learning, managing correlations, semantic variations, and irregularities in mobility data, and ii) a fusion module to combine multiple data sources with heterogeneous formats (e.g., weather data, information about points of interest, etc.), that help improving inference results. The proposed approach was validated on two real-world case studies, considering six months of the Yellow Taxi dataset and one month of the CitiBike trip dataset, both collected in New York, USA. An exhaustive comparison with 14 state-of-the-art statistical and leaning methods was performed, using the generated datasets for demand prediction. The proposed GAN-based approach computed the best Mean Square Error (RMSE) and Mean Absolute Error (MAE) results among the 15 studied methods.

Some recent articles have focused on protecting the privacy of mobility data. Liu et al. [11] proposed the TrajGAN framework, which applies GANs for privacy protection of trajectory data. The proposed model incorporates a geo-privacy protection layer for trajectory data and a traditional GAN architecture for generating synthetic trajectories that preserve the main features of real data. Authors described the main challenges for generating individual trajectories (i.e., with similar properties to each individual) and aggregated trajectories that approximate overall statistics of the training dataset, including the use of dense representations of trajectories as a fixed-length vector of numbers. Several validation metrics were proposed for both road- and place-based trajectories, including segment usage distribution and temporality, transportation mode, speed, time in transit, activity space, mobility motivations (for individual trajectories) and user distribution, driving behavior, temporal semantics of points of interest, trip-length distribution, and OD matrix comparison (for aggregated trajectories).

Yin and Yang [28] also addressed the problem of generating synthesized trajectories that properly protect the information of users, using GANs. The proposed GAN was evaluated on two real world mobile datasets: MoMo Mobile App Dataset, a mobile SC networking application in China containing GPS data (fields: user ID, timestamp, latitude, and longitude) and San Francisco Cabs Dataset, containing mobility trajectories of taxi cabs in San Fancisco, USA (fields: cab ID, timestamp, latitude, and longitude.) Authors performed a comparison with differential privacy (DP), a privacy preservation method based on adding noises into aggregated mobility data. Results showed that the proposed method was able to improve over the differential privacy approach, considering metrics related to data usefulness and robustness against attacks.

Other articles have focused on important related problems, for which generation/data augmentation approaches using GANs have been proposed. New synthesized data are useful for predicting the location of specific vehicles or individuals; performing crowd flow prediction, i.e., forecasting in-out flows on a given urban area [27]; and generating realistic trajectories for vehicles or fleets of vehicles. Furthermore, these specific problems are related to higher important issues such as air quality and pollution, public services and public resources (e.g., water, electricity, etc.) utilization, public health and the spreading of diseases, among others. The main challenges related to generation of mobility data to be applied to these problems are capturing the dynamic of mobility patterns, and learning the spatial-temporal correlations between data.

4   Case Study: The Public Transportation System in Montevideo, Uruguay

The Metropolitan Transportation System (STM) is a program whose objective is the integration of the public transportation of Montevideo and the metropolitan area into a common system. The system is aimed at improving mobility through-out the department of Montevideo and nearby population conglomerates.

STM proposed important investments in road infrastructure for public trans-portation. A significant modification of STM was including the use of new tech-nologies that allow a more efficient, rational and safe public transportation. In turn, the system provides effective control and enhanced convenience for users, through routes and costs according to their specific needs. A conceptual diagram of the STM is presented in Fig. 2.

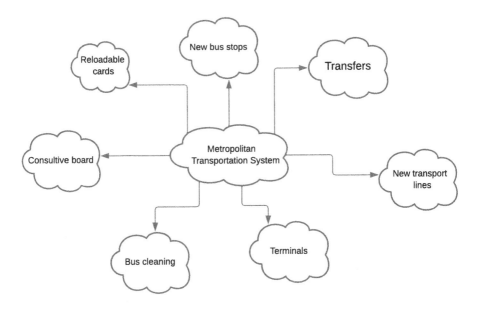

Fig. 2. Conceptual diagram of the STM (Montevideo)

A relevant change of STM was the incorporation of a smart card to pay for trips [13]. The smart card is an important technological tool to have control and knowledge about the trips or transfers for citizens of Montevideo and suburban areas [19]. Previous articles from our research group [2,4,7,13–16] proved that is possible to process the data of millions of trips using the STM card crossing various sources (geospatial data, bus information, etc.) and conducting a data cleansing process to maintain integrity between them. As a result, a set of tabular data of user trips was obtained.

Travel records are divided into categories of users, namely: public trans-portation employees, teachers, retirees, minors, common users, among others. It was recently identified that the records of users who are public transporta-tion employees are underrepresented, because the trips described do not faith-fully represent the movement routine in the city of said users. This under-representation has a negative impact on the statistical indicators that are obtained from the original travel data. To address the presented issue, this article proposes applying a methodology for building at a more complete version of the trip data for transportation employees by generating synthesized data, based on the original data set for all users. In particular, we are interested in the trips made by the employees of the transport companies, therefore, the false sample must be filtered by that value. Filtering the sample allows us to focus on those rows that interest us to make a better statistical study.

5   A Conditional Tabular GAN for Synthesized Data Generation for the STM

This section describes the data source and the methodology applied for synthesized data generation for the STM using a GAN approach.

5.1   Data Sources

The main source of data is the repository of urban mobility data for the public transportation system in Montevideo, Uruguay. The dataset consists of tabular data in csv format developed in a previous research effort by our group [13]. Data for a total number of 289 271 trips were reported, from trips paid using a smart card.

Relevant information considered in the analysis includes attributes that identify users, the bus lines (to know the route each passenger takes), the number of tickets paid using the smart card in each transaction, and the company operating each line. These attributes are categorical in the set and correctly describe the mobility patterns of users. In turn, geographical data sources (e.g., shapefiles containing the route of the considered bus lines) are used to properly locate bus lines and selecting relevant case studies for the analysis.

5.2   Overall Description of the Methodology

The applied methodology consists of eight activities, organized in three phases, as described next.

Phase 1: Data Analysis and Preprocessing. The first phase included two activities: statistical analysis of source data and grouping. The statistical analysis of source data studied the main features of the available data, including the number of lines and users of the STM, ticket types, user category and number of passengers. If necessary, attributes (or columns) of the sample that are not relevant for the proposed study (such as date and time of the trip, or patronymic data of the passengers) are eliminated. After that, the available data were grouped according to the type of user (i.e., transportation employees) to identify the most demanded lines in the city. Studying the composition of origin–destination for user trips in Montevideo is relevant from the study. From a quantitative point of view, it is recommended groping the individual records into groups of users to determine their proportion over the total number of trips and to account for all the different lines. For example, there should not be a majority of trips associated with lines in the metropolitan area, since they are the least requested trips. Furthermore, it should be analyzed whether the number of lines used by a group of users is representative of their usual trips.

Another relevant analysis for the characterization of public transportation systems is the identification of underrepresented sets. The statistical analysis detected that few information is available in the repository for some user categories. Some data are incomplete or do not represent the daily nature of the trips of those users. Identifying underrepresented categories is crucial, as they are the target categories for data augmentation using GANs.

Phase 2: Resolution. The resolution phase included three activities: selection of the GAN model and architecture, training, and generation of synthesized data. From the analysis, a conditional GAN for modeling and generating tabular data (CTGAN) was selected. CTGAN is specialized on the generation of tabular data. CTGAN has been applied to generate high-quality synthesized tables, including discrete and continuous variables. This property is very relevant for the reported research, to correctly generate new data based on the real samples available.

The applied CTGAN was trained considering relevant accuracy metrics and controlling overfitting. Finally, the CTGAN was applied to generate synthesized data from the real samples, with the main goals of respecting the distribution, proportions and fidelity of the original data.

Phase 3: Validation. The last phase included activities to analyze the quality of the generated data. First, specific metrics were applied to evaluate the distributions and features of the generated data and two-dimensional graphics were used to study the correlation with the attributes of real data. After that, cross-validation was applied combining the generated data with other sources of geographical information, to analyze the bus lines and passengers routes. Finally, visualization tools were used to generate maps for a proper visual evaluation of the generated data. Figure 3 describes the activities in phases 2 and 3.

5.3   The Proposed GAN for Synthesized Data Generation

The proposed approach consists in generating synthesized mobility data based on the information from all trips of the user groups. A supervised learning approach is applied, based on structured data. To properly capturing the class information associated with the groups of users in the considered problem, a conditional GAN is applied. The diagram of a conditional GAN is presented in Fig. 4.

The applied CTGAN uses the training-by-sampling approach and conditional generators to resample the training data, so that all categories in discrete variables have a fair chance of being included in the sample that GAN learns from.

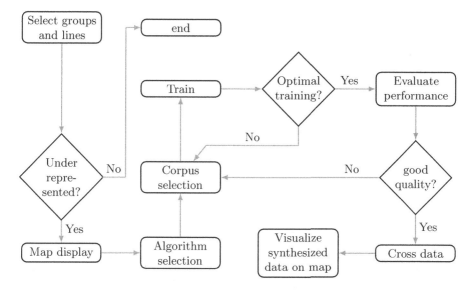

Fig. 3. Activities in the resolution and validation phases

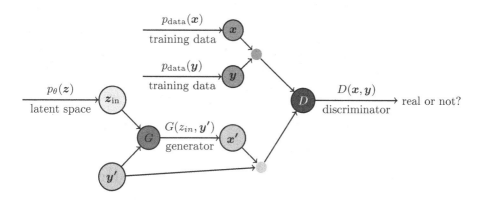

Fig. 4. Schema of a conditional GAN

6 Experimental Analysis and Discussion

This section describes the experimental evaluation of the proposed CTGAN approach. The obtained results are reported and discussed.

6.1 Development and Execution Platform

The proposed CTGAN was developed in Python3, following the replicable research approach. Specific libraries and packages were applied for processing geographic information (Geopandas) and for statistical analysis (scikit-learn). The library CTGANSynthesizer was used for the implementation and the table_evaluator library was applied to evaluate the correlations between the real samples and the synthesized data. The experimental analysis was performed on the high performance computing platform of National Supercomputing Center (Cluster-UY), Uruguay [18].

6.2   Problem Instances

The considered instances correspond to trip records of a particular month (April 2021). This month was selected since it is a representative month for bus trips, with a normal demand of mobility and activities in the city. Each instance was built considering a representative sample of trips, respecting the proportions of trips performed on each line. The proposed CTGAN was trained with this subset, which comprise about a fifth of the records in the complete repository.

Information in the considered problem instances includes:

– Type of the trip (TT): This attribute refers to the user category. The user category has the following values: common users (US), student (ST), institutional (OG), retired (RT), and transportation (TR).
– User group (UG): This attribute groups users according to the fare of the ticket. The considered groups are one hour (1H), two hours (2H), student A (STA), student B (STB), retired A (RTA), and retired B (RTB).
– Number of passengers (NP): This attribute indicates the number of tickets paid in each smart card transaction (between one and seven).
– Description of the company (CD): This attribute is the name of the transportation company that operates the line.
– Code of the line (CL): This attribute is a numerical code that allows linking the line with geographical data.

6.3   Results and Discussion

This subsection reports and discusses the results of the experiments performed to analyze the similarity and correlation between synthesized and real data.

CTGAN Training. The CTGAN was trained for 10 epochs, considering the loss functions defined for both the generator and discriminator. The training process was performed over a training dataset, defined by the following five categorical attributes: trip type, user group, number of passengers, company, and line, which define the characteristics of the passengers using each line. Figure 5 presents the evolution of the discriminator and generator loss in training experiments.

Results in Fig. 5 show that the generator loss reduced and that the loss of the discriminator and the loss of the generator have rather similar values after epoch 2. This results indicate that the generator is sufficiently well trained to generate synthesized data samples that are able to deceive the discriminator. Overall, the training was performed in an average execution time of ten minutes.

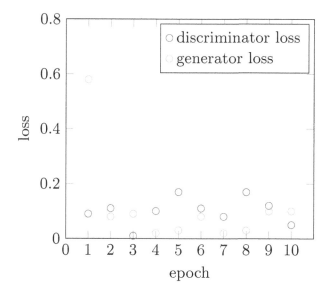

Fig. 5. Evolution of the discriminator and generator loss in training experiments

CTGAN Validation. The main goal of the validation experiments is to analyze the similarities of the synthesized data generated using the proposed CTGAN with samples of the real data. Three samples are considered in validation analysis, including 10000, 50000, and 100000 records. The table_evaluator library is applied to compute similarity metrics between synthesized and real data.

Modal Partition. The first study evaluates the modal partition of the categorical variables in the artificial set, compared with the ones in the real data. This analysis allows detecting if the proportions/relative distributions of each attribute are respected in the generated data. Figure 6 presents an example of the obtained results, regarding mode partition of the user category field. In turn, Fig. 7 presents the mode partition of tickets type for both real and synthesized data.

The graph bar in Fig. 6 shows that the synthesized data has a similar distribution (modal partition) for the different user categories. Some deviations are detected in medium-valued categories (ST, OG, and RT), where the proposed CTGAN generated larger values than real data. Deviations are below 5% in those cases. A similar situation is observed for ticket type RTB in Fig. 7.

Number of Passengers. Figure 8 compares the real and synthesized data regarding another relevant attribute for travel demand characterization: the number of passengers for each smart card transaction.

The most relevant results from Figs. 6, 7 and 8 are related to the most important categories (type of travel, group of users and quantity of tickets), which accounts for the larger proportion in previous analysis. These categories are considered for the analysis of correlations in both real and synthesized data.

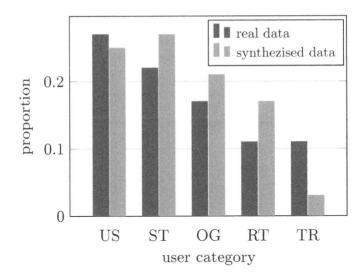

Fig. 6. Modal partition of user categories

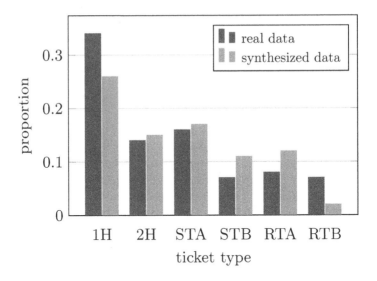

Fig. 7. Modal partition of ticket types

Summarizing, the computed results show that there is a great similarity between the real and synthesized data samples. This result suggests that it is possible to consider the generated samples as valuable data augmentation sets to compute accurate statistics about the STM utilization.

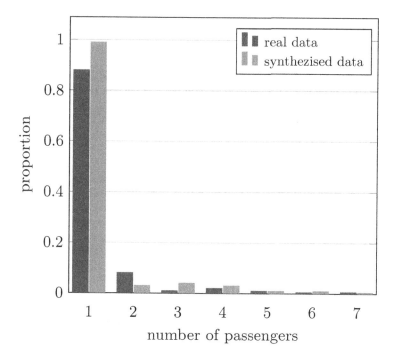

Fig. 8. Modal partition of number of passengers

7   Conclusions and Future Work

This article presented a study applying a GAN approach for generating synthesized data for public transportation systems.

A CTGAN neural network was applied to properly model tabular data from ticket sales of ITS. The model was trained with real data from the case study considered in the validation experiment: the public transportation system in Montevideo, Uruguay.

The main results indicated that the proposed CTGAN was able to generate accurate synthesized mobility data, according to the statistical analysis of correlations and the graphical analysis of distributions. Accurate values were obtained for the metrics used to analyze the results: up to 0.94 of mean correlation and up to 0.80 similarity score with real data. Summarizing, the computed results show that there is a great similarity between the real and synthesized data samples. This result suggests that The generated synthetic datasets are valuable inputs for data augmentation to be used for computing relevant metrics and statistics about the public transportation system in Montevideo.

The main lines for future work are related to expand the proposed methodology to better capturing the main features and attributes of real public transportation data, by applying other GAN models or other generative approaches.

References

1. Cervero, R., Guerra, E., Al, S.: Beyond Mobility. Island Press/Center for Resource Economics (2017)
2. Denis, J., Massobrio, R., Nesmachnow, S., Cristóbal, A., Tchernykh, A., Meneses, E.: Parallel computing for processing data from intelligent transportation systems. In: Torres, M., Klapp, J. (eds.) ISUM 2019. CCIS, vol. 1151, pp. 266–281. Springer, Cham (2019). https://doi.org/10.1007/978-3-030-38043-4_22
3. Emam, K.E., Mosquera, L., Hoptroff, R.: Practical Synthetic Data Generation. O'Reilly Media, Inc. (2020)
4. Fabbiani, E., Nesmachnow, S., Toutouh, J., Tchernykh, A., Avetisyan, A., Radchenko, G.: Analysis of mobility patterns for public transportation and bus stops relocation. Program. Comput. Softw. **44**(6), 508–525 (2018)
5. Foster, D.: Generative Deep Learning. O'Reilly Media, Inc. (2019)
6. Goodfellow, I., et al.: Generative adversarial nets. In: Advances in Neural Information Processing Systems, pp. 2672–2680 (2014)
7. Hipogrosso, S., Nesmachnow, S.: Analysis of sustainable public transportation and mobility recommendations for Montevideo and Parque Rodó neighborhood. Smart Cities **3**(2), 479–510 (2020)
8. James, S., Harbron, C., Branson, J., Sundler, M.: Synthetic data use: exploring use cases to optimise data utility. Discover Artif. Intell. **1**(1) (2021)
9. Jauhri, A., Shen, J.P.: Real-world data driven characterization of urban human mobility patterns. Technical report, Mobility21, Carnegie Mellon University, USA (2021)
10. Jauhri, A., Stocks, B., Li, J.H., Yamada, K., Shen, J.P.: Generating realistic ride-hailing datasets using GANs. ACM Trans. Spat. Algorithms Syst. **6**(3), 1–14 (2020)
11. Liu, X., Chen, H., Andris, C.: trajGANs: using generative adversarial networks for geo-privacy protection of trajectory data. In: Location Privacy and Security Workshop, pp. 1–7 (2018)
12. Machín, B., Nesmachnow, S., Toutouh, J.: Multi-target evolutionary latent space search of a generative adversarial network for human face generation. In: Genetic and Evolutionary Computation Conference (2022)
13. Massobrio, R., Nesmachnow, S.: Urban mobility data analysis for public transportation systems: a case study in Montevideo, Uruguay. Appl. Sci. **10**(16), 1–20 (2020)
14. Massobrio, R., Nesmachnow, S., Tchernykh, A., Avetisyan, A., Radchenko, G.: Towards a cloud computing paradigm for big data analysis in smart cities. Program. Comput. Softw. **44**(3), 181–189 (2018)
15. Massobrio, R., Nesmachnow, S.: Travel time estimation in public transportation using bus location data. In: Nesmachnow, S., Hernández Callejo, L. (eds.) ICSC-Cities 2021. CCIS, vol. 1555, pp. 192–206. Springer, Cham (2022). https://doi.org/10.1007/978-3-030-96753-6_14
16. Massobrio, R., Pías, A., Vázquez, N., Nesmachnow, S.: Map-reduce for processing GPS data from public transport in Montevideo, Uruguay. In: Simposio Argentino de Grandes Datos, 45 Jornadas Argentinas de Informática, pp. 41–54 (2016)
17. Nesmachnow, S., Baña, S., Massobrio, R.: A distributed platform for big data analysis in smart cities: combining intelligent transportation systems and socioeconomic data for Montevideo, Uruguay. EAI Endorsed Trans. Smart Cities **2**(5), 153478 (2017)

18. Nesmachnow, S., Iturriaga, S.: Cluster-UY: collaborative scientific high performance computing in Uruguay. In: Torres, M., Klapp, J. (eds.) ISUM 2019. CCIS, vol. 1151, pp. 188–202. Springer, Cham (2019). https://doi.org/10.1007/978-3-030-38043-4_16

19. Nesmachnow, S., Risso, C.: Exact and evolutionary algorithms for synchronization of public transportation timetables considering extended transfer zones. Appl. Sci. **11**(15), 7138 (2021)

20. Ng, A., Jordan, M.: On discriminative vs. generative classifiers: a comparison of logistic regression and Naive Bayes. In: Conference on Neural Information Processing Systems (2002)

21. Pan, Z., Yu, W., Yi, X., Khan, A., Yuan, F., Zheng, Y.: Recent progress on generative adversarial networks (GANs): a survey. IEEE Access **7**, 36322–36333 (2019)

22. Saxena, D., Cao, J.: Multimodal spatio-temporal prediction with stochastic adversarial networks. ACM Trans. Intell. Syst. Technol. **13**(2), 1–23 (2022)

23. Shi, R., Steenkiste, P., Veloso, M.: Generating synthetic passenger data through joint traffic-passenger modeling and simulation. In: Zhang, W., Bayen, A.M., Medina, J.J.S., Barth, M.J. (eds.) 21st International Conference on Intelligent Transportation Systems, pp. 3397–3402 (2018)

24. Sussman, J.: Perspectives on Intelligent Transportation Systems (ITS). Springer, Heidelberg (2005)

25. Toutouh, J., Esteban, M., Nesmachnow, S.: Parallel/distributed generative adversarial neural networks for data augmentation of COVID-19 training images. In: Nesmachnow, S., Castro, H., Tchernykh, A. (eds.) CARLA 2020. CCIS, vol. 1327, pp. 162–177. Springer, Cham (2021). https://doi.org/10.1007/978-3-030-68035-0_12

26. Toutouh, J., Nesmachnow, S., Rossit, D.G.: Generative adversarial networks to model air pollution under uncertainty. In: International Workshop on Advanced Information and Computation Technologies and Systems, CEUR Workshop Proceedings, vol. 2858, pp. 169–174. CEUR-WS (2020)

27. Wang, S., Miao, H., Chen, H., Huang, Z.: Multi-task adversarial spatial-temporal networks for crowd flow prediction. In: Proceedings of the 29th ACM International Conference on Information & Knowledge Management. ACM (2020)

28. Yin, D., Yang, Q.: GANs based density distribution privacy-preservation on mobility data. Secur. Commun. Netw. **2018**, 1–13 (2018)

Analysis of Public Transportation in Montevideo, Uruguay During the COVID-19 Pandemic

Andrés Collares[1], Diego Helal[1], Sergio Nesmachnow[1(✉)] ⓘ,
and Andrei Tchernykh[2] ⓘ

[1] Universidad de la República, Montevideo, Uruguay
{andres.collares,diego.helal,sergion}@fing.edu.uy
[2] CICESE Research Center, Ensenada, Baja California, Mexico
chernykh@cicese.edu.mx

Abstract. This article presents the analysis of the demand and the characterization of mobility using public transportation in Montevideo, Uruguay, during the COVID-19 pandemic. A urban data-analysis approach is applied to extract useful insights from open data from different sources, including mobility of citizens, the public transportation system, and COVID cases. The proposed approach allowed computing significant results to determine the reduction of trips caused by each wave of the pandemic, the correlation between the number of trips and COVID cases, and the recovery of the use of the public transportation system. Overall, results provide useful insights to quantify and understand the behavior of citizens in Montevideo, regarding public transportation during the COVID-19 pandemic.

Keywords: Public transportation · COVID-19 pandemic · Urban data analysis · Mobility patterns

1 Introduction

Mobility was significantly affected by the COVID-19 pandemic. Although all transportation means were affected worldwide, the impact was even more notable on public transportation. Despite the different sanitary measures taken by governments and local administrations, the number of trips on public transportation significantly reduced during the COVID-19 pandemic, mainly because citizens perceived a high risk of contagion when sharing a mobility mean [30].

The reduction on the number of trips was notable, reaching values over 90% during the hard restrictions, especially in countries that adopted lockdown as countermeasure. Trips on public transportation have not fully recovered, even in countries that have significantly lowered the contagion levels [9,19,27].

The analysis of urban mobility data is crucial to help public administrations and policy makers to improve public transportation systems [22]. Data analysis

S. Nesmachnow and L. Hernández Callejo (Eds.): ICSC-CITIES 2022, CCIS 1706, pp. 200–214, 2023.
https://doi.org/10.1007/978-3-031-28454-0_14

has been even more important as a tool to study and characterize the mobility patterns of citizens during the COVID-19 pandemic. A proper analysis via relevant indicators helps the authorities to identify citizens who are forced to move despite sanitary measures, understand their behavior, and adequately size the public transport system in this type of special situation, according to their needs.

In this line of work, this article presents a study to analyze the demand and characterize the mobility patterns of citizens using the public transportation system in Montevideo, Uruguay, during the COVID-19 pandemic. A urban data-analysis approach is applied to process and analyze available open data about trips performed in the public transportation system, geographical data, and statistics about the COVID-19 pandemic in Uruguay.

The main results indicate that the reduction of trips in public transportation was 71.4%, lower than the reductions reported in similar case studies. In turn, a negative correlation was detected between the use of the public transportation system in Montevideo and confirmed COVID-19 cases in Uruguay. A characterization identifies that neighborhoods with the higher correlation have lower levels of sociodemographic index, suggesting that low income citizens were the most forced to use public transportation. Finally, the analysis of the recovery of trips in public transportation indicate that citizens returned to use public transportation at a fast pace, significantly faster than in other capital cities. Overall, the study provides useful insights to understand the mobility patterns and the use of public transportation in Montevideo during the COVID-19 pandemic.

The article is organized as follows. Section 2 presents a description of the problem solved and reviews relevant related works. Section 3 describes the case study, the public ITS in Montevideo, Uruguay. The applied methodology and implementation details is presented in Sect. 4. The experimental evaluation of the proposed approach is reported in Sect. 5. Finally, Sect. 6 presents the conclusions of the research and formulates the main lines for future work.

2   Problem Definition and Literature Review

This section describes the addressed problem and reviews relevant related works.

2.1   Problem Description

The proposed problem is characterizing the use of public transportation during the COVID-19 pandemic in Montevideo, Uruguay. The main goal is to quantitatively evaluate the reductions of the use of public transportation after the national sanitary emergency was declared, characterize the mobility patterns during the different stages and waves of the pandemics, and how citizens returned to use public transportation when the sanitary conditions improved.

The problem is relevant considering two distinctive aspects of the case study addressed, in Montevideo, Uruguay, which are commented next.

On the one hand, in Montevideo there is a natural tendency of citizens to shift to public transportation and more sustainable transportation modes [15, 16], but this tendency significantly reverted during the COVID-19 pandemic when citizens decided to shift to car for commuting because of the perceived or suspected risk of shared transportation means as a vector for the spread of the virus, considering the practically impossibility of observing the recommended social distance. This fact is not new; as safety is one the main concerns that affect and determine the mobility behavior of citizens [5].

On the other hand, the model followed by the Uruguayan government to deal with the COVID-19 pandemic was different than in other countries. Instead of promoting a lockdown, the 'responsible freedom' (*libertad responsable*) model was adopted. The model was based in a voluntary quarantine, without limiting people mobility (i.e., people were never mandated to stay at home). A meticulous tracking of infected people was implemented, complemented by randomized COVID-19 testing and promoting the use of face masks, publicity campaigns to promote social distance and social responsibility, and a reasonable reduction of social activities. The model was successful to keeping infections controlled, even at zero during several days in the first few months of the pandemics. During the first eight months of the pandemic, active cases did not exceed a threshold of 200 [29]. The first wave of COVID-19 was this way postponed until mid-2021, when the influence of tourism and the fully recovered social activities played a role to help spreading the virus. The situation normalized in August 2021, until the second wave (Omicron strain) stroked the country in the summer of 2022. However, vaccination developed at a fast pace (more 50,000 shots per day) and the country was among the top of the list in terms of percentage of vaccinated population in the world [8]. The situation returned to normality in March 2022. The end of the sanitary emergency was officially declared on April 5th, 2022.

2.2   Related Work

Studies on the demand of public transportation during the COVID-19 pandemic in Europe, North America, and Asia concluded that the number of trips significantly reduced. The behavior of citizens varied depending on the type of lockdown implemented and also other cultural factors [10]. A reduction of 50% was reported in Australian cities [4], 60% in Stockholm, Sweden [17], and 80% (peak of 90%) in Budapest, Hungary [6]. Significant differences for the reduction of public transportation were reported in Poland, depending on the level of confinement [32]. Reductions between 50% to 85% were reported for Warsaw, later confirmed by an average of 70%, according to an online survey questionnaire [18]. The reduction was up to 90% in Gdansk, but 75% of the interviewed persons planned to return using public transportation when the sanitary situation improved [27]. In the Netherlands, reductions on public transportation usage up to 90% were reported, based on the analysis of data from 2500 Dutch citizens [9]. In all reviewed cases, the use of public transportation accounted for the largest decrease, when compared with other mobility means, such as private vehicles.

Similar reductions were reported in North America. Lui et al. [19] studied the impacts of the pandemic on public transportation demand for more than 100 cities in USA. Results shown that communities with higher proportions of essential workers and vulnerable populations had higher demand levels during COVID-19. A similar situation was detected for the public transportation systems in Toronto and Vancouver, Canada. Palm et al. reported that 63% of citizens stopped using public transportation during the first stage of the COVID-19 pandemic. During the second wave of the COVID-19 pandemic, 70% of citizens that stopped using public transportation returned [26].

In Latin European countries, where the behavior of citizens is more similar than in our Latin American cities, different considerations were analyzed. Carteni et al. [7] found a high correlation between COVID-19 contagion and the number of trips performed on public transportation 22 days before, during the second wave (without vaccination). In Spain, Rodríguez et al. [28] developed characterized the impact of the COVID-19 pandemic on public and private mobility in Fuenlabrada. The reductions at the peak of the pandemic were significant, 95% for public mobility and 86% for private mobility. Similar results were computed for the city of Santander by Aloi et al. [1], who also studied the impact on NO_2 emissions and traffic accidents. The average overall mobility reduced 76%, the demand of public transportation reduced up to 93%. In turn, NO_2 emissions and traffic accidents reduced up to 60%–67%. Awad et al. [3] studied the users behavior regarding public transportation and shared mobility in Spain. Results revealed that although the use of public transportation reduced significantly, citizens were still willing to use public transportation, as long as proper sanity measures are implemented without increasing the ticket prices.

Few articles have studied the impact of the COVID-19 pandemic in public transportation in Latin America. Andara et al. [2] presented a study of the impact of the COVID-19 pandemic on mobility in eight major cities in Latin America. The study focused on developing descriptive statistical models for the variation of motorized mobility in the period from March to September 2020. Traffic congestion and urban transportation were analyzed via regression models. The main results indicated that private mobility recovered faster than public transportation. Authors concluded that public transportation did not accounted as a relevant factor in the spread of the pandemic in the studied cities.

Gramsch et al. [13] analyzed the impact on public transportation of the dynamic lockdown strategy in Santiago, Chile. The main results reported a reduction of 72% on the demand for public transportation when strict lockdown measures were adopted, and a reduction of 12% when the dynamic lockdown strategy was applied. The study also detected a short-term effectiveness of lockdowns to reduce mobility. The implemented lockdowns had a greater impact on the demand for public transportation in municipalities with a larger elderly population and high-income households.

No studies have been published about the use of public transportation during the COVID-19 pandemic in Uruguay. This article contributes in this line of work, by applying a data analysis approach to characterize mobility in the public transportation system of Montevideo during the COVID-19 pandemic.

3 Case Study: The Public Transportation System in Montevideo, Uruguay

The public transportation system in Montevideo is within the Metropolitan Transportation System (STM), a program designed to integrate all public transportation of Montevideo and nearby locations and conglomerates.

The STM comprises 145 main lines, more than one thousand line variants, and five thousand bus stops, remarkable large numbers for a city like Montevideo. Figure 1 presents the bus stops of the public transportation system in Montevideo.

Fig. 1. Bus stops of the public transportation system in Montevideo

Among several features oriented to develop a more efficient, rational and safe public transportation, STM introduced a relevant technological improvement: contact-less smart cards to be used by passengers to pay for tickets, without using physical money [20]. Each smart card is linked to the identity of the owner, and the collected data are crucial to analyze the system performance, to determine the mobility patterns of citizens, and to identify issues that affect the quality of service offered to citizens.

The information about trips, collected by STM, is crucial to know relevant data, such as origin stop, destination, travel demand, bus line, date and time of travel, type of ticket or category of user, etc. These data allow computing important indicators, identify mobility patterns, and categorize the mobility demands. Previous research efforts from our research group [11,12,15,20–23] processed records of trips in the public transportation of Montevideo, and also crossing with other data sources (geospatial data, information on lines, etc.).

4 Analysis of COVID-19 and Mobility Information

This section describes the data source and the methodology applied for the analysis of public transportation in Montevideo during the COVID-19 pandemic.

4.1 Data Sources

The processed data to solve the problem was obtained from open data repositories provided by the Uruguayan government, under the National Open Data Catalog . Several data collections are free and fully available. In particular, the catalog includes data on trips made by bus, from the STM. The dataset of trips contains all the trips made on the lines of the public transportation system in Montevideo, including information on companies, lines, date and time, ticket categories and other relevant information, such as the origin bus stop for each trip and the payment method (smart card or cash). The information available for public transportation trips has data from November 2019 to June 2022.

Geographical information was obtained from shapefiles containing the location of bus stops in Montevideo and shapefiles containing the polygons of neighborhoods in Montevideo. In turn, free access data provided by the Uruguayan Interdisciplinary Group for COVID-19 Data Analysis (GUIAD-COVID-19) were also used. The extracted data from this dataset was the number of registered COVID-19 cases per day and department [14].

4.2 Overall Description of the Methodology

The applied methodology included three stages: data pre-processing, data processing applying parallel computing, and analysis of results.

Data Pre-processing. The data preprocessing stage included data cleansing and also associating the geographical location (neighborhood) to each registered ticket sale from the trips dataset. The shapefiles containing the location of bus stops in Montevideo was crossed with the shapefile containing the polygons of neighborhoods in Montevideo, to be used in the aggregation of results. The open-source cross-platform desktop geographic information system application QGIS was used for this task. A manual classification was performed for those bus stops that are located outside Montevideo. They were categorized as 'Canelones East' or 'Canelones West', according to their geographical location (Canelones is the department surrounding Montevideo).

Parallel Processing. A large volume of data was available to process in the proposed study. The size of the corresponding datasets for the analyzed period (2019–2022) was over 73 GB. In addition, there is a large flow of parallelizable operations, that fit on the using the MapReduce parallel computing paradigm. Examples of those operations are the grouping of data according to day and neighborhood (in order to analyze the daily mobility by neighborhood), the transformation of each trip into an integer for counting the number of trips that occurred each day, the grouping by day and user category, and the grouping by day and bus line.

Analysis of Results and Metrics. The final stage involved the computation of relevant metrics for the analysis and the application of statistics and time series analysis over the computed results.

4.3   Resolution Strategy

The parallel algorithm for data processing was developed in several stages:

1. An algorithm was implemented to compute the number of trips per day. The main goal was to find out how the start date of the pandemic and the declaration of the sanitary emergency impacted on the mobility patterns of citizens and determine the reduction of public transportation usage. For the implementation, the data about trips was separated by day to perform a parallelization of the computation and then a reduce operation was applied to group by day.
2. A second algorithm was implemented to calculate the correlation between reported COVID cases and mobility patterns of citizens.
3. In addition, an analysis of the mobility patterns of citizens during the COVID pandemic by neighborhood, bus line, and user category was carried out. Trip data was grouped by day and neighborhood, by day and line number, and by day and user category. The main goal was determining which category of users most needed to use public transportation, through the value of the correlation between COVID cases and trips for each case.
4. Finally, the recovery of citizens mobility in the city during the COVID pandemic was studied. The analysis studied the dates on which citizens returned to 'normal' levels of public transportation use, by analyzing how the monthly average of daily trips varied over time.

4.4   Implementation Details

The developed algorithms were implemented using the Scala programming language [25] and the Hadoop MapReduce framework [31]. The MapReduce framework adapts very well to the characteristics of the data processing problem and Scala offers a flexible and robust development and interoperability. Both are popular options in the field of big data.

The Hadoop Distributed File System (HDFS) was used for data storage. HDFS is a fault-tolerant system that uses data replication and was designed to be used as the storage system of Hadoop. Using HDFS allows for a robust and efficient design. On the one hand, if a processing node goes down, the data will be available on the other configured nodes. HDFS is optimized to store large amounts of data and maintain multiple copies to ensure high availability and fault tolerance. On the other hand, HDFS provides a very efficient access to data, granting a large bandwidth, so that MapReduce applications can efficiently process large volumes of data. It also uses the write-once-read-many storage model, so input data is written once and can be read as many times as needed.

The analysis of processed data and results was performed in Python, using the Pandas and Matplotlib libraries.

5   Experimental Analysis and Discussion

This section reports the results of the experimental analysis of COVID-19 and mobility information from the public transportation system in Montevideo.

5.1   Development and Execution Platform

The proposed big data processing approach was developed in Scala and Hadoop. The experimental analysis was performed on a HPE Proliant server with Xeon Gold 6138 processor, 40 cores and 120 GB of RAM memory from National Supercomputing Center (Cluster-UY), Uruguay [24].

5.2   Validation Results

The computed results are reported and discussed in the following paragraphs.

Effect of the Declaration of Sanitary Emergency. Figure 2 presents a comparison of the average number of trips performed on the STM before and after the sanitary emergency was declared in Uruguay.

The valley at the beginning of the year in Fig. 2 is seasonal: January and February are the holiday months, whereas most education activities (school, high school, university) started on March, 2nd, 2020. In a normal situation, bus trips peak in March, with a similar average than in November.

Figure 2(a) clearly shows the reduction on bus trips from the day when the sanitary emergency was declared (March, 13rd). The overall reduction was 71.4% with respect to the number of daily trips in 1–13 March. A different situation occurred for weekdays and weekends. In weekends, the reduction of trips was 54.1%, mainly because a significantly lower of bus trips are performed on weekends. Therefore, the reduction due to the COVID pandemic had a less significant impact. Figure 2(b) reports the analysis, separating weekday trips and weekend trips. The graph bar shows that the number of weekend trips reduced to approximately one half of the trips, considering the average trips in weekends from March 1–13.

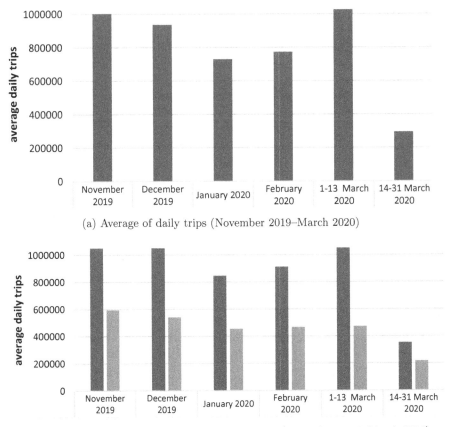

(a) Average of daily trips (November 2019–March 2020)

(b) Average of daily trips for weekdays and weekends (November 2019–March 2020)

Fig. 2. Comparison of average daily trips pre- and post-declaration of the sanitary emergency in Montevideo, Uruguay

The reported reductions on trips performed in public transportation are lower than other reported cases for similar cities in Europe and America. This result suggest that the risk perceived by citizens regarding trips in public transportation was lower than in other countries.

The use of public transportation steadily increased since the first week after the declaration of sanitary emergency. The evolution is reported and analyzed in the next paragraph.

Trips and COVID Cases. Figure 3 presents the evolution of the number of trips from May 2020 to May 2002 in the public transportation system on Montevideo, and the number of confirmed COVID cases, according to GUIAD-COVID-19 and the Public Health Ministry.

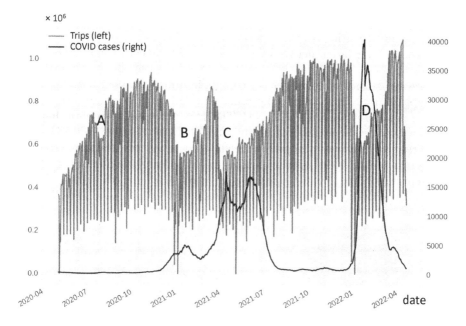

Fig. 3. Number of trips and COVID cases (April 2020 to May 2022)

Figure 3 shows a clear relation between mobility in public transportation and the number of COVID cases.

The number of trips reduced when a COVID outbreak happened, and the situation tended to normalize when COVID cases reduced. After the initial reduction of 70% in the first month after the sanitary emergency was declared, the number of trips recovered until the end of 2020. In Uruguay, the initial stage of the COVID pandemic was remarkable softer than in other countries. Only a minor increase of COVID cases was observed in August 2000, when the use of public transportation reduced about 10% (the small valley marked with 'A' in Fig. 3).

Then, the first wave of COVID occurred in December 2020. The number of cases increased up to 5000, and the use of public transportation reduced more than 20% (the first large valley marked with 'B'). A new outbreak in May 2021 reduced more than 40% the number of trips (the second large valley marked with 'C'). The number of COVID cases dropped significantly between August and December 2021, and the use of public transportation returned to almost normal levels (almost a million trips daily).

The second wave of COVID started in January 2022. The number of cases increased exponentially, up to almost 40 000 in January 2022. The use of public transportation decreased accordingly, almost 50%. When COVID cases reduced, citizens rapidly returned to their common mobility patterns using the public transportation system, with over one million tickets sold in May 2022.

Characterization of Daily Trips. Neighborhoods in Montevideo have different socio-economic realities. To characterize the mobility patterns from/to different locations, the correlation between trips performed from each neighborhoods was studied.

Since the dataset of trips does not contain information about neighborhoods, the shapefiles with the bus stops locations and with the polygons of each neighborhood in Montevideo were processed. The intersection between both shapefiles was computed to determine the neighborhood where each bus stop is located. The dataset of trips was grouped by neighborhood and the Pearson correlation between the number of trips from each neighborhood and the number of COVID cases reported in the city was computed. Figure 4 shows the correlation between trips for the 65 neighborhoods in Montevideo and COVID cases.

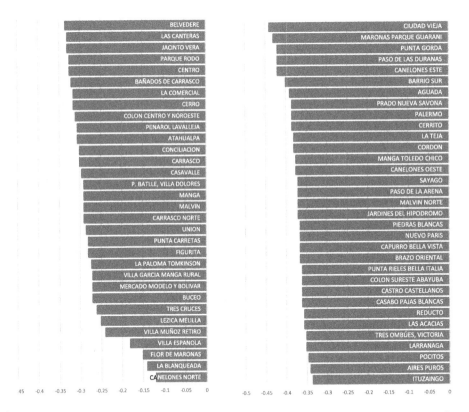

Fig. 4. Correlation between trips in the public transportation and COVID cases for neighborhoods in Montevideo

The correlation results in Fig. 4 shows three clear groups of neighborhoods: low negative correlation, medium negative correlation, and high negative correlation. Most neighborhoods with low negative correlation also have low socio-demographic indicators. These results are useful to perform an in-depth analysis of the impact of the pandemic on different neighborhoods, i.e., considering the average household income. This analysis is one of the main lines for future work.

Recovery of the Use of the Public Transportation System. The recovery of the public transportation system was significantly faster in Montevideo, Uruguay than in other reported capital cities around the world. Table 1 reports the number of average trips per day for each month in the period in which the sanitary emergency was in force, and the percentage over the average pre-COVID trips.

Table 1. Analysis of the recovery of trips in the public transportation system

2020								
pre-COVID	April	May	June	July	Aug.	Sept.	Oct.	Nov.
1024743	262008	357921	585612	860123	620732	805118	915852	925801
100.0%	25.6%	34.9%	57.1%	83.9%	60.6%	78.6%	89.4%	90.3%
2020	2021							
Dec.	Jan.	Feb.	March	April	May	June	July	Aug.
880519	650070	575294	720518	572381	590163	701371	738023	835182
85.9%	63.4%	56.1%	70.3%	55.9%	57.6%	68.4%	72.0%	81.5%
2021				2022				
Sept.	Oct.	Nov.	Dec.	Jan.	Feb.	March	April	
925830	996702	992601	990924	602185	712046	1050306	1082415	
90.3%	97.3%	96.9%	96.7%	58.8%	69.5%	102.5%	105.6%	

Table 1 indicates that after a slow period of two months after the sanitary emergency was declared, the number of trips recovered fast, i.e., 84% of the reference value in just four months (July 2020). Despite a reduction in August 2020, by the end of the year the number of trips was almost the same than pre-COVID (90% in November). Then, the first massive cases of COVID generated a reduction of up to 56% in February 2021, and the same pattern occurred again, users steadily recovered the confidence in public transportation, until the first wave stroked hard in April-June 2021, causing a decrease in the number of trips up to 56% of pre-COVID numbers. The recovery of the number of trips was significantly faster after the first wave, reaching values over 90% in just three months (September 2021) and a full recovery in the last months of 2021. The second wave (Omicron strain) reduced the number of trips to 59% in January 2022, but the recovery was very fast: the number of trips exceeded the previous pre-COVID value in just two months, in March 2022.

The reported values demonstrate that despite the reduction on trips in public transportation as a consequence of the increase of COVID cases, citizens rapidly trusted again in the public transportation system. The periods for the recovery of the number of trips was shorter in each wave, and just a month and a half in

2022. This pace is significantly faster than the ones reported for other similar case studies in the world [3,13,27]. These facts allows concluding that the responsible freedom model was not only successful in mitigating the impact of the spread of COVID, but also in guaranteeing a rapid recovery of mobility patterns and the use of public transportation in Montevideo.

6 Conclusions and Future Work

This article presented a study and characterization of the use of public transportation in Montevideo, Uruguay, during the COVID-19 pandemic. Following a urban data-analysis approach, available open data about trips and statistics about the COVID-19 pandemic in Uruguay were analyzed.

The analysis confirmed a reduction of trips in public transportation of 71.4%, lower than values reported for similar cities in related works. A negative correlation was detected between the use of public transportation and confirmed COVID-19 cases. Neighborhoods with the higher correlation have lower sociodemographic levels, suggesting that low income citizens were forced to use public transportation. Trips in public transportation indicate recovered significantly faster than in other capital cities.

The main lines for future work include expanding the analysis considering other categories (e.g., age and tariff type) and performing an in-depth analysis of the impact of the pandemic on different neighborhoods, i.e., considering the average household income. In turn, a throughout analysis of the post-COVID situation can be performed once more recent trip data are available.

References

1. Aloi, A., et al.: Effects of the COVID-19 lockdown on urban mobility: empirical evidence from the city of Santander (Spain). Sustainability **12**(9), 3870 (2020)
2. Andara, R., et al.: Behavior of traffic congestion and public transport in eight large cities in Latin America during the COVID-19 pandemic. Appl. Sci. **11**(10), 4703 (2021)
3. Awad, S., Julio, R., Gomez, J., Moya, B., Sastre, J.: Post-COVID-19 travel behavior patterns: impact on the willingness to pay of users of public transport and shared mobility services in Spain. Eur. Transp. Res. Rev. **13**(1) (2021)
4. Beck, M., Hensher, D.: Insights into the impact of COVID-19 on household travel and activities in Australia. Transp. Policy **99**, 95–119 (2020)
5. Bohte, W., Maat, K., van Wee, B.: Measuring attitudes in research on residential self-selection and travel behaviour: a review of theories and empirical research. Transp. Rev. **29**(3), 325–357 (2009)
6. Bucsky, P.: Modal share changes due to COVID-19: the case of Budapest. Transp. Res. Interdisc. Perspect. **8**, 100141 (2020)
7. Cartenì, A., Di Francesco, L., Henke, I., Marino, T., Falanga, A.: The role of public transport during the second COVID-19 wave in Italy. Sustainability **13**(21), 11905 (2021)
8. Costabel, M.: Uruguay emerges as a rare pandemic winner in Latin America (2021). Foreign Policy, 21 July 2020 (July 2022)

9. de Haas, M., Faber, R., Hamersma, M.: How COVID-19 and the Dutch 'intelligent lockdown' change activities, work and travel behaviour: evidence from longitudinal data in the Netherlands. Transp. Res. Interdisc. Perspect. **6**, 100150 (2020)
10. De Vos, J.: The effect of COVID-19 and subsequent social distancing on travel behavior. Transp. Res. Interdisc. Perspect. **5**, 100121 (2020)
11. Denis, J., Massobrio, R., Nesmachnow, S., Cristóbal, A., Tchernykh, A., Meneses, E.: Parallel computing for processing data from intelligent transportation systems. In: Torres, M., Klapp, J. (eds.) ISUM 2019. CCIS, vol. 1151, pp. 266–281. Springer, Cham (2019). https://doi.org/10.1007/978-3-030-38043-4_22
12. Fabbiani, E., Nesmachnow, S., Toutouh, J., Tchernykh, A., Avetisyan, A., Radchenko, G.I.: Analysis of mobility patterns for public transportation and bus stops relocation. Program. Comput. Softw. **44**(6), 508–525 (2018)
13. Gramsch, B., Guevara, C.A., Munizaga, M., Schwartz, D., Tirachini, A.: The effect of dynamic lockdowns on public transport demand in times of COVID-19: evidence from smartcard data. Transp. Policy **126**, 136–150 (2022)
14. Grupo Uruguayo Interdisciplinario de Análisis de Datos: Covid stats per department (2022). https://github.com/GUIAD-COVID/datos-y-visualizaciones-GUIAD/blob/master/datos/estadisticasUYporDepto.csv
15. Hipogrosso, S., Nesmachnow, S.: Analysis of sustainable public transportation and mobility recommendations for Montevideo and Parque Rodó neighborhood. Smart Cities **3**(2), 479–510 (2020)
16. Hipogrosso, S., Nesmachnow, S.: A practical approach for sustainable transit oriented development in Montevideo, Uruguay. In: Nesmachnow, S., Hernández Callejo, L. (eds.) ICSC-Cities 2021. CCIS, vol. 1555, pp. 256–270. Springer, Cham (2022). https://doi.org/10.1007/978-3-030-96753-6_18
17. Jenelius, E., Cebecauer, M.: Impacts of COVID-19 on public transport ridership in Sweden: analysis of ticket validations, sales and passenger counts. Transp. Res. Interdisc. Perspect. **8**, 100242 (2020)
18. Kłos, Z., Gutowski, P.: The outbreak of COVID-19 pandemic in relation to sense of safety and mobility changes in public transport using the example of Warsaw. Sustainability **14**(3), 1780 (2022)
19. Liu, L., Miller, H.J., Scheff, J.: The impacts of COVID-19 pandemic on public transit demand in the united states. PLOS ONE **15**(11) (2020)
20. Massobrio, R., Nesmachnow, S.: Urban mobility data analysis for public transportation systems: a case study in Montevideo, Uruguay. Appl. Sci. **10**(16), 1–20 (2020)
21. Massobrio, R., Nesmachnow, S., Tchernykh, A., Avetisyan, A., Radchenko, G.: Towards a cloud computing paradigm for big data analysis in smart cities. Program. Comput. Softw. **44**(3), 181–189 (2018)
22. Massobrio, R., Nesmachnow, S.: Travel time estimation in public transportation using bus location data. In: Nesmachnow, S., Hernández Callejo, L. (eds.) ICSC-Cities 2021. CCIS, vol. 1555, pp. 192–206. Springer, Cham (2022). https://doi.org/10.1007/978-3-030-96753-6_14
23. Massobrio, R., Pías, A., Vázquez, N., Nesmachnow, S.: Map-reduce for processing GPS data from public transport in Montevideo, Uruguay. In: Simposio Argentino de Grandes Datos, 45 Jornadas Argentinas de Informática, pp. 41–54 (2016)
24. Nesmachnow, S., Iturriaga, S.: Cluster-UY: collaborative scientific high performance computing in Uruguay. In: Torres, M., Klapp, J. (eds.) ISUM 2019. CCIS, vol. 1151, pp. 188–202. Springer, Cham (2019). https://doi.org/10.1007/978-3-030-38043-4_16

25. Odersky, M., Spoon, L., Venners, B.: Programming in scala: [a comprehensive step-by-step guide] (2008)
26. Palm, M., Allen, J., Liu, B., Zhang, Y., Widener, M., Farber, S.: Riders who avoided public transit during COVID-19. J. Am. Plann. Assoc. **87**(4), 455–469 (2021)
27. Przybylowski, A., Stelmak, S., Suchanek, M.: Mobility behaviour in view of the impact of the COVID-19 pandemic—public transport users in Gdansk case study. Sustainability **13**(1), 364 (2021)
28. Rodríguez, A., Wilby, M., Vinagre, J., Fernández, R.: Characterization of COVID-19's impact on mobility and short-term prediction of public transport demand in a mid-size city in Spain. Sensors **21**(19), 6574 (2021)
29. Taylor, L.: Uruguay is winning against COVID-19. This is how [corrected]. BMJ 370, m3693 (2020)
30. Tirachini, A., Cats, O.: COVID-19 and public transportation: current assessment, prospects, and research needs. J. Public Transp. **22**(1) (2020)
31. White, T.: Hadoop: The Definitive Guide, 4th edn. O'Reilly, Beijing (2015)
32. Wielechowski, M., Czech, K., Grzeda, Ł: Decline in mobility: public transport in Poland in the time of the COVID-19 pandemic. Economies **8**(4), 78 (2020)

Big Data Trends in the Analysis of City Resources

Regina Gubareva[1] and Rui Pedro Lopes[1,2]

[1] Research Center in Digitalization and Intelligent Robotics (CeDRI),
Instituto Politécnico de Bragança, Bragança, Portugal
{regina.gubareva,rlopes}@ipb.pt

[2] Institute of Electronics and Informatics Engineering of Aveiro (IEETA),
University of Aveiro, Aveiro, Portugal

Abstract. The operation and management of a municipality generate large amounts of complex data, enclosing information that is not easy to infer or extract. Their analysis is challenging and requires specialized approaches and tools, usually based on statistical techniques or on machine learning and artificial intelligence algorithms. These Big Data is often created by combining many data sources that correspond to different operational groups in the city, such as transport, energy consumption, water consumption, maintenance, and many others. Each group exhibits unique characteristics that are usually not shared by others. This paper provides a detailed systematic literature review on applying different algorithms to urban data processing. The study aims to figure out how this kind of information was collected, stored, pre-processed, and analyzed, to compare various methods, and to select feasible solutions for further research. The review finds that clustering, classification, correlation, anomaly detection, and prediction algorithms are frequently used. Moreover, the interpretation of relevant and available research results is presented.

Keywords: Big data · Smart city · Resources consumption

1 Introduction

The smart city concept is popular and common in scientific literature, characterizing a healthy environment that improves the quality of life and well-being of citizens [10]. Due to the diversity of services, resources, and projects, smart cities manage huge amounts of data, typically within the Big Data concept. One can argue what are the minimum conditions and characteristics for a city to become "smart". However, since nowadays most operations are controlled via comprehensive information and communication technologies, the need to collect, store, integrate, process, and analyze data is prevalent and important in most cities. Over the past ten years, the number of sensors and metering devices has been increasing geometrically. The intention to control and understand everything surrounding us became a significant step in the development of technologies of environmental sensors: smart houses, smart cities, smart devices, IoT,

S. Nesmachnow and L. Hernández Callejo (Eds.): ICSC-CITIES 2022, CCIS 1706, pp. 215–229, 2023.
https://doi.org/10.1007/978-3-031-28454-0_15

and many others. Legacy information is also laying around, in spreadsheets or databases, which can be valuable if correctly accessed and integrated. Citizens and institutions also make use of social networks to convey opinions, criticism, or information about resources, services, or events. The essential questions are how to use this data and how to extract practical and meaningful information from all these measurements. Big data is a set of technologies for processing large amounts of data. It refers not only to the amount of information but also to the data rate, meaning the multiple streams of data that should be processed in real-time. Moreover, large examples of data usually enclose hidden, potentially valuable, patterns. Several unique phenomena associated with high dimensionality, including noise accumulation, spurious correlation, and random endogeneity, make traditional statistical procedures difficult to use. In the Big Data era, large sample sizes allow us to better understand heterogeneity by shedding light on research such as examining the relationship between specific covariates and rare outcomes.

This work is developed within the project "PandIA - Management of Pandemic Social Isolation Based on City and Social Intelligence", which focus on providing detailed information, such as resource consumption trends, estimation of people in each area or household, a heat map of suspected outbreaks, and others to health and municipal authorities and to emergency personal. For that, it uses information from several sources, including pathogen characteristics, infection statistics, municipal information, social networks, and hospital information and statistics. The work described in this paper uses a systematic literature review to understand the nature and purpose of the data generated and collected in the context of a city. It aims to understand what types of data are usually considered, how they what collected, what algorithms are used, and for what purposes. We look for evidence and best practices for using city information in Big Data settings, the impact, and results. The authors do not set out to compare the algorithms with mathematical certainty, we just review various approaches and provide rough estimates of effectiveness. The article should give a base understanding of what to do with smart city data. Broadly speaking, the purpose of this paper is to systematize the basic principles of digital data handling in the formation and development of smart cities. The review summarizes the research being done for the last five years. The literature is categorized according to the algorithms used, the approach to handling data, the nature of data, and the results of the data processing.

The paper is structured in four sections, starting with this introduction. Section 2 describes the methodology followed in this study. The Result and Analysis follow, with the results and associated discussion and it finishes in Sect. 4 with some conclusions.

2   Methodology

The main objective of this literature review is to try to understand the data structure and nature, their sources, the processes of collecting and storing, the algorithms and tasks these are developed to do, and, finally, the purposes or intentions of the results. This literature review follows the approach suggested by Materla, Cudney, and Antony [11] and by Subhash and Cudney [14], including three phases: planning, operation, and dissemination (Fig. 1).

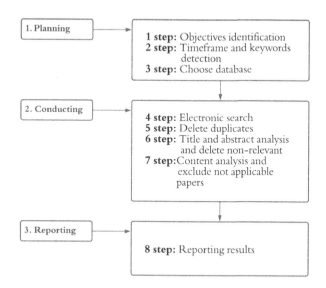

Fig. 1. Phases of the systematic literature review.

To guide the search, a set of research questions was considered:

1. What is the format, structure, and context of the data each paper uses?
2. What algorithms are used for urban data handling?
3. What is the complexity of each algorithm?
4. What are the results achieved after the analysis and what do they mean?

The papers were searched in Scopus and IEEEXplore. These databases were selected because they provide a wide set of areas and the key terms provide an initial focus on the main objective of this work. A total of 230 papers were identified in the first run (Table 1).

Only the papers retrieved from Scopus and IEEEXplore published between January 1st, 2015, and December 31st, 2020, whose text was available in the institutional repositories were considered. Moreover, papers without a peer review process and written in a different language than English were also excluded. After removing the duplicate entries, the total number of papers was 208.

Some guidelines were defined for the title, abstract, and text analysis. After a primary assessment, a detailed analysis of conformity to a chosen theme was made. The title's meaningfulness, associated with the abstract description helped with this. Next, the text was skimmed to assess if all the information needed could be found. So, in summary, the papers were analyzed according to the following steps:

Table 1. Search terms and the number of papers retrieved

Database	Search term	Results
Scopus	TITLE ("big data" AND ("urban data" OR "smart city" OR "geo data" OR "social network" OR "predictive maintenance" OR "algorithms"))	123
IEEEXplore	(("Document Title": "big data") AND ("Document Title": "urban data" OR "Document Title": "smart city" OR "Document Title": "geo data" OR "Document Title": "social network" OR "Document Title": "predictive maintenance" OR "Document Title": "algorithms"))	107
	Total	230

1. Searched articles were limited to the predefined time frame (2016–2021)
2. Papers with non-relevant titles, abstracts, and keywords were excluded
3. Text that did not mention the required subjects was excluded

After analysis of the title, abstract, and text, 196 more papers were excluded for being out of the scope of this work. A total of 12 papers remained for the analysis (Table 2).

Table 2. The results of the search by journals

Phase	Scopus	IEEEXplore	Total
search	123	107	230
del. duplicates	114	94	208
title	42	36	78
abstract	11	8	19
content	7	5	12

3   Analysis and Discussion

The analysis process started with the characterization of the selected references. Content analysis followed, to assess the context and definition of self-study and the purpose of the work described in the paper.

3.1   Characterization

In total, papers from 9 countries were found. Spain has 3 papers and China 2 papers. For United Arab Emirates, Denmark, Malaysua, South Korea, Taiwan, India and Greece, a single paper was found. It should be highlighted that the countries' distribution does not connect with cities' development in these regions.

The distribution by year reveals a peak number of papers in 2018, with 7 papers. The lowest amount of research is observed in 2019 (a single paper), which can reflect the exploration of new approaches in the area. The remaining years (2017 and 2016, two papers were accounted). Despite considerable attention from the scientific community to the issue of the impact of such a resource as digital data on the development of modern socio-economic systems, including cities, this area is only beginning to develop, and the understanding of the use of data as a tool for the development of smart cities remains limited in the scientific literature. In general, it can be noted that research is increasingly focused on the use of digital data as a new socio-economic phenomenon, and attempts are made to conceptualize, classify and evaluate the role of different types of data in socioeconomic processes. In most cases, such studies are related to the use of big data in certain areas of the urban environment, such as transportation, public safety, and environmental protection. At the same time, the literature lacks studies of a general systemic nature on the use of big data for smart cities regardless of the field of application.

3.2   Data Types and Sources

The smart city concept implies integrating multiple information and communication technologies for city infrastructure management: transport, education, health, systems of housing and utilities, safety, etc. Municipal governments collect numerous heterogeneous information, and an "urban data" term can mean various datasets: data from video surveillance cameras, traffic, air quality, energy and water consumption, and images for smart recognition. Therefore for this study, the essential is to recognize and classify different datasets utilized in considered resources.

Trilles et al. describe a methodology of (big) data process produced by sensors in real-time [15]. It assumes that it works with different sensor data sources with different formats and connection interfaces. Wireless sensor networks (WSN) are used for monitoring the physical state of the environment: air pollution, forest fire, landslide, and water quality. Although the system proposed by the authors is designed to process all data types, the WSNs mainly produce numerical data like water level, and the gas concentration in the air, mainly classified as quantitative information. An efficient method to derive spatio-temporal analysis of the data, using correlations was proposed by [3]. The authors use data from Bluetooth sensors installed in light poles. The data was collected from the road sensors in the city of Aarhus in Denmark. The measurements are taken every 5 min and the dataset includes a timestamp, location information, average speed, and a total of automobiles at the time of commit. The data were classified as numerical as there are no text, images, sound, or video information.

Bordogna et al. used in their paper big mobile social data, which included users-generated, geo-referenced and timestamped contents [4]. The content means text data that users posts in modern emerging social systems like Twitter, Facebook, Instagram, and so forth. Hereby, the dataset can be classified as heterogeneous by way of containing the text of social network posts and numerical data of location and time. Wang et al. considered another approach to analysis and evaluated the effectiveness of deep neural networks [16]. The aim of their paper was the monitoring and control of local HIV epidemics. The collection includes statistics on the number of morbidities, mortality, and mortality by region, age, sex, and occupation. The type of data is categorized as text and numerical.

The researchers from Spain, Pérez-Chacón et al., proposed a methodology to extract electric energy consumption patterns in big data time series [12]. The study used the big data time series of electricity consumption of several Pablo de Olavide University buildings, extracted using smart meters over six years. Karyotis et al. presented a novel data clustering framework for big sensory data produced by IoT applications [9]. The dataset was collected from an operational smart-city/building IoT infrastructure provided by the Federated Interoperable Semantic IoT/cloud Testbeds and Applications (FIESTA-IoT) testbed federation. The array is heterogeneous and represents measurements of different types: temperature, humidity, battery level, soil moisture, etc.

Azri et al. presented a technique of three-dimensional data analytics using a dendrogram clustering approach [2]. It is assumed that the algorithm can be applied to large heterogeneous datasets gathered from sensors, social media, and legacy data sources. Alshami et al. tested the performance of two partition algorithms K-Means and Fuzzy c-Mean for clustering big urban datasets [1]. Compared techniques can be applicable to huge heterogeneous datasets in various areas like medicine, business, biology, etc. In the paper, the authors utilized urban data from various data sources, such as the Internet of Things, LIDAR data, local weather stations, and mobile phone sensors.

Chang et al. developed a new iterative algorithm, called the K-sets+ algorithm for clustering data points in a semi-metric space, where the distance measure does not necessarily satisfy the triangular inequality [6]. The algorithm is designed for clustering data points in semi-metric space. To understand what semi-metric space is, it is necessary to briefly consider the concept of metrics in space. The metric is the mapping for some set $d : X \times X \rightarrow R$, for which the axioms of non-degeneracy and symmetry have to be satisfied but not necessarily the triangle inequality. If the distance between different points can be zero, the metric is semi-metric. The method was evaluated with two experiments: community detection of signed networks and clustering of real networks. The dataset included 216 servers in different locations, and the latency (measured by the round trip time) between any two servers of these 216 servers is recorded in real-time.

Chae et al. have compared the performance of the deep neural network (DNN), long-short-term memory (LSTM), and the auto-regressive integrated moving average (ARIMA) in predicting three infectious diseases [5]. The study uses four kinds of data to predict infectious diseases, including search query data, social media big data, temperature, and humidity. Data related to malaria, chickenpox, and scarlet fever, for 576 days, were considered. As a result, the data is partly numerical and partly text. The research of Chen et al. focuses on multi-source urban data analysis [7]. The points of interest are geographical, street view, road map, and real-estate data. The record comprises the road network of the city, longitude, latitude, name, and functionality of a structure in the urban environment, and imagery of locations. Obviously, the dataset is ranked as heterogeneous.

Simhachalam and Ganesan presented a multidimensional mining approach in a successive way by finding groups (clusters) of communities with the same multi-dynamic characteristics [13]. The data refers to the statistics of population, migration, tax capacity, dwellings, employment, and commuters.

The majority of the studies assume heterogeneous nature data. There are two research papers with only numerical data and one of the papers investigates image data processing. Text and numerical data are dominant and they are collected from multiple sources (Table 3).

Table 3. Data types and sources.

Paper	Data	Category
[15]	data from different sensors	heterogeneous
[3]	traffic data collected from the road sensors in the city: geographical location, time-stamp, average speed, and total of automobile	numerical
[4]	social networks posts, timestamp, geo-location	heterogeneous
[16]	10-year historical HIV incidence data: the number of morbidity, morbidity, mortality and mortality by region, age, sex, occupation	heterogeneous
[12]	electricity consumption for 6 years for several buildings	numerical
[9]	big sensory data, measurements of different types: temperature, humidity, battery level, soil moisture	heterogeneous
[2]	smart city data	heterogeneous
[1]	data from the Internet of Things, LIDAR data, local weather stations, mobile phones sensors	heterogeneous
[6]	locations and the latency (measured by the round trip time) between any two data points	heterogeneous
[5]	search query data, social media big data, temperature, and humidity	heterogeneous
[7]	geographical data, points of interests data(longitude, latitude, name, and functionality of a structure in the urban environment), street view data, real estate data, mobile phone location data, social network data, micro-blog data, taxi GPS trajectory data, taxi profile data	heterogeneous
[13]	the measurements of the blood tests as the corpuscular volume of test substances and the number of half-pint equivalents of alcoholic beverages drunk per day	numerical

3.3 Algorithms

In general, 12 different approaches to big municipal data processing were considered. The methods can be divided into groups depending on the manner of information handling: clustering, classification, correlation, deep neural network, frameworks, and community detection. Figure 2 illustrates the proportion between different techniques. The most popular approach is clustering, various algorithms of clustering utilized in 5 considered studies.

The approach followed by [15] includes three layers: content layer, services layer, and application layer. The content layer includes sensor network data sources, and the services layer provides database connection, transformations of data, and communications protocols for real-time data handling and processing. The last layer implies client application. The service layer implements the Cumulative SUM (CUSUM) algorithm of anomaly detection. The method considers

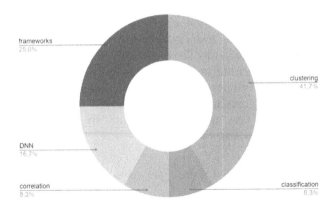

Fig. 2. Methods of urban data analysis

the set of observations following a normal distribution. For each collection of measurements, the cumulative sum is calculated. When the score overcomes the threshold, the algorithm detects anomalies. If the parameter exceeds the threshold, the anomaly will be due to the increase (up-event), and if the sum is greater than the threshold, it will be due to the decrease (down-event). Different data types from multiple sources are processed by a special wrapper and transformed into standard form. Transformed observation is encoded in line according to Open Geospatial Consortium (OGC) standard for Observations and Measurements.

The unique method used in [3] tried to apply correlation methods to urban data analysis. They suggested an efficient method to derive spatio-temporal analysis of the data, using correlations, with Pearson and Entropy-based methods and compares the results of both algorithms. Pearson's coefficient characterizes the presence of linear dependence between two values. The weakness of Pearson correlation is poor accuracy when variables are not distributed normally. Mutual information is the statistical function of two random variables, which describes the quantity of information of one random value in another. The constraint of mutual information is that it has a higher processing complexity than Pearson correlation. The technique continuously calculates the average correlation for sensory road data divided into two sectors until the data runs out. Different types of correlation were tested.

The Long short-term memory (LSTM) neural network models, autoregressive integrated moving average (ARIMA) models, generalized regression neural network (GRNN) models, and exponential smoothing (ES) models to estimate HIV incidence in Guangxi, China, and explore which model is the best and most precise for local HIV incidence prediction were used by [16]. ARIMA is the model used for time series forecasting. LSTM is a recurrent neural network, characterized by the ability to learn long-term dependencies. In this study, several models were built. The model with the lowest mean square error (MSE) was considered the optimal model. GRNN is a feed-forward neural network, which estimates values for continuous dependent variables. The principal advantages of GRNN are fast learning and convergence to the optimal regression surface as the number of samples becomes very large. GRNN is particularly advantageous with sparse data in a real-time environment because the regression surface is instantly defined everywhere, even with just one sample. The method is usually used for functions' approximation, so it can provide very high accuracy, but for huge samples is computationally expensive. ES model is one of the simplest and most widespread practices of series alignment. The method can be presented as a filter that receives the original series members as the input, and the output forms the current values of the exponential average.

The patterns in data related to electricity consumption were searched in [12]. The methodology describes all stages of data processing: data collection, cleaning, transformation, index analysis, clustering, and results. The first stage aims to pre-process the data so that they can be clustered. The second phase consists of obtaining the optimal number of clusters for the dataset by analyzing and interpreting various cluster validation indices. Next, k-means is used for clustering and, finally, retrieves the centroids for each cluster. The processing is done in Apache Spark and the algorithms include big data clustering validity indices (BD-CVIs) and k-means.

The community detection algorithm Girvan-Newman GN) [8] algorithm was modified for big data clustering of IoT sensors by [9]. Their method organizes complex data in blocks, called communities or modules, according to certain roles and functions, organized in a multi-graph. The problem is to find in a given multi-graph a partition of vertices where the objective function is minimized. To achieve this, the graph edges are deleted iterative, depending on the value of the metric. The Edge-Betweenness Centrality (EBC) is the most common metric used, but the computation for this is time-consuming. The authors suggested a new measure approximating EBC, which capitalizes on hyperbolic network embedding and can be considered as the "hyperbolic" analog of EBC. This measure is denoted as Hyperbolic Edge Betweenness Centrality (HEBC), and it is computed by utilizing the hyperbolic node coordinates assigned to the embedded nodes. The novel metric enhances the performance without harming accuracy.

The other technique of data organizing and processing proposed by [2] implies 3D data analytics using a dendrogram (hierarchical) clustering approach. 3D data represents a structure of information that combines, simultaneously, the classification and clustering tasks. The organized data is mapped to a tree structure and retrieved by tree traversal algorithms. Dendrogram clustering is a method of merging objects into bunches. In the study, the bottom-up algorithm of clustering is utilized, which means that each item in a class is assigned to a single cluster. Then combine the clusters until all objects are merged together. An important parameter is a distance between objects in a class. The metric shows a quantitative assessment of the items' similarity ratio according to different criteria. The given research does not provide a selection of the specific parameter, although the choice of metric occurs in the second step of the method. The ability to retrieve information and the efficiency of the structure were measured. In general, the technique demonstrates a good characteristic of information extraction but not the most attractive performance parameters.

Other clustering algorithms, Fuzzy c-Mean (FCM) and K-Means were tested by [1]. The k-Means algorithm is one of the simplest methods but at the same time the most inaccurate. The main idea is that at each iteration, the center of mass is recalculated for each cluster obtained in the previous step, then results are partitioned into clusters again under new centers. The algorithm ends when the cluster is not changed in iteration. The fuzzy c-Mean method allows for obtaining "fuzzy" clustering of large sets of numerical data and makes it possible to correctly identify objects at the boundaries of clusters. However, the execution of this algorithm requires serious computational resources and the initial setting of the number of clusters. In addition, ambiguity may arise with objects remote from the centers of all clusters.

A new approach for clustering data points was designed by [6]. In essence, the method is an extension of the K-set clustering algorithm for semi-metric space. The problem with the K-sets approach is that the triangle distance is not non-negative. Thus the K-sets algorithm may not converge at all and there is no guarantee that the output of the K-sets algorithm is clustering. For solving this difficulty, the definition of triangle distance was adjusted, so that the non-negativity requirement could be lifted. The experimental results confirm the proficiency of the method for the geographic distance matrix and the latency matrix. The deep neural networks for the prediction of infectious diseases were used in [5].

A visual analysis framework for exploring and understanding heterogeneous urban data was presented by [7]. A visually assisted query model is introduced as a foundation for interactive exploration coupled with simple, yet powerful, structural abstractions and reasoning functionalities.

One more clustering method is used by [13]. Fuzzy c-Means (FCM), k-means (KM), and Gustafson-Kessel (GK) clustering algorithms are implemented. According to the paper, the most accurate and effective algorithm is k-means clustering, but the other methods have their own advantages and show higher correctness in certain cases.

3.4   Algorithm Assessment

The algorithms described above have characteristics of performance and scalability that should be understood. Table 4 gives a comprehensive description of the complexity and accuracy of the considered algorithms. For many, it was not easy to evaluate the complexity since the time depends on the characteristics of the machine. Therefore we provide only rough estimates, and all presented assessments are for worst-case values.

The K-sets+ algorithm yields the highest performance from all cluster algorithms. The time complexity is linear $O((Kn + m)I)$, where I is the number of iterations. The other method with linear time is Fuzzy c-mean with $O(nCI)$, where C - number of clusters, I - number of iterations. If we compare the exponent for these two approaches, the apparent fact is that the K-sets+ gives a little

Table 4. Algorithms assessment

Algorithm	Purpose	Complexity	Accuracy	Ref
CUSUM algorithm	anomaly detection	$O(n)$	—	[15]
Mutual information and Pearson correlation	find correlation between sensory data	$O(n^3)$	+	[3]
LSTM	predict diseases	$O(w)$	85%+	[16]
ARIMA	predict diseases	—	80%	[16]
GRNN	predict diseases	—	76%	[16]
ES	predict diseases	—	74%	[16]
K-means clustering	to extract electric energy consumption patterns	$O(n^2)$	78%	[12]
modification of Girvan-Newman algorithm	community detection	$O(n^2)$	65%–100%	[9]
Dendrogram clustering	produce hierarchical tree structure for data for data retrieval and analytics	$O(n^3)$	—	[2]
K-Means	clustering	$O(n^2)$	87,94%	[1, 12]
Fuzzy c-Mean	clustering	$O(nCI)$	81,91%	[1]
K-sets+	clustering in metric space	$O(Kn + m)$	95%	[6]
DNN	predicting infectious diseases	$O(wnk)$	77%	[5]
VAUD	spatio-temporal data visualisation	—	78,6%+	[7]
K-Means	clustering	70,22%	60,41%–87,94%	[13]
Fuzzy c-Means (FCM)	clustering	68,54%	56,25%–81,91%	[13]
Gustafson-Kessel (GK)	clustering	60,68%	66,19%–95,83%	[13]
Similarity-Matrix-based Clustering	trip clustering	$O(n^3)$	—	[4]

advantage. Considering the accuracy, K-sets+ has 95% as the worst result. The Fuzzy c-Means algorithm gives the complexity on average 81,97%. It is note-worthy that the Girwan-Newman modification provides 100% accuracy for most datasets and only 50% in the case of outliers. It could be used for a dataset with low sparseness if high accuracy is required. The dendrogram clustering method is slower than the others but can produce a hierarchical tree structure for data. K-means clustering is the simplest method but has a quadratic complexity and an accuracy of not more than 88% for different input data.

The deep learning algorithms were compared by the set of parameters: MSE, Root-Mean-Square Error (RMSE), Mean Absolute Error (MAE), and Mean Absolute Percentage Error (MAPE). From the results given by the authors, it follows that the most accurate algorithm is LSTM, but at the same time, the slowest. The fastest method is ES, but with the worst accuracy. All deep learn-ing algorithms were used for predicting diseases. The accuracy of the ES and GRNN model was relatively poor [16]. The ARIMA model has several require-ments: the time series should be stationary with steadily changing differences, and only linear relationships could be captured [16]. The DNN and LSTM mod-els were observed to be sensitive to decreasing trends and increasing trends, respectively [5]. It is worth noticing that the time complexity for the deep neu-ral network is hard to evaluate with O notation. The authors provide real-time results, according to the considered research the fastest model is ES, and the slowest is LSTM.

The CUSUM algorithm is time linear complexity. The solution is straightforward and fast but has limitations that must be taken into account, such as the consideration that all the series must follow a normal distribution and a series of observations cannot have trends [15]. VAUD presents the visualization of heterogeneous urban data. The approach is based on queries to the database, hence the time complexity can not be estimated. The data gathered from mobile phones and stored in one database combines different queries and different results are obtained. The accuracy on average for queries is 76%.

One of the widespread statistical methods applied to big data is correlation. In the listed papers, there is one algorithm that considered the correlation applied to smart city data. The study compared two types of methods: Pearson correlation and Mutual information. The time complexity for both is a cube. But Pearson correlation can discover the linear distribution of data, and mutual information can discover dependencies in more general data distribution cases. However, if an application prioritizes real-time response over accuracy, Pearson correlation will be suitable as it will only give a few false negatives. In other scenarios with different types of data streams (temperature, pollution, etc.), it is better to use mutual information without a priori knowledge of the potential correlations because we do not know the percentage of cases where Pearson correlation will fail to detect the correlations [3].

The assessment of time and accuracy of all proposed algorithms demonstrate that if our purpose is prediction, the best variant for us is deep neural networks like LSTM. For effective clustering, the K-sets+ or Fuzzy c-Means algorithms are the most powerful. If it is necessary to obtain additional analysis, it is possible to find the correlation. Considering the context of municipal data the frameworks are beneficial, as they assume all stages of data processing from storage to visualizing.

3.5   Processing Outcomes and Purpose

The anomaly detection by CUSUM algorithm of the [15], creates the warning message for the client side in the case of rare events. Each event contains a sensor identifier (sender field) and the identifier of the particular observation that has caused the event (identifier field). An event dashboard visualizes this data. The panel shows all sensing nodes of a network on a map using markers. Inside each marker, the amount of events that have been detected for this particular sensing node appears. If this node triggers an event, the marker turns red, if not the marker remains blue.

The analyses based on the correlation and mutual information were used to monitor the traffic of the city. Three sets of experiments have been performed. In the first one, the performance of Pearson correlation and mutual information was compared [3]. The results were visualized on Google Maps. It can be concluded that the Pearson correlation is effective for the linear distribution of data, and mutual information is vital for nonlinear dependencies but requires more time.

The results obtained by [16] are predictions of HIV disease for two years. Each compared algorithm has its metrics. For example, ARIMA includes a moving average process, an auto-regressive moving average process, an auto-regressive moving average process, and an ARIMA process according to the different parts of the regression and whether the original data are stable. To evaluate data accuracy, they compared with original information about HIV cases for 2015 and 2016 years. The same type of outcomes data demonstrates the [5]. They compared the same parameters for LSTM, DNN, and ARIMA to evaluate infectious disease prediction correctness. All cluster algorithms give the same result as a count of clusters and their accuracy.

The electricity consumption data were clustered into 4 and then into 8 groups in [12]. The outcomes are presented as diagrams. The clusters are categorized depending on buildings, seasons of the year, and days of the week.

The modification of the Girvan-Newman method with a novel metric provided by [9], was applied to multidimensional data obtained from an operational smart-city/building IoT infrastructure. The authors presented an accuracy evaluation, modularity, and time comparison of HGN and GN, comparing the execution time of GN and HGN algorithms for graphs with known communities and modularity comparison for 5, 10, 20, 30, and 60-minute sampling. Given that statistics demonstrate the computational efficiency and that algorithm can give accurate outcomes.

The cluster visualization into dendrograms, as tested on the information about 1000000 buildings was presented by [2]. Response time analysis was provided as well, which exhibits that response time for the proposed method is 50–60% faster than non-constellated data.

4   Conclusion

The aim of the article was to figure out what is the trend in the city's infrastructure data processing. The authors were interested in consumption data of electricity, water, heat, data of city traffic, and the methods for creating predicting models, clustering, and classifying. Increasingly, big data are seen as a key resource for the development of the urban environment, which presents opportunities for the optimization of economic processes, the creation of innovations in the social sphere, formation of new management models. The literature review serves as a foundation for future work in resource expenditures data analysis and urban management system creation.

The article presents a detailed analysis of the twelve papers from the last five years. The authors considered the techniques of urban data processing. The input and output data, assessments of algorithms' effectiveness, and methods description are provided. The inspection gives the following results: 1 algorithm of correlation, 2 algorithms of classification, 1 method of anomaly detection, 2 approaches for data visualization, 5 algorithms of predicting, and 6 methods for data clustering. A disproportion between the number of reviewed articles and the number of techniques dues to the fact that more than one method in each research was provided.

The input and output data vary depending on the method and purposes of the research. Predominantly heterogeneous data sources are considered. In one case the images are exploited and in two cases the numerical information is leveraged. The heterogeneous data mean that the information of different bases is used: images, text, and numerical. The video or sound data is not used in reviewed papers. The major part of the investigation offers a clustering model in the capacity of output results. The second place in prevalence is frameworks. The remaining outcomes can be divided between deep neural networks, classification, and correlation models.

The most interesting approach is the leverage of LSTM. Based on surveyed articles LSTM gives the highest accuracy of prediction and is the fastest solution in comparison with similar solutions. The forecasting of social phenomena based on city data is the most desirable result. Although, in the context of the modern situation is a still challenging task, as the whole pipeline of the assembly, processing, and analysis is important. As the given review demonstrates, different data are necessary for various problems, different algorithms give diverse findings. The dilemma of the practical benefits and standardization in smart city data is still open.

Acknowledgments. This work has been supported by FCT - Fundação para a Ciência e Tecnologia within the Project Scope: DSAIPA/AI/0088/2020.

References

1. Alshami, A., Guo, W., Pogrebna, G.: Fuzzy partition technique for clustering Big Urban dataset, pp. 212–216 (2016). https://doi.org/10.1109/SAI.2016.7555984
2. Azri, S., Ujang, U., Abdul Rahman, A.: Dendrogram clustering for 3D data analytics in smart city. **42**(4/W9), 247–253 (2018). https://doi.org/10.5194/isprs-archives-XLII-4-W9-247-2018
3. Bermudez-Edo, M., Barnaghi, P., Moessner, K.: Analysing real world data streams with spatio-temporal correlations: entropy vs. Pearson correlation. Autom. Constr. **88**, 87–100 (2018). https://doi.org/10.1016/j.autcon.2017.12.036
4. Bordogna, G., Cuzzocrea, A., Frigerio, L., Psaila, G.: An effective and efficient similarity-matrix-based algorithm for clustering big mobile social data, pp. 514–521 (2017). https://doi.org/10.1109/ICMLA.2016.188
5. Chae, S., Kwon, S., Lee, D.: Predicting infectious disease using deep learning and big data. Int. J. Environ. Res. Public Health **15**(8), 1596 (2018). https://doi.org/10.3390/ijerph15081596. http://www.mdpi.com/1660-4601/15/8/1596
6. Chang, C.S., Chang, C.T., Lee, D.S., Liou, L.H.: K-sets+: a linear-Time clustering algorithm for data points with a sparse similarity measure, pp. 1–8 (2018). https://doi.org/10.1109/UIC-ATC.2017.8397636
7. Chen, W., Huang, Z., Wu, F., Zhu, M., Guan, H., Maciejewski, R.: VAUD: a visual analysis approach for exploring spatio-temporal urban data. IEEE Trans. Visual. Comput. Graph. **24**(9), 2636–2648 (2018). https://doi.org/10.1109/TVCG.2017.2758362
8. Girvan, M., Newman, M.E.J.: Community structure in social and biological networks. Proc. Natl. Acad. Sci. **99**(12), 7821–7826 (2002). https://doi.org/10.1073/pnas.122653799

9. Karyotis, V., Tsitseklis, K., Sotiropoulos, K., Papavassiliou, S.: Big data clustering via community detection and hyperbolic network embedding in IoT applications. Sensors (Switzerland) **18**(4) (2018). https://doi.org/10.3390/s18041205

10. Kwon, O., Kim, Y., Lee, N., Jung, Y.: When collective knowledge meets crowd knowledge in a smart city: a prediction method combining open data keyword analysis and case-based reasoning. J. Healthcare Eng. **2018** (2018). https://doi.org/10.1155/2018/7391793

11. Materla, T., Cudney, E.A., Antony, J.: The application of Kano model in the healthcare industry: a systematic literature review. Total Qual. Manag. Bus. Excellence 1–22 (2017). https://doi.org/10.1080/14783363.2017.1328980

12. Pérez-Chacón, R., Luna-Romera, J., Troncoso, A., Martínez-Alvarez, F., Riquelme, J.: Big data analytics for discovering electricity consumption patterns in smart cities. Energies **11**(3) (2018). https://doi.org/10.3390/en11030683

13. Simhachalam, B., Ganesan, G.: Performance comparison of fuzzy and non-fuzzy classification methods. Egypt. Inform. J. **17** (2015). https://doi.org/10.1016/j.eij.2015.10.004

14. Subhash, S., Cudney, E.A.: Gamified learning in higher education: a systematic review of the literature. Comput. Hum. Behav. **87**, 192–206 (2018). https://doi.org/10.1016/j.chb.2018.05.028

15. Trilles, S., Belmonte, O., Schade, S., Huerta, J.: A domain-independent methodology to analyze IoT data streams in real-time. A proof of concept implementation for anomaly detection from environmental data. Int. J. Digit. Earth **10**(1), 103–120 (2017). https://doi.org/10.1080/17538947.2016.1209583

16. Wang, G., et al.: Application of a long short-term memory neural network: a burgeoning method of deep learning in forecasting HIV incidence in Guangxi, China. Epidemiol. Infect. **147**, e194 (2019). https://doi.org/10.1017/S095026881900075X

Smart Monitoring and Communications

Detecting Air Conditioning Usage in Households Using Unsupervised Machine Learning on Smart Meter Data

Rodrigo Porteiro[1](✉)📷 and Sergio Nesmachnow[2]📷

[1] UTE, Montevideo, Uruguay
`rporteiro@ute.com.uy`
[2] Universidad de la República, Montevideo, Uruguay
`sergion@fing.edu.uy`

Abstract. This article presents an unsupervised machine learning approach for the problem of detecting use of air conditioning in households, during the summer. This is a relevant problem in the context of the modern smart grid approach under the paradigm of smart cities. The proposed methodology applies data analysis, a thermal inertial model for estimating the temperature inside a household, statistical analysis, clustering, and classification. The proposed model is validated on a real case study, considering households with known use of air conditioning in summer. In the evaluation, the proposed classification methodology reached an accuracy of 0.897, a promising result considering the very small cardinality of the set of households. The proposed method is valuable since it applies an unsupervised approach, which does not require large volumes of labeled data for training, and allows determining characteristics in the electricity consumption patterns that are useful for categorization. In turn, it is a non-intrusive method and does not require investing in the installation of complex devices or conducting consumer surveys.

Keywords: Unsupervised learning · Data analysis · Residential electricity consumption

1 Introduction

Currently, electricity utilities have advanced strongly in the deployment of various smart devices that assist monitoring and decision making. Final consumers have taken a very active role, given that there is greater knowledge of their behavior and their use of the electrical resource [23]. For utilities, it is essential to analyze the large amount of data gathered by using smart devices, to add value to the electricity business. In the residential sector, the existence of smart meters is crucial to improve management and profit. At the same time, it makes it possible to carry out commercial policies in which the consumer is a key player and feels part of the improvements.

© The Author(s), under exclusive license to Springer Nature Switzerland AG 2023
S. Nesmachnow and L. Hernández Callejo (Eds.): ICSC-CITIES 2022, CCIS 1706, pp. 233–247, 2023.
https://doi.org/10.1007/978-3-031-28454-0_16

Usually, utilities only consider the benefits obtained by being able to operate the smart meter remotely when analyzing the technical requirements of the smart meter to be deployed. For example, the benefits to obtain consume measurements without the presence of an employee in the field, to the detect blackouts remotely, or to perform remote power cuts in case of unpaid bills. For this reason, many electric utilities do not properly plan the selection of smart meters considering the benefit they will generate when analyzing the measured data. One of the features of smart meters that is not properly valued is the measurement frequency. Many of the tools that can be developed using consumption data require a high granularity in the values measured from smart meters. Another technical feature of smart meters usually underestimated for the creation of these tools, is the measurement of harmonics.

A very useful approach for building a detailed profile of consumers is to detect which electrical devices are in use. The literature shows that for obtaining a very precise disaggregation of the electrical appliances uses from smart meter data, very high measurement frequency and harmonic measurement are needed [9,10]. If the smart metering infrastructure is already deployed additional devices would need to be installed in households. However, this type of intrusive intervention is not always financially profitable and is often frowned upon by clients.

This article addresses the problem of detecting the use of air conditioning in summer, using the existing infrastructure of the Uruguayan electricity company (UTE). The company deployed smart meters on residential consumers, so replacing them would be very expensive. The meters are not capable of measuring harmonics, and have a quarterly consumption measurement frequency. However, despite the technological limitations, it is feasible to detect air conditioners using the available information and climate data. Detecting the use of this type of device, which is intensive in the summer, allows designing appropriate energy efficiency policies and commercial products, to optimize the electrical system and reduce the cost for the company, for consumers, and for the country [2,12].

An unsupervised machine learning algorithm is proposed to detect the use of air conditioning in summer. Given a household, the proposed methodology applies urban data analysis [15] over consumption measurements, and temperature and irradiance measured at the nearest weather station. An approximation of the internal temperature of the household is then obtained a simplified model of thermal inertia for a standard Uruguayan residential building. Thus, a function is obtained that approximates the internal temperature from the external temperature and the irradiance. With the fifteen-minute data on consumption and internal temperature, consumption measurements less than 10% of the average consumption are excluded, as a criterion to consider the moments in which there is activity in the household. The resulting data is classified into two sets using the k-means clustering algorithm, only considering its temperature. A set of consumptions for low temperatures and another one for high temperatures are obtained. The average consumption is calculated for each set and if the difference between these values is greater than a threshold value, the consumer in the studied household is classified as an air conditioning user.

A practical validation of the proposed methodology is presented for a case study with a set of 29 households for whom the use of air conditioning in summer is known. The main results of the research applying the proposed methodology to this set, yields an accuracy of 0.897. This result is promising, especially considering that the study could only be carried out on a very small set of households due to lack of labeled consumers. The proposed method is valuable since it applies an unsupervised approach, which does not require large volumes of labeled data for training and it is non-intrusive. Thus, it is a viable alternative to intrusive methods, which require replacing the currently installed smart meters with more sophisticated ones (a very costly task in economical terms). In turn, having labeled data to use supervised learning or to validate the presented algorithm requires conducting surveys that demand a hard and expensive task. Therefore, the proposed methodology has the advantage that it can be applied immediately using the current installed infrastructure, without incurring in significant investments costs.

The article is organized as follows. Section 2 describes the problem addressed in this article and reviews related works. Section 3 describes the proposed approach, including a description of data sources, the process of data preparation and the definition of the classification algorithm. Details of the developed implementation are provided in Sect. 4. Section 5 present the experimental evaluation of the proposed approach and discusses the obtained results. Finally, Sect. 6 present the conclusions of the research and formulates the main lines for future work.

2   Problem Definition and Literature Review

This section describes the general problem addressed problem and reviews relevant related works.

2.1   General Problem: Energy Disaggregation

Traditionally, electricity companies have mainly worked using static information from consumers. The only source of data that dynamically linked consumers to the company was the measurement that a company official obtained monthly from traditional meter. Nowadays, the massive deployment of smart meters has allowed companies in the energy sector to know in greater detail the behavior of consumers, regarding energy use. It is possible to detect various details regarding the behavior of consumers with greater or lesser accuracy, depending on the technical specifications of the smart meters deployed.

If smart meters with high metering frequency and harmonic measurement are available, it is possible to successfully address the overall problem of energy disaggregation. It consists of identifying the individual consumption of different household appliances, using only aggregate measurements of all the measured variables. Many studies have analyzed the problem of energy disaggregation using smart meters with advanced technological features.

2.2   Problem Description: Detection of Air Conditioning Usage

The addressed problem is detecting the use of air conditioners in summer, from smart meters with a measurement frequency of fifteen minutes and without measuring harmonics. Air conditioner is the only electrically-intensive device to lower the temperature of households in the summer. It is highly correlated with climatic variables and allows addressing the classification problem without the need to have labeled consumers or to have more advanced measurement devices. Then, the solution proposed is considered non-intrusive.

The input data consist of electricity consumption curves with quarterly frequency, the geographical location of the consumer, and weather information to approximate the temperature inside the household. One of the hypotheses assumed is that the only electrical device for thermal comfort in summer with a relevant consumption is the air conditioner. Other thermal conditioning devices for the summer have negligible power consumption respect to air conditioners. For example, the average power of fans is 50 W and coolers 100 W, compared to 1000 W to 2000 W for air conditioner. The other hypotheses is that its use is strongly correlated with the internal temperature of the household.

2.3   Related Work

The application of energy disaggregation tools to the residential sector has developed strongly after the high penetration of smart meters in electrical systems. The addressed problem is to estimate the consumption of each of the electrical devices in the household, considering as input the overall energy consumption. When disaggregation is coarse-grained, the main objectives are related to provide more information to consumers on energy bills, or even offer specific commercial products depending on the type of use. When the disaggregation problem is solved in real time, the main applicability is to identify problems such as electrical losses in the household, detection of overloads, and other relevant issues.

Non-intrusive load monitoring (NILM) and the dissagregation problem in households were introduced by Hart [11], as an alternative to existing intrusive, hardware-based monitoring approaches. The main advantages of NILM is that it does not require installing specific devices, but makes use of existing smart meters, focusing on more sophisticated software for data analysis. Hart also introduced the binary (ON/OFF) variant of the dissagregation problem and proposed the principle of continuity switch, i.e., assuming that in a given small time interval, few appliances change their status (from ON to OFF or vice versa).

Many recent articles have dealt with NILM as a learning problem, applying computational intelligence to solve it, both in supervised and unsupervised fashion. Supervised approaches (e.g., Bayesian learning, neural networks (ANN), patterns similarity) make use of specific datasets of electricity consumption of each device and the aggregate household consumption signal. Unsupervised approaches (e.g., Hidden Markov Models, HMM) seek to learn the ON/OFF state of devices from the aggregate consumption, without explicit knowledge about the consumption of each device [4].

Kelly and Knottenbelt [13] studied ANNs for the NILM problem, using the UK-DALE dataset, which includes the electricity consumption of appliances (fridge, washing machine, dishwasher, kettle, and microwave) in five houses in the UK. A denoising autoencoder ANN computed the best results, outperforming over a long short-term memory (LSTM) and a rectangles ANN. Kolter and Johnson [14] introduced the REDD dataset to study a HMM for the NILM problem. Mixed results were computed over two weeks of data from five households (64.5% accuracy on the training set and just 47.7% in the evaluation test).

Our previous articles [6,7] studied the dissaggregation of electricity consumption in residential buildings and proposed a method based on detecting similarities in the electricity consumption patterns from previously recorded labeled datasets. The method was evaluated over four different problem instances that model real household scenarios, reporting accurate results regarding standard prediction metrics.

Computational models are also very valuable for energy demand management and demand response [16,17]. Our previous articles [19,20] applied computational methods for defining a thermal index associated with an active demand management that interrupts domestic electric water heaters. Specific models using Extra Trees Regressor and a linear model were defined for water utilization and water temperature considering continuous power consumption measurements of water heaters, and Monte Carlo simulations to compute the proposed index. The approach was evaluated using real data from the ECD-UY dataset, Uruguay [8]. The thermal discomfort index correctly modeled the impact on temperature, providing accurate inputs for demand response and load shifting. Data analysis and computational intelligence techniques were also applied for the characterization and forecasting of short term electricity consumption on industrial facilities [21,22]. The model was validated for an industrial park in Burgos (Spain), the total electricity demand for Uruguay, and demand from a distribution substation in Montevideo (Uruguay).

3   The Proposed Approach for the Detection of Air Conditioning Usage in Summer

This section describes the data sources, the methodology to approximate indoor temperature, the data preparation and the methodology applied for the detection of air conditioning usage in summer.

3.1   Data Sources

The consumption data used in this article was provided by the Uruguayan National Electricity Company (UTE). It corresponds to "Total household consumption" and "Disaggregated electricity consumption by appliance", two of the three subsets included in the ECD-UY dataset [8]. The Total household consumption set gathers data of quarterly total consumption from 110953 households and Disaggregated electricity consumption by appliance contains data of 9 households with minutal measures and dissagegated consumption by appliance. These sets have measurements from January 1, 2019 to November 2, 2020. In turn, data obtained from 20 additional households from known consumers was used for validation. The overall dataset includes 29 labeled households (19 use air conditioning in the summer and 10 do not).

To approximate the temperature of the household, which is the variable that has the strongest correlation with the use of air conditioning, climate information on temperature and solar irradiance was used. The data used was obtained manually from Uruguayan Institute of Meteorology (INUMET), disaggregated by weather station. Only data from January 1, 2019 to November 2, 2020 were considered, to match with the consumption data. Therefore, the horizon of data analyzed in this article is determined by these dates.

Likewise, both the consumption and the climate information contains the location of the measurement, which allows households to be associated with the climate data obtained from the nearest station.

3.2 Approximation of the Internal Temperature of the Household from the External Temperature and Solar Irradiance

An approximation of the temperature inside each household is needed for the proposed model. The proposed approach consists in estimating the inside temperature from the curve of the outside temperature and the external solar irradiance.

The thermal inertia that occurs inside the household is considered. The most relevant factors to model this effect are the construction material, the number of windows, and the insulation. Cengel et al. [5] showed that the heat flux is proportional to the magnitude of the temperature gradient, and opposite in sign. This article only requires an approximation of the internal temperature, and for this purpose a simplified model, proposed by Absi et al. [1] is used.

The model by Absi et al. assumes that the effect of the walls of a house produces two transformations in the external temperature curve: a delay (thermal lag) and an attenuation in the amplitude of the curve. Fig. 1 shows that the amplitude of the indoor temperature (A_{ind}) is smaller than the amplitude of the external temperature (A_{ext}). It also shows that indoor temperature is lagged by $\beta \times w_{irr}$, the thermal lag considering the irradiance.

According to the aforementioned model, these parameters depend on the wall material, the wall thickness, and the solar irradiance. Intuitively, the flow of heat from outside to inside is more delayed (thermal lag) and also the indoor thermal amplitude decreases when thicker and more robust walls are used, and the lower the solar irradiance. For instance, if the wall is extremely thin, the indoor temperature and the external temperature are almost equal. This model provides a rough simplification of the real temperature dynamics, which is appropriate for the proposed case study, especially considering that there is not enough information about households to estimate the internal temperature using a more complex model.

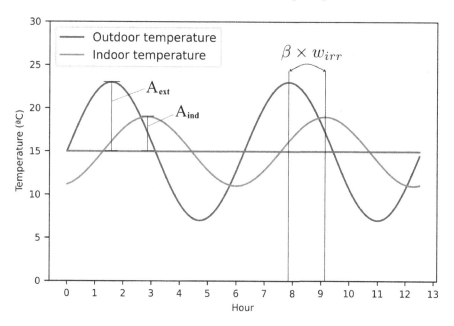

Fig. 1. Amplitude variation and thermal lag of indoor and outdoor temperature.

The internal temperature is represented as a function of the external temperature and the irradiance, according to the formulation in Eq. 1.

$$T_{ind}(t) = (T_{ext}(t - \beta \times w_{irr}) - \overline{T}_{24}(t))\rho \times w_{irr} + \overline{T}_{24}(t) \tag{1}$$

In Eq. 1, the function $T_{ind}(t)$ is the indoor temperature at time t and the function $T_{ext}(t)$ is the external temperature at time t. The function $\overline{T}_{24}(t)$ is the external average temperature of the last 24 h, used as a baseline to estimate the amplitude. Then, $\beta \times w_{irr}$ is the thermal lag and the parameter $\rho = A_{ind}/A_{ext} \times w_{irr}$ captures the amplitude reduction. Finally, $w_{irr} = 1$ when irradiance is 0 and a maximum value when irradiance reach its maximum. So β and ρ are the thermal lag and the amplitude reduction factor when solar irradiance is 0.

3.3 Data Preparation

The objective of preparing the data is to obtain a historical bivariate series for the summer, in the considered analysis horizon. The first variable of the series represents the electricity consumption of the considered household and the second variable is an approximation of the internal temperature. First, since the temperature and irradiance data are hourly, they are converted to quarterly simply by using the hourly value. There are no missing values in either the consumption data or the climate data.

To generate the series of indoor temperatures, the parameters β, ρ and w_{irr} must be estimated. β, ρ and w_{irr} are estimated by measuring real temperature curves in three types of buildings (considering the most used construction materials in Uruguay: brick, concrete and wood [3]. First, measures were performed during the night, so $w_{irr} = 1$ (since there is no irradiance).

According to Eq. 1, $\beta \times w_{irr}$ is the thermal lag between indoor and outdoor temperature, considering irradiance. The lag is calculated using the measured curves at night (i.e., the difference between T_{ext} and T_{ind} along the x-axis). Then, setting $w_{irr} = 1$, the value of β is determined. Analogously, $\rho \times w_{irr} = A_{ind}/A_{ext}$; A_{ind} and A_{ext} are measured, and $w_{irr} = 1$ at night, so, the value of ρ is determined.

Then, fixing β and ρ, the value of w_{irr} is estimated for a completely clear day using Eq. 1, so the maximum w_{irr} is determined (w_{irr}^{max}). All estimations are performed using real indoor and external temperature measures. To compute Eq. 1 for an intermediate value of irradiance I_{real}, w_{irr} must be calculated for I_{real}, proportionally. So $w_{irr} = I_{real} \times (w_{irr}^{max} - 1)/(I_{max} - 1)$, where I_{max} is the maximum irradiance measured in a clear day.

Once the three relevant parameters of the temperature model are estimated, the indoor temperature series is obtained from the outdoor temperature series and irradiance series applying Eq. 1. This procedure is performed for each household, using weather data of the closest meteorological station. Figure 2 presents the internal temperature curves for the same external temperature and solar irradiance, depending on the type of construction.

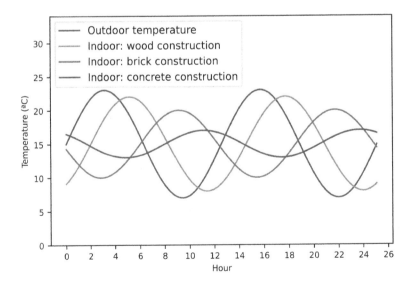

Fig. 2. Indoor temperature curves for wood, brick and concrete constructions.

The graphic in Fig. 2 shows that brick constructions present a thermal inertia between wood and concrete constructions. In the proposed study, since there is no information on the construction material of each household, the set of parameters estimated for a brick construction was used, considering that it represents a non-extreme thermal inertia. Also, brick is widely used in Uruguay, due to solidity and durability [3].

Finally, on the bivariate series with quarterly values, the data that do not correspond to the summer months (December, January, February, and March) are excluded, since they are not usseful for the proposed analysis. Then, the maximum consumption for the resulting data is obtained, and all data with consumption less than 10% of the maximum are excluded from the series, considering that in those cases there is no activity in the household.

3.4   Unsupervised Machine Learning Classification Algorithm

The unsupervised classification algorithm must take into account the high correlation between the consumption of the household and its internal temperature when there is activity in it. In the preparation of data, very low consumption was excluded, to focus on the correlation between consumption and temperature in the case of activity in the household. It is important to consider that if there is any device with relevant consumption not associated with thermal conditioning, it will not present a strong correlation with temperature.

The proposed algorithm consists of performing the following seven steps, including data preparation:

1. Construction of the indoor temperature curve of the analyzed household, using the technique described in Sect. 3.2 applied to the meteorological data of the nearest station. As a result, a bivariate quarterly series is obtained with consumption and indoor temperature variables.
2. From the series obtained, entries with consumption less than 10% of the maximum of the series are excluded.
3. A clustering is performed applying k-means, with $k = 2$ in the temperature variable. Thus obtaining a set of consumption values for low temperatures (L) and another set of consumption values for high temperatures (H).
4. A clustering is performed applying k-means, with $k = 2$ in the consumption variable for the set L (obtaining two classes, L_L and L_H).
5. A clustering is performed applying k-means, with $k = 2$ in the consumption variable for the set H (obtaining two classes, H_L and H_H).
6. $center_L = (T_L, E_L)$ is defined as the center of L_H and $center_H = (T_H, E_H)$ as the center of the cluster H_H
7. if $E_H/E_L \geq \Theta$, then the consumer is classified as user of air conditioning, otherwise it is classified as non-user of air conditioning. Parameter Θ must be calibrated considering the average increase in quarterly consumption when the air conditioning is on. The calibration methodology is described in Sect. 5.3.

Figure 3 presents the main steps of the algorithm. Figure 3a presents the original data for a consumer. Figure 3b shows the data after excluding low consumptions (step 2). Figure 3c presents the data after step 3, the class L in blue and the class H in orange. Finally, in Fig. 3d presents the four classes: L_L, L_H, H_L and H_H after step 6. The blue cross is $center_H = (T_H, E_H)$ and the orange cross is $center_L = (T_L, E_L)$. In this case, the value of E_H is significantly greater than the value of E_L, so with a value of Θ barely greater than 1, the condition $E_H/E_L \geq \Theta$ would be met and the consumer would be classified as an air conditioning user.

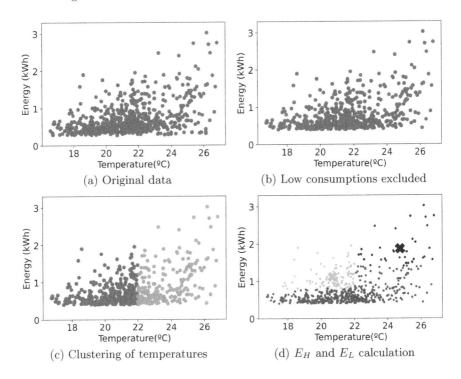

Fig. 3. Main steps of the proposed classification algorithm.

The rationale behind the proposed classification algorithm is that if there is indeed an intensive electrical use associated with thermal comfort, consumption at high temperatures tends to be greater than consumption at low temperatures. By separating the consumption by temperature (low and high) into two sets, and then taking the averages of the highest consumption foe each set, if the value associated with high temperatures is significantly higher than that associated with low temperatures, this is due to the use of air conditioning, since no other thermal conditioning device for summer consumes a significant amount of energy. However, if the averages are similar, there is not statistical significance in the reported electricity consumption values with respect to the indoor temperature and the consumer is classified as a non air-conditioning user.

4   Implementation

This section presents the implementation details of the proposed solution.

4.1   Implementation Details

The implementation of the proposed classification algorithm involved four stages, which are described next.

Construction of the Indoor Temperature Curve. The geographical coordinates of each consumer and the weather stations available were processed to find the closest station for each household. The curves of temperature and hourly solar irradiance are obtained from the corresponding station. Next, both curves are converted from hourly to quarterly, assigning each 15-minute time step the value of the corresponding hour. Finally, Eq. 1 is applied using the calibrated parameters to obtain the indoor temperature series. A new quarterly bivariate series S, is constructed with consumption and indoor temperature variables.

Selection of Relevant Consumption Entries. To properly capture the correlation between electricity consumption and internal temperature, the periods of time when there is activity in the household must be considered.
    To determine those periods, the method excludes entries from the series S with low consumption. Any entry with a consumption less than 10% of the maximum consumption existing in the considered time horizon is excluded from the series.

Classification by Indoor Temperature. To perform the classification according to the indoor temperature, the *Keras* library is used to apply the the k-means algorithm, using two clusters ($k = 2$). The resulting clusters represent consumptions with low temperatures, and consumptions with high temperatures.

Classification by Consumption. For each cluster found according to the indoor temperature, the k-means algorithm is applied again for classification according to the consumption variable, using two clusters ($k = 2$). The resulting clusters correspond to lower consumptions and higher consumptions values.

4.2   Final Classification

After determining the indoor temperature curve, the selection of relevant consumption entries, the classification by indoor temperature, and the classification by consumption, four sets are obtained. They represent:

1. Samples that have high consumption with high temperatures;
2. Samples that have low consumption with high temperatures;
3. Samples that have high consumption with low temperatures; and
4. Samples that have low consumption with low temperatures.

Sets 2 and 4 are ignored, because the focus is analyzing high consumptions depending on the temperature. The consumption average is calculate for sets 1 and 3. If the quotient between the average obtained for set 1 and the average obtained for set 2 is greater than a specified threshold Θ, the consumer is classified as user of air conditioning in the summer. The value of Θ must be estimated in such a way that it correctly considers the difference in consumption at high and low temperatures. In Sect. 5.3, a value of Θ appropriate for Uruguayan households is estimated.

5   Experimental Analysis and Discussion

This section presents the experimental analysis and discussion of the results.

5.1   Development and Execution Platforms

The proposed solution was implemented on Python. Many scientific libraries and packages were used to handle data, fit the models and visualize results, including Pandas and Matplotlib and Numpy. The experimental evaluation was performed on the high performance computing infrastructure of National Supercomputing Center (Cluster-UY), Uruguay [18].

5.2   General Considerations

The labeled data set, consisting of 29 users, was used for the analysis. In any case, for the calibration of the theta parameter, information from these users was not used, since in this way supervision would be introduced into the algorithm and, given the small amount of available data, this strategy would not have statistical support. For this reason, in this experimental analysis, the set of 29 consumers is used to evaluate the proposed unsupervised methodology but not for designing it. The vast amount of unsupervised data was used to perform an exploratory analysis to design the algorithm.

5.3   Parameter Calibration

To calibrate the parameter Θ, the maximum consumption of the considered household is considered. If it is a consumer that has a relatively low average consumption for the residential sector, the consumption of air conditioning will be relevant. However, if the household has a high base consumption, when turning on an air conditioner, the relative increase in consumption may be small. Therefore, if the parameter Θ is adjusted for households with high average consumption, it will be suitable for households with low consumption. Taking into account that the average energy consumed by an air conditioner in fifteen minutes on extreme situation is 300 Wh (standard power is 1200 W), and assuming an average intense consumption in peak hours of 1000 Wh, an appropriate value for theta would be $\Theta = 1300/1000$. But the costumer does not use the air conditioner in all extreme temperature situations. Therefore, a conservative Θ value could be estimated if it is assumed that on average 1 out of 10 times the costumer uses the air conditioner. Then, the average increase in consumption would be $300\frac{1}{7}10 = 30$, so $\Theta = 1300/1270 = 1.0237$. This value is the one used for the experimental analysis and subsequent evaluation.

5.4   Analysis of the Proposed Methodology

To validate the proposed methodology, two analysis are presented. On the one hand, to calculate the precision of the algorithm in the set of 29 labeled household data. On the other hand, apply the proposed classification algorithm to the complete set of non-labeled households of the data from ECD-UY and observe the percentage of households that results classified in the category of air conditioning use in summer. The purpose of estimating the number of households that use air conditioning in summer is to compare this value with the continuous survey of households carried out by the National Statistics Institute. To classify the unlabeled data, a sample of 1000 households is randomly taken. In both lines, the procedure described in the Sect. 3.4 is applied to the analyzed set.

5.5   Validation Results on Labeled Data

To validate the results of the application of the algorithm on the labeled data and considering that the sample is balanced, the accuracy metric is used. The result obtained on the set of 29 households is an accuracy of 0.897.

All 16 households were correctly classified as users of air conditioning in summer. However, of the 12 who were classified as not using air conditioning in the summer, 3 were misclassified. This shows that there were no false positives and also allows us to conclude that in order to improve the algorithm it is necessary to avoid the occurrence of false negatives. These considerations are preliminary, due to the small size of the sample used.

5.6   Validation Results on Unlabeled Data

According to the continuous household survey, by 2021, 53% of households have at least one air conditioner. When applying the developed algorithm to the sample of 1,000 non-labeled households, 497 households were classified as users of air conditioning in summer. Bearing in mind that most households that have air conditioning use it in summer, since there are no equivalent alternative thermal conditioning devices in this season (as is the case in winter), the result obtained of 49.7% is reasonable. This result is preliminary since there are no labels and it could happen that, although the total percentage is reasonable, many were misclassified. In any case, it could have happened that this analysis invalidated the algorithm if the percentage obtained was very different from the one shown by the survey.

6   Conclusions and Future Work

This article presented an unsupervised algorithm to detect the use of air conditioning in households, during summer. The proposed approach is valuable because it can be implemented in Uruguay with the existing infrastructure, without incurring large investment costs. The unsupervised algorithm applies the urban data analysis approach. First, it applies a filter by electricity consumption, then a chain of clustering, and finally estimates an indicator related to the variation in consumption with respect to temperature. As a result, the proposed algorithm classifies each consumer as a user (or not) of air conditioning in summer.

The proposed detection methodology was evaluated on a real case study considering data from 29 households in Montevideo, Uruguay. The unsupervised algorithm obtained an accuracy of 0.897 in the considered dataset. This is a promising result, considering the very small cardinality of the set of households.

The main lines of future work are related to improving the accuracy of the air conditioner detection tool, eventually using supervised learning. For this approach, communication with consumers (for example, through a mobile app) would be needed to allow a progressive labeling of households. Another line of future work consists of detecting the use of devices in real time, using the information from various sources and big data analysis.

Acknowledgments. We thank Pedro Moreno, from Universidad Autónoma del Estado de Morelos (México), and Carlos Torres, from Centro Nacional de Investigación y Desarrollo Tecnológico (México), for their valuable comments regarding the thermal inertia model and how to use it in the context of the proposed research.

References

1. Absi, R., Marchandon, S., Bennacer, R.: Thermal-electrical analogy and inertia for thermal performance of building envelops. In: MATEC Web of Conferences, vol. 330, p. 01037 (2020)
2. Al-Qawasmi, A., Tlili, I.: Energy efficiency and economic impact investigations for air-conditioners using wireless sensing and actuator networks. Energy Rep. **4**, 478–485 (2018)
3. Arias, C., Mujica, F., Nicola, C., Menini, A.: Tendencias de diseño, sector materiales de construcción (2019), cámara de Industrias de Uruguay/INEFOP
4. Bonfigli, R., Squartini, S., Fagiani, M., Piazza, F.: Unsupervised algorithms for non-intrusive load monitoring: an up-to-date overview. In: 15th International Conference on Environment and Electrical Engineering (2015)
5. Cengel, Y., Cimbala, J., Turner, R.: Fundamentals of Thermal-Fluid Sciences (SI units). McGraw Hill, New York (2012)
6. Chavat, J., Graneri, J., Nesmachnow, S.: Household energy disaggregation based on pattern consumption similarities. In: Nesmachnow, S., Hernández Callejo, L. (eds.) ICSC-CITIES 2019. CCIS, vol. 1152, pp. 54–69. Springer, Cham (2020). https://doi.org/10.1007/978-3-030-38889-8_5

7. Chavat, J., Nesmachnow, S., Graneri, J.: Non-intrusive energy disaggregation by detecting similarities in consumption patterns. Revista Facultad de Ingeniería Universidad de Antioquia (2020)

8. Chavat, J., Nesmachnow, S., Graneri, J., Alvez, G.: ECD-UY, detailed household electricity consumption dataset of Uruguay. Sci. Data **9**(1) (2022)

9. Chiang, J., Zhang, T., Chen, B., Hu, Y.: Load disaggregation using harmonic analysis and regularized optimization. In: IEEE Asia Pacific Signal and Information Processing Association Annual Summit and Conference, pp. 1–4 (2012)

10. Devarapalli, H., Dhanikonda, S., Gunturi, S.: Non-intrusive identification of load patterns in smart homes using percentage total harmonic distortion. Energies **13**(18), 4628 (2020)

11. Hart, G.: Nonintrusive appliance load monitoring. Proc. IEEE **80**(12), 1870–1891 (1992)

12. Hu, M., Xiao, F.: Price-responsive model-based optimal demand response control of inverter air conditioners using genetic algorithm. Appl. Energy **219**, 151–164 (2018)

13. Kelly, J., Knottenbelt, W.: Neural NILM: Deep Neural Networks Applied to Energy Disaggregation. In: 2nd ACM International Conference on Embedded Systems for Energy-Efficient Built Environments, pp. 55–64 (2015)

14. Kolter, J., Johnson, M.: Redd: A public data set for energy disaggregation research. In: Workshop on Data Mining Applications in Sustainability, pp. 59–62 (2011)

15. Massobrio, R., Nesmachnow, S.: Urban mobility data analysis for public transportation systems: a case study in Montevideo. Uruguay. Appl. Sci. **10**(16), 1–20 (2020)

16. Muraña, J., et al.: Negotiation approach for the participation of datacenters and supercomputing facilities in smart electricity markets. Program. Comput. Softw. **46**(8), 636–651 (2020)

17. Muraña, J., Nesmachnow, S.: Simulation and evaluation of multicriteria planning heuristics for demand response in datacenters. Simulation, p. 003754972110200 (2021)

18. Nesmachnow, S., Iturriaga, S.: Cluster-UY: collaborative scientific high performance computing in Uruguay. In: Torres, M., Klapp, J. (eds.) ISUM 2019. CCIS, vol. 1151, pp. 188–202. Springer, Cham (2019). https://doi.org/10.1007/978-3-030-38043-4_16

19. Porteiro, R., Chavat, J., Nesmachnow, S.: A thermal discomfort index for demand response control in residential water heaters. Appl. Sci. **11**(21), 10048 (2021)

20. Porteiro, R., Chavat, J., Nesmachnow, S., Hernández-Callejo, L.: Demand response control in electric water heaters: evaluation of impact on thermal comfort. In: Nesmachnow, S., Hernández Callejo, L. (eds.) ICSC-CITIES 2020. CCIS, vol. 1359, pp. 74–89. Springer, Cham (2021). https://doi.org/10.1007/978-3-030-69136-3_6

21. Porteiro, R., Hernández-Callejo, L., Nesmachnow, S.: Electricity demand forecasting in industrial and residential facilities using ensemble machine learning. Revista Facultad de Ingeniería Universidad de Antioquia (2020)

22. Porteiro, R., Nesmachnow, S., Hernández-Callejo, L.: Short term load forecasting of industrial electricity using machine learning. In: Nesmachnow, S., Hernández Callejo, L. (eds.) ICSC-CITIES 2019. CCIS, vol. 1152, pp. 146–161. Springer, Cham (2020). https://doi.org/10.1007/978-3-030-38889-8_12

23. Zafar, R., Mahmood, A., Razzaq, S., Ali, W., Naeem, U., Shehzad, K.: Prosumer based energy management and sharing in smart grid. Renew. Sustain. Energy Rev. **82**, 1675–1684 (2018)

SNS-Based Secret Sharing Scheme for Security of Smart City Communication Systems

Andrei Gladkov[1] , Egor Shiriaev[1]([⊠]) , Andrei Tchernykh[2,3] ,
Maxim Deryabin[4] , Ekaterina Bezuglova[5] , Georgii Valuev[5] ,
and Mikhail Babenko[1,3]

[1] Faculty of Mathematics and Computer Science, North-Caucasus Federal University,
355017 Stavropol, Russia
{agladkov,eshiriaev,mgbabenko}@ncfu.ru

[2] Computer Science Department, CICESE Research Center, 22860 Ensenada, Mexico
chernykh@cicese.mx

[3] Control/Management and Applied Mathematics, Ivannikov Institute for System Programming,
109004 Moscow, Russia

[4] Computing Platform Lab, Samsung Advanced Institute of Technology,
Suwon 16678, South Korea
max.deriabin@samsung.com

[5] North-Caucasus Center for Mathematical Research, North-Caucasus Federal University,
355017 Stavropol, Russia
{eksbezuglova,gvvaluev}@ncfu.ru

Abstract. A smart city has a complex hierarchical communication system with
various components. It must meet the requirements of fast communication, reliability, and security without compromising data. In the paper, we discuss methods
and techniques for increasing the speed and reliability of the mobile ad hoc networks with a sufficient level of security. We consider combining the secret sharing
schemes and residual number systems (RNS) as an efficient security mechanism
for a smart city dynamic heterogeneous network. We analyze the concept of data
transmission based on RNS that divides data into smaller parts and transmits them
in parallel, protecting them from attacks on routes by adaptive multipath secured
transmission. Proposed networks have the self-correcting properties that improve
the reliability and fault tolerance of the entire system.

Keywords: Smart City · Residue Number System · Secret Sharing Schemes ·
Distributed Storage System · Reliability · Mobile ad hoc network ·
Communication

1 Introduction

A smart city is a set of interconnected solutions of Information and Communication
Technologies (ICT) and the Internet of Things (IoT) integrated into the management
environment of city property and services. As the main assets, various city systems and
objects can act as distributed information systems, i.e., power plants, schools, transport,

© The Author(s), under exclusive license to Springer Nature Switzerland AG 2023
S. Nesmachnow and L. Hernández Callejo (Eds.): ICSC-CITIES 2022, CCIS 1706, pp. 248–263, 2023.
https://doi.org/10.1007/978-3-031-28454-0_17

law enforcement agencies, hospitals, and other public services. The main objective is to improve the living standard and urban service quality. ICT allows to analyze and manage the urban environment in real-time with a quick response. There are many scientific, commercial, and governmental solutions for implementing a smart city concept.

According to Deakin generalized definition [1], a smart city is a city that uses ICT to meet the needs of city residents. It is not only a set of technological solutions but the application of these technologies by local communities.

Let us consider the main hardware components of the smart city network. It consists of many elements, including video surveillance, emergency call systems, biometric systems, city and banking services, intelligent transport, and IoT solutions (Radio Frequency Identification [2], sensors for measuring temperature, illumination, pressure, etc.). The large-scale data sharing in a distributed environment is fraught with data security and privacy issues since data compromise can harm people and the entire system. Another important aspect is reliability. Failures can delay the response of emergency systems, medical, and rescue services. Thus, when building a smart city communication infrastructure, design methods that provide data security at the required level while having high reliability and speed are very important.

To solve this multi-objective problem, we consider the network as a distributed (DCS) rather than a centralized (CCS) computing system. It is well known that for large networks, centralized data processing imposes a large load on the central computing bottleneck slowing down the entire system. More detailed arguments about the positive and negative properties of a decentralized network can be seen in [3–5].

To ensure the security of such a network, we discuss a combination of the Secret Sharing Scheme (SSS) [6] and the Residue Number System (RNS). SSS is cryptographic technique that splits a secret into several shares and distributes them among participants, i.e., $S = \{s_1, s_2, \ldots, s_n\}$. In the original SSS, to restore the secret, all n shares are required. In the most used threshold SSS, k shares from n are needed to restore the secret, where $k < n$. RNS is one of the most common non-positional number systems that represents the number in a positional system as a tuple of n numbers $(x_1, x_2, \ldots, x_n)$, obtained by dividing numbers into residuals. Among many applications, we could mention the acceleration of operations due to the parallel implementation of basic arithmetic, information integrity control, digital signal processing, etc.

This paper is structured as follows: Sect. 2 considers data transmission in smart city networks. Section 3 discusses existing approaches to ensure security, as well as the advantages of SSS schemes based on RNS. Section 4 presents the RNS and SSS, as well as the proposed SSS-RNS. Section 5 discusses the SSS-RNS persistent. Section 6 is devoted to the presentation and analysis of the obtained experimental results. Section 7 presents the main conclusions and future work.

2   Data Transmission in Smart City Networks

A wireless ad hoc network (WANET) and MANET are important concepts of smart city communication widely used for ensuring self-configuring and dynamic connectivity between sensors, humans, and devices that send and receive information.

Lobo et al. [7] study the Quality of Service (QoS) of MANET in smart city networks with an emphasis on healthcare. Several frameworks were considered that improve the quality of transmission in MANET, as well as individual elements, such as video signal transmission. Cardone et al. [8] discuss the MANET and Wireless Sensor Network (WSN) hybrid network for fast data collection in the smart city. The authors provide a transmission protocol based on modern data transmission standards considering IPv6. Pandey et al. [9] study methods to improve the reliability of MANET networks and propose a method of self-healing knots.

In this work, our goal is to increase the speed and reliability of the MANET communication with a sufficient level of security. To achieve this goal, we propose the use of RNS in MANET. In the original version, MANET solves the minimax optimization problem of finding the shortest path in the network. The smart city network can be represented as a directed graph, where the vertices are the communication nodes (devices in the network), and the arcs are the data transmission between the nodes. Let's establish that $G(V, E)$ – smart city network graph, with flow $v_0 \in V$. With path cost function $c : E \to R$. We assume that the set of vertices V split into two non-overlapping subsets V_A and V_B ($V_A \cup V_B = V$, $V_A \cap V_B = \emptyset$). Now we fix a pair of mappings:

$$s_A : v \to V_G(v) \, for \, v \in V_A \backslash \{v_0\}; \quad s_B : v \to V_G(v) \, for \, v \in V_B \backslash \{v_0\};$$

where $V_G(v)$ – the set of ends of all arcs outgoing from a vertex v. We define the following subgraph $T_s = (V, E_s)$, generated by a set of arcs of the form $(v, s_A(v))$ and $(v, s_B(V))$. This subgraph has the property that for some given vertex $w \in V$, or there is a way $P_T, (w, v_0)$ from w to v_0 or there is no such path. In the latter case, moving from w along the outgoing arcs of the digraph T_s, uniquely get to some oriented cycle C_w. For an arbitrary vertex $w \in V$ define the value $\tilde{c}(s_A, s_B, w)$ as the sum of the costs of the arcs of the path $P_T, (w, v_0)$, if such a path exists T_s; if the path does not exist $P_T, (w, v_0)$ in T_s value $\tilde{c}(s_A, s_B, w)$ we will assume equal ∞ or $-\infty$ depending on the positivity and negativity of the sum of the costs of the arcs of the oriented cycle C_w; if the sum of the costs of the arcs of an oriented cycle C_w equals zero, then the value $\tilde{c}(s_A, s_B, w)$ equals the sum of the costs of the arcs of the path connecting the vertex w with cycle C_w. That is, a problem of the form $F(w) = \min_{s_A} \max_{s_B} \tilde{c}(s_A, s_B, w)$.

RNS allows us to approach the solution of this problem with less iteration. If, when solving the Minimak problem for one path, it is necessary to refine the optimal solutions up to one at each iteration, then in the case of RNS it is necessary and sufficient to refine such solutions to equal the number of modules in the RNS system. Thus, the use of RNS makes it possible to solve an optimization problem for a multiobjective problem. Consider the data transfer model (Fig. 1 and 2). It is known that MANET transmits using devices located on the infrastructure-less, distributed wireless networks without static located transmission stations.

It is an interesting and promising solution providing communication of a big variety of devices, from mobile devices to personal cars, from smart devices to public transport, etc. In addition, a smart city infrastructure also contains static nodes, such as data centers, storage, decision centers, etc. For such a dynamic heterogeneous network, we propose the concept of parallel data transmission based on RNS that divides data into smaller parts and transmit them in parallel. The self-correcting properties of RNS can improve the reliability and fault tolerance of the entire system [10–13].

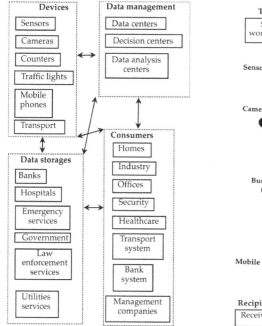

Fig. 1. General model of data transmission   **Fig. 2.** Data transfer model

Let us consider a conceptual model described above (Fig. 1). Here, we group the elements of a smart city according to common features. They can be separated from each other by large distances and distributed like data management modules.

However, this model gives a general idea of the transmission network complexity. Each group of components is connected to other groups, and control personnel can communicate to any device on the network. In such a data transfer model, MANET provides a definite advantage. Any device, such as a sensor, can send data to a destination, transmitting it through other devices within the network. Let us take a closer look at how the smart sensor transmits data over the network to the intended destination.

Figure 2 shows the data transfer model from the sensor to the recipient. The recipient can be a data warehouse, decision center, data processing center, cloud data analysis, etc. RNS allows you to transfer data in the MANET network in parallel breaking the message into several parts. It improves the system's speed since such parts are smaller than the message itself. The model of the data transmission packet is shown in Fig. 3.

Thus, the receiver collects pieces of information and combines them. The application knows how many parts have arrived and how many parts should arrive. If $k < n$ parts have arrived, the receiver recovers the entire message. Otherwise, it waits a certain time, and the packet is requested again or ignored. RNS is known to have self-correcting properties. This allows to recover the message if one or several parts are lost or intentionally changed. As a result, we can get a network with increasing speed and reliability.

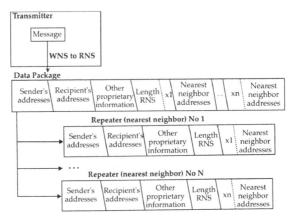

Fig. 3. Data packet model

3   DCS Security: Challenges and Solutions

Our main approach is to use SSS to ensure the security of data transmission. Let us discuss and compare well-known solutions for providing reliability and security of distributed data storage and transmission. Four main methods are used to ensure reliability [14]: Replication, Erasure code, Erasure code modifications, and Error correction code.

Chang et al. [15] presented a modified data replication method, providing a high encoding and decoding speed. But it requires additional cryptographic primitives to ensure security and has a high redundancy compared to erasure codes.

Many different modifications of erasure codes have been proposed to create reliable methods for distributed data storage. The joint use of error correction and erasure codes maintains system performance and minimizes the load on the data transmission network when recovering lost fragments [16, 17].

Erasure codes based on the Redundant Residue Number System (RRNS) [18] allow data to be processed in the encoded form [11]. So, it can be used both in the design of low-power wireless data transmission devices and distributed storage systems.

Secure distributed data storage and transmission systems are based on the use of cryptographic primitives - symmetric encryption algorithms (AES) and digital signatures based on RSA (Rivest, Shamir, Adleman) [19]. The advantages of these approaches are high speed of encryption and decryption and low data redundancy. The disadvantage is that an error in the encrypted data leads to its loss. To eliminate this shortcoming, the use of additional mechanisms for accessing data for a long time is required [20].

When building secure and reliable cloud storage, the following methods are used: Elliptic cryptography and erasure codes [21, 22], access structures [23, 24], error correction codes [25, 26], graph-based algorithms and modified data replication algorithm [27], attribute-based encryption [28], etc.

An alternative approach is to use recovery codes [17], erasure codes and error correction codes based on RRNS [16]. However, recovery codes and erasure codes do not allow encoded data processing. Homomorphic calculations process encoded data without additional computational costs for decoding.

A significant breakthrough in the field of homomorphic computing came from the work of Gentry [29]. The authors proposed a fully homomorphic scheme to perform both addition and multiplication. The main disadvantages of this algorithm are significant data redundancy and lack of control over the results of arithmetic operations.

Particular attention should be paid to the distributed data storage model proposed in [30], guaranteeing security, privacy, homomorphism, reliability, and scalability. The authors propose two approaches to building systems based on homomorphic access structures in RRNS, with RRNS moduli being used as secret keys stored by users. Data processing leads to an exponential increase in the load on the network and memory, which makes this model inapplicable in practice in modern conditions.

Access structures [31, 32] ensure data security and confidentiality. RRNS implements the same functionality as the Mignotte scheme but allows you to control the results of data processing. Distributed cloud storage is also characterized by collusion risks [33]. Several approaches have been developed to prevent cloud collusion [23]. As mentioned above, the non-stationarity of the cloud environment reduces the efficiency, performance, reliability, and security of the system. The adaptive paradigm reduces uncertainty but is rarely used in cloud computing [33].

Let us consider the following scenario. The user has sensitive data and decides not to store it in single cloud storage. He divides them into several parts and stores them in different clouds. There are several types of security threats in this scenario.

Deliberate threats include unauthorized access to information, interception, falsification, hacker attacks, etc., in one or more clouds.

Random threats include errors, crashes, etc. They can lead to the loss of one or more pieces of data, inconsistencies between different copies of the same data, and/or the inability to restore the original data. Collusion threats are an illegal agreement between two or more adversaries (in the context of multi-cloud storage, the adversaries are cloud services) to gain full access to personal data. Cryptographic protocols can be used to mitigate the risks of deliberate threats, but this is not enough for random threats. To improve the security and reliability of storage systems, distributed storage mechanisms based on access structures and error correction codes are used, which distribute data across multiple CSPs and minimize the likelihood of theft or loss of information in the event of deliberate and accidental threats. Examples of such mechanisms are RACS [34], DepSky [35], and RRNS, using Approximate Rank RRNS (AR-RRNS) [25].

Let us consider four schemes for data sharing (Fig. 4). The first thresholding structure (Fig. 4a) is a classic scheme where each store or channel has one share of data of the same size. An example of such a repository is DepSky [35]. The second threshold access structure (Fig. 4b) is an extension of the previous scheme, see Miranda-Lopez et al. [33], where each store has the same number of short shares. In both schemes, data can be recovered if the number of available shares exceeds a given threshold. Data splitting according to the traditional weighted access threshold structure means that the storages have one share of different sizes [6] (Fig. 4c).

Babenko et al. [12] proposed a weighted threshold access structure WA-RRNS (Weighted Access – RRNS) based on a redundant residue number system, where each store has several short shares (Fig. 4d). In the same work, a more efficient implementation WA-AR-RRNS was proposed, using an approximate value of the rank of the number represented in the RRNS to speed up the decoding procedure. With this approach, data can be recovered if and only if the sum of the share sizes is not less than a given threshold weight.

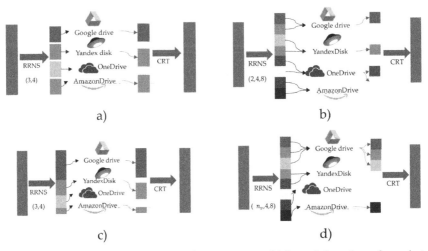

Fig. 4. Threshold access structure: a) One share per storage; b) Several short shares for each storage; c) Weighted threshold access structure (one share of different sizes per storage); d) Weighted threshold access structure (different number of shares of the same size per storage).

In the next sections, we show how the size and the total number of shares can change the reliability, security level, speed, etc. of data storage and transmission. These structures reduce the load on the transmission network compared to the classical replication mechanism and reduce the cost.

4   Residue Number System and Secret Sharing

RNS is one of the most common non-positional number systems [32]. Each specific RNS is determined by a system of coprime bases $\{p_1, p_2, \ldots, p_n\}$ and presentation range $P = \prod_{i=1}^{n} p_i$. Positional number X such that $0 \le X < P$, in this system is represented as a tuple of n numbers $(x_1, x_2, \ldots, x_n)$, obtained by the formula:

$$x_i = X \bmod p_i, i = 1, 2, \ldots, n.$$

RNS has many applications, among which we can note the acceleration of operations due to the parallel implementation of basic arithmetic operations, information integrity control, and digital signal processing.

Modular calculus is based on the Chinese Remainder Theorem (CRT) [25], according to which the number X, $0 \le X < P$, represented by remnants $(x_1, x_2, \ldots, x_n)$ in the system of moduli $\{p_1, p_2, \ldots, p_n\}$, then it can be uniquely calculated by the formula

$$X = \left| \sum_{i=1}^{n} \left| P_i^{-1} \right|_{p_i} P_i x_i \right|_P,$$

where $P_i = \frac{P}{p_i}$, $\left|P_i^{-1}\right|_{p_i}$ – multiplicative inversion P_i modulo p_i for $i = 1, 2, \ldots, n$. This method is called the CRT method or the Garner method. However, it is computationally complex, since it requires division by a sufficiently large number P. It is worth noting that there are many well-developed methods for converting numbers back from RNS to a positional system, together with an efficient implementation of calculating the remainder of the division, make this system suitable for use as the basics of a secret sharing scheme [12, 23, 25].

Let us consider SSSs using Shamir's threshold scheme as an example [24]. As mentioned above, threshold schemes allow you to restore the secret k the parties, and $k < n$. The idea of this scheme is that the secret is represented as a polynomial $k - 1$ degrees. Then, to interpolate the resulting polynomial, it is necessary k points, and the polynomial can be divided into n shares. Then the secret sharing process is as follows. Let's say we need to share a secret M on n shares. To do this, take a simple number $p < M$, which specifies the final size field p. The following polynomial is constructed over this field:

$$F(x) = \left(a_{k-1}x^{k-1} + a_{k-2}x^{k-2} + \cdots + a_1x + M\right) mod\ p$$

where $a_{k-1}, a_{k-2}, \ldots, a_1$ – random numbers that are only known when the secret is shared.

The secret recovery occurs due to the calculation of the Lagrange interpolation polynomial according to the following formula:

$$F(x) = \sum_i l_i(x)y_i\ mod\ p;\ l_i(x) = \prod_{i \neq j} \frac{x - x_j}{x_i - x_j}\ mod\ p,$$

where (x_i, y_i) – polynomial point coordinates. In addition, there is a limitation - all calculations are performed only in the final field p. In this scheme, an integer polynomial is used. Despite the low redundancy and high scalability, the field space p is not used efficiently.

Let us consider a scheme where a free coefficient represents information. This scheme was developed by Hugo Krawczyk in 1997 and, as in the case of the Shamir scheme, bears the name of its creator. Krawczyk scheme [36] appears to be a sharing scheme (k, n)- secret. It has a secret distribution protocol S among k participants randomly. In this case, the recovery of the secret is possible from k shares for a fixed value k, $1 \leq k \leq n$, while $k - 1$ shares do not allow you to recover the secret S. Thus, this scheme is a threshold.

Let us consider the information dissemination algorithm designated as *IDA*. This algorithm works for parameters n (total number of shares) and r (required number of shares for recovery). It includes a secure encryption function with a private key, which is designated as ENC. In addition, the algorithm implements a perfect (k, n)- secret sharing scheme, denoted as PSS. It is also worth noting that the space of both the secret and the message in this scheme is the same as for the encryption function *ENC*.

Share Algorithm:

1. Choosing a random encryption key K; secret encryption S with ENC turnkey K, then $E = ENC_K(S)$.

2. IDA shares the encrypted E on n fragments, then $- E_1, E_2, ..., E_n$.
3. Further PSS, create n key shares $K_1, K_2, ..., K_n$.
4. Shares are sent $P_{i_j, j} = 1, 2, ..., n$ to each participant, as well as $S_{i_j} = (E_{i_j}, K_{i_j})$. Shares K_i sent P_i in encrypted form.

Recovery Algorithm:

1. k Participants combine their shares $P_{i_j, j} = 1, 2, ..., k$ together with $S_{i_j} = (E_{i_j}, K_{i_j})$
2. UsingIDA, restoration is underway E from assembled parts$E_{i_j} = 1, 2, ..., k$.
3. Further PSS restores the key K from $K_{i_j} = 1, 2, ..., k$.
4. Using K, decrypted E, after which it recovers S.

Thus, the scheme is a computationally secure, ENC is a secure encryption function, and PSS is the ideal secret sharing scheme. Every share S_i has a length $|S|_k + |K|$. Evidence of this, as well as confirmation of the secrecy of the circuit, is given in [36].

In this section, RNS has been considered, as well as two threshold SSSs. Despite the obvious advantages of these schemes (low redundancy, scalability, flexibility), they have several disadvantages, such as the inability to add new participants without restoring the secret and re-sharing it. As mentioned above, this circumstance is unsatisfactory for building a smart city. The advantages of SSS-RNS schemes, as well as these schemes themselves, will be discussed in more detail in the next section.

5   Secret Sharing System with Residue Number System

In this section, we introduce the basic concepts used in constructing SSS based on RNS. The most famous SSSs on RNS are considered - the Asmuth-Bloom and Mignotte. The main approaches used for SSS security analysis and their extension for SSS on RNS are presented.

Let us consider SSS using RNS and RRNS. Let each participant in the scheme have a unique number or identifier, the entire set of which we will call the universal set of numbers and denote U (in the simplest case $U = \{1, 2, ..., n\}$, where n – number of participants in the scheme). The set of allowed coalition numbers is called the allowed subset of the set U and is denoted by I. On the other hand, an unresolved subset is a subset $\tilde{I}$ numbers of members of any coalition that does not have the right to restore the secret. Scope of the secret S in this case, we will call the set that combines all possible values of the secret s.

In the Asmuth-Bloom scheme, p_0 is selected first. It defines the set of all possible secrets. Arbitrary secret s should be chosen so that $s \in Z_{p_0}$. Further base system $p_1 < p_2 < ... < p_k < p_{k+1} < ... < p_n$ is chosen, so that $\prod_{i=1}^{k} p_i > p_0 \prod_{i=0}^{k-2} p_{n-i}$. The last inequality is usually called the Asmuth-Bloom condition. At the stage of sharing the secret, a random number is generated r such that $s' = s + rp_0 < \prod_{i=1}^{k} p_i$. Secret s is divided so that $s_i = s' \bmod p_i$ is a share for member i, where $i = 1, 2, ..., n$. In this method, any allowed set of participants with numbers from I can uniquely restore the secret; wherein $|I| = m \geq k$. First, using the Chinese remainder theorem, the position number is calculated x based on the modular representation $(s_{i_1}, s_{i_2}, \ldots, s_{i_m})$ in RNS with bases $p_{i_1}, p_{i_2}, \ldots, p_{i_m}$, where $i_j \in I$ for all $j = 1, 2, \ldots, m$. The original secret is restored as the remainder of the division of the number x on p_0: $s = x \bmod p_0$.

To discuss the security of the Asmuth-Bloom scheme, consider the shares of some unresolved coalition of participants with numbers from $\tilde{I}$. Then $\left| \tilde{I} \right| \leq k - 1$, let $P = \prod_{i=1}^{k} p_i$ and $\tilde{P} = \prod_{i \in \tilde{I}} p_i$. All that will be known in this case is the number $\tilde{s} = s' \bmod \tilde{P}$. According to the Asmuth-Bloom condition $P / \tilde{P} > p_0$ and $(\tilde{P}, p_0) = 1$, then the set of numbers $\tilde{s}$, such that $\tilde{s} \equiv s' \bmod \tilde{P}$ and $\tilde{s} < P$, covers all residue classes modulo p_0. Thus, as shown in [31], a coalition uniting less than k shares of the secret, does not receive any useful information about the secret, which indicates the strength of the scheme. However, its serious drawback is the increase in the size of the shares of the secret relative to the size of the secret itself, which leads to a significant excess of output information. The following threshold secret sharing scheme is free from this disadvantage., (k, n)-Mignotte threshold circuit.

In Mignotte's scheme, the base system $p_1 < p_2 < \ldots < p_k < p_{k+1} < \ldots < p_n$ is chosen as a Mignotte sequence, the numbers which satisfy the inequality

$$\alpha = \prod_{i=0}^{k-2} p_{n-i} < \prod_{i=1}^{k} p_i = \beta.$$

To achieve stamina secret s is selected. At the same time, for an arbitrarily secret s from the gap (α, β) numbers $s_i = s \bmod p_i$, there are secret shares for each participant with a number i, where $i = 1, 2, \ldots, n$. Any allowed set of participants with numbers can restore the secret. I, wherein $|I| = m \geq k$. Secret s is calculated using CRT number based $(s_{i_1}, s_{i_2}, \ldots, s_{i_m})$, presented in RNS with grounds $p_{i_1}, p_{i_2}, \ldots, p_{i_m}$, where $i_j \in I$ for all $j = 1, 2, \ldots, m$. To ensure a security, Mignotte sequences with a large value $(\beta - \alpha)/\beta$ should be used [32]. This scheme is not stable, but it has practical applications due to reducing the amount of output data [37].

Below, we consider the concepts that play an important role in the theory of the absolute security of a circuit. Based on this approach, we can estimate the entropy of secret sharing schemes. In the absence of information about the shares of the secret, we denote the information entropy as $H(s \in S)$, where s there is a secret distributed in the secret definition area S. In this case, the entropy is maximum since only public information is considered. The entropy of the secret is denoted as $H(s \in S | s_i : i \in I)$, when the shares of the secret belong to a certain known set $I \subseteq U$. If I is the set of numbers of the allowed subset of participants, then $H(s \in S | s_i : i \in I) = 0$ since in this case, the secret must be correctly restored. For the opposite case, in which an unresolved set of participants is combined, it is important to achieve the maximum conditional entropy. This condition leads to the formulation of the scheme perfection condition based on the probabilistic approach. At the same time, the most important concept of the SSS theory is the decrease of the uncertainty, which is understood as the quantity

$$\Delta(s_i : i \in I) = H(s \in S) - H(s \in S | s_i : i \in I).$$

The decrease of uncertainty in the case where I is the set of numbers of the allowed subset of participants is equal to the unconditional entropy of the domain of the secret:

$\Delta(s_i : i \in I) = H(s \in S)$. Now let the set of participants be unresolved. A secret sharing scheme is perfect if for all unresolved subsets of numbered participants $\tilde{I}$ should

$$\Delta(s_i : i \in \tilde{I}) = 0.$$

However, as noted earlier, to analyze the security of SSS based on RNS, an additional concept to study the properties of SSS of this type by conventional methods [38] was introduced. Therefore, the concept of an asymptotically perfect SSS was introduced. The scheme is asymptotically perfect if, for all unresolved subsets of participants with numbers $\tilde{I}$ and for any $\varepsilon > 0$, there is such p, that, for $p_0 < p_1 < \ldots < p_n, p_i > p$ $(i = 0, 1, \ldots, n)$, and $\Delta\left(s_i : i \in \tilde{I}\right) < \varepsilon$.

The question of how exactly it is necessary to choose the parameters of the SSS on the RNS so that it has the asymptotic perfection property remains open. The work [38] shows the asymptotic perfection of the Asmuth-Bloom scheme when using "sufficiently close" coprime as the RNS base system. The work [37] considers so-called compact sequences of coprime numbers with an initial value p_0 when $p_n < p_0 + p_0^\theta$ for some real number $\theta \in (0, 1)$.

Compact sequences of coprime numbers play an important role in studying the security of secret sharing schemes. The use of these sequences as a system of RNS bases makes it possible to build efficient and stable schemes, which is due to the proximity of numbers on the number line. The work [37] considers, it is shown that the Asmuth-Bloom scheme is asymptotically perfect when using compact sequences as the RNS base system. It should be noted that the Mignotte scheme is not asymptotically perfect. However, a robustness study would not be complete without an analysis of the computational robustness of the methods. In the future, we will assume that it is precisely the compact sequence of coprime numbers that are used as the bases.

Let us now turn to the concept of computational stability of a circuit. Let at some point in time some analysts managed to collect shares of an unresolved subset of participants with numbers $\tilde{I}$ for some SSS. The task of the analyst, in this case, is to recover the secret based on the available data. In a real situation, many S can be divided into two subsets. First subset S_1 will consist of all secret options that do not fit a secret role given the known data. Second subset S_2 will contain all remaining possible secret options. For example, if the Mignotte scheme knows the share of the secret s_j for module p_j, $0 \leq j \leq n$, then the secret must satisfy the condition: $s \equiv s_j \bmod p_j$. Therefore, in this case $S_1 = \{s : s \in S \wedge s \not\equiv s_j \bmod p_j\}$ and $S_2 = \{s : s \in S \wedge s \equiv s_j \bmod p_j\}$. Note that if the SSS is perfect, then for it $S_1 = \emptyset$ and $S_2 = S$.

Thus, to find the original secret, it is necessary to go through all the options included in S_2 and the stability of the circuit depends on the cardinality of this set and on the computational complexity of exhaustive enumeration. It is necessary to generate the scheme parameters so that the analyst cannot, using modern computing resources, pick up the secret in a reasonable time. A circuit that meets these conditions will be called a computational rack. As a measure of computational security, we take the cardinality of the set S_2: $f(\tilde{I}) = |S_2|$.

For the Asmuth-Bloom scheme, considering its asymptotic perfection and the Asmuth-Bloom condition, $f(\tilde{I}) = |S| = |Z_{p_0}| = p_0$ for anyone $\tilde{I}$. It is easy to see that not all secure circuits are computationally secure. But, on the other hand, computationally secure circuits are not always perfect. The most important in a practical sense is computational stability.

6 Modeling

In this section, an experimental study of the system considered above will be considered. The modeling was done by comparing two implementations of SSS-RNS, and is given: the Asmuth-Bloom implementation and the proposed implementation in Sect. 5 (RNS implementation). The study was conducted as follows: the number of modules is selected from 4 to 6; the input is images of various sizes from 6 MB to 146 MB. The study will take into account the following characteristics: coding and decading time, redundancy in coding and decading. Let's consider the obtained results (Fig. 5).

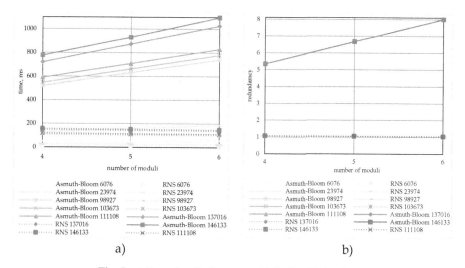

Fig. 5. a) Encoding Performance. b) Coding Redundancy

Analyzing the obtained results, we can say that the proposed implementation has a high performance. The encoding time of all images is in the range from 1 to 180 ms. When as the Asmuth-Bloom implementation is between 40 and 1100 ms. This result is achieved due to the applied RNS methods in our implementation. It allows you to reduce computational complexity due to a larger number of precomputed constants. However, because of this, it is also necessary to conduct studies of the redundancy that appears when encoding information. Consider this study (Fig. 5b).

Analyzing this illustration, we can observe that the redundancy of the proposed implementation remains approximately at the same level, while the redundancy of the Asmuth-Bloom implementation is 5 times greater and increases with the number of modules used. Thus, in addition to efficiency in terms of performance, the proposed implementation also has better coding redundancy properties. When conducting decadence, similar results were obtained (Fig. 6).

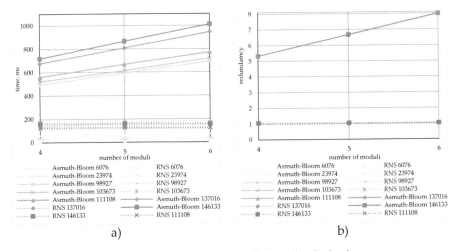

Fig. 6. a) Decoding Performance. b) Decoding Redundancy

Considering the result obtained for decoding, we can say that similar results were obtained, as in coding. The proposed RNS implementation also has performance and redundancy advantages.

Thus, we can say that using the proposed implementation of SSS-RNS, it is possible to increase the speed of the system, as well as the redundancy of the processed data. However, this requires a larger number of precomputed constants, which is a manageable disadvantage when using a static set of RNS modules, but if you need to change the set of these modules, all precomputed values must be recalculated for the new set.

7   Conclusions

In this work, we study mechanisms for protecting and accelerating smart city communication systems. Security mechanisms based on different methods are considered. We show that the most suitable method for a smart city dynamic network is SSS. RNS can be used as an adaptive mechanism to increase security and reliability through effective correcting management. We propose MANET with RNS to improve the quality of service for each application used in the self-configuring and dynamic connectivity heterogeneous networks. The main advantage of RNS is the versatility of the data representation. On the one hand, RNS is a highly efficient tool for error-resistant coding of information based on the corrective abilities of redundant RNS. On the other hand, it is the basis for designing secret sharing schemes, including efficient computationally secure schemes. The proposed approach can increase the network's resistance to attacks of various kinds and the transmission confidentiality, along with high reliability using multipath routing. This approach does not have the disadvantages of traditional encryption transmission methods: the key management problem is solved by using SSS, and the problem of possible attacks on routes is solved by using an adaptive multipath transmission.

Acknowledgments. This work was supported by the Ministry of Education and Science of the Russian Federation (Project 075-15-2020-788).

References

1. Deakin, M., Al Waer, H.: From intelligent to smart cities. Intell. Build. Int. **3**(3), 140–152 (2011). https://doi.org/10.1080/17508975.2011.586671
2. Weinstein, R.: RFID: a technical overview and its application to the enterprise. IT Prof. **7**(3), 27–33 (2005). https://doi.org/10.1109/MITP.2005.69
3. Weissman, J.B.: Gallop: the benefits of wide-area computing for parallel processing. J. Parallel Distrib. Comput. **54**(2), 183–205 (1998). https://doi.org/10.1006/jpdc.1998.1487
4. Lange, D.B.: Mobile objects and mobile agents: the future of distributed computing? Presented at the (1998). https://doi.org/10.1007/BFb0054084
5. Datla, D., et al.: Wireless distributed computing: a survey of research challenges. IEEE Commun. Mag. **50**(1), 144–152 (2012). https://doi.org/10.1109/MCOM.2012.6122545
6. Attasena, V., Darmont, J., Harbi, N.: Secret sharing for cloud data security: a survey. VLDB J. **26**(5), 657–681 (2017). https://doi.org/10.1007/s00778-017-0470-9
7. Lobo, P., et al.: Quality of Service for MANET based smart cities. Int. J. Adv. Comput. Eng. Netw. **5**, 2 (2017)
8. Cardone, G., et al.: Effective collaborative monitoring in smart cities: converging MANET and WSN for fast data collection. In: Proceedings of ITU Kaleidoscope 2011: The Fully Networked Human? - Innovations for Future Networks and Services (K-2011), pp. 1–8. IEEE, Cape Town (2011)
9. Pandey, J., et al.: Novel scheme to heal MANET in smart city network. In: 2016 3rd MEC International Conference on Big Data and Smart City (ICBDSC), pp. 1–6. IEEE (2016). https://doi.org/10.1109/ICBDSC.2016.7460339
10. Shiryaev, E., et al.: Performance impact of error correction codes in rns with returning methods and base extension. In: 2021 International Conference Engineering and Telecommunication (En&T), pp. 1–5. IEEE (2021). https://doi.org/10.1109/EnT50460.2021.9681756
11. Babenko, M., et al.: Algorithm for constructing modular projections for correcting multiple errors based on a redundant residue number system using maximum likelihood decoding. Program. Comput. Softw. **47**(8), 839–848 (2021). https://doi.org/10.1134/S036176882108 0089
12. Babenko, M., et al.: RRNS base extension error-correcting code for performance optimization of scalable reliable distributed cloud data storage. In: 2021 IEEE International Parallel and Distributed Processing Symposium Workshops (IPDPSW), pp. 548–553. IEEE (2021). https://doi.org/10.1109/IPDPSW52791.2021.00087
13. Tay, T.F., Chang, C.-H.: A new algorithm for single residue digit error correction in redundant residue number system. In: 2014 IEEE International Symposium on Circuits and Systems (ISCAS), pp. 1748–1751. IEEE (2014). https://doi.org/10.1109/ISCAS.2014.6865493
14. Nachiappan, R., et al.: Cloud storage reliability for big data applications: a state of the art survey. J. Netw. Comput. Appl. **97**, 35–47 (2017). https://doi.org/10.1016/j.jnca.2017.08.011
15. Chang, F., et al.: Bigtable: a distributed storage system for structured data. ACM Trans. Comput. Syst. **26**(2), 1–26 (2008). https://doi.org/10.1145/1365815.1365816
16. Dimakis, A.G., et al.: Network coding for distributed storage systems. IEEE Trans. Inf. Theory. **56**(9), 4539–4551 (2010). https://doi.org/10.1109/TIT.2010.2054295
17. Lin, S.-J., et al.: Novel polynomial basis and its application to reed-solomon erasure codes. In: 2014 IEEE 55th Annual Symposium on Foundations of Computer Science, pp. 316–325. IEEE (2014). https://doi.org/10.1109/FOCS.2014.41

18. Ye, R., Boukerche, A., Wang, H., Zhou, X., Yan, B.: RESIDENT: a reliable residue number system-based data transmission mechanism for wireless sensor networks. Wireless Netw. **24**(2), 597–610 (2016). https://doi.org/10.1007/s11276-016-1357-1

19. Stergiou, C., et al.: Secure integration of IoT and cloud computing. Futur. Gener. Comput. Syst. **78**, 964–975 (2018). https://doi.org/10.1016/j.future.2016.11.031

20. Lee, B.-H., et al.: Data security in cloud computing using AES under HEROKU cloud. In: 2018 27th Wireless and Optical Communication Conference (WOCC), pp. 1–5. IEEE (2018). https://doi.org/10.1109/WOCC.2018.8372705

21. Zhou, S., et al.: ESDR: an efficient and secure data repairing paradigm in cloud storage. Secur. Commun. Networks. **9**(16), 3646–3657 (2016). https://doi.org/10.1002/sec.1571

22. Lin, H.-Y., Tzeng, W.-G.: A secure erasure code-based cloud storage system with secure data forwarding. IEEE Trans. Parallel Distrib. Syst. **23**(6), 995–1003 (2012). https://doi.org/10.1109/TPDS.2011.252

23. Tchernykh, A., et al.: AC-RRNS: Anti-collusion secured data sharing scheme for cloud storage. Int. J. Approx. Reason. **102**, 60–73 (2018). https://doi.org/10.1016/j.ijar.2018.07.010

24. Shamir, A.: How to share a secret. Commun. ACM **22**(11), 612–613 (1979). https://doi.org/10.1145/359168.359176

25. Chervyakov, N., et al.: AR-RRNS: configurable reliable distributed data storage systems for internet of things to ensure security. Futur. Gener. Comput. Syst. **92**, 1080–1092 (2019). https://doi.org/10.1016/j.future.2017.09.061

26. Celesti, A., et al.: Adding long-term availability, obfuscation, and encryption to multi-cloud storage systems. J. Netw. Comput. Appl. **59**, 208–218 (2016). https://doi.org/10.1016/j.jnca.2014.09.021

27. Shen, P., et al.: SpyStorage: a highly reliable multi-cloud storage with secure and anonymous data sharing. In: 2017 International Conference on Networking, Architecture, and Storage (NAS), pp. 1–6. IEEE (2017). https://doi.org/10.1109/NAS.2017.8026878

28. Radha Devi, G., Kumar, A.: DROPS: division and replication of data in cloud for optimal performance and security. Adv. Math. Sci. J. **9**(7), 5075–5083 (2020). https://doi.org/10.37418/amsj.9.7.73

29. Gentry, C.: Computing arbitrary functions of encrypted data. Commun. ACM **53**(3), 97–105 (2010). https://doi.org/10.1145/1666420.1666444

30. Gomathisankaran, M., et al.: HORNS: a homomorphic encryption scheme for cloud computing using residue number system. In: 2011 45th Annual Conference on Information Sciences and Systems, pp. 1–5. IEEE (2011). https://doi.org/10.1109/CISS.2011.5766176

31. Asmuth, C., Bloom, J.: A modular approach to key safeguarding. IEEE Trans. Inf. Theory. **29**(2), 208–210 (1983). https://doi.org/10.1109/TIT.1983.1056651

32. Mignotte, M.: How to share a secret. In: Beth, T. (ed.) EUROCRYPT 1982. LNCS, vol. 149, pp. 371–375. Springer, Heidelberg (1983). https://doi.org/10.1007/3-540-39466-4_27

33. Miranda-López, V., et al.: Experimental analysis of secret sharing schemes for cloud storage based on RNS. In: Mocskos, E., Nesmachnow, S. (eds.) CARLA 2017. CCIS, vol. 796, pp. 370–383. Springer, Cham (2018). https://doi.org/10.1007/978-3-319-73353-1_26

34. Abu-Libdeh, H., et al.: RACS. In: Proceedings of the 1st ACM symposium on Cloud computing - SoCC 2010, p. 229. ACM Press, New York (2010). https://doi.org/10.1145/1807128.1807165

35. Bessani, A., et al.: DepSky. ACM Trans. Storage **9**(4), 1–33 (2013). https://doi.org/10.1145/2535929

36. Krawczyk, H.: Secret sharing made short. In: Stinson, D.R. (ed.) CRYPTO 1993. LNCS, vol. 773, pp. 136–146. Springer, Heidelberg (1994). https://doi.org/10.1007/3-540-48329-2_12

37. Barzu, M., et al.: Compact sequences of co-primes and their applications to the security of CRT-based threshold schemes. Inf. Sci. (Ny) **240**, 161–172 (2013). https://doi.org/10.1016/j.ins.2013.03.062
38. Quisquater, M., et al.: On the security of the threshold scheme based on the Chinese remainder theorem. Presented at the (2002). https://doi.org/10.1007/3-540-45664-3_14

Application of LPWAN Technologies Based on LoRa in the Monitoring of Water Sources of The Andean Wetlands

Luis González[1]([✉]), Andrés Gonzales[1], Santiago González[1],
and Alonso Cartuche[2]

[1] Department of Electric, Electronic and Telecommunication Engineering,
Universidad de Cuenca, Av.12 de Abril, 010203 Cuenca, Ecuador
{luis.gonzaleza,amauta.gonzales,santiago.gonzalezm}@ucuenca.edu.ec
[2] Carrera de Ingeniería Ambiental y El Centro de Investigaciones Tropicales del
Ambiente y Biodiversidad (CITIAB), Universidad Nacional de Loja, Ciudad
Universitaria Guillermo Falconí, 110150 Loja, Ecuador
victor.cartuche@unl.edu.ec

Abstract. This paper presents the design of a water source monitoring system based on LoRa technology for the Tres Lagunas Andean high-altitude wetlands ecosystem (Ecuador). The solution has been implemented using mainly an ATmega1284p microcontroller, an SX1278 transceiver and hydrological sensors. The data is transmitted from the study site to the TTN server and sent via the MQTT protocol to the Node-RED platform. On the other hand, a graphical interface has been developed that allows analyzing historical data of temperature, dissolved oxygen (DO), oxidation-reduction potential (ORP) and hydrogen potential (pH). Furthermore, energy consumption tests and LoRa physical layer experiments have been performed with the prototype. Results reveal the proper operation of the prototype. In particular, it has been observed that SF9 and SF10 present packet reception rates higher than 97%. Regarding SF7 and SF8, they was discarded for this type of scenarios due to the packet loss rate higher than 10%. The main contribution of this work is the proposal of a portable, low-cost and open source prototype, focused on the transmission of hydrological data obtained in Andean high-altitude lakes through IoT technologies for the administration, management and control of water resources that represent a fundamental component of a smart city.

Keywords: LoRa · Monitoring system · Wetlands ecosystem

1 Introduction

Applications based on IoT (Internet of Things) technologies constitute a fundamental piece in the field of innovation and sustainable development [1]. In particular, water resource management technologies are vital components of Smart Cities [2], promoting the use of real time data through online platforms with

© The Author(s), under exclusive license to Springer Nature Switzerland AG 2023
S. Nesmachnow and L. Hernández Callejo (Eds.): ICSC-CITIES 2022, CCIS 1706, pp. 264–278, 2023.
https://doi.org/10.1007/978-3-031-28454-0_18

significant efficiency compared to traditional methods [3]. These data are usually hydrogen potential, conductivity, dissolved oxygen, among others. These data are measured through sensors and allow determining the water quality [4]. As for water sources, they are usually located in remote areas of the city and lack services such as Internet access, electricity, among others, therefore, solutions based on IoT and sensor networks (WSN) would allow the creation of monitoring systems that improve the management of water resources.

On the other hand, the water resources of aquatic systems are vulnerable to climate change due to several factors, for example, the increase in temperature can contribute to the evaporation of the lagoons, reduction of the water table and alterations in water quality [5]. In this context, an economic valuation of water and carbon storage in the Ecuadorian wetlands was carried out in [6]. The study area covered the wetlands of the cantons of Nabon, Oña, Saraguro and Yacuambi, specifically the sectors of Tres Lagunas and the Shincata river. It should be noted that despite the existence of two INAMHI (Instituto Nacional de Meteorología e Hidrología) stations, one in Oña (M421) and the other one in San Lucas (M32), due to the location of these stations, it is not possible to determine the exact climatic conditions of the study area and therefore the understanding of these aquatic ecosystems is almost null. That is, the stations only cover the slopes of the Pacific and Amazon water systems in the study area. The data collected from these stations, possibly present discrepancies with the real conditions of the site, due to the contributions of rainfall, fog and drizzle.

In relation to Tres Lagunas, this ecosystem contributes to the subsistence of nearby populations due to its great ecologic, economic, social, and cultural value. The main contribution is the supply of water for domestic consumption and crop irrigation. In addition, it is a place of great cultural importance for the 3 cantons because it is considered a magical place, linked to ancestral religious traditions, the manifestation of power and energy of mother earth [7]. Currently, this wetland complex is threatened by several factors, for example, the road that connects Saraguro and Yacuambi crosses this area and represents a great risk for the conservation and protection of this sector. In this sense, it is essential to know the status of the lagoons in order to prevent a deficit of water resources, improve water quality, and mitigate the effect of anthropogenic contamination such as vehicle traffic, tourist waste, among others.

Tres Lagunas does not count with a system to monitor weather and water conditions; the nearest stations are located several kilometers away. Factors such as distance, adverse weather conditions, limitations in access to the mobile network and the Internet have prevented the implementation of any type of meteorological station in the lagoons of interest. Therefore, the deployment of monitoring stations in the sector represents a contribution to determine the current state and vulnerabilities to which the aquatic ecosystems of the site are exposed and to provide data that will allow us to assess the current state of the lagoons and the vulnerabilities to which they are exposed.

The company's strategic management and conservation of natural resources is a key factor in the implementation of the decisions of the government institutions.

In this context, the present work focuses on a technological solution to monitor the Tres Lagunas site, through a data acquisition and transmission device, from the study site to the Internet. This document is divided into 5 sections, the second section presents the state of the art, the third section indicates the monitoring architecture, the fourth section presents the results and the fifth section concludes with the conclusions.

2   Related Works

The integration of IoT solutions in Smart Cities allows the improvement of different services through new technologies. For example, the monitoring of water resources allows a sustainable management of water services. The best option when these sites are in remote areas is to use long-range networks such as LPWAN (Low Power Wide Area Network). For example, networks based on LoRa (Long Range), have characteristics to be able to adapt to various scenarios. In this context, relevant studies related to such applications are discussed below.

In relation to the recording of water parameters, data collection devices require special equipment called probes that are usually very expensive [8]. Therefore, it is essential to develop prototypes that offer greater accessibility for their use. In terms of implementation, the recording of these environmental data is performed by devices such as microcontrollers (MCUs), where the information measured by the sensors is preprocessed and stored internally in the station also known as node [9]. When the nodes are used in remote locations, the power supply is provided by batteries, in this context there are several works that have managed to increase the battery life time for periods longer than one year [10,11].

In this sense, in [12] a prototype is described, where low-cost sensors are used for the acquisition of physicochemical water data. During a period of 45 days, the device was tested together with a professional team, obtaining a high correlation between the data of both teams, verifying the quality of the prototype information.

On the other hand, monitoring of water ecosystems is very costly in terms of resources when sites are remotely located and manual access is required to collect data [13]. One solution is to use wireless communication technologies. In this context, a suitable transmission technology would be LoRa/LoRaWAN. The communication protocol and architecture of this technology support low-cost, mobile and secure bidirectional communication and is optimized for low power consumption and designed to scale easily [14]. Therefore, the use of LoRa/LoRaWAN is becoming more and more frequent in different applications and is adaptable to a wide range of applications.

For example, [15] highlights the importance of the advantages of LoRa in terms of coverage and energy efficiency, which facilitates its operation in poorly characterized sites, such as high mountains and glaciers, allowing to open new fields of research in these areas.

Regarding remote sites where there is no access to the power grid, the energy resource of the batteries is crucial for their operation, as discussed in [16], a study in which groundwater monitoring is performed, where the nodes record the variables and transmit them to a LoRa Gateway, obtaining 8 days of energy independence. Other methods increase the energy resources of the nodes through a combination of energy sources, for example solar and hydroelectric, as presented in [17], which provides up to 432 h of autonomy to its nodes.

In this sense, one of the factors of higher energy consumption in LoRa nodes is generated in the transmission stage. In [18], the importance of selecting the appropriate transmission parameters is highlighted, otherwise the useful life of the node is shorter. For example, the increase of power for packet transmission drastically affects the energy consumption as reported in [19], where their study focuses only on the rest of the parameters to improve communication. In this context, the use of low SF (Spreading Factor) values would allow improving the energy efficiency. For example, in [20] the authors recommend using low SFs (high data rate) and high transmit power only for nodes that are far away from the gateway. Another approach is described in [21], where different payload lengths and physical layer parameters were evaluated to reduce the ToA (Time on Air), the authors recommend leaving the BW (Bandwidth) fixed and only focus on the SF and CR (Coding Rate), on the other hand they indicate that it is necessary to decrease the payload.

Regarding mountain scenarios, in [22] an evaluation of LoRa parameters is presented, the authors show that the radio transmit power is not a dominant parameter affecting the network, instead BW, SF and CR play a more relevant role. In these mounting scenarios, 3 km coverages have been achieved as reported in [23], where they evaluated the LoRa technology using three data rates in the 433 MHz band, with a transmit power of 20 dBm, highlighting that line-of-sight is a relevant factor for this transmission technology.

In this context, it is observed that the use of LoRa for environmental data transmission is feasible and allows an adaptation to different environments due to its variety of properties that can be configured according to the requirements. In the present study, a prototype of physicochemical data acquisition focused on lagoons of the Andean wetlands in southern Ecuador was developed using LoRa transmission technology for monitoring water sources.

3   Monitoring Architecture

This section details the operation of the monitoring architecture, from the implementation of the prototype to the presentation of the data using cloud services.

3.1   Prototype Implementation

The hydro station was implemented using hardware and software tools that facilitate its reconfiguration. In the central part of the station, an ATmega 1284p MCU of the Pico Power family [24] is used. On the other hand, the measurement of physicochemical variables of the water is performed with analog and digital sensors. Figure 1 shows the integration of the prototype.

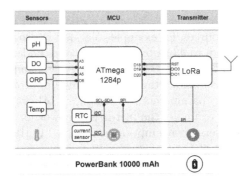

Fig. 1. Prototype design.

As shown in Fig. 1, the prototype consists of 4 sensors, three are analogical: Gravity pH [25], DO [26], ORP [27], and a digital temperature sensor DS18B20, the most relevant technical characteristics of these devices are presented in Table 1. On the other hand, a current sensor INA219 is added to measure the energy levels consumed by the peripherals and the water station in general. Additionally, a DS3231 RTC (Real Time Clock) module is incorporated to provide time stamps to the system. For the control of the sensors, open-source libraries available in [28] were used. Regarding the communication protocol, the digital sensors use the i2C protocol and the analog sensors are read with the 10-bit ADC (Analog-to-Digital Converter) incorporated in the MCU.

Table 1. Technical characteristics of the sensors

Parameter	pH	ORP	DO	DS18B20	Unit
Measurement range	0.1 a 14	−1500 a +1500	0 a 700	−55 a +125	pH, mV,%, °C
Accuracy	± 0.2	± 1	± 2	± 0.2	pH, mV,%, °C
Response time	0	0	0	750	ms
Energy consumption	3	3	3	1	mA

Regarding the network layer, it is composed by the LoRa RA-02 module [29] and its configuration is done through the MCCI-LoRaWAN-LMIC [30] libraries to work in a LoRaWAN network. This way the data is transmitted wirelessly to a Gateway that uploads the data to The Things Network (TTN) server. For the power supply, a PowerBank of 10000 mAh. Finally, a printed circuit board (PCB) was designed which collects all the components that facilitates the prototypes usage. Figure 2 shows how the PCB and its components are implemented.

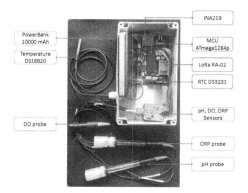

Fig. 2. Prototype components.

3.2   Water Monitoring System

Figure 3 shows a functional diagram of the monitoring system. For the programming of the ATmega, the Arduino IDE platform [31] was used, in this way the management of sensors and modules is more flexible from libraries available for the devices, promoting a more efficient development.

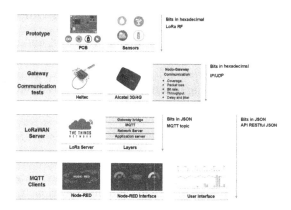

Fig. 3. Functional diagram of the system.

As for the TTN server, it is required to configure the LoRaWAN network equipment. In particular, first the node is configured in ABP (Authentication By Personalization) mode and its AppSKey and NwkSKey credentials are registered in TNN as well as in the node software, with these credentials the information is encrypted and travels from the node to the server. On the other hand, the Gateway is configured in TTN by means of the MAC (Media Access Control) address and is accesses the Internet through the mobile network.

The TTN data are decrypted and sent through a MQTT (Message Queuing Telemetry Transport) server to the Node-RED platform, where an API (Application Programming Interface) is implemented with the network nodes: http in and http response that provide endpoints with the stored data, which could be visualized in a more user-friendly way through an interface developed with JavaScript using the APEXCHARTS.JS library. Currently, for the purposes of the application, only one endpoint has been deployed with the GET method, which allows retrieving all the data of the available variables. In this interface the user can observe the changes of the variables with respect to time, analyze statistical results of the information, access historical data and download them easily. In this way the system is able to measure, transmit and present to the user physicochemical variables obtained in high Andean lakes.

4   Evaluation and Results

This section presents the characterization of the prototype, both at the network level and in the data acquisition process.

4.1   Analysis of LoRa Prototype Performance in Different Scenarios

This section examines the performance of the prototype under different meteorological weather conditions, distances and configurations of the SF and CR parameters both in a rural area and in the high plains, examining the PRR (Packet Reception Rate), throughput/bit rate, RSSI (Received Signal Strength Indicator), delay and jitter metrics, by means of histograms with confidence intervals.

Rural Area. It was first considered evaluating the rural area instead of the wetlands because of the ease of locating the Gateway-node and thus obtaining reference data such as bit rate, coverage, antenna location, which allow us to appreciate the capabilities of the prototype when faced with different environments. The rural area was the Urdaneta parish in the Saraguro city.

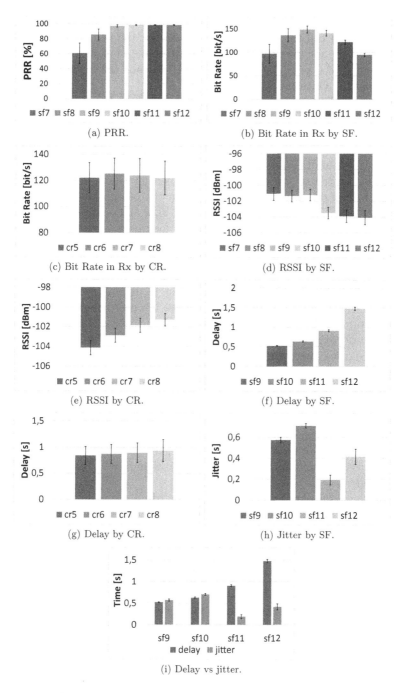

(a) PRR.

(b) Bit Rate in Rx by SF.

(c) Bit Rate in Rx by CR.

(d) RSSI by SF.

(e) RSSI by CR.

(f) Delay by SF.

(g) Delay by CR.

(h) Jitter by SF.

(i) Delay vs jitter.

Fig. 4. Results of the metrics obtained in the rural area.

Urdaneta is located approximately 30 km away from Tres Lagunas with an altitude of around 2490 m m.a.s.l. Regarding the environment in the rural area, many bushes and tall trees were observed between the node and the Gateway, however; they do not directly interfere with the line of sight. The experiments were conducted at 4 points at 500 m, 1 km, 1.7 km and 2.2 km distance between the node and the Gateway.

The general histogram of each SF is shown in Fig. 4a. It can be seen that both SF7 and SF8 have the lowest rate, therefore, they are the least recommended for this scenario. From SF9 onwards, an average PRR greater than 97 % is obtained with a very low confidence interval, which shows stability in the connection.

As for the overall results of the bit rate for each SF, Fig. 4b shows a bell shape, which is due to the packet loss obtained for the case of SF7 and SF8, therefore the bit rate is directly affected. On the other hand, for SF10, SF11 and SF12, the PRR is 99%. However, the bit rate at the transmitter decreases as the SF increases, therefore, the best choice for this case are the values of SF9 or SF10, since they are at an intermediate point and allow to obtain the highest possible bit rate. On the other hand, the bit rate decreases as the denominator of the CR increases (see Fig. 4c), with the exception of CR5.

In the results of the RSSI for each SF in Fig. 4d, it is observed that the power data have varied very little among themselves, however; it is clear the trend of RSSI reduction as the SF value increases. That is, the signal is slightly stronger when the SF decreases, while a higher denominator in the CR improves the signal power (see Fig. 4e), generating changes between each CR of approximately 1 dBm difference.

Figure 4f shows the average delay values for each SF. There is a clear tendency for the delay to increase as the SF increases, which corresponds to the theory, since a larger SF represents higher ToA. As for the CR, it can be seen in Fig. 4g that the delay is higher when the denominator of the coding rate is larger, since there are more bits for transmission. However, the variation is very small, going from 0.84 s to the maximum value of 0.94 s, so the impact of the CR on the delay is not considerable.

As for the results presented in Fig. 4h regarding the jitter, such behavior is related to the accuracy of the RTC. In particular, the RTC device (DS3231) has a minimum scale given in seconds, so the minimum delay is 1 s, which makes delays of milliseconds or more undetectable. Then, the closer the average delay is to integer values, the less probability of variance in the delay. As shown in Fig. 4i, the lowest jitter corresponds to the SF with the promised delay closest to 1 s, in this case SF11. But this does not mean that using SF11 will have less jitter and a more reliable connection, but it is an error in the accuracy of the RTC. However, the jitter does affect the communications with high bit rates or applications requiring real-time data, so for this case the jitter behavior does not affect the network.

High Wetlands Area. In the wetland zone, the environment is suitable for LoRa, as the results from the rural area show an excellent performance when the line of sight is completely clear and in Tres Lagunas there are no considerable interferences. The site is mostly covered with grass, small bushes and wild plants that do not represent an obstacle. The two points chosen for the location of the node and the Gateway are 1 km and 1.2 km apart.

Figure 5a shows the overall PRR result for all points and CR combinations. The PRR tends to increase as the SF increases, reaching an average of 100 % of packets received in SF11 and SF12. In addition, it is observed that SF9 and SF10 have an excellent performance, presenting an average PRR of 99 % with confidence intervals close to zero. Therefore, with respect to PRR, it is recommended to use any SF greater than 9.

The overall throughput for the SF and CR values are presented in Figs. 5b and 5c, respectively. The bit rate tends to decrease as SF increases, with the exception of SF7 and SF8, due to packet loss. Therefore, SF9 remains the best choice with respect to bit rate for this scenario, since it provides the highest possible bit rate. Regarding the CR, the bit rate decreases as the denominator of the CR increases, but the variation between each CR is very small.

With respect to the RSSI values for each SF, the graph in Fig. 5d presents a clear trend of decreasing RSSI as the SF increases. However, the degradation is quite small, e.g., SF10, SF11 and SF12 have approximately the same mean. The CR values obtained in Fig. 5e show that the RSSI increases as the denominator of the CR is larger, although the difference is minimal. As in the rural area, a larger CR denominator improves the signal power.

Figure 5f shows the delay results for this scenario. The data corresponds to the theory, because as the SF increases, the ToA also increases, which generates a higher delay. The most interesting result is observed in SF9, where there is a delay of approximately 10 ms and a reduced variability, which is reflected in the confidence intervals. Looking at SF9 and SF10, it is evident that the delays are also very small compared to the rural area, reiterating the importance of line of sight for LoRa. With respect to SF12, the delay is approximately 1s. In contrast, Fig. 5g shows that as the denominator of the CR increases, so does the delay. However, in this case the confidence intervals are very wide as a consequence of the SF values, since the result corresponds to the mean of all the CRs for each SF and test point.

In Fig. 6, photographs taken during the development of the experiments in the study scenarios are presented.

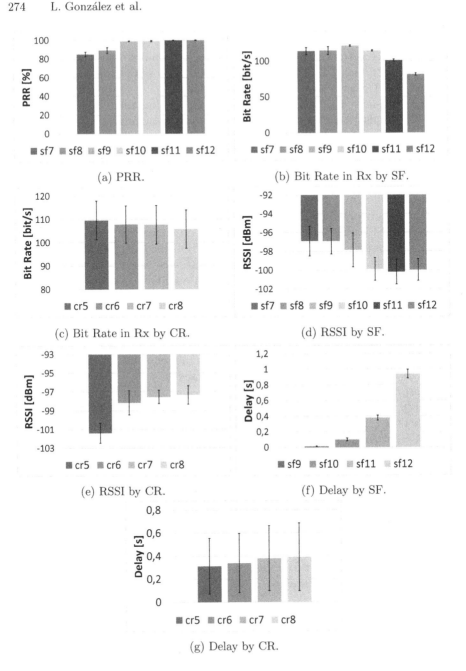

(a) PRR.

(b) Bit Rate in Rx by SF.

(c) Bit Rate in Rx by CR.

(d) RSSI by SF.

(e) RSSI by CR.

(f) Delay by SF.

(g) Delay by CR.

Fig. 5. Results of the metrics obtained in the high wetlands zone.

4.2   Energy Consumption

Considering that the prototype is powered by a battery, it is very important to have an overview of the power consumption during operation. Figure 7a shows the current consumption of the prototype during a 30 min period, the measurements were taken with a 1 s interval and the confidence intervals were plotted with 95 % reliability. As for the LoRa interface, SF9, BW 125 kHz, CR 4/5 and a power of 14 dBm at 433.175 MHz frequency are used.

(a) Rural.   (b) Wetlands.

Fig. 6. Experiments carried out in both scenarios.

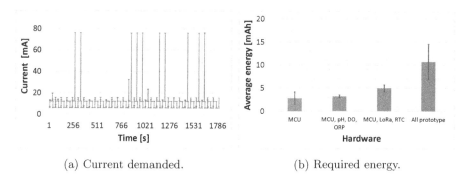

(a) Current demanded.   (b) Required energy.

Fig. 7. Energy consumption of the prototype.

Figure 7a also shows maximum currents of 76.26 mA and minimum currents of 6.18 mA, the maximum is due to the current peaks caused by the LoRa transmission stage and the minimum is during the low power stages.

As for the modules, sensors and peripherals of the prototype, in order to determine the current power they require, several measurements were made, whose average current levels are shown in Fig. 7b. In relation to the MCU, its power consumption is 2.84 mAh and when adding the sensors its increase was not significant, reaching 3.22 mAh, on the other hand, when using the LoRa module with the RTC, it reached 4.99 mAh and the consumption of the entire prototype was 10.7 mAh.

Finally, tests were performed with a 10000 mAh power supply to verify the correct operation of the prototype, where only approximately 8 days of autonomy were obtained. Due to the internal losses of the PowerBank it was not possible to take advantage of all its capacity, however, the time was enough to perform the installation and evaluation of the prototype.

5 Conclusions

In this article we have presented a LPWAN application based on LoRa whose function is to monitor water sources in the Andean pampas, where the results show that it is possible to implement the system in these scenarios. During the analysis it was observed that in general SF7 and SF8 have the worst performance, also the PRR less than 85% is the most relevant aspect that forces to discard these factors. Among the remaining options: SF 9, 10, 11 and 12, all of them would be a good option, however, the bit rate decreases as the SF increases, for example SF12 in the span presents a bit rate of 81 bits/s and for SF10 of 114 bits/s, which evidences less packets transmitted and therefore, less received even though the PRR is almost 100%. Regarding the delay, it also increases as the SF increases, and this is clearly observed in the section, where there is a difference of almost one second between SF9 and SF12. These results reflect that higher SFs produce higher energy consumption, because they require more time for transmission. In the case of RSSI, it is observed that lower SFs have a stronger signal power, however, there is a higher packet loss. It is important to remember that low SFs are less resistant to noise and have fewer redundant bits. Then, based on the above considerations, the most appropriate is to choose the lowest SF that presents a high PRR, in the case of the rural area it would be SF10 and in the SF9 sector. With respect to the CR, the difference between choosing one or the other is minimal in all cases, unlike the SF, which does affect the network considerably.

Comparing the results for each point facilitates the choice of the best scene for LoRa, concluding that the best performance corresponds to those places that have a wide area free of interference and with a clear line of sight between the node and the Gateway. This is clearly reflected in the rural area, where the farthest point from the node presents better results than closer points, this is thanks to the free line of sight, since in addition the node and the Gateway were approximately at the same height.

The energy consumption analysis shows that by using a Power Bank, the prototype reached an autonomy of 8 days, which would limit its installation within months. To overcome this, other batteries could be evaluated and a charging system could be added, for example, using solar panels.

This study did not develop the design of a LoRa Gateway and was limited to the operation of only one node. As for future work, it is proposed to evaluate the network using multiple nodes and gateways, allowing to increase the number of monitoring points and a better coverage of the network.

References

1. Bellini, P., Nesi, P., Pantaleo, G.: IoT-enabled smart cities: a review of concepts, frameworks and key technologies. Appl. Sci. **12**(3), 1607 (2022)
2. Li, C., Su, Y., Yuan, R., Chu, D., Zhu, J.: Light-weight spliced convolution network-based automatic water meter reading in smart city. IEEE Access **7**, 174359–174367 (2019)
3. Li, X.J., Chong, P.H.J.: Design and implementation of a self-powered smart water meter. Sensors **19**(19), 4177 (2019)
4. Ramírez-Moreno, M.A., et al.: Sensors for sustainable smart cities: a review. Appl. Sci. **11**(17), 8198 (2021)
5. León Ortiz, P.: Influencia del calentamiento global en los ecosistemas terrestres del perú (2021)
6. Castro, M.: Proyecto "creación de capacidades para la valoración socioeconómica de los humedales altoandinos": Una valoración económica del almacenamiento de agua y carbono en los bofedales de los páramos ecuatorianos (2011)
7. Briceño Salas, J.P.: Percepción de los cambios ambientales en los humedales de Oña-Saraguro. Ph.D. thesis, Universidad Técnica Particular De Loja (2014)
8. Ahmed, U., Mumtaz, R., Anwar, H., Shah, A.A., Irfan, R., García-Nieto, J.: Efficient water quality prediction using supervised machine learning. Water **11**(11), 2210 (2019)
9. Mao, F., et al.: Moving beyond the technology: a socio-technical roadmap for low-cost water sensor network applications. Environ. Sci. Technol. **54**(15), 9145–9158 (2020)
10. Pieters, O., et al.: MIRRA: a modular and cost-effective microclimate monitoring system for real-time remote applications. Sensors **21**(13), 4615 (2021)
11. Wild, J., et al.: Climate at ecologically relevant scales: a new temperature and soil moisture logger for long-term microclimate measurement. Agric. Forest Meteorol. **268**, 40–47 (2019)
12. Méndez-Barroso, L.A., Rivas-Márquez, J.A., Sosa-Tinoco, I., Robles-Morúa, A.: Design and implementation of a low-cost multiparameter probe to evaluate the temporal variations of water quality conditions on an estuarine lagoon system. Environ. Monit. Assess. **192**(11), 1–18 (2020). https://doi.org/10.1007/s10661-020-08677-5
13. Menon, G.S., Ramesh, M.V., Divya, P.: A low cost wireless sensor network for water quality monitoring in natural water bodies. In: 2017 IEEE Global Humanitarian Technology Conference (GHTC), pp. 1–8. IEEE (2017)
14. Moya Quimbita, M.A.: Evaluación de pasarela lora/lorawan en entornos urbanos (2018)
15. Kimothi, S., et al.: Intelligent energy and ecosystem for real-time monitoring of glaciers. Comput. Electric. Eng. **102**, 108163 (2022)
16. Kombo, O.H., Kumaran, S., Bovim, A.: Design and application of a low-cost, low-power, LoRa-GSM, IoT enabled system for monitoring of groundwater resources with energy harvesting integration. IEEE Access **9**, 128417–128433 (2021)

17. Bathre, M., Das, P.K.: Water supply monitoring system with self-powered LoRa based wireless sensor system powered by solar and hydroelectric energy harvester. Comput. Stand. Interf. **82**, 103630 (2022)

18. Bor, M., Roedig, U.: Lora transmission parameter selection. In: 2017 13th International Conference on Distributed Computing in Sensor Systems (DCOSS), pp. 27–34. IEEE (2017)

19. Ko, S., et al.: Lora network performance comparison between open area and tree farm based on PHY factors. In: 2018 IEEE Sensors Applications Symposium (SAS), pp. 1–6. IEEE (2018)

20. Cattani, M., Boano, C.A., Römer, K.: An experimental evaluation of the reliability of LoRa long-range low-power wireless communication. J. Sens. Actuator Netw. **6**(2), 7 (2017)

21. Lopez Chalacan, V.H.: Performance evaluation of long range (LoRa) wireless Rf technology for the internet of things (IoT) using Dragino LoRa at 915 Mhz (2020)

22. Iova, O., et al.: Lora from the city to the mountains: exploration of hardware and environmental factors. In: Proceedings of the 2017 International Conference on Embedded Wireless Systems and Networks (2017)

23. Zhang, Z., Zhang, B., Zhang, X.: Performance research of LoRa at high transmission rate. In: Journal of Physics: Conference Series, vol. 1544, p. 012177. IOP Publishing (2020)

24. Microchip: ATmega1284P. http://www.microchip.com/en-us/product/ATmega12 84P. Accessed 18 Jun 2022

25. Atlas-Scientific: Gravity^{TM} pH. http://www.atlas-scientific.com/kits/gravity-ana log-ph-kit/. Accessed 10 Sept 2022

26. Atlas-Scientific: Gravity^{TM} DO Sensor. http://www.atlas-scientific.com/kits/grav ity-analog-do-kit/. Accessed 10 Sept 2022

27. Atlas-Scientific: Gravity^{TM} ORP Sensor. http://www.atlas-scientific.com/kits/gra vity-analog-orp-kit/. Accessed 10 Sept 2022

28. Atlas-Scientific: Gravity Analog Sensor/Meter Sample Code. http://www.files. atlas-scientific.com/atlas_gravity.zip. Accessed 10 Sep 2022

29. Ai-Thinker: Módulo LoRa SX1278 433 Mhz. http://www.docs.ai-thinker.com/en/ lora/man. Accessed 10 Sept 2022

30. Github: User-friendly library for using arduino-lmic with The Things Network and other LoRaWAN® networks. http://www.github.com/mcci-catena/arduino-lorawan. Accessed 18 Sept 2022

31. Arduino IDE. http://www.arduino.cc/en/software. Accessed 10 Sept 2022

Author Index

A

Albornoz, Enrique Marcelo 173
Araya-Solano, Luis Alonso 110
Arbeláez-Duque, Cristian 77
Arizmendi-Peralta, Paris 95

B

Babenko, Mikhail 248
Bello, Hugo Jose 3
Bezuglova, Ekaterina 248
Bove, Maximiliano 61

C

Callejo, Luis Hernandez 3
Cardeñoso-Payo, Valentín 3
Cardinale-Villalobos, Leonardo 110
Cartuche, Alonso 264
Chicano, Francisco 46
Collares, Andrés 200

D

del Carmen Peralta-Abarca, Jesús 95
Deryabin, Maxim 248
Draper, Martín 61
Duque-Ciro, Alejandro 77

E

Estrada-Esquivel, Hugo 123

F

Flores-Sedano, Juan José 123

G

Gallardo, Cesar 173
Gil-Merino, Rodrigo 46
Gladkov, Andrei 248
Godoy, Diego Alberto 173
Gómez, Federico 185
Gomez, Victor Alonso 3

G

Gonzales, Andrés 264
González, Lucas 31
González, Luis 264
González, Santiago 264
Gubareva, Regina 215

H

Helal, Diego 200
Hernández-Aguilar, José Alberto 95

I

Ibarra, Nicolas 173

J

Jaramillo-Duque, Álvaro 77

L

León-Hernández, Viridiana Aydeé 143
Lopes, Rui Pedro 215

M

Massobrio, Renzo 17
Moreno-Bernal, Pedro 95, 143

N

Nesmachnow, Sergio 31, 61, 158, 185, 200, 233

P

Peralta-Abarca, Jesús del Carmen 143
Perera, Sara 17
Plaza, Alberto Redondo 3
Porteiro, Rodrigo 233
Prieto, Juan José Jassón Flores 123

R

Rebollar, Alicia Martínez 123
Rebollo, Miguel Angel González 3
Risso, Claudio 158

© The Editor(s) (if applicable) and The Author(s), under exclusive license
to Springer Nature Switzerland AG 2023
S. Nesmachnow and L. Hernández Callejo (Eds.): ICSC-CITIES 2022, CCIS 1706, pp. 279–280, 2023.
https://doi.org/10.1007/978-3-031-28454-0

Romero, Héctor Felipe Mateo   3
Rossit, Diego   158

S
Selva, Ricardo   173
Shiriaev, Egor   248
Solís-García, Luis Antonio   110

T
Tchernykh, Andrei   200, 248
Toutouh, Jamal   31, 46

V
Valuev, Georgii   248
Velásquez-Aguilar, J. Guadalupe   95
Villa-Acevedo, Walter   77

Printed in the United States
by Baker & Taylor Publisher Services